Instructor's Manual to Accompany

PURCHASING
AND SUPPLY
MANAGEMENT

TEXT AND CASES

Sixth Edition

DONALD W. DOBLER
Colorado State University
Emeritus

DAVID N. BURT
University of San Diego

LAMAR LEE Jr.
Late Professor of Management and Director of Purchasing
Stanford University

The McGraw-Hill Companies, Inc.

New York St. Louis San Francisco Auckland Bogotá
Caracas Lisbon London Madrid Mexico City Milan Montreal
New Delhi San Juan Singapore Sydney Tokyo Toronto

McGraw-Hill

A Division of The McGraw·Hill Companies

Instructor's Manual to Accompany
PURCHASING AND SUPPLY MANAGEMENT
Text and Cases, Sixth Edition

ISBN 0-07-037090-7

234567890 GDP/GDP90987

PREFACE

This *Instructor's Manual* is designed to assist the busy instructor. To this end, the major components of the Manual are:

- Proven *suggestions for organizing and teaching* a course in Purchasing and Supply Management
- Detailed *instructor's teaching notes* for all cases (123 cases in total)
- Thirty-one *cases not contained in the textbook*—"old chestnuts" identified by past users
- Examination or quiz *questions and answers* for all chapters

In addition to these major items, the Manual contains illustrative student analyses of two sixth edition cases, along with easily reproducible guidance on the case method. The exam questions are also formatted for ease of reproduction.

Although not a part of the Manual, the instructor should be aware of the package of six video tapes that come with adoption of the text. These tapes deal with specialized aspects of purchasing and supply management—and are excellent supplementary teaching tools.[1]

The authors would be remiss if they failed to acknowledge the work done by Elaine Dobler—she handled all the review and initial production work for the manual. We sincerely thank her for an excellent job.

---

[1]These tapes are developed and produced by the National Association of Purchasing Management.

TABLE OF CONTENTS

PART III: INSTRUCTOR'S TEACHING NOTES

EXAMPLES OF STUDENT-DEVELOPED CASE ANALYSES

PART IV: EXAMINATION QUESTIONS AND ANSWERS

PART I

Objectives and Suggestions
for a Course in
Purchasing and Supply Management

Overview

A course in purchasing and materials management should be one of the most exciting, provocative, and insightful learning experiences students have. Conducted properly, in practice purchasing[1] demands analytical ability, creativity, the ability to use logical reasoning to convince others, and general competence of the highest order.

A good instructor recognizes the importance of motivation in the learning process. Purchasing can be a lively and vital subject. The successful instructor is the one who brings his or her subjects to life. The dramatic, exciting learning experience will have a far greater impact and be retained longer than will the boring or routine one. It is likely that few of the basic principles and techniques in any area—whether purchasing, marketing, finance, or engineering—are really exciting. But their applications in a real world setting can truly be exciting.

A course in purchasing is important *both* to students majoring in that field and to those concentrating in other areas. Purchasing is the one business function that provides its executives, early in their careers, insight into all other business functions. Careers in purchasing offer responsibility, excitement, the enjoyment of exploring new products, the stimulation of working constantly with different personalities, and the challenge of integrating all of the purchasing and supplier management activities into a smoothly operating system.

Many students enrolled in a purchasing course will not make their careers in the purchasing and supply management field. Nevertheless, the course should be of vital importance to them. After all, purchasing typically spends approximately 60 percent of the firm's revenue! It can and does have a major role to play in the firm's efforts to improve product quality and, in turn, market share. Good purchasing greatly improves the firm's productivity, profitability, and return on investment. Students concentrating in fields such as marketing, operations, finance, and engineering will be greatly handicapped if they do not understand the purchasing function and its interrelationships with their own functions. In this era of cross-functional teams, "functional silos" are rapidly disappearing.

Methods of Teaching

Purchasing and Supply Management: Text and Cases has been designed to give maximum flexibility to the method of teaching that works best for individual instructors and for individual student groups. However, for instructors teaching the course for the first time, the following thoughts may be helpful:

1. With respect to the substantive content of the course, the instructor should consider doing as the authors have done in the text—*focus on basic concepts and underlying principles.* In a fast-moving technological society, practices and procedures are subject to rapid and constant change. Principles and concepts undergo change also, but only through slow, evolutionary processes. However, it is not usually possible to teach purchasing meaningfully by limiting discussion to principles and concepts in the abstract. Purchasing concepts become more real for most students (at all levels) after they acquire an understanding of the realistic working environment in which the principles and concepts are applied. Therefore, typical purchasing operating procedures, as they occur in the business world, should be integrated with the study of purchasing principles. This can be accomplished by studying

---

[1]Throughout the Instructor's Guide, the term "purchasing" normally includes the broader term "purchasing and supply management."

the cases, actually viewing a purchasing department on a field trip, or by reading about specific purchasing operations in such magazines as *NAPM Insights* and *Purchasing,* the *Harvard Business Review,* and the *International Journal of Purchasing and Materials Management.*

2. In *Purchasing and Supply Management: Text and Cases,* the cases and the text material have been written to be complementary. Together they form a comprehensive basis for a complete purchasing and supply management course. Many instructors make use of a combination method of teaching involving text reading and case analysis by the student, and lecture and case discussion by the instructor. When cases are used, it is important for the instructor to make frequent summaries of the points covered during the case discussion; otherwise, it is possible for the discussion to drift aimlessly.

    It is often of interest at the close of case discussion to reveal what the company in the case actually did. However, during the case discussion period the student's interest should not be focused on any "school solution." In fact, one of the outstanding features of the case method is the recognition that most business problems have more than one workable solution. The student is, therefore, allowed to bring his or her breadth of experience and study to bear on each problem posed. This forces the student to present his or her own ideas and thoughts in a logical manner, realizing that both contemporaries and the instructor are evaluating the presentation. A major objective of a case discussion should be the evaluation of the alternate solutions proposed by the participants.

3. While teaching the course, the instructor should not view purchasing as a specialized activity, that is an end in itself. Rather, purchasing should be viewed as an integral part of a firm's total operation. This means that the course should assume a *management* orientation. It also means that the instructor should, in a general way, stress Frederick Taylor's theory of the specialization of work and its application to the purchasing function. To accomplish this end, each purchasing topic can first be observed in the broadest perspective possible, investigating its relationship to other functional activities and other purchasing activities. Then, the topic can be studied in detail, delving into its unique technical problems. The "teaching-mix" used should be geared to the background and to the needs of each specific group of students.

Use of the Text Material

Purchasing and Supply Management: Text and Cases is an adaptable text. For the beginner, it provides a sound and complete introduction to the purchasing and supply management function. For the sophisticated reader, the book offers advanced discussions and cases focusing on many of the subject's important concepts and more subtle issues. Consequently, the book can be a useful text for a basic course in the community college or the four-year undergraduate curriculum. It also is appropriate for a more advanced course in the MBA curriculum or in training programs for industrial or government buyers. It has wide use in many technical schools and institutions. Undergraduate schools offering a course in purchasing may choose to cover only part of the text and cases. For this reason, the book is designed so that specialized activities may be omitted if time does not permit use of the complete book.

The book is used in many different academic settings. Accordingly, no one group or selection of topics and chapters is universally appropriate. We believe that for a comprehensive two-semester program, coverage of chapters 1–16 in the first semester and 17–32 in the second is appropriate. For an introductory one-semester course, chapters 1–4, 6, 8, 9, 11, 12, 14–17, 20, 21, 27, 30, and 31 should be considered. For a more advanced course, the following chapters can be used to supply a more sophisticated learning experience: 1–3, 5, 7–9, 28, 10–17, 20, 21, 27, 29, and 31.

Written Assignments

A purchasing course lends itself well to a "project" or a "depth-research study" on the part of the student. Each student can be given an opportunity to conduct a research project in depth in an area of special interest. Four types of projects are suggested:

1. *The Product Buying Report.* In this type of report, the student is asked to assemble and present all of the information a buyer needs to purchase intelligently a specific product or commodity such as transistors, automobiles, pumps, or peanut oil. In selecting and presenting the assembled facts, the student should indicate what use a buyer might make of these facts. For example, to list only a few, the student might report on the following questions:

   a. The intended use of the product and the requirements to be met by the items purchased.

   b. The available products which might meet these requirements and the characteristics of these products. In discussing the characteristics of these products, the grades, classifications, and properties which distinguish one product from another should be defined. One of the available products may be selected for detailed investigation.

   c. The technical data required in specifying and inspecting the selected product.

   d. The materials or parts entering the selected products and an analysis of their sources and availability.

   e. The methods of manufacture, provided they are significant in selecting suppliers or in appraising quality.

   f. Sources from which the product can be obtained.

   g. Factors affecting the supply, demand, price, and inventory of the selected product (an analysis of general business conditions is not intended in this question); however, substitute possibilities and value-analysis considerations should be covered.

   h. Detailed sources of information on the selected product.

2. *The Area Specialization Report.* In this report, the student is asked to make himself or herself an "expert" in one specialized area of the purchasing and supply management function. For example, he or she might choose or be assigned the *Make or Buy* area. The project would involve learning about this subject from the literature available, perhaps visiting several industrial firms for first-hand discussions, and then reporting the findings and conclusions in a report. After the area specialization report is completed, the student should be able to answer with reasonable ease many penetrating questions in his or her field of study. In grading this second kind of report, the following guidelines can be used and should be made known to the students at the time the assignment is made:

   a. Has the writer performed adequate research on this subject?

   b. Is the research well documented?

   c. Does the writer fully comprehend this subject?

   d. How well has the writer explained this subject?

   e. Are there parts of this subject which should have been covered and are not covered?

   f. Is the report free from excessive wordage?

3. *Discussion Questions.* Many of the discussion questions at the end of each chapter are suitable topics for assignment as written reports. Also, these questions can be substituted for cases as assignments for brief written reports.

4. *Case Reports.* In addition to, or in lieu of project reports, several written analyses of the cases in the text are also recommended.

The Case Method

Purchasing and Materials Management: Text and Cases provides a treasury of cases that allow the instructor to bring the course to life. These cases, when used as the basis for classroom discussion, draw on and complement the text. Proper use of the cases results in a very meaningful and exciting learning experience.

The instructor plays a key role in achieving this learning experience. He or she must be sensitive to several prerequisites to learning through the use of cases: preparation by both instructor and student, and the student's needs for security, challenge, recognition, self-esteem, and the need to help others. Thus, the use of the cases becomes a balancing act. The instructor will want to stretch the student and to motivate him or her to be well prepared. But needless embarrassment can be dysfunctional.

We have found that undergraduate and community-college students may be reasonably well prepared but are hesitant to perform in front of their peers. If this appears to be a problem, dividing the class into small groups provides a safer and more supportive environment for the shy student.

Also, we have found that the cases can be employed in a variety of ways. All of the cases lend themselves to classroom discussion through the use of the questions raised at the end of each case. Many of the cases lend themselves to rigorous case analysis. The instructor may choose to reproduce and distribute the following case instructional material when making an assignment requiring a traditional case analysis. Recognizing that a picture may be worth a thousand words, copies of actual student analyses of two cases are contained in Part II of the *Instructor's Manual.*

If a project report is not assigned, four or five written case assignments can be appropriately made. If a project report is assigned, two written cases should suffice. The written solutions should be kept as short as possible without diluting the quality of the analysis. Brevity forces the student to organize and present his or her thoughts concisely.

In preparing to discuss a case, the student follows a simple problem-solving outline in writing it up. The write-up contains four sections: (I) the facts; (II) the major problem statement; (III) possible solutions with a listing of advantages and disadvantages of each; and (IV) justification for the decision to select one of the possible solutions. A fifth section, implementation, may be required by the instructor at the outset. The student is required to list the major facts in the case. From these facts he or she then develops a written problem statement. Ideally, this should be one sentence long! Based on the problem statement, a possible set of solutions must be developed. This is important because in real on-the-job situations there are a number of solutions to each problem situation. Too often a preconceived solution is the only one given serious consideration. Little thought is given to looking for the better solution from among possible alternatives. The principle advantages and disadvantages of each possible solution should be listed briefly. In the last section of the paper, the student writes out what he or she considers to be the best solution—and justifies the selection.

Development of this four-section structured outline is mandatory. This classroom practice in problem identification, search for solutions, and documentation and justification of decisions builds a bridge from the classroom to "on-the-job" performance. Documentation and justification of decisions achieve a two-fold purpose: (1) they sharpen the learner's decision-making process, and (2) in real life they provide data that general management can understand concerning the "what" and "why" of the actions that take place in the decision-making process of the organization.

MANDATORY OUTLINE FOR CASE ANALYSIS

Case Name:

I. *Major Facts*

(State here the major facts as you see them. Make statements clear and concise for your own understanding as well as for the understanding of the other students and the instructor.)

II. *Major Problem*

(State here the major problem as you see it. Emphasize the *present* major problem. You may wish to phrase your statement in the form of a question. In a few cases, there may be more than one major problem. A good problem statement will be concise, usually only one sentence.)

III. *Possible Solutions*

    A. (List here the possible solutions to the major problem. Let your imagination come up with alternative ways to solve the problem.

    B. Do not limit yourself to only one or two possible solutions. These solutions should be distinct from each other.

    C. However, you may wish to include portions of one solution in another solution, as long as each solution stands alone. Only in this manner will your subsequent choice be definitive.

    D. Briefly note advantages and disadvantages of each possible solution.)

        etc.

IV. *Choice and Rationale*

(State here your choice, A or B, or ___, and the detailed reasons for your choice. You may also state your reasons for not choosing the other alterative solutions.)

V. *Implementation*

(When requested, prepare a plan to implement your choice.)

Name

Date

INSTRUCTOR'S EVALUATION FORM

A. Presentation   30 points
1. Organized in a logical manner
2. Neatly typed and presented.
3. Appropriate punctuation, spelling and phrasing.

B. Content   70 points
1. Identifies *the* problem.
2. Good, concise businesslike analysis.
3. Conclusions logically flow from the analysis.
4. Integrates relevant text and classroom material.

Overall evaluation of this paper:

| Unsatisfactory | Poor | Average | Good | Very Good | Excellent |

SUGGESTED CASE ASSIGNMENTS FOR EACH CHAPTER

Chapter 1: Profession in Transition

Q–4: The Outsourcing of Information
     Technology
Rommy Picks a Career
Sheer Elegance
Sunspot

Chapter 2: The Role of Purchasing

The Centennial Company
The Privileged Fly
Metropolitan University

Chapter 3: Objectives/Policies

Sampson Products Corporation
Pacific Healthcare
Mississippi Mutual Life Insurance Co.
Senator Foghorn
The Old Oak Furniture Company

Chapter 4: Procedures

Blozis Company
Tokisan Corporation
The Office Supplies Hassle
WVC Industrial Chemicals Company
The Oakland School District
Metropolitan University

Chapter 5: Computer/EDI

Julberg, Inc.
New Valley Power Corporation

Chapter 6: Organization

Northeastern Equipment Company
Blozis Company
Smith-Jones Electronic Corporation
G.A.R. Manufacturing Company

Chapter 7: New Product Development

Mazda Electronics
Elite Electronics
Fauquier Gas Company
The Dear John Mower Company
Dynamic Aircraft
Signal-Tek Corporation
Hy Tech

Chapter 8: Specifications

Fauquier Gas Company
Dynamic Aircraft
The Big "O" Company
SMC Turbines
The Peach Computer Company
OCR, Inc.

Gotham City Buys Fire Engines
The Case of the Unruly Spider

Chapter 9: Standardization

National Computers
Brothers Mowers
Signal-Tek Corporation
Holy Cross Health Care, Inc.
Fauquier Gas Company

Chapter 10: Outsourcing/Make-or-Buy

Main-Barnes Limited
Futronics, Inc.
Krause Company
Donley Brothers
The Munster Pump Company
Universal Motor Company Acquires
     Semiconductors

Chapter 11: Sourcing I

Nadia Develops a Commodity Study
Ripley Engine Company
Donley Brothers
Dynamic Aircraft
Ruhling Manufacturing Company
Sheer Elegance
Delta Steel Company
Vigard Manufacturing Company
Springfield Purchases a Garbage
     Truck
Sunspot, Inc.
Printed Circuits—Components for a
     JIT Factory
SMC Turbines

Chapter 12: Sourcing II

Collier Company I
Selection of a Pressure Vessel
     Manufacturer
Sampson Products Corporation
Lion Industries
Microcomp, Inc.
Pegasus Technologies
Black Motor Company
Great Western University
Alpha Omega Corporation

Chapter 13: International/Global

The Dutzel Diesel Case
National Machine and Electronics
SDC Corporation
The Wide, Wide World of
     Purchasing

EXAMINATIONS

Many of the questions at the end of the chapters have been used successfully as examination questions. Generally, the questions most suitable are those requiring broad, subjective answers that test the student's comprehension of concepts. A few short questions requiring specific answers may be added to give variety to the examination. The cases not covered in class can also make excellent examination material.

Part IV of the Instructor's Guide contains representative multiple-choice and true–false questions which can be used either alone or in conjunction with questions and/or cases for quizzes and examinations. The questions have been prepared so they may be easily reproduced.

FIELD TRIPS

Most schools offering a course in purchasing at the undergraduate or graduate level are located near an industrial activity with a purchasing or materials management department. Although most purchasing executives are busy people, they usually are pleased to be host to a purchasing class.

A two-hour visit to a purchasing or materials management department can give students a good look at the purchasing function in action. It is usually helpful if the host explains to the students before the tour of the plant begins exactly what they will see on the tour. It is also beneficial if the host holds a question-and-answer period after the tour is complete. Field trips seem particularly effective near the beginning or the ending of the course. If field trips are made at the beginning of the course, the stage is set for the reading and lectures to follow. If field trips are made near the end of the course, the students can then see for themselves in practice the theory being learned.

THE NATIONAL ASSOCIATION OF PURCHASING MANAGEMENT

The National Association of Purchasing Management (NAPM) has many affiliate purchasing associations located in most principal cities throughout the United States. These NAPM affiliates are often particularly active in working with community colleges and four-year colleges. Any teacher of purchasing certainly should make contact with the purchasing management association in his or her area. Regional purchasing associations are good sources of guest speakers as well as good contacts for field trips.

Full-time faculty members teaching purchasing courses are currently eligible for a complimentary academic membership in their local purchasing management association.

The National Association of Purchasing Management is a good potential source of many supplemental teaching aids. The Association has interesting and highly informative pamphlets covering a wide variety of purchasing topics. Also available are video and audio tapes. Most of these materials are available to purchasing instructors on a free/loan basis. Please contact the NAPM at (602)752-6276 for the latest materials available.

PART II

Additional Cases Not in the Text
The "Old Chestnuts" Identified
By Past Users

ALPHA OMEGA CORPORATION

The Alpha Omega Corporation, one of the world's largest computer manufacturers, faced increasing challenges from a number of competitors for the market share needed for profitability and success. In recent years the company had undertaken several efforts aimed at improving its profit margin and increasing sales.

One such effort was the centralization of a group of talented procurement and component engineering personnel from around the country to one site. This new organization, known as CXO, had its humble beginnings in 1982 with a mere six procurement people and twenty component engineering personnel. Being the "darling" of the corporation, CXO added employees at a rate exceeding any other organization in the company; the head count now exceeds 150—20 of whom are employed in purchasing functions.

Within the procurement department of CXO, there are seven commodity managers, eight buyers, and five support personnel. The organization has responsibility for the procurement of all integrated circuits used throughout the corporation as well as for negotiation of corporate pricing agreements in effect for most other repetitive purchases. The number of part numbers that CXO procures is approximately 2,000, of which all are received at CXO, tested, warehoused, and ultimately shipped to manufacturing plants worldwide. Other components used in Alpha Omega products are purchased and received directly by the system plants, against corporate pricing policy agreements negotiated by CXO.

CXO procurement, in negotiating all pricing agreements, utilizes a materials requirements forecasting system created and installed by a team of in-house management system specialists at every manufacturing plant in the United States. This forecasting system collects data from each plant's own master schedule system—extracting the data in such a way that when data from all plants are combined, the information is homogeneous. The data collected are the basis of the forecast for the next eighteen months.

CXO buys against plant forecasts and requires its customers (the manufacturing plants) to place delivery orders against CXO contracts to cover the next five to nine weeks' requirements. On an individual plant basis the orders seldom match the forecasts, which are obtained monthly and are probably outdated almost immediately; however, on an aggregate basis the total quantity ordered for any given part number roughly approximates the total forecast for all plants.

CXO procurement negotiates future contracts with qualified suppliers using aggregate forecasts. Typically, an RFQ is sent out to all potential suppliers, many of whom respond with a bid. When the bids are received, purchasing manually compiles the data in the first step of the award process. Second, purchasing queries engineering and procurement personnel from all plants in an effort to obtain a service rating of the prospective suppliers. Test data likewise are collected from the test database and massaged to eliminate erroneous data. All this is a very time-consuming process and renders purchasing almost incapable of processing any new purchase requisitions during the pre-award period.

Eventually the contract is awarded to one or more suppliers based on several factors: qualification by engineering, price, past service, and quality ratings. Suppliers who have not yet been qualified are tentatively awarded a portion of the contract, but no deliveries will be requested or accepted until the supplier is qualified.

Once the contract is awarded, purchasing hopes that suppliers will perform up to the wording of the contract. Unfortunately, in spite of agreeing to make on-time deliveries of the right quantity and the right quality level, suppliers are often late or early, often deliver below what was ordered, and frequently ship parts that subsequently fail testing.

Guy Craig, commodity manager for memory and microprocessor devices, was quite concerned. His buyers spent hundreds of hours determining which suppliers should be awarded contracts. In spite of this effort, the suppliers performed at an acceptable level only so far as price was concerned. Guy shared his dissatisfaction in quarterly reviews with the suppliers. He had nothing quantitative to back up his claims, with one exception: test histories were available, but were skewed on the negative side by lots purchased as "standard product" due to unforecast orders. These parts were tested to Alpha Omega specifications and results had been erroneously counted against the supplier's quality rating. (Normally when a supplier supplied to an Alpha Omega spec, it special-tested the parts in-house at the same parameters used by Alpha Omega.) Consequently, before test data could be shared with potential suppliers, manual manipulation of the data was required to properly document quality levels.

The purchasing database used by CXO contained all information pertinent to a purchase order and subsequent receipt of material. Guy, while not a computer whiz by any means, was knowledgeable enough to realize that with the help of management systems, he could obtain information on supplier performance by purchase order (i.e., on-time versus early or late delivery, and receipt in full versus partial receipt of the quantity ordered).

The finance and materials departments both shared purchasing's concerns about supplier performance. Safety stock inventory levels had increased to guard against suppliers who did not deliver to contract. The desired inventory level was three weeks of material at an estimated cost of $3 million per week. CXO inventories had climbed to five weeks, clearly a detriment to a company with cash flow difficulties. The cost of this idle inventory was enormous. But the potential costs associated with lower inventories (production disruptions and possible lost sales) were even greater.

In recent supplier reviews, some of the suppliers expressed the idea that if parts were sample-tested rather than 100 percent tested, the test cycle could be shortened, resulting in lower work in process inventory levels. The Alpha Omega quality department was not ready to go to sample testing except on parts that consistently achieved test failure rates of no more than 500 parts per million. The suppliers then suggested that if commercially standard products were specified, no additional testing should be required at either the supplier's site or Alpha Omega's. This would result in lower-cost purchased material and shorter lead times as well. Guy agreed with their ideas. He established an additional objective of obtaining engineering concurrence with the adoption of standard products in lieu of specially tested parts when possible. Engineering was less than enthusiastic about Guy's involvement in "its area."

As Guy sat in a deserted building late one Friday evening, he looked at the list of objectives to be accomplished by CXO purchasing this year. One jumped out at him: CXO had stated that it would save the corporation $10 million this year in favorable material price variance. Guy also knew that the corporation expected CXO to become 10 percent more productive this year. He felt that there was a significant amount of money to be saved throughout the organization if suppliers met their contractual obligations with regard to quality, quantity, timeliness, and service. His estimate was that 25 percent savings could be achieved if suppliers performed as stipulated. But how could be get there from here?

1 What is the basic reason that suppliers have consistently failed to meet their contractual obligations?
2 What can be done to ensure adequate supplier performance in the future?
3 On what basis should contracts be awarded?

BLACK MOTOR COMPANY

Harper South, senior electrical buyer at Black Motor Company, was discussing an interesting situation with some of this fellow buyers. Mr. South, along with most of his fellow buyers, had always considered that a fixed price contract under competitive bidding conditions was the best possible method of arriving at a price that would be fair to both the seller and the buyer. It was Mr. South's contention that under these conditions, a bidder would receive a fair profit on his work, since he would not reduce his bid below a point that enabled him to make a fair return. A bidder could make more than a "fair" profit, Mr. South realized, when an entire industry "fixed" prices or was operating in excess of planned capacity. Conditions of this sort were rare, Mr. South believed. On the other hand, a bidder might be willing to make less than a fair profit (or no profit at all) under conditions of fixed price and competitive bidding when he needed work to keep his plant operating. Under these conditions he might bid abnormally low. Yet, in most cases, Mr. South believed that the lowest bidder was the most efficient producer and, as a result, was able to make a satisfactory dollar profit. This profit, by the very nature of competition, was also fair to the buyer since he was still obtaining the item at a lower price than competing firms could offer. But something had just come up to cause Mr. South to question this widely held belief.

For several years, Mr. South had been purchasing a number of different items from White Generator Company. White was a leader in the field of automotive and truck electric motors, controls, and special equipment. It sold these items on a nationwide basis. Many of the articles that Black purchased from White were specially designed items used in the manufacturing of Army tanks and personnel carriers.

Mr. South had always purchased from the White Generator Company on a fixed price basis. As might be imagined, White's competition consisted of some of the largest and most successful corporations in the United States. Thus, it was with some surprise that Mr. Jones, the purchasing manager at Black, received a sharply worded letter from the Army. The letter pointed out that a team of Army auditors had just completed an audit of all Army work in the White plant. The Army was extremely perturbed to discover that the White Generator Company was making, on the average, 45 percent profit on its sales to the Black Motor Company.

Enclosed with the letter was a complete list of all the purchase orders issued to White by Black Motor Company and the amount of profit that had been made on each one. For example, the following figures were submitted on one item, a switch block:

Amount	Manufacturing cost	General expense	Development	Total	Price to Black	Total
500 blocks	$20.28	$3.85	$1.33	$25.46	$93.94	$46,970

On another item the profit, as a percentage of selling price, was 60.8 percent, and on still another, 73.7 percent. The Army intimated that the high profit figures at White were the result of poor buying on the part of the Black Motor Company and requested that steps be taken immediately to improve the situation.

Mr. South and the Black management were inclined to feel that if White were so efficient that it could consistently bid low against difficult competition and still make a 45 percent profit on sales, more power to the company. On the other hand, the Army was one of the company's best customers. It was thought wise to call a conference with the management of the White Generator Company to discuss the problem posed by the Army auditors.

In preparation for the conference, the purchasing personnel at Black were puzzled as to just what approach to take to the problem. As one of Harper's colleagues said, "How the devil are we going to tell another private corporation that it isn't enough just to be the low bidder. Now, we've got to tell them that they can't get our business unless they're at least 20 to 30 percent lower than everyone else?"

Harper then asked, "What is a fair profit for a manufacturer? Is it a fixed amount? Should it vary with total sales or total capital invested? Is a percentage of cost an adequate way of computing profit when one manufacturer may spend $100 to produce an item and a competitor may be able to produce the same item for $80? If a profit of 10 percent of cost is allowed, should the high-cost producer receive $10 for his inefficient work and the low-cost producer only $8 for his efficient efforts? Is a percentage of profit based on selling price a more satisfactory method of determining a fair profit than one based on cost?"

As might be expected, the White management objected to the findings of the Army audit. They pointed out that the Army had disallowed a whole series of costs that White's public accountants had accepted as being fully justified. In particular, the Army auditors had disallowed large sums for research and development (R & D) expenditures. The management at White stated, "Our policy over the years has been a conservative one with respect to the risk factors involved in the defense equipment business. We speak of risk in the sense that it is not uncommon for suppliers to be called on to establish prices on the basis of specifications which do not lend themselves to accurate cost analysis. Design changes, not to mention the expenses connected with correcting difficulties which appear only after the equipment is in service, result in a quotation based on considerable guesswork.

"The situation is further aggravated by the fact that the rapidly changing character of the defense business has created entirely new problems for which there is no experience on which to draw. Nevertheless, the last few years in particular have better prepared us to appraise the risk aspects involved. We now have a better understanding of what defense manufacturers must require of their suppliers. Moreover, we have had the benefit of the costly education entailed in becoming familiar with inspection, performance, and qualification test procedures required to satisfy the government authorities and our customers.

"In addition to improving our position with respect to the factors which affect costs, we have been urged to rebate to our prime contractors any cost savings we are able to effect, so as to assure the Army the best use of the funds appropriated to it. Henceforth, it will be our policy to review all government contracts as production progresses and our actual costs become known. Whenever possible, price adjustments will be volunteered for the benefit of the Army, or whichever branch of the Department of Defense is affected."

The Army administrative contracting officer at the Black Motor Company was satisfied with the explanation made by the White management. Basically, he agreed with the general feeling of the Black purchasing department that Black was in no position to dictate to another company what it could charge for an item after a fixed price bid had been accepted. However, both Black and the Army had a vested interest in reducing Black's costs. Most of the Black contracts with the Army were of the fixed price incentive type. Under a typical fixed price incentive contract, every dollar of savings below target would increase Black profits by $0.30 and reduce Army expenditures by $0.70.

1 What is the purpose of a "profit"?

2 When a buyer is deciding on an adequate profit to promote his or her own interests, what points should be kept in mind?

3 In this case, should a cost breakdown have been considered?

4 Discuss ways of obtaining fair and reasonable prices as applied to this case.

5 What method of pricing do you believe should have been used?

BRANSON ELECTRONICS COMPANY (A)

Founded in the late 1960s by William Morgan, a brilliant engineer, the Branson Electronics Company has experienced tremendous growth as a producer of specialized components for the computer industry. But like many companies which have experienced this type of growth, Branson has reached near-capacity conditions in its plant. Undertaking an expansion of new capacity will be at least sixteen months in the future. Known for its high quality and innovative approaches, Branson has been forced to subcontract some work. Recently, one of the major computer manufacturers approached Branson to design and build a subsystem. While capacity could be made available for almost all of the subsystem at the Branson facility, it became apparent that one key component, a rather intricate and yet very inexpensive circuit board, would have to be subcontracted. The boards were under a government contract which would make Branson a subcontractor. All of Branson's suppliers are also subcontractors. This would mean "tons of forms" to be sent to suppliers but would also give Branson some leverage. On the basis of the projected value of the order, it would be necessary for each supplier to provide a cost and price breakdown on the SF 1491. From this breakdown Branson could estimate the reasonableness of the price.

Branson engineers would provide the design to meet the customer's specs, and, in turn, it would be purchasing's responsibility to handle the contracting aspect. Since the board is custom designed, it would require a fair degree of interaction between the potential suppliers and Branson's engineering staff. Cost was also a factor. Thus, there would have to be both an engineering evaluation with respect to technical aspects of the part as well as a cost analysis made.

Ralph Wilson, the Purchasing Manager of Branson Electronics, concurred with the Vice President of Engineering that it would be best to seek competition on the design and fabrication of the board. In concert with engineering, it was decided that three suppliers would be selected by engineering based on the engineers' technical knowledge. Upon receipt of the proposals, a technical evaluation would be made of the proposals to identify the best design. Cost proposals would be cost analyzed and an appropriate team would negotiate the purchase with one or more of the proposers. Wilson felt that this would insure a reasonable price for the board.

Branson design engineers prepared the specifications in great detail and sent them along with a list of three potential suppliers to Wilson. Wilson, in turn, prepared the rest of the proposal package and specified a July 30 deadline for proposal submission. He also indicated that proposers would be able to meet with Branson engineers anytime between receipt of the request for proposal and July 30 by simply contacting Wilson to arrange such meetings. Wilson also stated that after 15 August, final negotiations on purchase of 500,000 of these parts would begin. The following is a sequence of the events leading up to the present time.

1 April – Stockbridge, Crow and Shawnee are sent proposal packages

12 April – Stockbridge responds and requests meeting on 18 April to discuss the design

15 April – Crow calls and sets up meeting on 20 April

16 April – Shawnee responds with meeting set for 3 May

18 April – Stockbridge engineers meet at Branson Company—indicate the part can be produced, but much of it will be custom designed due to Branson specs. Several technical problems are resolved, and Stockbridge requests a second meeting in late June to review preliminary designs

20 April – Crow engineers meet and clarify some details.

When asked if they desire a second meeting, Crow engineers decline, indicating they have enough information and will submit a proposal by 30 July

3 May – Shawnee engineers meet with Branson engineers and indicate some basic changes in the Branson specs which could be made without altering part quality or reliability and probably reduce the final cost by using off-the-shelf components. After a careful review of the specifications, Branson engineers agree that these changes will still meet overall specs and give Shawnee a go-ahead to incorporate the proposed changes.

20 June – Stockbridge engineers return with a final design. Branson engineers are impressed by it since it exceeds many of the performance parameters specified. A Branson engineer comments on the excellence of the design.

30 July – All bids are received with the following results

Stockbridge – $11.34 per unit
Crow – $12.09 per unit
Shawnee – $10.54 per unit

1 Aug – Proposals sent to engineering for technical analysis

8 Aug – Report from engineering:

Stockbridge proposed design—exceeds almost all performance parameters, excellent technical approach, 100 percent custom-made components for the subassembly—long lead times for all parts

Crow—meets all performance parameters, good technical approach, 50 percent custom-made components

Shawnee—altered basic design slightly to reduce costs but met or exceeded specifications on performance. An innovative technical approach by this potential supplier. The supplier showed us some ways to increase reliability of the subassembly

Technical recommendation: Shawnee.

Prior to acceptance of the technical recommendation, a cost analysis must be performed since the anticipated value of the contrast is in excess of five million dollars and small errors can cost huge amounts. The summary information on price structure for all three bids appears in table 1 as exhibit #7. Stockbridge has estimated the learning function (curve) at 95 percent after the manufacture of 100,000 units. Stockbridge will be carrying the inventory on a no charge basis with assurance of a no cancellation clause in the contract. Delivery is scheduled for 100,000 units per month from March to July. No design changes will be allowed beyond the date of contract signing since all the boards are custom fabricated. Supplier also requires a cash advance of $2,000,000 for purchase of long lead time components by 1 September. Stockbridge will submit samples for reliability testing by January 15th.

Crow, using 50 percent custom-made components, estimates a learning curve of 95 percent after the manufacture of 200,000 units. Crow will begin production in January. This will allow for acquisition of long lead time items. Shipments will be made as completed in batches of 100,000 units. First 100 units of each batch will be used for reliability testing and will be billed at materials and labor only at the end of the total run. Due to the presence of custom made components it is necessary for Crow to receive $3,000,000 in advance (upon contract signing) to cover long lead time procurements. Crow's bid contains a 50 percent of contract value cancellation clause or 100 percent of all completed, whichever is greater. Redesign costs will be billed at $75 per hour plus Crow reserves the right to quote on the basis of any new design with Branson paying full price for all units produced prior to redesign if they must be scrapped.

Shawnee has projected a learning curve of 98 percent. Almost all the components are off-the-shelf and therefore Shawnee's operation is an assembly operation. The assembly is quite simple and therefore the training of personnel will be very rapid with the possibility of reaching the curve at 60,000. Shawnee will begin production within one month with the option of stocking for Branson at the rate of 3.5 percent per month on the average value of inventory carried for that month. Since the original specifications were modified by Shawnee, they have indicated they own the design. They would be willing to sell the design rights for $260,000. Redesign costs would be no more than $100 per engineering hour with a maximum of 8000 hours and would be Branson's intellectual property. Design changes which caused material to be obsolete would be the responsibility of Branson for either use, disposal or return to Shawnee's suppliers. Shawnee wants a 25 percent of contract cancellation clause plus cost of all materials on hand and on order.

Wilson, after reading over the bids, has decided that a complete proposal comparison should be made to evaluate all potential suppliers on "an equal" basis.

He looks at the information available to him:

1. Proposal from Stockbridge Computers—Exhibit #1
2. Proposal from Crow Computer—Exhibit #2
3. Proposal from Shawnee Electronics—Exhibit #3
4. Financial Information on Stockbridge—Exhibit #4
5. Financial Information on Crow Computer—Exhibit #4
6. Financial Information on Shawnee Electronics—Exhibit #4
7. Excerpts from Branson Electronics Proposal—Exhibit #5
8. Selected Industry Data—Exhibit #6
9. Summary of Price and Cost Data—Exhibit #7

Wilson feels under some pressure since he knows there will be no follow-on business for the winning supplier. He is also uneasy about the relative closeness of the bids and the apparent differences between the suppliers in terms of responding to the original request for proposal. Wilson feels negotiation must be the real key to the best possible deal for Branson. However, the question is, "With whom do I negotiate?"

This case was developed by Professor Richard G. Newman of Rockhurst College.

EXHIBIT 1

Stockbridge Computers, Inc.
P.O. Box 117
Fond-du-Lac, WI 55129

Mr. Ralph Wilson, Purchasing Manager
Branson Electronics Company
2178 High Street
Grandview, MO 64102

Dear Mr. Wilson:

Stockbridge Computers is delighted to respond to the recent request for proposals tendered by the Branson Electronics Company for 500,000 units of your proposed model #CB 1002-2. As you know, Stockbridge has spent several person-years of effort coming up with what we feel is the best design. In fact your engineers were kind enough to recognize that effort. All this means little if we are not competitive. Thus we are quoting a firm, fixed price of $11.84 per unit F.O.B. our facility at Fond-du-Lac. We feel that this bid is reasonable and reflects a 95 percent learning curve being reached at 100,000 units.

Like you, we are concerned with delivery. We can meet your requirements and reach the desired level of 100,000 units per month. We can either produce at the delivery rate or in one batch all within the price envelope quoted. We are confident of smooth sailing since the materials are being purchased from our subsidiary in Green Bay. We see no materials problems. In that light, we are forced to ask for a line of credit guaranteed by Branson for $2,000,000 to cover the purchase of a large quantity of expensive, customized components. In addition, once the contract is signed, it will specifically omit any cancellation clause. Changes in design which necessitate alterations in the flow of work will be charged on a time and overhead rate at $100.00 per hour plus the applicable overhead.

As far as quality and reliability are concerned, we shall have samples ready for testing three months after contract signing. We look forward to working with Branson Electronics Company. Any other issues or questions can easily be resolved. Since we are so isolated, we would be happy to send the corporate jet to Kansas City to bring you and your associates for a plant tour. Give me a convenient date and I will go from there.

Sincerely,

Wilson Embry, Vice President
Sales

EXHIBIT 2

Crow Computer Components
1818 Broadwell Road
Cincinnati, Ohio 43207

Mr. Ralph Wilson, Manager
Purchasing Department
Branson Electronics Company
2178 High Street
Grandview, MO 64102

Dear Mr. Wilson:

Crow Computer Components is happy to respond to your Request for Proposal and offer our solution to the design specifications given in your proposal. We have made every effort to be competitive and based on a guaranteed purchase of 500,000 units, we offer our units at the competitive price of $12.09 per unit F.O.B. our plant in Cincinnati, Ohio. Since the vast majority of the parts in your boards are custom made, we shall need a cash advance of $3,000,000 or a line of credit backed and supported by Branson Electronics to cover the purchase of long lead time items.

Additionally, we feel that we need some form of protection against cancellation of the contract. We must insist on a minimum of 90 days warning on cancellation as well as your guarantee that all units produced to date, both in the form of finished goods and work in process, as well as nonreturnable raw materials, will be your responsibility. This may seem like a great deal to ask from you, but you are getting priority service from us. We are prepared to begin shipment in February on the first 100,000 units. While this may appear premature to your needs, we feel that our material in your shop is material worth having.

There are additional considerations which I must insist upon. These include a $75.00 per hour fee for costs incurred through redesign or design changes on your part as well as reliability testing units billed at 75 percent of our price.

With respect to questions on the learning curves, we do not find that concept really applicable toward our operation. We take our time to build high quality parts and such techniques are for shoe manufacturers, not a precision house like us. However, I know you need some estimate. Let us say 95 percent reached at 200,000 units of production.

We at Crow are ready to start tomorrow, if necessary. Just send me a fax authorizing start up and we can take care of the remaining paperwork later.

Sincerely,

Waldo Keester
National Sales Manager

EXHIBIT 3

Shawnee Electronics
2625 Waymen Drive
Shawnee Mission, KS 65008

Mr Ralph Wilson, Purchasing Manager
Branson Electronics Company
2178 High Street
Grandview, MO 64102

Dear Mr. Wilson:

Shawnee Electronics is pleased to bid $10.54 for the manufacture of 500,000 units of CB 1002-2. This is the delivered price at the Branson plant. We can begin delivery in January, a full two months ahead of schedule. With respect to the learning curve, we estimate a 98 percent curve to be reached by 60,000 units of production.

There are several other factors which must be included in our response to the bid. Since Shawnee engineers spent a considerable amount of time in the redesign of the board, we feel it is our design at this stage and it meets or exceeds all your specifications. If any redesign is done as a result of changes in specifications, then engineering time would have to be billed at $100.00 per hour for a maximum of 8000 hours. In addition, we must insist on a cancellation clause in the contract which would be at the rate of 25 percent of the value of the contract at the time of cancellation as well as payment for material on hand and on order. Obsolete units due to design changes would be paid for at full price and would be the property of Branson.

In addition, we reserve the right to undertake price redetermination upon completion of 75 percent of the contract. Given our efforts on your behalf, we feel this is applicable and appropriate.

Finally, we would be happy to inventory the board for you at the rate of 3.5 percent per month of the value of the finished goods. We look forward to working with you and Branson.

Yours truly,

Charles Walters, Vice President
Marketing

EXHIBIT 4

Selected Financial Data for Suppliers
(in thousands of dollars)

Data	Stockbridge	Crow	Shawnee
Current Assets	154,315	59,497	35,770
Current Liabilities	70,490	23,598	12,751
Inventory	101,248	39,266	17,829
Receivables	41,777	14,734	16,651
Total Assets	240,957	85,200	48,122
Net Sales	333,317	94,470	40,905
Cost of Goods Sold	293,603	71,494	24,079
Sales, Gen & Admin	23,795	23,722	12,489
Profit before tax	6,402	1,634	1,613

EXHIBIT 5

Selected Portions of Branson Bid

Price

The price paid by Branson will be competitive and will reflect the cost to produce the product plus coverage of normal overhead costs plus a profit. The bid price should reflect the increasing productivity of the labor force of the supplier as more boards are produced.

Delivery

In order to achieve the best use of funds, Branson expects its supplier to undertake a JIT posture. Units will be delivered at the rate of 100,000 per month with no overages or back-orders allowed. Any units which the supplier builds beyond the stated monthly level are the property of the supplier and Branson assumes no financial responsibility for these units.

Quality

Branson expects the supplier to employ SPC techniques in the manufacturing process and will expect a "zero defect" shipment each time. Since reliability is the key factor in customer acceptance, the supplier will supply an agreed upon number of units from each batch for reliability testing. These units will be supplied at the cost of labor and material only and will be so indicated in the bid. They will be used for MTBF testing and will not be used in the final product.

Payment

Payment will be in accordance with Branson's usual policy of 2/10, net 30 on completed portions of the order. Bidders should be aware of Branson's policy of requiring an escrow account of 5 percent of the value of the order to be used to defray warranty call work associated with part failure. These funds will be deposited to an accessible, interest bearing account. At the end of the warranty period any unused funds plus interest will be returned to the supplier.

Warranty

The supplier warrants the product to operate properly for a period of one year. Warranty shall cover defects in workmanship and defective parts or components. Parts or components which fail will be replaced free of charge. Subsequent installation of these parts will be done by Branson at the supplier's expense. Labor charges for installation will be charged at the prevailing rates charged by Branson to its customers.

Termination

Usual and customary business practices will be observed and Branson reserves the right to cancel the order with 30 days notice. Branson assumes the responsibility of all finished goods and work in process inventories built to Branson specifications and schedules. A supplier engaging in a "build ahead" program assumes the associated risks.

Branson reserves the right to audit all termination claims above $10,000. Final payment for termination will be made no later than 60 days after the completion of the audit or 90 days after termination notification, whichever is sooner.

Design Modification

Branson encourages suppliers to be creative and innovative in seeking better ways to design and build their products. This does not imply that Branson will assume any responsibility for engineering or design work done without prior approval by an appropriate officer or agent of the Branson Electronics Company. In those instances where suppliers are building to Branson specifications, all designs shall be the intellectual property of Branson Electronics.

Rebid/Negotiation

Branson reserves the right to rebid in the case of nonresponsive bids and/or negotiate with any or all suppliers.

EXHIBIT 6

S1C 3672—Printed Circuit Boards

Industry Data

In 1995 the Census of Manufactures developed a new category named Printed Circuit Boards. Thus the aggregate data for this census only includes a single set of data points.

1995 industry expenditure on material	= $ 1820.	(millions)
1995 industry expenditure on production labor	= $ 758.6	(millions)[1]

Cost of Material per dollar of shipment   = .46[2]

Source: 1. 1994 U.S. Industrial Outlook, U.S. Department of Commerce
Bureau of Industrial Economics

2. 1995 Census of Manufactures, U.S. Department of Commerce

EXHIBIT 7

Branson Electronics-Part A

Summary of Cost & Price Data by Supplier

	Shawnee	Crow	Stockbridge
Cost Elements			
Direct Labor	$1.05	$1.48	$1.50
Materials	$3.00	$3.10	$2.80
Factory Overhead	$2.63	$3.26	$3.00
Tooling	$0.75	$1.44	$1.22
S,G & A & Profit	$3.01	$2.69	$3.20
Transportation	$0.05	$0.06	$0.06
Packaging	$0.05	$0.06	$0.06
Bid Price	$10.54	$12.09	$11.84

All the above data are with application of learning curves

BRANSON ELECTRONICS COMPANY (B)

After awarding the bid to Shawnee on the basis of price and quality, the contract proceeds without incident for the first two months of production. Boards are produced and the quality and reliability testing proves that Shawnee indeed does have the capacity and capability to meet their promises. Early on the morning of the fifth day of the third production month, Ralph Wilson, Purchasing Manager at Branson receives and urgent phone message from Charles Walters, VP Marketing at Shawnee. Wilson returns the call and Walters appears distraught over the phone. It seems that Elmo Pinch, Comptroller at Shawnee, has dropped the proverbial "bomb" in the midst of the monthly management meeting. Due to higher than expected start up costs and an overly optimistic estimate of the learning curve as well as labor content in the product, Shawnee is *losing* money on every unit being produced for Branson. The best estimates now show the following cost structure for Shawnee:

Direct Labor	$ 1.50
Materials	3.00
Factory Overhead	3.10
Tooling	1.20
S,G & A and Profit	2.81
Transportation	.06
Packaging	.05
Total	$ 11.72

From the data presented, Shawnee is losing $1.18 per unit and will therefore sustain a total loss on the order in excess of $600,000. Wilson, a veteran of twenty years of Purchasing is somewhat wary of the numbers and suggests that Walters fax him a copy of the calculations for his review. Walters agrees and skillfully reminds Wilson of the price redetermination clause in the original proposal. He also comments that Shawnee is a small company and a loss of this magnitude could mean financial trouble for the company to the degree that it could jeopardize their stability in the market place.

Walters suggests that price renegotiation begin immediately. Wilson says that the whole matter of the contract would have to go to top management for a high level determination of the next course of action. He promises to get back to Walters in no more than 24 hours. Wilson calls the office of the company president and a top level meeting is called for 3 pm that afternoon. Wilson is told to have his people prepare a cost analysis and recommendations for the meeting as well as an impact statement on the problems of price negotiation.

Wanting to cover "all the bases", Wilson calls Keester at Crow and Embry at Stockbridge asking each if they would be interested in rebidding the project at a reduced level of output, say 300,000 units. Keester declines over the phone, citing a new contract just received that will tie up the plant for the next six months. He hints that they could put on a second shift or pull out all the stops on overtime and help out Branson, but the price would have to be on a time and overhead basis with Branson buying and stocking the material. In addition, no learning curve was possible.

Embry practically leaps through the telephone and promises to be ready to start production in five business days after receipt of the order. He guarantees delivery as per the first bid. The costs will have to be renegotiated, but he promises an upper maximum not to exceed 110 percent of bid price plus pass through on overtime costs to catch up the five days make ready time. Wilson is not terribly excited about the prospect of a 10 percent price increase, but that is better than a breach of contract lawsuit for Branson should Shawnee "bite the dust."

Wilson calls in his bright assistant, Walter Able, and assigns Walter the task of preparing the analytical portion of the presentation. Referring to part A of the case, prepare the analytical segment plus the appropriate recommendations.

This case was developed by Professor Richard G. Newman of Rockhurst College.

CAMPBELL TYPEWRITER CORPORATION

The Campbell Typewriter Corporation was enjoying the biggest year in its history. High production made its unit costs low. It was the successful bidder for the National Mail Order Corporation's annual typewriter contract—the largest single typewriter sale in the world each year.

Campbell Typewriter Corporation, in order not to interfere with the sales of typewriters under the "Campbell" brand name, modified the appearance of the "National" model from the appearance of the Campbell regular line of typewriters. Part of the appearance change was in the color and shape of the keyboard key tops.

Typewriter key tops are usually double-injection-molded. This means that first, the individual letters themselves are injection-molded, for instance, in a light color such as white. Then, the white letters are used as inserts around which the body of the key is molded, in a dark color such as green, for instance. It is a patented art in which there are a small number of skilled suppliers. Campbell Typewriter molded its own key tops, except under overload conditions.

In order to meet the initial delivery deadline to National Mail Order Corporation, the Campbell Typewriter Corporation had to "put a new dress on the old lady" in a hurry—by changing the housing, the key tops, and the carrying case. The shape of the carrying case was a rather simple matter to change, since it was fabricated by hand on a bent plywood frame. It was decided to change the appearance of the housing by using the lower portion of the housing from the preceding model, and just building one new tool for the "mask"—the top part of the housing that covers the type basket and the ribbon spools. This meant that the time squeeze would be concentrated on the double-injection-molded key tops. Campbell Typewriter's own key top molding department could not handle the National order. It would have to be placed outside.

Because of the tight schedule, it was essential that purchasing delay as little as possible in selecting a source for the key tops and placing the purchase order. Of the double-injection-molding plants available, only four were large enough to handle the key tops in the necessary quantities. Three of the four sources contacted either refused to quote on so short a schedule or else were fully loaded and unable to consider the order. The only exception was the Ingborg Key Top Company, a highly reputable concern with a wide reputation for reliable work and strict adherence to promised delivery dates.

The Ingborg Key Top Company was run by Niels Ingborg, a Swede by birth, who was indeed a master craftsman and a man of personal integrity and honesty. However, Ingborg was a businessman of the old school and ran his operation on a tight-fisted, closed-mouth basis. He knew his business and insisted on running his business as he saw fit. He sought advice from no one, and recently, when he was told by one of his customers that his prices were too high, he was heard to have said, "I produce a quality product, and I meet my delivery dates. I know my business, and I know what I should charge as a price. You get what you pay for, and if you're looking for bargains or cut-rate prices, I would rather not have your business."

This, then, was the only supplier willing and able to consider the key top procurement. Jim Smith, the Campbell Typewriter purchasing manager, opened discussions with Ingborg expecting at best a difficult time. At the outset, the meeting was noticeably strained. Several months previously, Campbell Typewriter had canceled a sizable order with Niels Ingborg and returned the work to its own shops to relieve what was then an underload condition. As could be expected, Ingborg was most unhappy on that occasion, and Smith was aware that now the shoe was on the other foot.

It was with a sense of uneasiness, therefore, that Smith asked Ingborg to submit a quotation on the mold-making and molding of the key tops. However, Ingborg was the epitome of politeness and seemed sincere and anxious to be helpful and cooperative. They key top letters were a fancy style—created by Campbell's industrial designer and approved by National Mail Order. Ingborg cited the fact that the Campbell letters were difficult to make, and that more time was needed than Smith was prepared to allow in order to develop a realistic quotation. As a consequence, he proposed that Smith tell him what the job was worth, and that would be the price he would quote. This approach on the part of Ingborg caught Smith completely off balance. It was the last thing he expected to hear, and although he liked to believe that the "old man had mellowed," his intuition told him to be more wary. To aggravate Smith's dilemma further, Ingborg then proposed an alternative—$33 per hour straight time and $40 for overtime, based on the actual hours spent on the job.

1 What is your opinion of Ingborg's two proposals? Which, if either, would you accept, and why?
2 Are there any other choices open to Smith for arriving at an equitable agreement?
3 How would you have handled the procurement if you were Smith?
4 What should Campbell do in an effort to get better competition?

THE CASE OF THE UNRULY SPIDER

Allen Jones, the buyer of tooling and subcontract material for Alex Precision Manufacturing Company, received a routine rejection notice from the inspection department. This notified him that thirty-two spider gears, which had recently been received from the Speedy Tool Company, had been rejected. There were two reasons for the rejection. First, the 1 1/8-inch-diameter holes had a rough finish on the bore. Second, the magnaflux mark was not clearly legible on all the pieces. Before Jones had a chance to go to the receiving department to examine the pieces, he received a telephone call from the production superintendent demanding immediate replacement of the parts because they were holding up the shipment of a substantial spare parts order. The parts were needed for a foreign shipment.

As soon as he got a chance, Jones went to the receiving department and examined the spider gears. He called to the attention of the chief inspector the fact that there was no notation on the drawing calling for any finish on the bore of the three holes. This dimension called for an extremely tight tolerance of 0.0004-inch. All the parts met this requirement when measured with an inside micrometer. However, he could see that the inside surface of these holes was slightly rough from the boring operation. Jones did not feel that this roughness was adequate grounds for rejection; however, he suggested that the inspector call the engineer responsible for the part to see if it would be possible to use the part.

A meeting was quickly arranged with the engineer, who took one look at the spiders and said that they were absolutely unsuitable for use. The dimension he objected to was a bearing seat. The engineer said that he could not afford to take a chance on a fit which could become loose in service. He felt that any respectable supplier would produce a smooth surface on this type of hole without any notification on the drawing. He felt that the rough surface showed inferior workmanship. The engineer refused to accept the parts as they were and suggested that the supplier prepare new ones with a ground finish on the bores. Jones asked the engineer to add a suitable finish indication on the drawing, so the supplier would know exactly what finish was required. This indication would give the inspection department a definite standard for inspection. The request was refused because the engineer felt that any good subcontractor would immediately identify the holes as bearing seats and would produce a 64-micro-inch finish without any special note. Moreover, these parts had been in production for several years and he had never experienced this trouble before; the engineer felt that it must be the fact that there was a new supplier that was causing the trouble.

Allen Jones put a telephone call to Mr. Speed of the Speedy Tool Company and described the situation to him. Mr. Speed objected strenuously to the rejection on the basis of the rough finish. He said that he had been furnished a plug gauge to check this dimension and that the parts had all been checked satisfactorily with this gauge before they had been shipped. Nothing had ever been said to Mr. Speed about the necessity for a ground finish on the bores. Since the holes were already at the proper dimension, it would be impossible to grind them further to salvage the 32 units without an expensive chromeplating operation. Mr. Speed agreed to change his procedure in the future, so that these holes would have a ground finish. The fixture for this operation would cost at least $2,000, and Speed felt that he would probably have to spend about $25 a unit for additional labor in the grinding operations.

In regard to the magnaflux marking, Mr. Speed pointed out that the marking stamp had been furnished by the Alex Company and that the drawing called for it to be applied to a curved surface. Mr. Speed agreed that it was not very legible, but said that it was the best they could do under the circumstances without damaging the stamp.

Mr. Speed said that he was able to make the new grinding operation effective on 100 pieces that were in process and thought that he could deliver these within a week.

The Speedy Tool Company was a major supplier of production tooling, particularly dies, jigs, and fixtures. The two companies had had a very favorable relationship for ten or twelve years. Mr. Speed called on Mr. Jones about once a week in regard to the many items of tooling which were on order, and the two men had come to know each other very well. Speedy Tool had done very little production work for Jones, but its precision work on tooling had always been well done and it had a very good delivery and quality record.

The spider had become active at the time of the introduction of the Alex offset press. It had been necessary to subcontract this item because no facilities were available internally. At that time, the drawings, specifications, and gauges were furnished to the original subcontractor, the Wilson Automatic Machine Company. Wilson had built the original tooling. When Alex had dropped this press from the product line, the part had become inactive. A demand had only recently occurred for spare parts. Jones had found that Wilson had virtually gone out of business on subcontract precision work. In fact, he had had considerable difficulty in getting the original gauges and tooling back from the Wilson Company. Speedy had quoted on the basis of tooling to be furnished, but when the tools had been received from Wilson, they were found to be in very poor condition. In fact, some of the tooling had not been modified to bring it up to the marked revision of the drawing. It had been necessary for Mr. Speed to spend over $25,000 in repairing the tooling before he could use it.

Allen Jones was puzzled as to the action he should take. He did not think it would be completely fair to Speedy to reject the thirty-two units, because he felt that Alex Precision Manufacturing Company had some responsibility for the loss. He also knew that Mr. Speed had spent considerably more than he had anticipated on getting adequately tooled for the job. He was debating in his own mind the advisability of permitting Mr. Speed to raise the price to compensate him for this change in circumstances.

1 What are the sources of this problem?
2 What do you think would be an equitable solution to the problem?

CHEAPER BY THE DOZEN

Irene Johnson has just been promoted from expediter to assistant buyer. Irene is responsible for the purchase of roughly $1 million of maintenance, repair, and operating supplies at the Coal Dust Mining Company.

The Coal Dust Mining Company uses approximately 16,000 wood shores each year. Irene recently forwarded a request for bids to four suppliers of this commodity. The low bid is as follows:

0–399	$7.50 each
400–599	$7.00 each
600 or more	$6.75 each

Transportation costs are: 0–399, $1.25 per unit; 400 or more, $1.00 per unit. Inventory carrying costs are 30 percent of the value of the average annual inventory. Variable order processing costs are estimated to be $60.

Irene is familiar with EOQ concepts, but she has never been exposed to a problem just like this.

1 What items should be considered when determining the optimal order size?
2 What is the optimal order quantity for Coal Dust's shores? (Show your work.)

COLLIER COMPANY II

Assume that instead of pricing the purchase for stools by competitive bidding, as was done in Collier Company I, the purchasing manager (PM) decided to negotiate this purchase. All the facts that applied to Collier Company I (text page 800) also apply to this case with one exception. Instead of requesting bids, the PM requested quotations, and all suppliers were advised that the purchase would be negotiated.

After receiving the quotations from the competing suppliers, the PM made the following listing to help him start his analysis:

- Supplier A's price of $55.92 is 140% of G's price of $39.00.
- Supplier B's price of $44.70 is 115% of G's price.
- Supplier C's price of $39.48 is 100.13% of G's price.
- Supplier D's price of $45.36 is 116% of G's price.
- Supplier E's price of $43.86 is 112% of G's price.
- Supplier F's price of $38.70 is 99% of G's price.
- Supplier H's price of $42.78 is 110% of G's price.
- Supplier I's price of $48.60 is 124% of G's price.

From the above listing, it was clear to the PM that suppliers C and G were the suppliers with whom he should negotiate. Other suppliers were asking from 10 to 40 percent more money than these suppliers. Although supplier F submitted the low bid, this supplier was considered to be unsatisfactory because of labor troubles that had occurred after he had been invited to bid. Therefore, his bid was rejected.

After carefully considering his initial analysis, the PM decided that his first negotiation step would be to request a cost breakdown from suppliers C and G. At this point, the PM did not know how much lower he could get these companies to go. However, he did know the pricing theory involved, and he knew that he must apply this theory to the practical situation at hand. For good negotiation, he also knew that a knowledge of variable and fixed costs was essential.

In response to his request for a cost breakdown, the PM received the following information:

	Company C cost	Company G cost
Labor	$13.20	$ 9.00
Material	13.08	12.00
Overhead	13.20	18.00
	$39.48	$39.00

1 What are some of the most important factors that will influence the cost for both C and G of the stools that are being purchased?

2 How can the PM use the cost breakdown information that he has available to help him negotiate the price he wants?

3 What principal negotiation arguments should the PM present to the two low bidders before requesting their final quotations?

4 Approximately what dollar profit do you believe the successful supplier will most likely receive from this order?

DELTA STEEL COMPANY

The Delta Steel Company produces a large annual tonnage of sheet steel, tin plate, galvanized sheets, black plate, merchant bar, and other products. Company operations are on a substantial scale, as indicated by the fact that annual purchases, exclusive of capital equipment, average $200 million.

Purchasing is centralized in a department headed by the director of purchasing, who reports directly to the president of the company. The director of purchasing is, therefore, on a coordinate organizational level with the executives in charge, respectively, of operations, engineering, marketing, and finance. The purchasing department personnel consists of the director, the assistant director, buyers, clerks, and typists. The director, in addition to his responsibility for general administration of the purchasing function, formulates purchasing policies, handles the major problems of coordination with various departments of the company, and represents his company in those industrial, governmental, and other external activities involving important procurement matters. Although thousands of different items are bought during the course of a year, the director concerns himself with the purchase of such principal items as major capital equipment, construction, and raw materials, including those requiring contract negotiation, such as steel scrap and sulphuric acid.

It was the purchasing department's normal practice to have several sources of supply for all important materials and continuously to seek new and better sources. For the past fourteen years, however, the Delta Steel Company had contracted for its entire requirements of sulphuric acid from the Eureka Chemical Corporation, a subsidiary of a large metal mining and smelting company. Because of the fact that the Eureka Chemical Corporation produced sulphuric acid as a by-product from smelter stack fumes, its costs were appreciably less than those of several local chemical companies that manufactured the acid from natural sulphur. In fact, the price of locally produced sulphuric acid was from 15 to 20 percent higher than the delivered price of the Eureka Chemical Corporation, although its plant was several hundred miles distant. Delta did purchase excess requirements from either of two local suppliers on occasion.

Despite the price disadvantage that they faced, the local chemical companies had regularly and aggressively solicited the sulphuric acid business of the Delta Steel Company. They pointed out the hazards of a single source of supply and the propriety of patronizing local industry. Sulphuric acid is not only a critical item in the manufacture of certain steel products, but one involving considerable annual expenditure. In the case of the Delta Steel Company, purchases of this acid amounted to $1.7 million or more in a year of capacity operation.

Sulphuric acid is used for the pickling of strip steel after the steel has been hot rolled. The long strips of steel are passed through a 25 percent solution of acid, which removes scale, oil, grease, and dirt. This surface cleansing is essential before tin plate or galvanized sheets can be made, since otherwise tin or zinc would not adhere properly to the steel. Even for steel sold in the form of black or uncoated sheets, the surface must be similarly pickled before the subsequent operation of cold rolling. For pickling purposes, only the highest grade of sulphuric acid is usable. In trade terms this grade is specified as pure virgin acid or 100 percent H_2SO_4.

Sulphuric acid is essential to the manufacture of a wide variety of products other than steel. Among them are gasoline, paper, fertilizer, and chemical products ranging from rayon to explosives, dyes, rubber, and paint.

During a current period of scarcity of sulphuric acid, the plant of the Eureka Chemical Corporation was closed down by a strike. The Delta Steel Company had experienced no shortage, however, as the Eureka Chemical Company, in order to fulfill its contract obligations, had purchased sulphuric acid from the local manufacturers and absorbed the difference in price.

As the strike extended well into the second month, the vice president of operations of the Delta Steel Company became increasingly concerned over the situation. He voiced anxiety as to whether there would be an interruption in the shipments of acid. Steel companies do not store large quantities of sulphuric acid, depending instead on scheduled daily receipts.

The director of purchases stated that he had implicit confidence in the Eureka Chemical Corporation's management and that, in accordance with the terms of the contract, three tank cars of acid had been received at the steel mill daily. Moreover, he said that the contract contained a cancellation clause that permitted either party to withdraw from the agreement on ninety days' notice and, as yet, the supplier had not availed itself of this privilege. The vice president of operations still had some misgivings. He argued that the strike could well be a protracted one, and the Eureka Chemical Corporation could properly exercise the ninety-day cancellation provision. At the end of that period, the Delta Steel Company would have to rely on local suppliers. The present scarcity of acid, together with the vulnerable position of the company, might well mean a substantial increase in the price of acid, with a resultant increase in steel production costs.

The director of purchases took the position that his company had benefited financially and in other ways from its long and satisfactory relationship with the Eureka Chemical Corporation. He did not feel, after fourteen years, that such a relationship should be abandoned when that particular supplier had the misfortune to be shut down by a strike that might be settled at any time. He also pointed out that any purchasing transaction is a two-way proposition and should be mutually advantageous to buyer and seller. He stated that trade relationships developed on this basis are invaluable, and related the instance in which he had voluntarily testified in a freight-rate case on behalf of the Eureka Chemical Corporation a year or so ago. The local manufacturers of sulphuric acid had petitioned the Interstate Commerce Commission for an increase in freight rates on acid into the local territory. If the increase had been granted, the delivered price of sulphuric acid for the Eureka Chemical Corporation to the plant of the Delta Steel Company would have been 10 percent more than that of the local manufacturers. This would undoubtedly have precluded the Eureka Chemical Corporation from participation in the local business. Finally, the director of purchases expressed confidence in being able to negotiate a contract with either or both of the local suppliers in the event that the Eureka Chemical Corporation terminated its contract.

The vice president of operations remained unconvinced and continued to question the practice of concentrating the purchases of a vital commodity with a single supplier—a commodity, furthermore, for which there was no substitute. In his judgment there was a long but indefinite period of capacity operations ahead, and every means practicable should be taken to prevent any interruption to production. He suggested that in view of their opposed opinions, he and the director of purchasing take the matter before the president of the company.

1 If you were the president of the Delta Steel Company, what decision would you make regarding this controversy? Explain why.

2 With respect to sulphuric acid or any other item of major importance, what are the advantages and the disadvantages of concentrating purchases with a single supplier?

3 What are your reactions to the proposition of patronizing home industries as advanced by the sales representatives of the local acid manufacturers?

4 The director of purchasing in the Delta Steel Company reported to the president. Under what circumstances do you think the purchasing function should enjoy equal organizational status with such other functions as engineering, production, marketing, and finance?

DIATECH VERSUS RPM

Diatech, Inc., was becoming the market leader in the growing clinical diagnostics industry. The company develops and manufactures reagents used in the detection of pregnancy, heart disease, infectious diseases, and cancer. Hospital laboratories are provided with instruments to run the manufacturer's test as a standard marketing practice. Diatech introduced a new instrument, the Spectrum, two years ago in order to be more competitive in this market.

The Spectrum was placed in laboratories with an agreement to purchase a minimum number of kits monthly. This program was an effective way to gain new customers as well as to introduce new products to existing accounts. Altanta Scientific manufactured the Spectrum for Diatech at a price of $3,500 per unit. Placement rate was forecasted to be 100 units per month.

Atlanta Scientific and Diatech developed the Spectrum II, taking advantage of design and technology improvements, lowering unit costs to $2,500 per unit. Cost savings were estimated at $100,000 per month.

Diatech's senior buyer, Paula Green, identified Roland Plastic Molding (RPM) as the prime candidate to supply the required molds to Atlanta Scientific. A contract was negotiated to manufacture three tools (molds) for components of the case. The terms of the contract included:

1. A physical description and performance criteria for the mold. Drawings were to be provided by Atlanta Scientific.
2. A maintenance agreement with RPM while parts are manufactured at RPM.
3. RPM would construct the mold so it could be used in other injection molding machines. Diatech would be the sole owner of the tools.
4. The price was $44,202 and payment terms were:
   a. The first third due with the purchase order, $14,734.
   b. The second third due on 50 percent completion of the mold.
   c. The final payment on acceptance of the first article.
5. The mold fabrication time was to be ten to twelve weeks after receipt of the first payment.

Three months after the first purchase order was placed, Sam Colousseau, the sales manager at RPM, called Paula demanding the second payment. Paula contacted Bob Potter, the vice president of engineering at Atlanta, to determine whether RPM deserved to be paid. Bob claimed the first article parts did not meet dimensional specifications and insisted payment should not be made until the problems were corrected. Bob also said work had not begun on the bottom of the case. The bottom was crucial, since all pieces fit into the case bottom. Bob further stated RPM insisted that the parts must be manufactured at RPM, since the contract specified Diatech owned only the tool and not the tool block. The tool block allowed the mold to be interchanged with other machines. Paula decided to report the situation to her superior, the vice president for operations, Ron O'Grady. O'Grady was very upset. He asked, "Why did you let that incompetent at Atlanta monitor the contract for you?" Paula was directed to assemble a task force consisting of representatives from quality control, engineering, and marketing to resolve the situation in two weeks. The introduction of the Spectrum II was due in ten weeks. Paula had her work cut out for her to resolve this problem, or Diatech would lose $100,000 per month in cost savings.

1 What alternatives are available to Diatech at this stage?
2 Which alternative should Paula choose?

DYNAFLIGHT, INC., CALIFORNIA DIVISION

Part I

Mary Williamson was in a dilemma. As the facilities subcontract administrator within the purchasing department at Dynaflight, she was responsible for all contracts pertaining to facilities maintenance at the California Division. On her desk was a request for a $40,000 open-ended contract with an electrical company to perform repairs on an as-needed basis. The request had been submitted by the facilities manager and recommended that the Eveready Electrical Company be awarded the project. Williamson knew that the facilities manager was outside of the purchasing department and had no authority to award business, yet the manager, Ron Tyler, had already promised the job to Eveready, a company owned by a close personal friend. Williamson also knew that Eveready was not the optimum source for electrical repair contracting. Having previously conducted a market survey, Williamson had determined that the Shining Light Electrical Company could perform the same work at a rate 27 percent lower than Eveready. Furthermore, Shining Light had performed the initial electrical installation within the building and had thus been certified by the Dynaflight purchasing department. Yet the facilities manager had been vociferous in his support for Eveready.

The California Division

Dynaflight, California Division, operated a support system whose principle product was the development of flight simulators for various commercial aircraft. These simulators were purchased by commercial airlines for pilot training and were considered indispensable by the airlines for providing a relatively inexpensive means of ground training in sophisticated and realistic scenarios. The California Division was an "old boy" network that had not adapted to the transitions that had taken place within the last two years. Dynaflight had been acquired in a financial merger that left the parent company with a heavy long-term debt. Dynaflight had always been a profitable operation, but the new owners brought their own mandates for lean and cost-effective measures, value analysis, and increased attention to budgets and expenditures. The California Division employed about 2,500 people and continued to hold on to old methods of operation.

Mary Williamson

Mary Williamson had come to Dynaflight from a senior buyer position with a major defense contractor. During this time Williamson had been impressed with company policies of operating "by the book." Tight control over all company procurements was necessary in the cutthroat world of government military contracts, an environment coming under increasingly close scrutiny by public and private organizations.

When Williamson had interviewed with Dynaflight, she felt she had satisfied herself that the company operated along clearly defined policies of procurement and that Dynaflight held the highest standards of conduct. She also had made it very clear that Dynaflight was aware it was getting a buyer accustomed to making multimillion dollar decisions and that the position she would be moving into would utilize these skills. She was impressed with the potential she saw in Dynaflight, and the California Division offered what she believed to be a good opportunity to begin in the company.

A Collision of Worlds

When Williamson relocated to California she was unprepared for the conditions that awaited her. The division ran as its department heads saw fit, and the purchasing department was in complete disarray as a result. Procurements were routinely made by engineers and rubber-stamped by the purchasing department. The underlying modus operandi in purchasing was "Don't make waves." Approximately one year prior to Williamson's arrival, purchasing had balked at confirming decentralized procurements and promotions within the department had subsequently ceased. Turnover was running at 25 percent, and conditions were so bad when Williamson got there that no records existed of contracts held for current facilities maintenance. She had little recourse other than to call companies whose representatives she found in the building and ask if contracts were held with Dynaflight, and if so, what the terms and conditions were. Williamson would then develop fair market values for the contracts and reissue them to the companies. In this manner she began to establish some order to maintenance contracting.

Although improvements were made, Williamson soon became disillusioned with the division. Despite clear company policies that purchasing was the only department authorized to make acquisitions, Williamson saw herself as little more than an implementor of buying decisions made by engineers and division department heads. Several departments were in an ongoing process of acquiring computer workstations for their engineers. The procurement process consisted of the engineers selecting the systems and suppliers they desired and then purchasing issuing confirmation orders. Williamson strongly felt that either company policy should change to accommodate these and other practices at the California Division or the practices should cease. She was very uncomfortable with the wink-and-nod procedures she saw at the division and felt that purchasing not only was being poorly utilized but also was forced to cover up for other departments overstepping their boundaries. In the four months she had been at the California Division, Williamson had clashed numerous times with her purchasing department head over the rubber-stamping issue. She felt that the contract request for Eveready Electrical had gone too far.

Williamson's boss, Lou James, had been with Dynaflight for just four years, yet he had risen quickly in purchasing. James saw himself as a team player and attributed his advancements to keeping the engineers happy. The division had been a leader in flight simulator development and production; it was critical to get to market ahead of the competition; and James felt that the working relations at the division contributed to its ability to put out quality products. He was aware of the mandates introduced after the merger, yet it was hard to argue with success. When the "brass" had visited California after the merger, James put his house in order to display compliance with the new directives. Afterward, it was business as usual.

1 What are the options that Williamson faces in writing up the electrical contract?
2 What are the principle sources of conflict that Williamson faces in preparing purchasing contracts?
3 What resources are available to Williamson to support her desires to reach a fair and equitable contract for the electrical maintenance?

DYNAFLIGHT, INC.

Part II

The facilities manager was quite surprised. Word had gotten to him that purchasing was about to issue the electrical repair contract to Shining Light Electrical Company. Robert Tyler was not a little angry that, as facilities manager, his recommendations in a matter of building maintenance were being so casually ignored. He also had heard that a newcomer to the department had suggested that Shining Light be awarded the contract. Tyler had been with Dynaflight for 12 years and had amassed considerable influence in a great many of the division's operations. He prided himself on his ability to "get things done" and enjoyed a good working relationship with numerous department heads at the division. These were individuals who had been with the company for a long time and admired the energy and the hours that Tyler put into his job. These individuals shared Tyler's disregard for red tape when it got in the way of making things happen for the company. Tyler felt as if the purchasing department decision was a challenge to his influence. He knew that purchasing was well within its rights to award the contract to whomever it chose, yet he felt as if something was being taken away from him.

Tyler discussed the situation with some of the department heads. Although he expressed no outrage himself, he raised the question of why purchasing was suddenly ignoring the wishes of the shakers in the division. The department heads with whom Tyler conferred shared his concern. They were very accustomed to having their wishes carried out, and did not like the idea that suddenly there were going to be consultations and questions over their decisions. They decided to talk to the head of the purchasing department and set things straight.

When the department heads confronted James with the issue of the electrical contract, he quickly acquiesced and decided to rewrite the contract, giving a $40,000 contract to Eveready and a $40,000 contract to Shining Light. He certainly didn't need a storm brewing over what he felt had been a very good working relationship. Furthermore, James informed Williamson that any correspondence from or to other departments would have to pass through James's desk for routine review.

4 What is the prevailing attitude at the California Division regarding purchasing's role?
5 Do you think the department heads would view their actions to circumvent company policy regarding purchasing as unethical?

DYNAFLIGHT, INC.

Part III

After the merger, a rigid and clearly established code of conduct was introduced to those subsidiaries that had been taken over. The parent company was committed to a policy of integrity and had set up a corporate ethics hierarchy, headed by an ethics administrator and composed of group ethics administrators. These persons were available to answer any questions regarding proper behavior and would hold all reports in the strictest confidence.

Williamson found herself in an untenable position. She had lost the support of her boss over the electrical contract issue, and had lost her power to conduct procurement independent of outside influence. Having considerable experience in conducting multimillion dollar contracts, she was certainly not going to accept having her every move overseen. Williamson felt that the old boy network was too entrenched to take on, and did not relish making accusations of a purchasing department casually disregarding company policy. The fact division practices had continued in the face of company-wide mandates to revamp operations convinced her that a stand would either be fruitless or, even if successful in the short run, would jeopardize her chances of future advancement. She felt that any reports to the ethics administrator would easily be traced to her.

Less than four months after she reported to the California Division, Williamson resigned from Dynaflight.

6 What elements contributed to the breakdown in the ethics policy at the California Division?

7 Do you think the company ethics department is aware of the goings-on at the California Division?

       If so, why have no actions been taken?

       If not, why not?

8 How can the company change the existing atmosphere at the division?

ELITE ELECTRONICS

Management at Elite Electronics is faced with a golden opportunity—or is it only fool's gold? Six months ago, marketing research indicated a potential market of 10,000 oscilloscopes per year, if Elite's selling price could be brought down to $1,000 per unit. (Elite's lowest-priced model, the EE201, currently sells for $1,485.)

Engineering had been working day and night to develop a new model whose variable production cost would be no more than $700. Purchasing had been working with present and potential suppliers to lower the total cost of purchased material. Recently, purchasing learned of the possibility of a breakthrough on material costs for the new oscilloscope. Gamma Conglomerates, working on the development of an analog-to-digital (ADC) module for three years, developed a revolutionary new process that allowed it to produce 1,000 modules a month. In order to guarantee the amortization of its research and development and setup costs, Gamma offered a price of $90 per unit F.O.B. the Elite plant if Elite would agree to purchase all of its ADCs for the new oscilloscope from Gamma for a period of five years. Full-scale production could begin in three months.

Incorporation of the new ADC would allow the elimination of four modules required in the present model EE201 oscilloscope with only a slight loss of resolution. This would result in a system whose variable production cost would be between $650 and $700, including $200 for assembly and testing. Allocations for fixed general, administrative, and marketing expenses would add approximately $200 per unit. Five prototype oscilloscopes incorporating the new ADC were built and tested. The new system was an engineering success!

Both engineering and marketing were very enthusiastic about the new system. Purchasing, manufacturing, and quality control shared their enthusiasm, but with some reservations. Purchasing was concerned that Gamma Conglomerates would be the sole source of supply for the ADC. Purchasing, quality control, and production shared another concern: the quality of incoming materials. Production already had experienced unpleasant situations with new "state-of-the-art" materials. Many electronics items and the systems that incorporate them are extremely complex and interdependent. It is not always possible to detect defective items until they are incorporated into larger modules or even the complete system. This is an inherent aspect of the sophisticated state-of-the-art production processes used to produce modern electronics components. Things go along fine for a while, and then for no apparent reason defects get completely out of control. It often takes ten to fourteen months to stabilize new production processes and eliminate the problems.

Great amounts of test and rework time may be required of Elite's production department to locate and correct this type of problem. For example, Elite currently is experiencing just such a situation on a new premium-quality oscilloscope. Test, rework, and assembly time is running at 400 percent of the work hours budgeted for the new oscilloscope. On the basis of his experience with previous state-of-the-art materials, Elite's production manager estimates that there are two chances in five of such a situation occurring with the new low-cost model if it incorporates Gamma's new ADC.

The high cost of such test and rework time can have disastrous implications for a firm like Elite. Items projected to make a profit contribution can wind up as losses. And, in some ways even more damaging to such a firm, promised delivery dates might not be met. As a result, current sales, customer goodwill, and future business all can suffer.

In many industries, the first firm to market a new product successfully is able to build and maintain a much stronger market position than firms that enter the market later. Elite believes that its likely market would be 10,000 units of the new low-priced oscilloscope for the first year of production and 6,000 per year for the following four years *if* it is the first firm to market such a low-priced oscilloscope. However, *if* the introduction is not successful (for quality or manufacturing reasons), the negative impact would reduce likely sales to 4,000 units for each of the five years. Production estimates that it would take approximately one year to clear up the problem. Accordingly, it appears realistic to assume that some 4,000 units would require excessive test, rework, and assembly time. The unit variable cost of the 4,000 units would be an estimated $1,275. Marketing believes that likely sales would be 6,000 units per year for four years if Elite were to wait for the ADC production process to stabilize or if a less risky approach became available in approximately ten to fourteen months. Purchasing is confident that alternatives to the ADC will be available at that time. These alternatives will use proven technology and cost approximately $45, lowering variable production costs to about $630 per unit.

Management at Elite truly is in a predicament. Should it grab the new ADC and run for the pot of gold, or should it play things safe and wait for more proven technology and competitive sources?

1 Should Elite proceed with the new low-cost oscilloscope incorporating the new analog-to-digital module (ADC)?

2 Who should be involved in the decision-making process? Who has the final responsibility for the decision?

3 What other issues related to this problem should be of concern to purchasing and materials management?

FLORIDA RETAIL COMPANY

Overview

The Florida Retail Company is a collection of small consumer electronic retail stores. The company is known for its personal and efficient service. Susan Bender, the Vice President of Operations, prides herself on running one of the most efficient operations in the electronics retail industry. One of the main tools for this efficiency is a computer system which allows FRC to closely monitor sales progress and inventory turnover rates.

The computer system in operation was bought and is currently maintained by ACME Retail Computer Services. ACME and Florida Retail have had an excellent and mutually profitable relationship for the past 10 years. FRC maintains a small staff of three people to run the ACME retail system.

New Strategy

The Florida Retail Company is planning a bold strategic move into the consumer electronic retail industry. The company plans to phase out all of its current smaller retail stores and mold its business around large super-stores. The first store will be the showcase and model for future stores. Jack Murphy, the owner of FRC, has envisioned a futuristic computer system to support his new store concept. The new computer system will provide all the functionality of the current system (accounts payable, accounts receivable, general ledger, purchasing, inventory control, sales analysis) and have a fully integrated point-of-sale function. Jack envisions a "paperless" sales floor where all transactions and merchandise reservations are handled by the computer system. Additionally, the new computer system will have an optical bar code reading capability to facilitate customer transactions.

The first super-store will open at this time next year. FRC plans to open at least two other super-stores in the year following.

Need for New System

Susan Bender, the vice president of operations, realized that the current computer system supplied by ACME would not support the larger operations of the future super-store. After some inquiries, Susan believed that ACME was the only supplier capable of offering the software needed. ACME was currently in the process of developing a software package that would provide all the functions of the current systems for larger operations.

Susan contacted David Lansing, the CEO of ACME, to discuss a possible deal. The two quickly agreed that ACME would supply the needed computer software system for FRC. Susan would be involved initially to help develop the customized point-of-sale system for FRC. Beyond that, ACME agreed to deliver a new software system capable of all functions the old system provided plus integrating the customized point-of-sale system. FRC was to be the first ACME customer to use the new computer system. It was agreed that the software was to be in place two weeks before opening day of the new super-store and the hardware needed for the software was to be in place one month prior to opening day.

A fixed price of $350,000 for the software was proposed by ACME based on a $3 million estimate for total development costs. The price of the software was derived by prorating the development costs (including the point-of-sale system) over the expected number of customers and adding 15 percent for profit. ACME required that 50 percent of the purchase price was to be paid up front and the remainder was to be paid upon delivery of the software system.

Susan thought that the price was fair and the terms and deadlines of the agreement were satisfactory. Close monitoring of ACME's progress would not be necessary since Susan has always relied on ACME to successfully solve FRC's computer system problems; besides, nobody at FRC knew much about developing computer software systems.

Opening Day (Six Months Later)

Susan was a bit nervous this morning. Everything about the store was ready, but there had been some problems with the computer system during these past two weeks. Her system manager, Helen Cooley, as well as two ACME representatives had been spending many sleepless nights fixing and tuning the system. Susan hoped all the major problems were resolved.

A long line of people were waiting to get into the store when the doors finally opened. Right away there were problems with the computer software system supplied by ACME. The first customer to be serviced at the cashier's station took 20 minutes to finally get out of the store due to the slowness of the computer software system. Salespeople were complaining about slow computer response time when they tried to reserve merchandise through the system. Soon, there was a long line of people at every cashier station and with every salesperson. Customers were leaving the store due to long lines at the cashier stations and slow salespeople. The computer system finally "crashed" in midafternoon and became inoperable. The employees of FRC had no idea what to do next.

That evening, Jack Murphy had a meeting with Susan, Helen, and two ACME representatives. Jack told them that the computer system was going to put him out of business and they had better do something about it.

1 Do you feel that the fixed price contract agreed to by Florida Retailing Company was the best way to procure ACME's computer system?
2 Where did FRC go wrong in purchasing the software system?
3 Was the Statement of Work sufficient? What could or should have been added?
4 What are the problems encountered in purchasing a high-technology software system?
5 How could the problems on opening day have been avoided?

This case was developed by David Strangland and Barbara Meehan under the direction of Professor David N. Burt.

G.A.R. MANUFACTURING COMPANY

The G.A.R. Manufacturing Company is a producer of toys and small appliances with a seasonal sales pattern. Its sales are about $120 million a year. Recently the board of directors decided that G.A.R. should diversify, so it acquired the Wonder Chemical Company, a firm with $40 million sales of resins and chemicals. Wonder's market is mainly industrial, with an even year-round sales pattern, and the company has the reputation of being a fast-growing outfit in the field. Its one plant is located about 100 miles from G.A.R.'s factory, in the same state.

When the acquisition was completed, the president of G.A.R. said to Ralph Foster, his purchasing director, "I wonder if we should combine the purchasing departments of the two companies. I know both companies make widely different product lines, but there ought to be some economies, maybe in personnel and paperwork. Perhaps we could work out some transportation deals. For that matter, there may be some overlap in buying maintenance supplies.

"I understand that Wonder's purchasing manager is a very good man, and of course, you know that we've promised to retain all their executives. But I would like you to look into the situation and let us know what you recommend. I've told them you'll be coming over."

Ralph's department consists of himself, four buyers, and five clerks and secretaries. It is responsible for buying all materials, components, and operating supplies, as well as inbound traffic. However, Ralph knows that his department has no experience in purchasing chemical industry raw materials, equipment, or supplies. Wonder's purchasing department includes five people and is responsible only for buying.

1 If you were Ralph Foster, what facets of the situation would you explore in order to make an intelligent report?
2 What recommendations would you put into a formal report to your president?

GOTHAM CITY BUYS FIRE ENGINES

Mayor Harold Goodfellow of Gotham City is faced with a touchy situation involving a City Hall dispute between his newly appointed city purchasing manager, Ed Frisby, and Gotham's venerable fire chief, Willard Clark.

It all started soon after Mayor Goodfellow hired Frisby following a favoritism scandal linked to the purchases of the previous city purchasing manager. To prevent a recurrence of the problem, the mayor gave Frisby instructions to set up a standards committee and gave the new city purchasing manager full backing in enlisting assistance from other city employees.

In accordance with the mayor's instructions, Frisby formed a committee consisting of a Fire Department representative selected by Chief Clark, an engineer from the Public Works Department, a woman from the Finance Department, and himself. The group began working on the high value purchases, and the first on the agenda was the purchase of ten new fire pumping engines and five extension ladder trucks, involving an estimated expenditure of approximately $600,000 for the pumpers and another $1 million for the ladder trucks.

Frisby got together with the standards committee and representatives of firefighting equipment suppliers. Through these meetings the committee prepared open specifications, to which all agreed.

Bids were received, opened publicly, and then analyzed. The purchasing manager, in accordance with the unanimous findings of the committee, recommended that the city accept the lowest bid that met the minimum specifications in all respects. There was considerable spread between the lowest and the next lowest bids.

Then the trouble began. Shortly after making this recommendation, purchasing manager Frisby learned that Chief Clark had sent a resolution to the City Council recommending rejection of all the bids and award of the contract to another higher-priced supplier. Clark told the City Council that he would not be responsible for fighting fires unless his selection of equipment was approved by the council.

The mayor called Frisby. "Look, Ed," he said, "I'm in the middle of this fire equipment dispute. I think you're right in this hassle, and I want to support your work on the standards committee. But Chief Clark is a respected old-timer around here, and I think he's got some of the City Council on his side. Do you have any ideas on how to settle this difficulty and keep the chief happy too?"

1 What should Frisby tell the mayor?
2 How should the city purchasing manager help solve the fire equipment dispute to the satisfaction of the fire chief and the city council?

GREAT WESTERN UNIVERSITY

Dan Summerfield just recently took over as director of purchasing for Great Western University. Great Western spent roughly $400,000 a year for the purchase of various kinds of plumbing supplies. These supplies included such items as pipe, tees, elbows, and many small plumbing repair parts. However, they also included some expensive items such as large valves and water heaters. Because its plumbers were poor planners, Great Western maintained approximately a $240,000 inventory of plumbing supplies in its stores system. The university purchased its plumbing requirements from four plumbing supply houses.

Mr. Summerfield believed that if the university could consolidate its plumbing purchases with a single supplier who could supply all its needs, Great Western could save money two ways: first, by getting lower prices, and second, by reducing inventories. Within the geographical area where Great Western is located, there were two very large plumbing suppliers and six small plumbing suppliers. Mr. Summerfield visited each and carefully reviewed its managerial, technical, and financial capabilities.

The closest plumbing supplier to Great Western University was Bumble Bee Plumbing Services. This company was owned by the Bee family, and last year sales were roughly $64 million. Although Bumble Bee had many warehouses and offices throughout the state, one of its largest outlets was in Red City, just a few miles from Great Western. In fact, it was so close to the university that the plumbers regularly went there to pick up plumbing parts and participate in the free coffee and soft drinks Bumble Bee made available for its pick-up customers.

Bumble Bee was managed by Mr. John Bee, age 74 and senior member of the Bee family. John Bee had worked in the family business since he was fifteen years old. His desk was located just inside the front door of the company's largest branch, where he was readily available to all who wanted to see him. Also, as he stated, "From here I can keep an eye on everything going on in the business." When questioned about the size of Bumble Bee's inventory by Dan Summerfield, Mr. Bee stated that he didn't know the exact size because he used no formal inventory control system, but he figured the inventory to be about $80 million, or a little over a year's supply of *everything*. Bumble Bee had excellent young managers, but for the most part Mr. Bee would not let them manage. For example, the purchasing manager told Dan Summerfield that only a few months ago he showed Mr. Bee a plan for reducing inventory by $20 million with little or no loss in customer effectiveness or product cost. Mr. Bee would have none of the plan. The company's controller told Summerfield that Bumble Bee's financial position was unbelievable. The "Old Man" had no interest in financial ventures outside the company, and for years he had just let its cash position grow until it now exceeded $30 million in cash assets. Total liabilities were less than $4 million.

After proposing an annual contract with Bumble Bee, Mr. Summerfield was told by Mr. Bee that his firm *never* sold for less than wholesale list price, and it would not sell to Great Western for anything less than that. With great pride Mr. Bee stated that Great Western might pay a little more for material from Bumble Bee, but his company *never* would be out of anything Great Western might need. Although Mr. Bee would not reduce prices to get an annual contract, he would give daily delivery service to Great Western in consideration for such a contract. Mr. Summerfield estimated that daily delivery from Bumble Bee's huge back-up inventory would permit him to reduce his own inventory from the present $240,000 to $80,000.

The largest plumbing supplier in Great Western's area was Automated Plumbing Supply. This was a widely held corporation with a staff of professional managers, the majority having been trained in well-known graduate schools of business. Automated's sales throughout the state last year totaled $100 million. Automated's closest outlet to Great Western was 12 miles away in the city of Dumbarton. That branch was not large; however, it could be resupplied daily from Automated's large central warehouse in the city of Field. Field is a large industrial center about 30 miles from Great Western.

Automated had experienced rapid growth during the past ten years, its compounded growth rate being approximately 20 percent per year. Members of the management team at Automated pointed with pride to their new computer, which was located at their headquarters in Field. The computer, in addition to providing reports to guide the company's overall operations, controlled the inventory in all twelve Automated branch warehouses. By use of the computer, Automated was able to turn its inventory roughly five times per year, which meant it had on hand about $20 million of inventory at all times. Mr. Summerfield was told that stock-outs averaged about 5 percent. However, use of the computer might lower the percentage of stock-outs for the specific items Great Western buys. Automated's management was superb. Their capability and drive really impressed Summerfield. The management was young, aggressive, and very knowledgeable concerning the company's problems, how they could be solved, and where they were trying to take the company. Because of the company's rapid growth, finances in terms of accounting ratios appeared weak. Summerfield commented on this fact to the financial vice president. The latter readily admitted the weakness, explaining how the company planned to handle its finances to assure continued rapid growth. So sure of ultimate success were the managers that all had agreed to relatively low salaries with high stock options. This faith removed Summerfield's doubts.

Because of Automated's efficient operations, the company felt able to offer Mr. Summerfield a very attractive discount schedule, averaging 15 percent below wholesale list price, if he would sign a year's contract to purchase all his plumbing supplies from Automated. Under the contract, Automated would deliver twice a week. Mr. Summerfield believed that semiweekly deliveries and a 5 percent stock-out level at Automated would enable him to reduce his inventory from $240,000 to $160,000.

The other plumbing supply firms in the area typically had sales of less than $4 million. Some of these firms had only one office, but others had several branches. All of them were owner-managed and prided themselves on their "personalized" service. Several of these firms offered Mr. Summerfield a flat 25 percent discount if he would sign up with them. Typically, these firms had average stock-out levels exceeding 10 percent. Each of these firms could deliver only once weekly to Great Western. Therefore, Summerfield could not reduce his inventory meaningfully, if at all, were he to contract with one of the smaller firms. However, the substantial 25 percent discount was attractive and interesting to Summerfield.

What should Dan Summerfield do? Should he contract with Bumble Bee? Automated? A small supplier?

HARTINCO, INC.

John Angst, purchasing director at Vista Junior College, was in the process of developing a pricing mechanism for a contract for information retrieval and reporting services. Hartinco, Inc., was established two years ago by Jennifer Hart, a recent M.B.A. graduate. The company specialized in information retrieval and report preparation for a variety of clients. There were two production cost centers: Information Retrieval and Report Writing. To assist these production centers the company had two service centers, namely, the Data Processing and Library Services. Costs of these service areas were charged to the two production centers at the end of the month. The allocation was based on the amount of direct labor hours spent on the projects by each center. Each project was then charged an amount per direct labor hour for each production cost center's overhead. Indirect costs included rent, utilities, and labor. Rent and utilities were allocated to the four cost centers according to square footage of office space; indirect labor was assigned to each department as incurred. Information Retrieval and Report Writing each occupied 5,000 square feet. Data Processing occupied 1,250 square feet, and Library Services occupied 10,000 square feet.

Jennifer had approached John's request for cost data in a very open manner. She provided the following data on January transactions:

1. $560 (80 hours) of direct information retrieval labor were incurred for Project A.
2. $175 (25 hours) of direct information retrieval labor were incurred for Project B.
3. $1,120 (160 hours) of direct information retrieval information were incurred for Project C.
4. $140 (20 hours) of direct report preparation labor were incurred for Project A.
5. $70 (10 hours) direct report preparation labor were incurred for Project B.
6. $350 (50 hours) of direct report preparation labor were incurred for Project C.
7. Rent was $2,000.
8. $3,200 for indirect Data Processing labor expenses.
9. $1,380 for indirect Library Services labor expenses.
10. $350 for indirect Information Retrieval labor expenses.
11. Utilities were $400.
12. $1,000 for other Data Processing expenses.
13. $100 for other Library Services expenses.

Jennifer and John were to meet to develop a pricing mechanism for the college's contract.

1 Determine the amount of direct costs for each project for the month of January 1989.
2 Calculate the indirect costs for each of the production and service departments for January 1989.
3 Calculate the rates at which indirect costs should be allocated to each project for each of the two production departments.
4 What is the full (total) cost of each of the three projects that were performed in January?
5 Develop a logical pricing mechanism for Vista's contract with Hartinco.

HYDROSUB'S UNFLOATABLE AMPHIBIOUS ASSAULT VEHICLE

Kathleen Johnson started her new job as chief buyer at Hydrosub in San Francisco. Her day was without incident until she received the following telephone call.

Voice on phone: Good afternoon, Ms. Johnson. I am Burt Lauderas, project supervisor at Bolger Shipyards in Tacoma. The design changes for the A.A.V. are not part of our current contract. We need to renegotiate the contract before instituting the changes. Completion of the A.A.V. will be delayed an additional four weeks.

Kathleen Johnson (mildly concerned): Is it really necessary to renegotiate the current contract before beginning the work?

Voice on phone: Yes, Ms. Johnson, the contract states that every design change must be renegotiated.

Kathleen Johnson (more concerned): Why will it take four additional weeks to complete the project?

Voice on phone: It will take time to renegotiate the contract and hire replacement welders, and approximately two weeks to do the rework.

Kathleen Johnson (completely bewildered): Thank you for calling, Mr. Lauderas. I'll contact you tomorrow.

After recovering her composure, she opened the A.A.V. file and started the formation of her first ulcer. Status reports showed that progress toward completion had been slow. The last chief buyer had been "retired" when costs exceeded the original estimate of $9 million. Revised cost estimates revealed expected expenditures to exceed $23 million. Particularly despairing was the fact that the completion date had already been revised four times and the current completion date was listed as "unknown."

After hours of reviewing the A.A.V. project file, Kathleen understood Burt Lauderas's concerns. The project involved building a prototype amphibious assault vehicle for the U.S. government. It had been Hydrosub's intent to build a premium product, without concern for cost. If Hydrosub received the subsequent production contract, the company's financial stability would be greatly enhanced. However, due to in-house capacity problems, Bolger Shipyards had been contracted to build the prototype.

Hydrosub engineers designed the prints and specifications for the prototype. These specifications incorporated the latest in high tech design and utilized the best materials available. Design specifications had changed innumerable times over the project's life. Continual rework and time delays had hampered progress. Bolger had reported design errors that necessitated the refitting of complex equipment and rework of the aluminum welding.

Materials requirements included the use of welded aluminum. Bolger normally employed only steel welders; aluminum welders were in short supply and impatient during work stoppages.

On the A.A.V. project, Bolger Shipyards currently employed 150 people on two shifts. Often Bolger required overtime work. The Bolger contract was cost-based plus a fixed fee.

A particularly disturbing problem was Bolger's cost reporting system. Bolger contract negotiators waited for up to three weeks for cost data. Weekly time cards, bimonthly reporting, and periodic analysis greatly hindered preparation for the contract talks.

As Kathleen Johnson reflected on the facts, her phone rang again.

Voice on phone: Hello, Ms. Johnson, welcome to Hydrosub. This is George Rope, president of Hydrosub.

Kathleen Johnson: Thank you, Mr. Rope.

George Rope: Mr. Johnson, I feel uneasy burdening you with the Bolger Shipyards problem, but I haven't any other choice. Your hiring was based on your tremendous qualifications. We had hoped to acclimate you to your responsibilities; unfortunately, there is no time. The A.A.V. project must be concluded soon. Over 100 Hydrosub employees are currently working on this project; they are discouraged. The government is very anxious, and we are competing for the future sales of this product. Utilize all your expertise and finish the prototype.

1 Who is responsible for the poor performance of the Bolger contract?
2 What caused the production delays and cost miscalculations?
3 What can Kathleen Johnson do now to ensure completion of the project and prevent further problems?
4 How should Hydrosub's staff have prepared for negotiations with suppliers on this contract?

This case was developed by Valerie Johnson, Karen Landgraf, Chelly Bolger, and Richard A. Harris under the direction of Professor David M. Burt.

HY TECH

Hy Tech is one of those fast-growing high technology firms that have sprung up like weeds around the Boston, Massachusetts, and Palo Alto, California, areas. In the past seven years, Hy Tech sales grew from $45 million to $750 million.

The success of firms such as Hy Tech depends on their abilities to produce an ever-increasing line of sophisticated products made from increasingly sophisticated parts and components. Consequently, new products and new ideas are the wellhead of Hy Tech's future prosperity.

Ed Williams, director of purchasing for Hy Tech, was a most conscientious purchasing manager. He realized that to keep up with new materials and products it was necessary for him to read prolifically, to talk with engineers and scientists whenever possible, and to attend electronic and similar trade shows several times a year. He also knew that he and his fourteen buyers had to see approximately seventy-two salespeople a day. To establish good supplier relations, Ed had established as one of his principal policies that every supplier calling at Hy Tech would receive a prompt and courteous hearing. He believed such a policy would guarantee Hy Tech a first chance at new items as quickly as they were invented.

The encouragement Ed gave potential new suppliers to bring their new ideas and their new products to Hy Tech caused the firm to be swamped with visiting sales representatives. Keeping track of them was difficult; evaluating them was almost impossible. One particular difficulty continuously perplexed Ed. When should he send sales reps with especially good new ideas or products to talk directly with Dr. Schmidt, Hy Tech's director of research and development? Dr. Schmidt was well known for his short temper and for not always being objective.

One afternoon in June, a salesman from Advanced Electronics, a small supplier, turned up with what appeared to be an outstanding new analog-to-digital converter. "Ed," the salesman said, "this new converter is exactly what Hy Tech has been looking for. However, it is extremely complicated; therefore, I think much time could be saved by you, me, and Dr. Schmidt if you would send me to talk directly with him." Ed reasoned with himself, "Should I call Dr. Schmidt and risk making a fool of myself if this converter is really a dud, or should I take a chance and ask the old boy to have a look at it in case it's as good as the Advanced salesman says it is?" Ed decided to call Dr. Schmidt.

Later that afternoon, in a high state of agitation, Dr. Schmidt called Ed. "Ed," he said, "Hy Tech pays dearly for my scientific knowledge and ability. To waste my time talking to screwball salesmen is really cheating the company. That salesman you sent to me early this afternoon was an absolute idiot! Besides that, my office and laboratory are filled with confidential company information, and I don't want any salesmen snooping around there. None of them can be trusted, and under no circumstances do I want to see any more of them."

Ed was crushed by Dr. Schmidt's phone call. He and his buyers were consciously aware that they lacked scientific training. Nonetheless, all were experienced in production, and up to this time they thought they had been doing their job of locating and screening new ideas and products very well. After reflecting back on previous experiences, Ed became a little hot under the collar. He deliberated, "Old Doc Schmidt really gets under my skin! He obviously has forgotten the time that purchasing discovered the key component that put our major product on the map and made Hy Tech wealthy and highly respected. That component practically had to be rammed down his throat. Although the discovery was worth millions of dollars to Hy Tech, Old Doc Schmidt just kept grumbling that he had not heard of the supplier."

Ed also was rankled because of what had happened at a staff meeting the week before. Hy Tech's president complained, "How come research and purchasing let that new gamma gobbler get away from us? Our competition has it, and they are building a whole line of highly profitable products with it. We will be lucky if we can catch up in two years! What has happened to our profitable policy of always being the first company to get new products?"

1 What generally happens when purchasing departments fail to pay prompt and courteous attention to potential suppliers and their offerings?
2 What can Ed Williams do to develop an effective new product screening system?

THE INVENTORY OCTOPUS

Tom Johnson, newly hired purchasing director at Smithers Industries, Inc., was about to tackle an inventory octopus. Word had just come from the board room that the directors had decreed a $1 million raw materials and supplies inventory reduction to conserve the company's working capital.

Smithers's president, Brashly Wintersee, had told Johnson during the hiring interview that inventory was one of their biggest problems, and that's why they were looking for a purchasing and inventory control person who could show them how to work some of the fat off the company's inventories. Johnson's background and experience were expected to turn the trick.

Johnson started to dig into the problem via a visit to each of Smithers's divisions: Mill Machinery Division, Whizzo Tool Division, and Aerlectro Division.

At the Mill Machinery Division, he heard from Elihu Adams, purchasing superintendent, "Don't know as how the home office can give us much help on inventory, Johnson. We've been making machinery here since 1887, and every customer knows he can get a replacement part from us for almost every machine we've ever made. That's the real service that sells our machines. See that pile of raw castings and plates out there? Don't imagine there's another company in the country that has such a complete stock of material all ready to be made up to customer orders. It's taken years to build this up, and it's worth millions! We figure it's all gravy after depreciation, too."

Jean Rogers, the purchasing manager at Whizzo Tool Division, told him, "Sure, I'm trying to get our inventory-sales in line with what the top brass at headquarters want. It's not purchasing materials that's out of the line now on Whizzo home hobby shop tools. Our big materials stock last quarter is now in production or in finished tools. Look at them in the warehouse, all backed up for the Christmas selling rush. We've been building up finished stock for a big season all summer. I sure hope our sales forecast is right."

Their Aerlectro purchasing manager, Nelson Briteway, told Johnson, "We don't have any inventory problem here in purchasing. All our money is out there on the shop floor in custom-built components. All gear we buy goes directly into a government space black box. Since our customer is Uncle Sam, we don't have any finished goods inventory and darn little in the stockroom."

Smithers's divisions ran under separate division vice presidents, so Tom couldn't tackle the inventory problem himself at each plant. Because he was close to the top brass as a brand-new, high-powered expert, he was expected to help the purchasing managers come up with some results—and fast.

1 What are the company's inventory troubles?
2 How can Tom cure them?

METROPOLITAN UNIVERSITY

In early March, senior buyer Daniel Bluestone was reviewing information he had collected about the purchasing function at Metropolitan University as part of his first major work assignment in the university's purchasing department. Much of the data suggested that adequate controls did not exist for the purchasing process.

Metropolitan University

Metropolitan University was a private educational institution located in New York City. Last year, the university's twenty-two schools, 25,000 undergraduates and graduate students, and 6,000 employees occupied 390 buildings on a sprawling urban campus.

The Purchasing Environment

University policy clearly stated that all buying responsibility rested with the purchasing department, and gave the department a "classic" charter to obtain the best quality, price and delivery for needed materials and services.

In the calendar year just passed, 30,000 purchase orders were issued, with an aggregate value of $35 million. Both the number of individual orders and the dollar value had been growing at an annual rate of 20 percent, and it was expected that this would continue for the foreseeable future as the university maintained its planned expansion. A new $150 million capital improvement plan was under consideration.

The purchasing organization consisted of thirteen people, six of whom had specific commodity buying responsibilities. Department head count had not changed in four years because of strict budget constraints imposed by the university administration. When there was an occasional vacancy, attracting qualified purchasing professionals to the academic environment was difficult.

Purchasing faced an increasing sophistication of the supply and service needs of the Metropolitan community as technology levels rose. Greater buyer breadth and expertise were required just to stay current with user demand. The purchasing department was using temporary personnel and student aides to stay current with the workload.

Three months ago, Daniel Bluestone came to the university with about a dozen years of industrial procurement experience. When he was hired, the director of purchasing asked him to take on a six-month overview assignment to look at current purchasing policy and procedure.

The Purchase Order Process

The purchasing system at Metropolitan University was paper-based and manually operated. When a need was identified, the requester filled out a preprinted and prenumbered requisition form, obtained necessary approvals, and transmitted the completed form to purchasing. Blank forms were widely available.

Incoming requisitions were sorted by commodity area and given to the appropriate buyer on a first-come, first-served basis. No priority was assigned and each requisition got the same attention. Buyers would complete the purchase, adding their identifying letter code to the six-digit number already on the form.

Receiving documents and invoices were matched with purchase orders in the purchasing department, sent to the requisitioner for approval, and, subsequently, to accounting for payment.

The Control Problem

Requisitioners complained that purchasing was not responsive to needs, was taking too long to handle emergencies, and was unable to provide status information on requisitions and purchase orders in process.

The situation at the present time was such that a significant number of requisitioners had "broken" the buyers' letter codes, and were beating the system by adding the appropriate buyer code to purchase orders and placing their own orders directly with suppliers.

Suppliers voiced common complaints that payments were continually late, and that questions about invoice status went unanswered.

Daniel Bluestone felt that the rest of his six-month departmental analysis project would be wasted if purchasing management did not address the control issue immediately.

1 Assume you are a consultant called in to work with Daniel Bluestone. List and discuss in some detail the major problems you see in the present Metropolitan University purchasing operation.

NAVAL OPERATING BASE, ARKLADELPHIA

Lieutenant June Early, a Navy contracting officer, was perplexingly involved in a difficult sole-source negotiation. The Trustworthy Equipment Company, with whom she was negotiating, was really giving her problems.

The Trustworthy Equipment Company was the only supplier of a special machine costing tens of thousands of dollars. This machine was useful in the maintenance and repair of nuclear submarines. Using the machine, it was possible for three or four mechanics to complete in an afternoon a job that would otherwise require a week or more. Thus, the purchase of Trustworthy machines would not only save the Navy money but would also reduce substantially the "downtime" on submarines. The Navy Purchasing Office, where Lieutenant Early worked, had been requested to obtain 100 Trustworthy machines.

In conducting the negotiations, Lieutenant Early encountered the following overhead rates, which the company willingly provided as part of a cost breakdown to explain its fixed price quotation. The Navy considered this quotation to be too high.

- Manufacturing overhead: 170 percent of direct labor
- Engineering overhead: 93 percent of direct engineering labor
- General and administrative expenses: 25 percent of operating cost (i.e., materials, direct labor, and manufacturing overhead)

Additionally, the company had included a contingency allowance of approximately 3.3 percent of all other costs.

Compared with other firms in the same general line of business, the overhead rates seemed unusually high. Therefore, Lieutenant Early requested detailed statements of the cost included in each of these overhead pools. After receipt and review of this information, Lieutenant Early concluded that many of the costs were highly questionable. An inspection of the company's facilities further confirmed this conclusion. It was the inspector's impression that inattention to duties, loafing around the soft drink machines, and similar practices were standard operating procedures. For these reasons, Lieutenant Early asked a representative of the Trustworthy Company to come to Arkladelphia to discuss the breakdown of costs with her.

When the representative arrived, Lieutenant Early pointed out to him the items that she regarded as questionable. She questioned the necessity for the company to employ one stenographer for every five production workers. She questioned the need in a small company for Trustworthy's elaborate management structure with its three separate echelons of management. Moreover, Lieutenant Early pointed out that members of the Hawthorn family, who owned the enterprise, seemed to occupy positions in management that duplicated those of other people in the management hierarchy. Lieutenant Early was particularly interested in one item of salary that she learned was being paid to the estate of an individual who had died over two years ago. When Lieutenant Early suggested that the Trustworthy Company must be a most pleasant place to work, the representative smiled and agreed with her. "People have a good time at the company," he said, "and there are lots of opportunities for relaxation and sociability."

Throughout the negotiation, the Trustworthy representative was pleasant and amiable, but he insisted that the costs the company had submitted were necessary and justified. Although Lieutenant Early succeeded in eliminating a few dollars in the cost of producing the item, she was unable to achieve any substantial reduction. She realized that the Navy needed the equipment and that use of the machines would save the Navy many times their cost. Yet she also recognized that the Navy's purchasing policy was based on the assumption that prices should reflect reasonable costs. With these thoughts in mind, Lieutenant Early, as the negotiator, wondered what her next step should be.

1 Should Lieutenant Early question costs that appear to be caused by "inefficient management"?

2 What action should Lieutenant Early take with respect to the contingency allowance of 3.3 percent?

3 What can Lieutenant Early do if the Trustworthy representative is unwilling to eliminate some of the unusual cost items?

OCR, INC.

OCR, Inc., produced a wide line of optical character recognition products. One of its new models, the 501, had been in development for two years. By the time the 501 was considered ready for production, demand for other OCR products completely filled the firm's production capacity. Management decided to subcontract the assembly of the 501. OCR would select and qualify all components going into the 501 assembly. Based on the urgency of the situation and the limited competition available, competitive negotiations were used to select the subcontractor. Jones Electronics was selected as the 501 assembler. Jones agreed to purchase all components (except the optical character recognition unit, which was to be supplied by OCR, Inc.) from sources shown on the OCR print. Jones's price for the delivered, assembled 501 was $872.

One of the components in the assembly was a plastic base, molded to an OCR design. The plastic base was to be produced on supplier-developed tooling. The tooling was to become the property of OCR on completion of the supplier's production run. Four suppliers had been invited by OCR to submit prices for the plastic base and the tooling under a request for competitive bids. The low bidder was Brown Molding Co., a leader in the field of precision molding. Brown's bid was $3.60 per unit as a rate of 1,000 units per month. Brown's price for the tooling was $47,750.

A purchase order was issued by OCR to Brown for the tooling and two sample bases. The samples were approved by OCR's quality control department. Brown was qualified as the source of supply for the base, and its name was inserted on the assembly drawing. Once Brown had been approved by OCR, Jones Electronics placed an order with Brown for a three-month supply of the bases.

An interesting procedure was established whereby duplicate gauges and fixtures were provided to both Jones and Brown. These were patterned to master gauges and fixtures at OCR. All the gauges and fixtures were new.

The relationship between OCR, Jones Electronics, and Brown Molding was as follows:

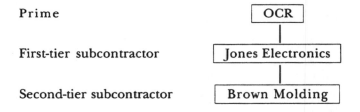

Prime   OCR

First-tier subcontractor   Jones Electronics

Second-tier subcontractor   Brown Molding

Thirty days after issuing a purchase order to Brown, Jones received the first shipment of 1,000 plastic bases. All other components required for the model 501 were received by Jones by the end of the following week. Twenty days later 1,000 assembled 501 units were shipped to OCR. They arrived in good condition. Inspection by OCR revealed that the Jones-assembled 501's did not conform with the OCR drawing. Detailed investigation revealed that a dimensional error in the Brown-supplied base was the culprit.

1 Comment on the manner in which the purchase was made. Could the problems have been minimized—or eliminated—by some other approach?
2 What was the extent of Jones's liability? of Brown's?

THE OLD OAK FURNITURE COMPANY

The Old Oak Furniture Company of High Point has been making quality Early American reproductions for seventy-five years. Two years ago, Silas Milo III, grandson of the founder of Old Oak, instituted a major reorganization. This reorganization resulted, among other things, in the establishment of a separate purchasing department. Previously, the three buyers and two clerks who were responsible for purchasing reported to the director of manufacturing operations. With some reservations, Silas hired Petula Petrie, who had been purchasing manager at Great American Furniture Company. Great American had become High Point's largest employer after only ten years of operations. Silas held much contempt for the Great American management—nothing but a bunch of over-educated college kids. No tradition, no roots. Silas had hired Petula as much to rile the management at Great American as anything. But after Petula had been on the job for only a year, Silas began to realize that he had made another shrewd management decision in hiring her. She had forcefully taken hold. Expenditures for purchased materials had remained constant while production and sales had risen by 6 percent.

More recently, Petula had eased two of the buyers she had inherited into retirement. They were replaced by a graduate of Western State University with a major in materials management and a 22-year-old former secretary who had just completed her A.A. degree in purchasing. Purchases, as a percentage of sales, continued to decrease.

But now Silas began to wonder if Petula was being a bit too aggressive. He had just received a letter from a long-time Old Oak supplier, Upholstery Suppliers of America (USA). The letter read, "I have just lost a $20,000 order from your company because my bid was $75 over the lowest quotation. I have been supplying your firm for over twenty years and I don't understand why I've been cut off without even the chance of discussing my bid. Most of the people I used to do business with in purchasing are retired. We used to talk over your company's needs, and I often advised them on how much to buy and at what price.

"Now I am asked only to bid on a specific quantity by a set date, and any remarks by me as to quantity, quality, or delivery are not accepted. I have tried to talk with these kids now in purchasing as I used to with the old-timers, but they want none of it. They tell me the policy of the company is to keep a minimum inventory and to buy on bids, and the lowest bidder gets the business.

"In time they will find out that buying on price alone will be an expensive business. It may fit some things, but it will not work for the kind of upholstery I furnish. Furthermore, the outfit that undercut my bid has been in business only three years. How can you depend on a firm like that? I'm not going to do business unless there is a reasonable profit over a period. Certainly, I have got to be competitive, but I think my whole performance and capability should be considered. I have been a dependable supplier for twenty years, and it's unfair to cut me out for only $75."

Silas called Petula into his office to discuss the situation. He said, "We may have treated this supplier unfairly, and I would like to see if this complaint is justified. His letter suggests that we do not have a policy on evaluating our suppliers, particularly where intangibles like service, technical information, and advice are important. Just how should we weigh these points along with financial stability, delivery performance, price, and quality?

"We buy about $300,000 a year of upholstery. We could give USA an order for next month's requirements if it has been hurt. Send me a memorandum on what you think we should do."

1 What would Petula's memorandum to the president contain?
2 Who should answer the supplier's letter and what should the answer say?

PRICE PRINTING SERVICE

Company Background:

Price Printing (PP), located in Novato, California, is a local advertising magazine company. Once a week it prints and distributes to its customers a free copy of its magazine FOR SALE, which is filled with advertisements for employment opportunities, cars and trucks for sale, household goods and rummage sales, and so on. It also provides a listing of the next week's local events, such as concerts and trade shows. Its revenue is derived from those businesses and individuals who place ads in the magazine. Started over four years ago by some students as a way to earn extra money, it has grown from a typewritten, six-page "flyer" to a printed magazine with an average of fifty pages. PP purchased its own warehouse a year ago to serve as its printing and distribution center. The debt the company incurred from buying the building has made cash a very important asset to PP, and management has made every employee aware of the fact.

Printing Production

The printing of the magazine starts two days before its scheduled distribution date. All copies of the magazine are picked up by a local distribution company on Wednesdays, the night before FOR SALE is actually put on the stands. When PP purchased its printing presses, it could not afford new equipment and instead obtained eight-year-old presses from a newspaper company. No warranties exist. Since the original purchase time, PP has purchased one new press, and though similar to the older presses, it was made by a different manufacturer. One of the production managers, Joe Printer, has been with PP for three and a half years. He handles the 1 to 10 P.M. shift and is known for his efficiency and productivity.

Purchasing at PP

In the past, the procurement function at PP has been very informal, with the owners doing all the buying. However, two months ago the owners decided to formalize the process, and last month Gregg Adams was hired as the new (and first ever) purchasing agent. Gregg, hired right out of college, impressed the owners with his knowledge of procurement processes and terms, his eagerness, and his proactive thinking. The owners gave Gregg any paperwork from past purchases they could find, which included old invoices, receipts, and price catalogs. Gregg's first job was to sort through these things and locate suppliers' names, prices, and recurring orders. The owners told Gregg that they wanted him to upgrade and improve on the present procurement system but that they must approve any changes. Gregg knows his performance evaluation will revolve around how well he has been able to decrease costs in the procurement area.

Tuesday Afternoon, 3:30 P.M.

Gregg is at his desk when he receives a call from Joe.

"Gregg, I need you to call Print Fixers, our printing press repair company. A rolling mechanism just broke on the older press. I need it fixed within four hours or we'll run into late production costs."

"O.K., Joe, I'll get on it right away. Let me take a look at some of the old PO's and I'll get right back with you."

After looking through some paperwork, Gregg was disturbed. From what he could gather, past emergencies were handled in this way: Joe called the owners, they cut a blank PO for the company of Joe's choice (four companies had been used in various instances in the past), and the PO amount was filled in after the bill was received. To verify this process, Gregg called Joe back.

GREGG: "Hi, Joe. I'm looking through some papers here and am a bit confused. How have you handled printing emergencies in the past?"

JOE: "Pretty much like I'm handling it now. I'd call the office to have a PO cut, and get the machine fixed. I was told that now I can't call the repair company myself but that you had to deal with them. So I called you and didn't call Print Fixers."

GREGG: "Do you know how long it should take to fix this machine?"

JOE: "Maybe two hours. I'm usually too busy to really watch repairs, so the repair man just pages me when he's done. I've never had a repair run over three hours."

GREGG: "I understand, Joe, but I have one last question. I notice that there are two other companies that you've dealt with in other emergencies. Can they all repair the older presses?"

JOE: "Well, yes. But Print Fixers is the company I recommend for this particular repair. Can you get them for me?"

GREGG: "I'll check right now. Thanks for the information and I'll call you back ASAP."

JOE: "O.K., but this is an emergency, Gregg. I've never been late on production and I don't want to be late this time."

Gregg hung up the phone and got to work. He called all three repair sources. The information he gathered is shown in figure C-1. Other facts he discovered are listed below.

- Maintenance Plus is the same company that handles the new press warranty.
- Print Specialists currently has a contract with PP for regular maintenance on the older press.
- PP must pay 5 workers $10.00/hr each for any overtime wages
- For every hour the magazine is late on the racks, PP loses an estimated $398.00 in advertising revenue.

Figure C-1

Supplier:

1. Print Fixers
   - Can be in plant within 1/2 hr
   - Estimated repair completion time is 2-1/2 hrs
   - Cost is $900.00/hr, parts & labor
   - No maximum fixed price given

2. Print Specialists
   - Can be in plant in 3 hrs
   - Estimated repair completion time is 2 hrs
   - Cost is $345.00/hr plus parts
   - Guarantee maximum fixed labor cost at $790.00, even if the repair takes more than 2 hrs
   - Materials estimated at $750.00

3. Maintenance Plus
   - Can be in plant in 6 hrs
   - Estimated repair completion time is 2 hrs
   - $750 per hour, including parts

All three repair shops are willing to work with Gregg on setting prices for future emergency repairs.

Gregg took a quick glance at his watch and found it was now 4:30 P.M. This meant that three hours remained before Joe would run into late production.

1 What is Gregg's first objective in this situation?
2 What action should Gregg take to meet his immediate objective?
3 What long-term action should be taken on procurement for emergencies?

This case was developed by Illyana Aasen and Mike Collies under the direction of Professor David N. Burt.

RIO VALLEY STATE UNIVERSITY

In late October, 1989, Eileen Boyd, a buyer for Rio Valley State University (RVSU), received a phone call from the auditorium coordinator. One section of the new carpet had repeated "bubbling" problems, and he felt that the installer was not taking care of the problem. Eileen wondered how she should handle the situation with the installer.

Rio Valley State University

Rio Valley State University, founded in 1885, was located in Bay Side, Washington, near the heart of Seattle. The campus, with over 40,000 students, had expanded with the growth in the Northwest, adding to the educational and cultural environment in the greater Seattle area.

RVSU Purchasing Department

The purchasing department had grown with the university throughout the years. The total purchases for the 1988–89 year were over $45 million, resulting from some 33,000 purchase orders.

All of this business was placed by a relatively small group headed by the director of purchasing, Gerald Morse, who started with the department after joining the university in 1945. Under Mr. Morse were Bruce Conners, purchasing agent; six buyers; and a clerical staff.

Eileen Boyd, one of the six buyers, was in charge of buying interiors for the university during the past four years. Interiors consisted of furniture, carpeting, draperies, and other interior furnishings for offices, classrooms, and dormitories across the campus.

Babson Memorial Auditorium

The Babson Memorial Auditorium, designed by Frank Lloyd Wright, was one of RVSU's landmarks. In the spring of 1987, problems with the ceiling resulted in damage to the carpeting in several areas of the auditorium. Eileen Boyd was called upon to replace the original carpeting with an exact duplicate. This resulted in a major research project which took over three months. The total replacement cost was estimated at more than $85,000.

Once the carpeting was delivered, a sealed bid package went out to interested carpet layers. The carpeting was to be installed in two phases due to budget restrictions and because of the high auditorium usage. A complete list of contractor instructions which explained the limitations and liabilities was included with the Request for Quotation (see Exhibit 1).

After the bids were returned, the contract was awarded to Prestige Carpet Installers, Inc. They began work on Phase One in late September, 1987, and finished later that fall. Phase Two began in 1988. Work was occasionally held up by bubbling problems. Bubbling occurred in spots where the carpet did not properly adhere to the floor.

Eileen had been paying the installers as the work was completed. When the bubbling occurred, she would withhold five percent of the payment until the installers repaired the area in question. The last payment was released in March 1989, when the work was completed and approved.

Prestige Carpet Installers, Inc.

Prestige Carpets was a small firm of fifteen employees specializing for over thirty years in commercial and residential carpet installation and cleaning. They were unique in the Seattle area in that the owner paid his employees by salary, not by the square yard laid, as did other installation companies. The average Prestige Carpet installer had approximately fifteen years experience with the company.

The owner and his employees had a good reputation in the Seattle area. The firm had installed many jobs for RVSU since the early 1970s. The university had been satisfied with the work.

Until Eileen received the call in October from the auditorium coordinator, she was not aware of a reoccurrence of the bubbling problem in one section of the carpet. The coordinator had personally contacted Prestige Carpet Installers after the March completion date, but he was not able to resolve the problem. Eileen was now faced with the situation.

1 What should Eileen do to overcome the immediate problem?
2 What should be done to ensure that such problems do not reoccur?

RIO VALLEY STATE UNIVERSITY
EXHIBIT I

Contractor Instructions

Qualifications of Contractor

This contract will be awarded to a responsible contractor, qualified by experience, and in a solvent financial position to perform the work. The successful contractor will be approved by Rio Valley State University. All installers and contractor must have a minimum of five years experience for this job. Installation crew must have an on-site supervisor at all times.

Guarantee

Contractor is to *guarantee* for one year all workmanship and supplier materials used.

Glue

Acceptable brands: Patterson or Riley or as recommended by Mfg.

RVSU-Furnished Carpeting

Carpet Manufacturer: Mohassco Fiber, 100 percent virgin wool, velvet construction, round wire, Roxbury Cinnamon.

Carpet Location

RVSU carpeting is stored at RVSU's warehouse on 1st Street and Price Road in Bay Side. Successful contractor is to pick up carpeting from warehouse as needed for job completion. List of roll information will be available from the purchasing office. One roll of carpeting is at Babson Center for on-job site inspection.

Misc.

Exact yardage and installation plan will be determined on first working day.

Clean-Up and Salvage

Installation crew is to haul away all rubbish and scraps. Babson Center will determine what is salvage and will retain possession of all salvage. Installation crew is to exercise as much care as possible to salvage old carpet to be used as patching.

Schedule

Installation must be accomplished during the following schedule. Babson Center is available from 6 A.M. to 10 P.M. on the following days:

Sept 19–24	Must be cleaned up by noon Sept. 24
Sept 27–29	Must be cleaned up by noon Sept. 29
Sept 30–Oct 1	Must be cleaned up by noon Oct. 1
Oct 4–14	Must be cleaned up by noon on Oct. 14

Contact Jose Curling of Babson Center to view carpet and installation area at 565-6182.

SPRINGFIELD PURCHASES A GARBAGE TRUCK

Sam Springer, the purchasing manager of the City of Springfield, has a hot political potato on his hands. The situation sort of reminds Sam of an experience he had when he tried out for his high school football team. Sam was the fourth team left guard. One day in a practice scrimmage, Sam picked up a loose ball. Unfortunately, Sam didn't know which way to run.

Last month, Sam had solicited bids for a highly automated garbage truck. Only three responsive bids had been received by the specified bid opening date. The prices, F.O.B. Springfield, were as follows:

Mangler Garbage Trucks	$ 95,472
Springfield Sanitation Trucks, Inc.	$ 99,712
Chattanooga Cruncher Company	$110,000

Mangler Garbage Trucks was located in Warren, a city some 300 miles from Springfield. The second lowest bidder was Springfield Sanitation Trucks, Inc. SST, as the firm was known to most locals, was Springfield's largest employer.

Sam checked with the chief of the Sanitation Department. The chief said that although he would like to see SST get the order, any of the three trucks would be fine with him. He felt that they were about equal in performance, quality, and maintenance cost.

When the contents of the bids were made public, SST's president, Paul Percivel, contacted Sam's boss, Tim Johansen, the city manager. Mr. Percivel acknowledged that his bid was higher than Mangler's. He then pointed out that SST recently had to lay off workers due to slack orders. He concluded by saying, "Tom, you and I both know that unemployment is the number one problem in Springfield. How can we get manufacturers to locate here if we don't show them that Springfield takes care of its own?" The city manager winced on this one. He currently was engaged in extended discussions with the vice president for logistics of one of the Fortune 500 companies. This firm had narrowed down its alternatives for a new 2,000-employee plant to Springfield and Warren.

After Mr. Percivel left, Mr. Johansen stopped by Sam's office and discussed the situation. After hearing what the city manager had to say, Sam threw another coal on the fire by reporting on a discussion he had had with the sales manager of Mangler Garbage Trucks. The sales manager had opened the discussion by saying that he expected Springfield Sanitation Trucks to exert political pressure on Sam to buy its trucks. He continued by saying, "Not only will we save you nearly $5,000, but don't forget that Mangler purchases $3 to $4 million of components each year from Springfield manufacturers."

That evening, Sam attended the monthly meeting of the Springfield Purchasing Management Association. He asked three of his dinner companions what they thought about the situation.

Wilbur Wilson, purchasing manager of Eagle Tool and Die, offered his advice. "I'd give the order to SST. You've got to do business with your friends here in Springfield. We've got to keep Springfield dollars in Springfield. We've been operating this way at Eagle for years."

On the other hand, Chuck Connors of Excalibur, Inc., insisted, "Sam, if you compromise now, you'll start something you can't stop. Every fly-by-night outfit in town will hound you for a piece of city business. I'd keep Springfield's good name in mind. Suppliers tell me they think we're an honest bunch. That's why they always give us such good service and help so much on the standardization and value analysis committees."

Roscoe Stevens of Needmore Corporation added this diplomatic note. "You can't throw the bids out, Sam, but you've got to watch your step. The Taxpayers' League will scream if you give the order to SST, because they were not the low bidder."

1 What factors should Sam consider in making a decision?
2 What should that decision be?
3 What should have been done to avoid some of the problems Sam faced?

THREE VENDORS AND A TUB

Charlie Harris, tub buyer at Rub-A-Dub Washing Machine Company, faced a tough negotiation problem. Rub-A-Dub needed major tub assemblies for a new low-priced model designed to improve Rub-A-Dub's share of the market. Quality and reliability were musts. But so were rock-bottom costs. Not a penny could be wasted.

In fact, purchasing and engineering had developed a cost program for suppliers that they felt was tight but fair. Harris emphatically was told to stay within the maximum that they had worked out.

The figure was $160 per unit, broken down thus:

Estimated supplier costs	
Material	$40
Labor	60
Overhead and profit	60
	$160

Harris first asked himself, "What if we make our own assemblies?" But he discarded this idea when he found out that Rub-A-Dub's tooling costs would be twice those of outside suppliers.

Meantime, the sales department was flowing with enthusiasm, hoping Harris would come through.

Sales target	
1st year	50,000
2nd year	150,000
3rd year	300,000
4th and 5th years	200,000

Harris figured the sales projections were impressive enough to make the tub contract very attractive. So he invited three old-time suppliers to review the specifications and submit informal proposals for 50,000 units.

Joe Wilson of BMT Company presented setback No. 1. He said that his company could not go lower than $180. He stated that packaging costs were higher than Harris figured. If a three-year contract for 500,000 units was given, Wilson thought he could spread tooling costs and get the price down to $168.

Sam Newson of IND Company was disappointment No. 2. Newson offered a 100 percent return policy on rejects and quoted $196. Newson said that anything cheaper would just be junk, and that Harris wouldn't dare put it on the market.

George Withers of IRT Company would not quote at all. Withers told Harris that he thought the engineering department was pulling his leg. Withers suggested that Harris and Slim Boggs, IRT sales manager, get together to review the prints and the figures.

Harris told the three salesmen he would think over their proposals and get in touch with them soon. Then he wrote a digest of the situation and showed it to Donald Kingman, purchasing director. Kingman reiterated the fact that if they could not get $160 tubs, the new machine would be dead (and so would purchasing!). Kingman felt that the suppliers were a pretty short-sighted crowd, and maybe purchasing should teach them a lesson. In any event, Rub-A-Dub needed good $160 tubs—and fast!

1 What factor must Charlie consider now?
2 How should Charlie prepare for and conduct new negotiations?

THE TIDEWATER GAS AND ELECTRIC COMPANY

Customers of the Tidewater Gas and Electric Company (TG&E) were up in arms. Electric rates had gone up over 100 percent in two years. The State Assembly was considering a bill to do away with the state public utility commission (PUC) and place approval of rate increases under the direct control of the Assembly.

The PUC responded by conducting an extremely thorough management audit of TG&E's operation. One of the findings of this audit is quoted as follows:

Area: Contact management

Findings: The management of equipment and construction contracts ranges from poor to none at all. Cost overruns and schedule slippages on construction and equipment contracts are common occurrences. Such mismanagement causes two types of cost increases, which necessitate higher electric rates:

1. The cost of completed projects is far higher than it should be.
2. Electricity must be purchased from neighboring utilities at higher rates for unnecessarily long periods of time.

Recommendation: Policies and practices to ensure efficient contract management should be established and implemented immediately.

Savings potential: $10 million a year

1 Explain your understanding concerning the importance of contract administration or contract management. Have you noticed that in the help wanted ads of big-city newspapers there are always many ads for contract administrators?
2 When does the purchasing department prepare for its expediting responsibilities?
3 Assume that you are a management consultant. Develop a list of recommendations for TG&E's purchasing management.

VIGARD MANUFACTURING COMPANY

Mr. Jesse Krause, purchasing manager of the Vigard Manufacturing Company, was faced with the problem of selecting a source to prepare a technical manual for a winder that the company was planning to sell nationally.

The Vigard Manufacturing Company was formed four years ago by Edward Vigard, an engineer who had previously been employed by a large electronics manufacturer in the New Jersey area. Mr. Vigard's company concentrated on the production of a special type of wound magnet that had wide application in military and commercial electronics equipment. The company had grown from two employees to a present work force of seventy-five. In addition to Mr. Vigard and Mr. Krause, the management of the company included a sales manager and a production manager. The president, Mr. Vigard, handled design and engineering matters.

The magnets that the company produced were wound on a machine that Mr. Vigard had designed. The machine consisted of a specially designed casting, a high-speed motor, and a small core around which the finely spun copper wire was wound in order to produce the magnet. Mr. Vigard had fabricated a number of these winders for use by his company. Successful production of the magnets required proper operation of the winders and this, in turn, depended on continual servicing to maintain required speeds and accuracy.

Last year Mr. Vigard and his management group decided to manufacture the winders for sale to electronics, aircraft, missile, and instrumentation firms, many of which produced their own magnets on equipment that Mr. Vigard believed was inferior to his own winder. Cost analyses and projections indicated to Mr. Vigard that sales of the winders might constitute a substantial new source of volume and profit. When a decision to produce the winder had been reached, Mr. Vigard invested a substantial portion of the company's funds in the castings and other components needed to manufacture the winders. As production proceeded, the sales manager made preparations for marketing the new product. First, he undertook exploratory discussions with potential customers in the immediate area of the Vigard plant. Second, he negotiated an agreement with a sales representative to handle sales in the western part of the United States. Third, he initiated an advertising campaign, by means of direct mail and announcements in trade papers, stating that the winders would be ready for delivery on June 1st of that year.

The Vigard Manufacturing Company proceeded satisfactorily with the manufacture of the winders. Although the sales manager found that there was a substantial amount of interest in the new product, he learned that the winders could not be sold unless they were accompanied by an illustrated operation and maintenance manual. For example, the western sales representative informed him that the manual was not only essential to the user but also needed for demonstrating the winder. Moreover, an eastern customer had placed an order for several of the winders contingent on their being delivered with a suitable manual. These contingent orders were of great importance to the Vigard Company because the cost of the manufacturing program had required an additional bank loan and had seriously depleted the company's working capital.

Accordingly, Mr. Vigard and his associates prepared the technical descriptions that the manual would contain. Mr. Krause, the purchasing manager, was directed to locate a source that could prepare approximately 180 illustrations and technical drawings and have the manual ready for the printer on the first of May so that it would be available for the June 1 deadline.

Although he had never before had occasion to place artwork contracts, Mr. Krause found that he was able to locate a number of potential sources through the use of the "yellow pages" and the telephone. The companies that he located were of two general types: (1) commercial art companies that prepared mail order catalogs and (2) art companies that specialized in the preparation of technical manuals. He found that most of the commercial art companies showed little interest in the work because they were busy preparing catalogs and promotional pamphlets for their regular clients. Two large concerns that specialized in the preparation of technical manuals seemed anxious to obtain the work.

In addition to these two broad classes of companies, Bullock Art, a small organization that was attempting to expand, gave promise of being able to handle the work. This company consisted of Mr. Bullock and a group of freelance artists he employed whenever he obtained a contract requiring their help. Mr. Bullock had been employed as a freelance artist by several companies, which, upon telephone inquiries by Mr. Krause, reported favorably on the quality of Mr. Bullock's work. In addition, he taught commercial art at a well-known trade school and had developed his own production methods, which appeared to be superior to those used by most other art concerns.

Mr. Krause's preliminary survey indicated that four companies were interested in undertaking the work: Bullock Art; Webster, Inc., and Hershey Associates (the two concerns specializing in the production of technical manuals): and The Catalogue Corporation, a large commercial art concern. Mr. Krause decided to visit each of these companies.

Webster, Inc., the first company visited, was the largest art concern in the city, employing approximately 150 artists and book designers. The company had excellent facilities, including the latest art and layout equipment and its own photographic laboratories. The operations of the company appeared to be efficiently organized and well managed. Although the company was then operating at capacity, Mr. Krause learned that approximately 80 percent of its business had been with one large manufacturer that had recently informed the Webster management that it was shifting its technical manual and work to another firm. The general manager of the company estimated that he could complete Mr. Krause's work on schedule. He stated further that the company would undertake the work on an hourly basis with a guarantee that the total time would not exceed a specified number of hours. He informed Mr. Krause that he could submit a definite quotation within forty-eight hours.

Hershey Associates was visited next. Although considerably smaller than Webster, Inc., the company had been doing the same general type of work. After examining samples of the company's previous work, Mr. Krause concluded that Hershey Associates was qualified to prepare the artwork for the manual, and invited the company to submit a quotation.

Mr. Krause then called on The Catalogue Corporation. Although this company was well known as a publisher of mail order catalogs, it had never produced a technical manual. The company representative saw no problem in meeting Mr. Krause's requirements, however, He said that if any specialized talent was required, he would have no difficulty in obtaining needed personnel inasmuch as several qualified people had called on him that week in search of employment. In view of these assertions and the general reputation of the company, Mr. Krause asked The Catalogue Corporation to submit a quotation.

The pressure of other work prevented Mr. Krause from visiting Bullock Art. However, Mr. Bullock telephoned to ask if he might visit the Vigard Manufacturing Company to analyze the job and submit a quotation. He stated that if he were given an opportunity to study the work, he was confident he could demonstrate his ability to handle the contract within the time limit and at a lower cost than his competitors. Although Mr. Krause did not believe that an additional quotation was necessary, he agreed to let Mr. Bullock analyze the work and submit a quotation.

The following day the general manager of Webster, Inc., called on Mr. Krause to present his quotation. The quotation stipulated a rate of $17.60 per hour with a maximum guarantee of $72,000. The quotation was contingent, however, on weekly progress payments based on the number of hours spent on the contract. In submitting the quotation, the general manager stated that the hourly rate should be considered as the significant figure, since the maximum guarantee provided a margin of safety for contingencies. Mr. Krause took exception to this statement, pointing out that a company employing more highly skilled personnel might complete the job in fewer hours and at a lower total cost, even though it had a higher hourly rate. He concluded, therefore, that the maximum guarantee was the more important figure. In addition, Mr. Krause stated that although the artwork would not necessarily be awarded to the lowest bidder, it was going to be placed on a competitive basis, and he advised the Webster general manager to eliminate any 'water' that might be in his bid. After making a few computations on a scratch pad, the general manager stated that he could reduce the maximum guarantee to $48,000. Thereupon Mr. Krause told him to prepare a new quotation and to submit it as soon as possible. The following morning, the general manager returned with a new quotation containing the same hourly rate but with a new maximum guarantee of only $22,500. When Mr. Krause remarked, "There must have been enough 'water' in the previous quotation to float the manual," the general manager replied that he expected to lose money if he received the contract. He said that in view of this, he was unwilling to assume the burden of financing the work. Mr. Krause explained that this was an important issue to him and that his award of the contract might well hinge on this provision. The general manager pointed ut that his company typically received weekly progress payments and that without them he was not willing to accept the contract. Mr. Krause then stated that he would make his decision and place the contract within forty-eight hours.

In the meantime, Mr. Bullock had visited the Vigard Company and had spent several hours analyzing the work and preparing his quotation. In the course of analysis, Mr. Bullock made a number of suggestions that not only improved the style of the manual but simplified the production of the artwork. For example, Mr. Bullock suggested that certain expensive airbrush operations could be replaced by relatively inexpensive screening techniques. He also demonstrated that through more careful "eye control" many of the sketches could be improved: This would result from a rearrangement of details so that they were placed at a point in the illustration where the eye naturally fell first. He stated that if he were given the contract, he would improve the layout and general appearance of the manual and eliminate difficult production problems. Mr. Bullock examined the rough sketches for the manual and discussed them briefly with Mr. Vigard and the sales manager. When Mr. Krause discussed Mr. Bullock's qualifications with these two officers of the company, they both expressed the opinion that he possessed an unusual ability and seemed to be well qualified to undertake the work.

Bullock Art's quotation specified an hourly rate of $18 and a maximum guarantee of $21,060. Mr. Bullock explained in detail how he had prepared the quotation and how the production shortcuts he had developed would enable him to make a fair profit on the contract. Although Mr. Krause was convinced that Mr. Bullock had a better understanding of the job to be done than any other bidder, he questioned his ability to acquire an organization and get it in operation in time to meet the required production schedule. Mr. Bullock countered by saying that this was the normal manner in which he worked and that he was confident that he could get the personnel and equipment needed on a moment's notice. He stated further that if he needed additional funds to finance the work, he could borrow the money from his brother-in-law. In the event that he fell behind schedule, he could work nights and weekends.

During the day, the quotations of the other two companies were received. The Catalogue Corporation offered to take the contract at an hourly rate of $21.00 and a maximum guarantee of $32,130. The quotation of Hershey Associates stipulated an hourly rate of $18.90 and a maximum guarantee of $33,750.

Although Bullock Art submitted the low quotation, Mr. Krause was somewhat reluctant to place the contract with the company. He did not question Mr. Bullock's personal ability, but he doubted that Mr. Bullock could expand his organization fast enough to meet the desired production schedule. On March 22, because of this doubt, Mr. Krause decided to visit Bullock Art. His visit disclosed that Bullock Art did not possess adequate space in which to do the work. However, Mr. Bullock showed him an unoccupied basement in a building down the street that could be rented, cleaned up, and put to use if needed.

After his visit to Bullock Art, Mr. Krause wondered if the potential savings of an award to Bullock justified the risks that were involved. He needed to place the contract immediately in order to allow sufficient time for the completion of the artwork and delivery of the manual to the printer by May 1. Unless the manual reached the printer by this date, it would not be available on the first of June, the day on which the winders had been promised for delivery.

1 If you were Mr. Krause, what action would you take and why?

THE WIDE, WIDE WORLD OF PURCHASING

Charley Ruggles, purchasing manager at the Newton Manufacturing Company, was wondering whether to take the plunge into worldwide purchasing. A salesman from Eurofabrik, Ltd., a foreign producer of small assemblies and stamps, had just left a proposal on his desk for one of Newton's major purchases, the transklutch. Eurofabrik's price was 35 percent below what Charley was paying to a local supplier—even figuring in the extra cost of duty, ocean freight, and overland transportation to the Newton plant.

Newton used this assembly, a combination of stampings and turnings, in all its "Powermaster" assemblies sold both for use in consumer and industrial end-products. The transklutch was half of the unit cost of a Powermaster final assembly. Charley had instructions from Slaterer P. Colby, Newton's president, to cut costs. "Charley, the cost-price squeeze on the Powermaster really hurts. Purchasing is responsible for half the cost of this product, and you have got to get your material cost down. *But don't cut corners on quality!* We can't afford to lose our reputation for a quality Powermaster! Give me a report at our meeting in two weeks!"

Ruggles had just started to work on the problem when the Eurofabrik salesman called. "Our plant is one of the most modern in the Common Market, and that's why we can give you such a low price. We have all the latest equipment, and our quality reputation is well known. In three months you will have the first shipment made exactly to your specifications."

Charley talked it over with several of his closest purchasing management friends at lunch: Ralph Wilson, purchasing director of ABC; Gene Nelson, purchasing manager for Universal Manufacturing; and Larry Smith, purchasing manager for the local electric utility.

Ralph: "I'd rather look into it, Charley. You know we have been buying foreign on some of our raw materials and metals for years. You have to get used to some of the delays and red tape, *but it's sure worth it!* I got a promotion out of my foreign buying record."

Gene: "Whoa! That's just on commodities, Ralph, not components! We got stung when we couldn't get foreign suppliers to stick to our specifications on components. The late deliveries and headaches aren't worth it. We had to go back to our U.S. suppliers after that adventure!"

Larry: "There's another side, too, Charley. We believe in 'buying American' and supporting local industry. Say, don't you purchase transklutches from Merit Machine here in town? That makes it a pretty touchy political issue then, I'd say."

Transklutch quality was important. If a Powermaster failed in service, the final customer usually complained to Newton. Deliveries had to be on schedule to prevent assembly line downtime and minimize expensive safety stock inventory. Technical service had never been a problem, as their supplier, Merit, was just down the street.

Ruggles knew he had to have an answer for the president in ten days, and the Eurofabrik proposal might be it. He could not go in half-cocked, but neither could he look into all aspects of the problem in this short a time.

1 What key issues and figures and information should Charley pull together?
2 What sources should Charley use for his information?
3 What should Charley recommend?

PART III
Instructor's Teaching Notes

AAA, INC.

(A SERVICES CONTRACT MANAGEMENT CASE)

Purpose

The purpose of this case is to discuss the buyer's role in managing a services contract. Specifically, the case addresses the appropriate level of buyer involvement in a supplier's problems, and effective methods of avoiding problems. The case examines source selection and the disadvantages of cost plus percent of cost contracts.

Discussion

The case asks the following questions:

1. How could the supplier problems be avoided in this particular case?

    This question points out the importance of sufficient bid time, being sensitive to the supplier's limitations, and contract terms and conditions which give the appropriate level of control to the buyer.

2. What are the potential implications of a cost plus percent contract?

    This question addresses the issue of providing proper incentives to the supplier and the disadvantages of cost plus percent contracts. It examines cost plus incentive fee contracts when the buyer has an objective other than price (in this case, schedule).

3. What type of sourcing procedure should have been used?

    This question examines sourcing methods and the use of source evaluation criteria.

4. In this particular case, what should the buyer do?

    This question examines the advantages and disadvantages of cancelling the services contract and selecting a new source.

Question 1:

How could AAA have avoided the problems it experienced with Comstock?

Comment:

At the outset, AAA placed itself in a disadvantageous position by not ensuring hat there was sufficient time for the source selection process. In addition, AAA placed an unnecessary restriction in its specifications by stipulating that the contractor would have to perform all work in-house. If Comstock had been permitted to subcontract for the talent it could not provide from within, it could have avoided many of the problems encountered. AAA could have retained control over the subcontracting process by requiring that it have final approval of subcontractors.

Finally, there was no clause in the contract to prevent Comstock from delaying or asking for relief from the contract provisions. AAA's only legal recourse was to sue Comstock for breach of contract. AAA's objective, however, was the timely completion of the modernization project, not a court victory. AAA would have been more in control had the contract specified a plan of action and key milestones for the project. The significant milestones, in turn, should have been tied to progress payments, with penalties for noncompliance. Ideally, such provisions would inspire the desired performance.

Question 2:

What are the potential implications of the type of contract AAA used? Discuss.

Comment:

The terms of AAA's contract with Comstock are cost plus a percent of cost with a cap of $3.3 million. This means that Comstock receives, as profit, a percent of what it spends. Obviously, with this type of contract there is no incentive for Comstock to control costs. In fact, there is an incentive to increase costs since profit increases as costs increase. However, in this case, low cost was not the primary objective. With time being the main focus of attention, it would be safe to assume that AAA would allow Comstock the entire $3.3 million as long as the project is completed on time. AAA may even tolerate cost overruns to obtain time savings.

AAA should have considered the use of another type of contract which would have rewarded Comstock not for cost efficiency, but for time efficiency—e.g., a cost plus incentive contract. Tying Comstock's profit to milestones would have greatly increased the likelihood of completing the project on schedule.

Clearly, with a cost plus percentage contract, there is no incentive for the supplier to perform efficiently. AAA, in turn, was slow to react to Comstock's sluggishness.

Question 3:

How could AAA have improved its approach to sourcing?

Comment:

As suggested earlier, AAA could have prevented many of the problems encountered later by allowing more time during the source selection process. Influenced by a tight timetable and a strong desire to maximize coordination with the project team, AAA appears to have chosen the first acceptable solution to its sourcing needs. In so doing, AAA severely limited its options and ignored sources of information which could have been very valuable in the source selection process. Even a cursory analysis of key financial data and ratios could have provided important information on the relative financial condition and the managerial ability of the potential suppliers.

In addition, AAA should have asked all potential suppliers for data regarding projected utilization and backlog for the next 12 months. This information would have placed AAA in a better position to evaluate the relative capabilities of the prospective suppliers.

Use of a multiple sourcing strategy probably would have improved AAA's source selection. This sourcing alternative could have been accomplished by contracting with firms specializing in either electrical, mechanical, or civil engineering, with AAA acting as the project coordinator. Another option would have been to award the contract to one engineering company which would subcontract with specialized engineering companies required for the project.

Question 4:

What should AAA do now? Discuss.

Comment:

AAA has two basic choices: remain with Comstock or develop a new source. What are the format advantages and disadvantages of remaining with Comstock; of changing to a new firm?

Remain With Comstock:

+ AAA will not incur changeover costs associated with obtaining a new supplier.
- AAA probably will experience more and continued problems with Comstock, which leads to $1.2 million/month lost opportunity costs.
- AAA will be without electrical engineers until Comstock's efforts to transfer and recruit come through.
- Comstock may lack adequate incentive to complete the AAA project on schedule.

Change To Another Firm:

+ AAA may obtain a properly staffed firm.
+ AAA may obtain a contract that is less costly.
- The time necessary to find a new firm may set AAA's project schedule back.
- The new firm may be more costly and just as bad as Comstock.
- It will take extra time for the new firm to sift out what Comstock has completed and where it left off.
- When Comstock learns of AAA's search for a new firm, the quality of Comstock's work will suffer.

AGE BUILDERS, INC.

Purpose

The purpose of this case is to provide an introduction to the understanding of value analysis and the decision making process involved.

Discussion

Part of the decision making process for AGE will involve careful analysis of quality, economic, and reputation factors that will have a tremendous impact on their company if the proper decision is not made. In discussing this case the following should be kept in mind:

> When considering the use of a product or service stemming from value analysis work, it should be considered an upgrade. It is not and should not be something that will reduce quality. It should improve it and make it a more economic process.

Question 1:

What are the advantages and disadvantages of using waferboard?

Comment:

Waferboard is less expensive. It is a much more consistent material than plywood, as far as having no core voids and knotholes, which makes it easy to work with. Because of its makeup, the waferboard also tends to be much more weather resistant than the plywood. All this seems to confirm is that it is a quality product, but there is still the big drawback that it is a new product in the industry. Another disadvantage of the waferboard is its appearance. It doesn't have a finished appearance as does plywood. It also resembles a type of board used by the industry for nonstructural items, known as particle board. This in itself creates an image problem with the individual home buyers because most home buyers are not familiar with waferboard. They are accustomed to seeing nice, clean looking plywood. This could create a negative attitude toward the builder as having poor quality which leads to a bad reputation.

Question 2:

If AGE Builders does not use waferboard, does it risk falling behind competition?

Comment:

This depends on whether the industry has accepted the use of waferboard as a standard. AGE will have to do research to see if the product conforms to Building Code. If competitors are using it and passing inspections, and sales are consistent, it clearly will reduce costs. Then AGE may seriously want to consider the use of waferboard. But like most new products there is always hesitation. Sometimes an innovative start is what makes the difference between competitors.

Question 3:

In this situation how would you determine if value analysis could be beneficial for AGE?

Comment:

The concept of value analysis is improvement, with efficiency. This includes quality as well as cost factors. the problem with many companies today is that they do not implement value analysis in their daily operations. If this concept were implemented properly companies would experience tremendous savings, and be more efficient and effective in the process.

Question 4:

How can AGE obtain additional information on this new product? What information would be useful?

Comment:

AGE needs to use its suppliers to the fullest; this includes obtaining any information from them. AGE needs to discuss with Bayord the disadvantages of waferboard as well as the advantages. AGE also needs to consider what competitors are using; are they using the waferboard? Why and why not? AGE can also get information from the County Building and Safety Department to determine the extent to which it is accepting this as a substitute for plywood. The standards association for the lumber industry is also a good source for information of this type.

Question 5:

Are there other alternatives for the use of waferboard which AGE may consider? Can AGE implement further value analysis studies on the use of waferboard?

Comment:

Waferboard can be substituted for anything plywood can be used for, from roof sheathing to cabinets. The use depends on how much AGE wants waferboard to be seen by buyers, since the appearance is not very enhancing. The more AGE can use waferboard, the more potential it has in achieving greater cost savings.

ALPHA OMEGA CORPORATION

Purpose

The purpose of this case is to provide insight into some of the factors other than price which should be considered in awarding contracts to suppliers. Additional costs associated with late deliveries, poor quality and receipt of less than the full quantity ordered are very real and can have significant impact upon the corporation.

Discussion

When used with textbook material on presourcing and/or supplier motivation, this case allows students to consider the impact of supplier performance on product cost. It demonstrates that beyond the material price, there is a cost associated with quality, timeliness, service, and delivery quantities. As such, if these or any other similar costs are important to a company in managing its suppliers or awarding future contracts, the company must evaluate the suppliers against known criteria and make awards consistent with the suppliers' previous performance.

Students should be encouraged to develop a rating system which attempts to quantify important factors of performance. Further, to do a good job in all aspects of purchasing, there must exist either manual or automated systems which can be utilized to produce accurate performance information as desired. Alpha Omega has some shortfalls in this regard but by supplementing the work force sufficiently, accurate data can be obtained.

Question 1:

What is the basic reason that suppliers have consistently failed to meet their contractual obligations?

Comment:

Suppliers are no different from other people: they pay attention when there is reinforcement for doing so. In this case, suppliers performed as promised on price because they were aware of the direct impact price had—the higher the price the less business was awarded them by Alpha Omega.

Procurement at CXO included wording in purchase orders covering supplier requirements in the areas of quality, quantity, timeliness and service. Unfortunately, during reviews with the suppliers on their performance, few non-price data were available to back up claims of poor performance. The consequence was that the supplier's data presented in support of his position was no more or less acceptable than Alpha Omega data and they carried as much credence.

When contract awards were made, here again the emphasis was placed on price—consequently supplier performance on price was always adequate while other factors slipped further. Suppliers were allowed to skirt the quality issue somewhat by being required to take back all test rejects. More emphasis should have been applied to having suppliers deliver good quality the first time.

Question 2:

What can be done to ensure adequate supplier performance in the future?

Comment:

Following directly from question 1, the obvious answer is to monitor supplier performance against those criteria deemed most important—realizing the potential for over-monitoring which will, in and of itself, adversely impact cost. In this case Guy Craig as well as the finance and materials departments were most concerned with the impacts of quality, timeliness, quantity, and service upon costs. Each of these factors needs a target performance goal and measurement criteria. Guy developed what is called a Supplier Effective Model, which addresses each of these factors with costs applied that are appropriate to Alpha Omega. It is anticipated that each company developing such a model will arrive at different weights and costing methods.

Quality

There are various target limits which can be used in this area. The goal chosen by Guy Craig is a zero PPM reject rate at incoming electrical test. At reject rates of up to 500 PPM, sample testing can be employed which will result in a substantial reduction in inspection costs compared with 100 percent testing. Also, inspection cycle time will be reduced, thereby allowing a reduction in inventory. Further, at 100 PPM and lower, supplier certification will be possible—resulting in no in-house testing.

Measurement of quality should be recorded for a particular supplier if the parts are being tested to the same parameters specified in the specification to which the supplier has agreed. Parts purchased as "standard product" should be screened by the supplier in accordance with the appropriate specification. The supplier should be held accountable for quality deficiencies for such items in the same manner as for defects under CXO-designed specifications.

In determining a cost factor to apply to a given quality level, consideration should be given to the actual cost to test devices. At Alpha Omega the figure used is 21.4 percent value added. Other companies will likely have different rates; no matter what the rates are. they must be applied to the units tested in order to arrive at a realistic test cost. Further, poor quality probably will require that higher safety stock levels be carried by the firm, thus resulting in more unproductive assets.

Timeliness

The goal for any firm in this area should be to have 100-percent on-time delivery. Deviations from this—either early or late—will result in additional costs from either having more WIP inventory than planned and budgeted for or having to increase safety stock to cover potential shortages due to late delivery.

Measurement is most likely to be made in terms of days early or late with a cost factor being applied to the number of days in deviation from the scheduled delivery dates.

Quantity

The goal of almost every company is usually to receive 100 percent of the expected delivery volume. Volume of less than 100 percent probably will require additional safety stock in order to meet customer orders and production build cycles. Measurement of this factor will most likely be a percentage of order received/not received and again should be costed at an appropriate figure to result in a delivery volume figure.

Service

Service tends to be very subjective but if the proper evaluation tools are provided, the resulting quantification can be meaningful. Alpha Omega has determined five criteria upon which a supplier is evaluated by purchasing and engineering representatives from each plant. The criteria include local representation, follow-up service, application assistance, representative available when requested and representative responsiveness.

Since measurement of service is subjective, it is likely that other companies will want to measure other criteria. The important idea is that if performance by suppliers in certain areas is required, that performance should be measured.

Question 3:

On what basis should contracts be awarded?

Comment:

Contracts should be awarded based upon those factors determined by the company to be the most important in terms of meeting or achieving financial and nonfinancial goals and objectives. For Alpha Omega, price, quality, quantity, timeliness and service are the most important performance areas. Consequently, Alpha Omega suppliers should be monitored against target ratings and awarded contracts based upon historic performance levels. Up until the time Guy obtained initial management concurrence with the Supplier Effectiveness Model (Exhibit 1), Alpha Omega was not evaluating suppliers formally against identified important areas. As a consequence, performance was only acceptable in those areas measured.

For Alpha Omega, each measurement factor has been found to impact every other factor and consequently in arriving at a final rating, all intermediate ratings are multiplied to yield that Supplier Effectiveness Rating. This number is then multiplied by the price per unit to get an adjusted price per unit which purports to represent the actual cost of doing business with that supplier.

Recent Events

Guy Craig has spent the past several years developing the Supplier Effectiveness Model. This model quantifies the impact of delivery quantity, quality, service and timeliness upon the cost of doing business with each supplier. For the first time, in the latest quarterly review held with the top ten suppliers, Guy shared his model and informed suppliers that they would be measure against the criteria included in the model. He also alluded to the desirability of awarding future contracts based upon the final rating for each supplier as determined by the model.

In order to obtain a Supplier Effectiveness Rating, all intermediate factors are multiplied, representing their true dependent nature as far a Alpha Omega is concerned. This measure is then multiplied by price to achieve an adjusted price for that supplier. The supplier with the lowest adjusted price for any component should be the one awarded the bid.

Included in one of the factors is the cost of money—taken as CXO's normal cost of capital figure used for determining the net present value of projects. One can make a good argument that the delivery volume factor should include the cost of capital. Without it, delivery volume appears to be disproportionately important vis-a-vis delivery timeliness. It is also not clear how these two measures interrelate with one another—i.e., is the second part of a partial delivery subject to the timeliness criteria or is the whole delivery quantity penalized for being late?

Management at Alpha Omega has not yet agreed to base future contracts upon the SEM because it has not yet been convinced that costs, other than material and quality, can be measured effectively. Further, management is not convinced that such "costs" are, in fact, true incremental costs. The next round of contract reviews is upcoming soon; it will be interesting to see whether management sees the wisdom of the Supplier Evaluation Model.

THE APEX AVIATION CASE

Purpose

The Apex Aviation case provides a realistic opportunity for advanced students to apply the principles of negotiation in a challenging situation.

This case was developed for a purchasing workshop conducted at Stanford University. The participants were experienced purchasing managers. They and subsequent workshop attendees claimed that the case provided an excellent hands-on negotiating experience. Several participants stated that they thought they had understood negotiating principles. However, after the role-playing of this case, they stated they realized there was considerably more for them to learn!

Mechanics

The roles for the buyer, Richard Raymond, and the seller, Ralph Hawk, follow. The case lends itself both to one-on-one negotiations and to team negotiations. If a good level of experience is present, one-on-one negotiations may provide the greater level of learning. If the case is used by less-experienced individuals, it may be desirable to divide the class into an even number of teams, each consisting of three to five students. This approach reduces the possibility of frustration setting in.

Due to the complexity of the case, it is recommended that the roles be distributed near the close of one class for use in the next class. The students then have time to analyze the material, develop negotiation objectives, and develop their tactics. The instructor should assign roles to all students and discuss the nuances of role-playing. The students are instructed to study the role assigned and to digest the facts in preparation for face-to-face negotiations. They should be encouraged to "get into the spirit of things"—to act as they would if they were the buyer or seller. They have concrete facts in their roles. They are free to ad-lib, as appropriate. They are *not* to share their roles. Each role has privileged information. But neither role has facts or information which is in conflict with the "opponent's" role. Now, the roles can be distributed.

Some students may request permission to conduct their negotiations in another room. Don't let this happen! A high level of energy is achieved when several pairs are negotiating in the same room simultaneously. A synergism results. Interest increases.

Approximately 30–45 minutes of the next class should be allocated to the face-to-face negotiations. The instructor will require 15–30 minutes to discuss the findings and implications.

On completion of the negotiation, the instructor should lead a group discussion. The following questions are suggested:

1. What negotiating strategy did Raymond use?
2. How did Raymond gather information?
3. How did Raymond deal with the uncertainty on the number of hours required to develop the tooling? (If Hawk is unwilling to base his cost for the tooling on approximately 3100 hours, his estimate for the most likely number of hours, then a fixed price incentive or even a cost plus incentive fee contract should be considered by Raymond for this portion of the work.)
4. Who retains title to the tooling? (Since Apex is to pay all costs, Apex should take title in order to avoid any sole source situation on follow-on purchases.)
5. Was a firm agreement reached on the delivery schedule?

6. What role did the learning curve play in the negotiations? Raymond's data indicate that it should take an *average* of 50 hours per strut when 100 struts are machined. Hawk's data are slightly more complex. He estimates that it will take 100 hours to produce the *first* strut if it is produced on hard tooling. Nothing is said about the learning curve in Mr. Hawk's role. It is Raymond's job to introduce the concept of the learning curve and then to convince Hawk to apply the principle of the learning curve.

Role for Richard Raymond, Buyer

On receipt of a properly prepared purchase request together with specifications for 100 landing outer cylinder struts, you developed a Request for Proposal which was sent to eight machining firms. Only three firms responded to the RFP and only one of these was willing to meet the required delivery schedule. Calls to the two nonresponsive suppliers confirmed their inability to meet the required delivery schedule. Although Apex has the ability to do the work in-house, a decision has been made to subcontract the work for two reasons: (1) Apex is nearing capacity on other work; and (2) Apex's hourly rates and overhead are approximately 50 percent higher than those of smaller suppliers.

Apex has had a continuing relationship with the only responsive proposer, Hawk Manufacturing of San Mateo, California. Last week you visited Hawk and performed a mini-preaward survey which convinced you that this source will be able to satisfy your requirements if awarded a contract. Because the machining industry is operating near capacity, you carefully reviewed Hawk's schedule. You are satisfied that Hawk will be able to meet your schedule. However, inclusion of your order will bring Hawk to full or near-full loading. A copy of Hawk's proposal is attached (attachment 1.1).

You are scheduled to meet with Mr. Hawk, owner of Hawk Manufacturing Co., in your office tomorrow morning. Information on the cost of manufacturing the struts last year is provided in attachment 1.2. Relevant learning curve data is in attachment 1.3. Extracts of rates from recent machining jobs is contained in attachment 1.4.

Hawk Manufacturing Co.
700 El Camino Road
San Mateo, California

January 10, 19XY

Mr. Richard Raymond
Purchasing Department
Apex Aviation Co.
2777 Imperial Highway
Hawthorne, CA 92050

Dear Mr. Raymond:

Reference is made to your Request for Proposal #29–74. We are confident that we can meet all the terms and conditions of your request for a total price of $696,400.

As we see the job, there are two components: (1) development of special tooling and (2) production of the outer cylinder struts.

Based on our past experience, we estimate that the special tooling will cost $310,000. If you would prefer, we will develop special tooling on a time and material approach. The hourly rate, including overhead, G & A, and profit, will be $45.00 per hour. Material will be at cost plus a 10-percent handling charge. We estimate material costs to be $140,000.

The actual machining of the struts should take 100 hours per strut. Our cost for this portion of the contract is as follows:

100 hours per strut, 100 struts; 10,000 hours	
direct labor cost, at $12 per hour	$120,000
overhead, 150%	180,000
total cost to manufacture	300,000
G & A, 15%	45,000
Subtotal	345,000
Profit, 12%	41,000
Total cost for struts	386,400
Special tooling	310,000
Total	$696,400

If awarded the contract, we will be able to begin work on the special tooling immediately and on the production of the outer cylinder struts in six months.

Thank you for the opportunity to do business.

Sincerely,

Ralph Hawk
President
Hawk Manufacturing Co.

attachment 1.1

Apex Aviation

January 15, 19XY

MEMO

FROM: D. Jones
         Director of Manufacturig Operations
TO: Richard Raymond
         Purchasing Department
SUBJECT: Costs for Manufacturing Outer Cylinder Struts

During the past year, we machined 50 identical struts.* The average strut required 65 hours to machine. We found that a 90 percent experience curve approximated the learning achieved in this process. Fully burdened direct labor currently is $55 per hour.

The special tooling, which was since converted to manufacture of another job, required 3,000 man-hours of tool-and-die-makers' time. Their hourly rate including applicable overhead is $70 per hour. Cost of materials for the special tooling was $130,000.

David Jones

*This was done on a single production line.

attachment 1.2

Learning Curve: Cumulative Values

Unit Number	Slope		
	0.80	0.85	0.90
1	1.0000	1.0000	1.0000
2	1.8000	1.8500	1.9000
3	2.5021	2.6229	2.7462
4	3.1421	3.3454	3.5562
5	3.7377	4.0311	4.3392
6	4.2994	4.6881	5.1008
7	4.8339	5.3218	5.8447
8	5.3459	5.9359	6.5737
9	5.8388	6.5333	7.2898
10	6.3153	7.1161	7.9945
11	6.7774	7.6860	8.6890
12	7.2267	8.2444	9.3744
13	7.6646	8.7925	10.0515
14	8.0922	9.3311	10.7210
15	8.5104	9.8611	11.3836
16	8.9200	10.3831	12.0397
17	9.3217	10.8977	12.6898
18	9.7161	11.4055	13.3342
19	10.1037	11.9069	13.9734
20	10.4849	12.4023	14.6076
21	10.8602	12.8921	15.2371
22	11.2299	13.3766	15.8622
23	11.5943	13.8560	16.4831
24	11.9538	14.3307	17.1000
25	12.3086	14.8009	17.7131
30	14.0199	17.0908	20.7267
35	15.6427	19.2940	23.6658
40	17.1934	21.4254	26.5425
45	18.6835	23.4958	29.3655
50	20.1216	25.5134	32.1416
55	21.5147	27.4847	34.8762
60	22.8678	29.4147	37.5735
65	24.1852	31.3077	40.2371
70	25.4708	33.1669	42.8699
75	26.7273	34.9955	45.4745
80	27.9573	36.7960	48.0530
85	29.1629	38.5705	50.6072
90	30.3460	40.3207	53.1388
95	31.5081	42.0484	55.1488
100	32.6509	43.7550	58.1399
150	43.2338	59.8901	82.1539
200	52.7203	74.7908	104.9614
300	69.6637	102.2341	148.1968
400	84.8495	127.5737	189.2588
500	98.8480	151.4560	228.7746

attachment 1.3

Extracts of Rates from Recent Machining Jobs

Name:	Jones Manufacturing Co.	Ryan & Sons	Southeast Tool & Die
Location:	San Francisco, CA	Springfield, OH	Atlanta, GA
Date Purchase Order Awarded:	June 19xx	October 19xx	December 19xx
For:	Machining Pistons	Outer Cylinders	Brake Cylinders
Hourly Rate:	$11.50	$10.00	$10.20
Overhead:	160%	150%	140%
G&A:	17%	16%	15%
Profit:	10%	10%	12%

attachment 1.4

Role for Ralph Hawk, President
Hawk Manufacturing Co.

You recently submitted the attached proposal (attachment 2.2) to the Apex Aviation Company for machining outer cylinder struts. Your proposal is composed of two elements: one for special tooling and one for manufacturing. Several days ago, Mr. Raymond, of Apex's purchasing department visited your plant to check on loading and capacity. You have had a continuing and reasonably satisfactory relationship with Apex.

Your estimate of the most likely number of hours required to prepare the special tooling was 3100. You were fairly certain that no more than 4000 hours would be required. Accordingly, you used the value 3750 hours as a conservative, but realistic, estimate. Your hourly rate for tool and die personnel, overhead, G & A and profit rates are $14 per hour, 150 percent, 15 percent and 12 precent respectively.*

In order to estimate the amount of time required to manufacture an outer cylinder strut, you had one of your machinists use soft tooling and actually produce a strut. It required 200 hours to produce the test strut. Based on past experience on the relative efficiency of labor using hard tooling versus soft tooling, you divided the required hours by two, giving you 100 hours if the test item had been produced using hard tooling.** All of your rates are shown in the proposal.

You would like to get this job because it complements your present schedule. In fact, if you get this job, you will be operating at nominal capacity. However, things are good in the machining business and you feel reasonably confident that if you don't get this job at a reasonably healthy profit, something just as good will come along.

* Materials will cost approximately $140,000.

** You plan to use a single production line with no parallel stations if you received this order.

attachment 2.1

Hawk Manufacturing Co.
700 El Camino Road
San Mateo, California

January 10, 19XY

Mr. Richard Raymond
Purchasing Department
Apex Aviation Co.
2777 Imperial Highway
Hawthorne, CA 92050

Dear Mr. Raymond:

Reference is made to your Request for Proposal #29–74. We are confident that we can meet all the terms and conditions of your request for a total price of $696,400.

As we see the job, there are two components: (1) development of special tooling and (2) production of the outer cylinder struts.

Based on our past experience, we estimate that the special tooling will cost $310,000. If you would prefer, we will develop special tooling on a time and material approach. The hourly rate, including overhead, G & A, and profit, will be $45.00 per hour. Material will be at cost plus a 10-percent handling charge. We estimate material costs to be $140,000.

The actual machining of the struts should take 100 hours per strut. Our cost for this portion of the contract is as follows:

100 hours per strut, 100 struts; 10,000 hours	
direct labor cost, at $12 per hour	$120,000
overhead, 150%	180,000
total cost to manufacture	300,000
G & A, 15%	45,000
Subtotal	345,000
Profit, 12%	41,000
Total cost for struts	386,400
Special tooling	310,000
Total	$696,400

If awarded the contract, we will be able to begin work on the special tooling immediately and on the producton of the outer cylinder struts in six months.

Thank you for the opportunity to do business.

Sincerely,

Ralph Hawk
President
Hawk Manufacturing Co.

attachment 2.2

BACK BAY UNIVERSITY

Purpose

The   purpose of this case is to explore the opportunities and problems of initiating a surplus disposal program.

Discussion

The large number of companies and institutions that have not instituted aggressive surplus and salvage programs is nothing short of amazing. Part of this problem stems from a misunderstanding of the high value of surplus. A typical example happened recently at one large university. Temporary metal buildings purchased during World War II were to be demolished to make way for a large, new library for the school. The immediate thought was to obtain bids from wreckers to demolish the buildings and haul the debris away. Fortunately, this university previously had instituted a surplus disposal program with a full-time surplus and salvage coordinator. This individual immediately perceived that the buildings had value as surplus material. The buildings were sold on an "as is, where is," basis and were moved by the buyers at no cost to the university. In fact, rather than payment of an anticipated $10,000 demolition bill, the university received several thousand dollars from the sale of the buildings. This same university was throwing away, as scrap, high-grade carbon cutting tools from its machine shops and surgeon's instruments from its hospital. This metal is valuable; it sells for a high price. Monsanto Chemical Company saved $400,000 in just one plant in the first year it installed a comprehensive salvage program. Savings similar to these are available to companies and institutions when they install a surplus disposal program.

This case also brings up the interesting subject of fringe benefits. Fringe benefits are important to all employees. In the past twenty years, fringe benefits in industry have risen at a far faster rate than wages. However, all personnel authorities are in agreement that fringe benefits should be administered with impartiality and with some relationship to assigned tasks and length of service. Certainly it is unwise to relate fringe benefits to the probability of an individual being physically near enough to a piece of capital equipment to obtain it as a gift or at an unrealistically low price. Such a practice can only lead to unhappiness among the vast number of employees who are not able to share in a fringe benefit program of this kind.

Question 1:

What arguments are there in favor of a formal salvage program at Back Bay University?

Comment:

The major argument favoring such action is the increased revenue for the university. A second argument is that such a formal program will avoid the possibility of fraud or favoritism which exists under the present "program."

Question 2:

What arguments are there in opposition to such a program?

Comment:

The two major arguments in opposition to such a program are:

1. It may not be cost effective.
2. The present program has become something of an employee fringe benefit.

More extensive research needs to be conducted into the likely annual salvage value of the materials presently being disposed of informally. Then an estimate should be made for the likely cost of a formal program. This estimate should include the intangible costs as well as the tangible costs. For example, the salary and expenses of any employee assigned to a formal disposal program should be included as well as any extra salary or other expenses that might be incurred because of a change in the present disposal system. It may be that one of the primary things that retains one of the university's outstanding researchers or technicians is the opportunity he has had each year to buy a piece of equipment at a reduced price.

Question 3:

Assume that a salvage program is to be implemented. Which department at the university should be responsible for it? Why?

Comment:

Administrative services (or the department responsible for providing such support) is a logical candidate. Many heterogenous activities frequently are planned under such a department.

Purchasing also is a likely candidate. Normally, a salvage program includes sales, either by auction or sealed bid. Frequently, the most cost effective way of disposing of surplus is to use it as a trade-in on new equipment. One of the authors had the experience of using surplus automotive parts as trade-ins on new parts. Items which had been selling for 10¢ on the dollar through sealed or spot bids returned 25¢ on the dollar when used as trade-ins. Thus, there are arguments favoring the assignment of the salvage program to purchasing.

A third alternative would be to assign the salvage program to the materials management division (if one exists at Back Bay U.). Surplus and scrap are materials. The director of materials is the person best qualified to oversee this material function.

Question 4:

Develop an implementation plan for such a salvage program.

Comment:

A good way to initiate a disposal program is to have an individual within the appointed department act as part-time or full-time coordinator of a salvage unit. The person selected should have tact, imagination, and business acumen. He or she should operate under the authority of a new policy requiring that all surplus material be disposed through the new salvage unit. Slowly, he or she should develop programs for collecting and selling surplus items in the most profitable manner for the university. Department heads will soon support the program because of their recovery of funds.

THE BETTER-LATE-THAN-NEVER BID

Purpose

This case provides an opportunity to discuss the competitive bidding process in a public institution. Purchasing practices and an ethics issue are involved.

Analysis

An experienced professional who serves as Purchasing Director for a public institution was asked to study the case. A summary of his analysis follows.

Lisa Needs A Lesson

Lisa did the right thing only in correcting her own lapse. But it's still sloppy purchasing. If Prairie was the source she considered potentially the most competitive, she should have assured that they were going to respond *before*, rather than *after*, the bid opening. this is part of the buyer's responsibility.

Lisa may have been within her legal rights to reject all bids, but she was lucky that the second go-around produced a $6,000 variation. Had it only been $100 or so, she would have been hard pressed to assert that the original bids were unreasonable.

The lesson? If all the bids are not in your hand several days before closing, get on the phone! The lesson may also involve an ethics issue.

Purchasing Director
Bucks County Community College

THE BIG D COMPANY

Purpose

The purpose of this case is to explore and apply to a growing company the concepts of inventory control and to review the inextricable interdepartmental implications. The need for effective inventory control in this company clearly illustrates the interrelationship of all the material functions and the advantages to be gained from a materials management organization.

Discussion

Inventory control has four primary objectives:

1. To have on hand, when needed, materials, parts or finished goods required by production or sales
2. To keep the investment in inventory at a minimum
3. To provide proper protection against loss, theft, and spoilage
4. To provide the necessary controls at the least possible cost

The first objective is relatively the most important, for the costs of production stoppages, emergency purchases, overtime, or lost customers are usually greater than the costs of excessive inventories. But this objective is, of course, in conflict with the second and fourth objectives. Any inventory control program therefore represents a compromise, based upon calculated risks.

Inventory control is inevitably and inseparably coupled with purchasing and production control. Therefore, frequent excursions into these functional areas are necessary to emphasize this interrelationship.

Ideally, the materials management activity includes the following functions: purchasing, production planning and control, inventory control, traffic, salvage and surplus, receiving, and warehousing. Some companies also include customer services, scheduling, shipping, materials handling, and physical distribution. The organization of such an activity and decision as to which responsibilities to include depends on local conditions, including politics and the capabilities of a firm's present employees.

It should be pointed out that there is no single correct answer to this case. Various feasible approaches may be taken which will improve the existing situation. The important thing, however, is that the student carefully analyze the situation and clearly define the problems inherent in the existing system. His or her recommendations, then, should focus on the problem areas. It is essential that he or she offer sound, realistic justification for the suggestion; at the same time, the student must point out the weaknesses of the recommended courses of action as well as the strengths.

Question 1:

What specific action should the company take in the area of inventory control? Support your proposal with an analysis of its strengths and weaknesses.

Comment:

a. There is a definite need for a record of purchased items and components. At the outset the record can be a very simple one.

b. The company should definitely attempt to forecast its sales demands for individual products; this forecast should then be translated into an estimated demand schedule for individual raw materials and component parts. While the demand for some finished products and parts cannot be forecast with great accuracy, the demand for many individual materials and parts often is more stable than is at first apparent and can frequently be determined well in advance of the need. Even though the demand for some finished products (while forecastable) is not stable, certain individual components are used in a number of different products, and in the aggregate the demand for many such components will be much more stable than the demand for each of the finished products.

The purpose of attempting to forecast sales is twofold:

1. It permits the firm to plan parts manufacturing activities in advance. This planning can subsequently be translated into the purchasing area.

2. It permits a current ABC analysis of production inventories. It also provides current data necessary to determine the approximate stability of demand for each individual item. These investigations constitute the starting point in developing an inventory control system. The final system must be based on this data.

c. The company should attempt to develop a one- or two-week cyclical control system for those items that are most expensive and are used in the greatest quantities.*

d. The company should attempt to use a fixed order quantity control system for the balance of the items failing in the B and C categories that exhibit reasonably stable usage and lead time characteristics. Order quantities for those items should be determined, using an EOQ approach.

e. All highly unstable items should be placed on a cyclical type of control system, using approximately a one-month review period.*

This and foregoing recommendations require that the company maintain more precise loading and scheduling control of its production operations than is now being done.

The production control activity must be coordinated with the inventory control activity in order to ensure efficient utilization of production facilities. The production control analyst should from time to time authorize premature production of stable items when the shop has excess capacity available. The objective of the above recommendations is to promote advance planning of production and purchasing requirements by placing inventory control and production control responsibilities in the hands of a centralized staff group (or groups). This will relieve the superintendent of this responsibility, giving him more time to manage the production operations (his major interest). At the same time this will provide specialized talent to handle inventory control and production control.

---

* As the volume of business increases, Big D may find it profitable to develop a simple MRP system for production planning and control purposes. An MRP system would be a very good approach for managing these inventories.

f.   The finished goods inventory record should be posted as completed orders are delivered to stock. This delivery should take place on a daily basis where the duration of production runs exceeds one day.

g.   All "overruns" should be brought under formal stores control, and inventory records of the items should be maintained.

The preceding items deal largely with production parts and components. The student must clearly distinguish between the need for this inventory control system and the need for an inventory control system for finished goods. A similar system, however, must be tied in closely with production control activities and shop capabilities in the various production areas. The case does not give sufficient detail on these latter matters to permit more than a general discussion of the type of system which might be used.

Question 2:

What is your reaction to the argument of those who oppose tighter controls?

Comment:

a.   Obsolescence is a valid consideration because of rapid design change of some items. But this can be predicted by engineering and can be controlled by coordinating the timing of engineering decisions with inventory control requirements. A good communication system is required. Control can also be facilitated by setting lower limits for fast-changing items.

b.   If the firm's working capital is very low, it may not be able to carry as much production or finished goods inventory as it would like. It is very likely, however, that inefficiencies of the existing uncontrolled system are costing the company substantially more than they realize (in excessive setup costs for underruns and in excessive carrying costs for overruns of certain parts on which the superintendent "guessed" incorrectly on the order quantity; this latter inefficiency also needlessly ties up valuable working capital).

c.   It is true that investment of funds in buildings, equipment, research, and so on, yields a return. It is also true, however, that investment of funds in inventories yields a return. The opponents apparently fail to recognize this fact. Inventory yields returns on investment through (a) lower manufacturing costs resulting from longer runs, (b) reduced purchasing costs resulting from planned and volume buying, as well as more efficient use of purchasing and related personnel, (c) shorter delivery time, and greater customer satisfaction. In Big D's case, the question to be decided is, how significant is this return and at what inventory level does the rate of return fall below that produced by other investments?

Question 3:

How would your recommendation in answer to question 1 differ if this company were making a single product?

Comment:

If the company made only a single product, sales forecasts would be much easier to make, and the demand for individual production materials and components would be much more stable. This would clearly simplify the inventory control situation. Some of the major materials could undoubtedly be "flow-controlled" on a JIT basis, reducing the required inventory investment. Most other materials could be controlled by an MRP system or a simple fixed order quantity system. Economic order quantities could be easily calculated for most of the items. In many cases it might be possible to develop suppliers who would be willing to carry a significant portion of Big D's inventory in their own stock, thus relieving Big D of some of its required inventory investment.

Question 4:

How does the inventory control problem change as the company's overall volume of business increases?

Comment:

As sales volume expands, more working capital and higher inventory levels are required; however, inventory levels increase less than proportionately as volume increases. This is true because the EOQ varies with the square root of the usage factor, not directly with usage. Likewise, as usage increases, the safety stock required for a given level of protection increases less than proportionately. Additionally, increased volume permits larger order quantities and larger production runs, thus reducing unit costs of production.

Control of inventories will also tend to be easier and less costly as volumes rise. As sales volume increases, the aggregate demand for individual production materials usually tends to become more stable. This permits the use of simpler, semiautomatic types of control.

Question 5:

Do you believe that this company would benefit from the establishment of a materials management activity? If so, what functions do you think it should include?

Comment:

The answer to this question is an emphatic "YES!" It is amazing that the Big D Company has grown, let alone survive. Conservatively, the introduction of an integrated materials management system at Big D should reduce material-related costs by 10 to 20 percent. Waste is present in all of the materials areas.

Ideally, the materials management activity at Big D should include: purchasing, production planning and control, inventory control, traffic, salvage and surplus, receiving, and warehousing.

The following additional questions can be used for discussion purposes:

a. How does inventory control in a small company differ from that in a large company?
b. What is the relationship between inventory control, production control, and purchasing?
c. This is a fairly small company. To what extent can it employ a sophisticated control system? What problems arise? Outline a realistic approach the company might take in developing an effective yet simple and inexpensive inventory control system.

THE BIG O COMPANY

Purpose

The purpose of this case is to discuss the rights and obligations of a buyer and a seller under a purchase contract when quality specifications are changed before delivery is completed.

Question 1:

What are Barry's legal obligations in this matter?

Comment:

Barry's legal obligations depend largely upon the exact language of the specifications contained in the original Procurement Standard, and those contained in the new standard. Since these are not detailed in the case, students usually express conflicting points of view on the matter. Some will contend that Barry only agreed to meet original specifications. Having done so, it discharged its obligations, and was under no further obligation to correct, replace, or reproduce castings to the new standard.

The instructor should seek to develop these opposing points of view fully. In so doing, he will probably want to relate question 1 to question 2, particularly as it pertains to the possible extent of Barry's responsibility.

Question 2:

Comment on the fact that Barry had already produced the full order quantity of 4,000 well in advance of actual delivery requirements.

Comment:

Consideration to the buyer under a purchase agreement is delivery of the purchase quantity in accordance with the contract schedule. Unless there is specific language to the contrary, this is the extent of the buyer's claim on how the seller produces. Accordingly, Barry is free to plan and schedule its production in whatever sequence or flow is "reasonable" to its "normal" manufacturing process. This means that if Barry's continuous-line operation was, in fact, a reasonable technique of manufacture, production of 4,000 units in one batch was not contrary to the spirit of the contract. Again, so long as Barry maintained the inventory of finished castings, and delivered solely in accordance with the order schedule, it did not violate the letter of the contract.

However, if Barry's actions were "unreasonable" in terms of "normal" manufacture, then production in anticipation of delivery might well have been at its own risk, so that the buyer would be justified in rejecting claims for units in excess of normal flow quantities.

The instructor should seek wide discussion on this question. Some buyers assume that delivery schedules firmly establish supplier manufacturing schedules. This assumption should certainly be brought out in the open for criticism and comment.

Question 3:

What does the buyer do now?

Comment:

Although legal issues are important to any consideration of this case, it should be apparent that a purely legal resolution of the problem is impracticable. The case describes a situation demanding a negotiated settlement. The Big O Company must seek compliance with the new Procurement Standard, and castings produced in deviation to that standard must be rejected. On the other hand, Barry is entitled to normal costs incurred in producing castings to the original purchase specification. The intent of any settlement should be the satisfactory achievement of both objectives, with minimum loss to either party.

As a negotiating aim, the buyer should seek to have all castings now produced to the original specification reannealed so as to meet the new standard. Any costs experienced by Barry in the reannealing should become the basis of upward price revisions on the completed castings. If the quantity produced in anticipation of delivery was "unreasonable" to Barry's "normal" manufacturing process, then the formula for settlement should be applied only to those units "reasonable" for Big O's delivery schedule.

Although this approach increases the price of the castings, it is justified by the increased scope of work demanded in the new Procurement Standard. Also, it is preferable to and less costly than a termination settlement, which is the only alternative under the circumstances described.

BLACK MOTOR COMPANY

Purpose

The purpose of this case is (1) to explore the question of what constitutes a fair and reasonable profit and (2) to discuss the merits and limitations of competition and negotiation as methods of establishing prices.

Discussion

This case realistically illustrates one of the common, repetitive errors of purchasing, i.e., the recurring mistake of confusing "competitive bids" with "adequate competition." Mr. South is not the only person confused concerning this issue. Sellers will normally bid on anything they are asked to bid on. However, when costs are unknown, specifications are not clear, etc., contingencies for every conceivable unknown will be included in the bid price. Competitive bids result in genuine competition only when the five criteria (as discussed in the text) that correctly dictate the use of this method of pricing prevail. In short, getting bids is always possible; however, if bids are obtained under improper circumstances, negotiated prices will invariably be lower than such bid prices.

Question 1:

What is the purpose of a "profit"?

Comment:

Underlying the discussion of much of this case are the factors which determine the reasonableness of profit.

Basically, a profit is allowed for two purposes: (1) to persuade the seller to accept the contract, and (2) to persuade him or her to perform it well and as efficiently as possible. This implies at once that it is not possible to set reasonable profits simply by making them a certain percentage of the cost or selling price of the product. If an efficient manufacturer produces an article at a cost of $1,000 per unit, while a less efficient manufacturer produces the same article at a cost of $1,500 per unit, the result of a flat profit rate of 10 percent for both would be that the efficient producer would receive a reward of $100 per unit for his or her management, while the inefficient one would receive $150 per unit for his. The flat profit rate would be even more absurd if the efficient producer should reduce his total costs to $800 per unit. The reward would be a reduction of $20 per unit in profit on the next contract.

Another type of flat profit rate is a percentage of the cost of the contractor's facilities or of his investment therein (net worth). This method is not better than the flat percentage of cost of sales. If an article can be produced for $100 in simple facilities worth $1 million while another contractor with facilities worth $2 million cannot produce it for less than $1150, there is certainly no reason why the latter should receive the greater profit.

The true purpose of profit is to promote efficiency of production, and it must be determined upon this basis. If greater investment really produces greater efficiency it is upon demonstrated efficiency that the greater profit should be earned. Stated differently, in normal circumstances profit should be correlated to efficiency.

Question 2:

When a buyer is deciding upon an adequate profit to promote his own interest, what points should be kept in mind?

Comment:

The following brief outline lists some of the points to be borne in mind by the buyer when deciding upon a profit adequate to promote the interests of the purchaser.

a. Initial orders: A fairly high profit may be necessary on an initial contract in order to persuade the supplier to undertake the risks and problems of a new kind of production.

b. Size of order: Expressed as a percentage of cost or price, the profit rate on a small order will often, if not always, be justifiably higher than on a larger order.

c. Kind of management talent demanded: Production calling for an unusually high degree of design or production engineering skill on production carried out under unusually difficult circumstances merits a profit adequate to retain this management for the purchaser's requirements. On the other hand, production which consists largely of the assembly of subcontracted components requires less effort from management and justifies less profit, unless the subcontracting is pursued in the interests of government policies.

d. Reliability of performance: A contractor who has demonstrated reliability of performance on past contracts should not be lost to the purchaser through inadequate profits, and conversely the purchaser can probably afford to discourage an unreliable performer until he improves.

e. Reliability of cost estimates: Since cost estimates are more important than profit estimates in determining real profits, a past record of excessive cost estimates calls for reducing both cost and profit estimates in new contracts, whereas a record of accuracy in this respect permits the buyer to award a reasonable profit without fear that it will become excessive.

f. Risks involved in the contract: If there are unusual risks involved in the contract because of the nature of the product or a long delivery schedule, then a higher profit may be called for than in more normal cases. It may often be more desirable, however, to remove the risk by allowing price redetermination or some other means, rather than to pay the contractors for risk assumption.

Question 3:

In this case, should a cost breakdown have been considered?

Comment:

For the moment, forgetting the broader implications of the question, strong arguments can be advanced that the dollar value of the purchase was too small to warrant a cost breakdown. The total order cited by the Army auditors was for $46,970. Some class members probably will maintain that it is uneconomical for White to expend the time and money necessary to prepare a cost breakdown. Or can Mr. South afford the time to analyze costs in connection with each bid received? If this argument is raised, the instructor might ask the class if there is a specified dollar amount below which it is economical to ask for a cost breakdown. The conclusion which will probably be reached is that there are many factors other than the size of the order which must be considered in making the decision to ask for a cost breakdown.

The broader implications of the question are these: Mr. South holds that the best way to insure a fair and reasonable price is to obtain competition and select the lowest bidder. Under such circumstances, the profit return the supplier receives is not a factor that need be considered because the total price can be assumed to be reasonable, since it resulted from competition. Implied in his reasoning was the opinion that it was unfair to negotiate the low bidder's price downward, since the low bidder had already won the contract from his competitors. A further argument is that if Mr. South refused to allow White the profit that competition and the company's efficiency afford it, White would not sell to Black because it could get a greater return from its other customers. Black would then be saddled with the higher cost owing to inefficient producers. On the basis of this reasoning, a cost breakdown would be unnecessary. As a matter of basic strategy, cost breakdown, if desired, should always be requested before orders are given, not after they are given.

Question 4:

Discuss ways of obtaining fair and reasonable prices as applied to this case.

Comment:

In order to discuss Mr. South's stand, it is necessary to explore the relative merits of competition and negotiation as methods of establishing fair and reasonable prices. There can be no argument that effective competition is the best method of establishing such prices. But what is effective competition? Effective competition results only when all of the following conditions are present: (a) an adequate number of qualified suppliers actively compete for the order; (b) suppliers are willing to price competitively; (c) definitive specifications exist; (d) there is time for this method of purchase; (e) the dollar amounts involved justify the administrative expense involved. Conversely, where one or more of these conditions is lacking, negotiation is necessary to obtain fair and reasonable prices. Although the case is silent on the number of South's competitors or their qualifications, it does indicate that the specifications may not have been adequate for complete reliance on competition. White stated:

> Our policy over the years has been a conservative one with respect to the risk factors involved in the defense business. We speak of risk in the sense that it is not uncommon for suppliers to be called upon to establish prices on the basis of specifications which do not lend themselves to accurate cost analysis. Design costs, study models, tooling, short run requirements before tools are completed, and finally, production costs, not to mention the expenses connected with correcting difficulties, which appear only after the equipment is in service, result in a quoted price based on considerable guesswork.

From this statement it can be concluded that Black was wrong in relying on competitive bids as a means of obtaining reasonable prices in many of its procurements with White. Admitted, White was including many contingencies in its estimates and was probably submitting unrealistically high bids. Further, if White has made the exact item before, we do not know whether the other companies submitting bids had made this item previously. Consequently, the bids of the other companies may be unrealistically high because of the inclusion of contingencies, developmental expenses, and setup costs, and as a result, offer no reliable standard by which to judge the reasonableness of White's bid. If such is the case, Mr. South would be justified in asking for a cost breakdown as a step in negotiating a reasonable price.

The case presents an opportunity to emphasize the importance of keeping accurate records in order that the buyer may justify the action he takes. He should keep a complete record of all bids received on each transaction. Besides providing a means of justifying his actions, a list of all bids received represents a good source of information to the buyer on the efficiency of his suppliers and the trends of their prices.

It might be noted that had White manufactured a standard commercial item that was manufactured by many companies and had a wide market, Mr. South's position would have been changed. Then his argument concerning the usefulness of competition as a means of establishing a fair and reasonable price might be justified. However, under the circumstances, it is still possible for a low bidder to make what appears to be an exorbitant profit of 40 to 50 percent because of its unusual efficiency. If such a company can undersell its competitors, a real question is raised as to whether its profit is too high.

Question 5:

What method of pricing do you believe should have been used?

Comment:

A more appropriate method of pricing would have been a negotiated fixed price with redetermination downward only or a fixed price incentive contract. Remember, negotiation can start with quotations, just like competitive bidding. The mistaken belief that negotiation means the elimination of competition is fallacious.

BLOZIS COMPANY

Purpose

The purpose of this case is to outline the steps in the purchasing procedure and to illustrate the importance of adequate procedures and forms in effecting good communications and control within the organization. The astute student will deduce that the type of organization in question influences the procedures which should be used and that the procedures used largely determine the number and types of forms required to assure sound communication and control.

Question 1:

If you were the purchasing manager, what recommendations would you have made?

Comment:

It is evident in this case that existing procedures, documents, and forms leave much to be desired in the realm of interdepartmental communication and materials control. By initiating a few simple changes in procedure and responsibility assignment within the purchasing department, the purchasing manager can develop a system which will convey to all interested parties the information they require regarding materials orders and costs, and definitely fix responsibility for all materials at each stage of the process. The revised purchasing procedure should include the following elements:

A. Complete stores catalog

All items carried in stores should be listed in easily accessible fashion and should be completely described, with applicable specification identification. This should be very helpful to operating and technical personnel, and should relieve the expediter of some of his "extracurricular" duties.

B. Purchase requisitions

1. These may be made out by any personnel management feels desirable, but should be subject to approval of respective department heads for two reasons:
   a. To give department managers control over department expenses
   b. To insure that all requisitioned data are included on the requisition and that items are properly described
2. All items requisitioned must be defined by specification number or by an adequate description of the technical characteristics the item must possess in order to fulfill its function.
3. The correct cost center identification or capital job charge should be included on the requisition for each item.
4. Minimum distribution of copies includes:
   a. Using department
   b. Purchasing

C. Purchase orders

1. Authorization for purchase order preparation should reside solely with the purchasing manager or his assistant.
2. All purchase orders should bear the proper accounting charge for each item.

3. Emergency orders should receive special attention:
   a. A special requisition form may be used, on which the department head must justify his request for rush treatment.
   b. Only the purchasing manager and his assistant should be authorized to place phone orders, unless the purchasing manager delegates this authority to a department head in a given special situation.
   c. All phone orders must be covered by a purchase order number to insure control over the order.
4. Blanket orders may be used for small-value, rush items which can be procured locally from a single source. However, adequate control must be incurred by use of signed receipts, company receiving reports, and so on.
5. Minimum distribution of copies includes:
   a. Purchasing department
   b. Accounting department
   c. Using department
   d. Supplier

D. Receiving and delivery
1. All purchased items brought into the plant, whether emergency or routine, must go through the standard receiving procedure.
2. The following signatures are required on receiving department records:
   a. Receiving clerk must sign receiving report.
   b. Delivery man must sign for items picked up for delivery outside the warehouse area.
   c. The user must sign for receipt of an item when delivered or picked up.
3. Minimum distribution of receiving report copies includes:
   a. Using department
   b. Purchasing department
   c. Accounting department
   d. Receiving department

E. Specifications

When an internal material specification is drawn up (for both stores and nonstores items), purchasing should have an opportunity to review it and make suggestions regarding the commercial and cost aspects of the specification. A formal procedure for specification development and approval by all interested departments will greatly facilitate coordination of the efforts of all departments involved. When the specification has been finalized, copies of the completed specifications should be distributed to all interested departments, including purchasing.

If purchasing is to operate effectively, one step in this process must be a general familiarization of the buyer of the item with the technical provisions of the specification. Otherwise it is virtually impossible for purchasing to translate accurately the specification into commercial standards. If the purchasing manager does not have the time or technical skill required, he must employ someone who does.

F. Slow-moving and obsolete materials
1. Stores or inventory control personnel should issue a monthly report to the purchasing manager, listing all slow-moving stock. Without such information the purchasing manager can establish no systematic procedures for the needed revision of inventory levels of certain slow-moving materials.

2. In order to uncover and dispose efficiently of obsolete materials the purchasing manager should establish a systematic procedure whereby all departments periodically report such materials to the purchasing manager. Before external disposal of such materials is made, the purchasing manager might consolidate these reports and notify all department heads of the availability of materials which they might be able to use. This entire operation could be accomplished by means of a simple reporting procedure utilizing standardized forms.

Questions 2 and 3:

At what point does this purchasing department exhibit weak control over (1) materials, (2) overall purchasing performance?

How could these weaknesses be corrected?

Comment:

As outlined in the comment to question 1, this company displays weak control over materials all along the line. Overall purchasing performance could be improved by taking the action suggested. Note, that under the present system there exists a needless opportunity for the expediter to steal company funds.

Question 4:

What activities should the expediter be responsible for in this organization?

Comment:

The expediter probably would make a good engineering buyer. He appears to have some of the necessary skills, and such a buyer is obviously needed in this company's purchasing department.

Question 5:

What is the purchasing department's responsibility in establishing and interpreting technical specifications?

Comment:

The engineering department can ask for help from purchasing in establishing specifications, but the final responsibility for setting specifications must rest with engineering.

THE BOARD ROOM

Purpose

This case addresses the need for project coordination and the buyer's role in ensuring that someone is in charge. As is so often the case, there is an immediate problem which requires an immediate fix and a longer-term responsibility problem.

Discussion

Ideally, management should appoint a project manager to coordinate the interdependent activities of independent suppliers (i.e., constructors and equipment suppliers) each of whom is under contract to the firm. All too often such appointments are not made and problems arise. The buyer frequently is in a position of seeing where such coordination is required. He or she should either step into the vacuum or ensure that a coordinator is appointed.

Question 1:

What alternatives are open to Tom?

Comment:

Three alternatives are listed and discussed:

Redesign Floor

The building contractor could tear up the existing floor and redesign and rebuild. The new design will take into account the engineering characteristics of the chairs. The chairs will be installed properly according to the original intentions of the architect and the executive working group.

This option will obviously take a significant amount of time. The executive directors want this resolved—and quickly. This will also cost a lot of money. The architect probably will claim that he should be paid to redesign and the contractor must be paid to rebuild. Additionally, there is no guarantee that the chairs ordered will work under any circumstances.

Pay Local Installer $15,000

Tom has the option of paying a local installer $15,000 to install the chairs. The advantages of this option are time and money. The installer can install the chairs quickly since he has already worked with the chairs and floor. The cost is inexpensive relative to other options.

There is a question as to whether the local installer can actually do the job. According to the case, satisfaction may be impossible. Assuming that the installer will not come up with a miraculous way of installing the chairs, this is a false option. Most likely, the chairs will be installed with only temporary satisfaction before they fail.

Procure Another Chair

Tom can procure another set of chairs in a smarter way by considering the total cost of the procurement and selecting the source based on some major factors. The operating characteristics and the engineering features of the new chairs must be considered. A chair will not be chosen unless it can be installed in the existing floor. Qualitative factors must be considered when choosing a source: Does the supplier work with the buyer to ensure a good fit? Will a warranty be included? Does the supplier have a policy of service and reliability? The all-in-cost of the chairs must also be considered when choosing an option. The all-in-cost includes initial cost of the chairs, delivery, installation, and maintenance.

This option will ensure a quality chair installed properly. Tom can work with the architect and the original working group to find an acceptable alternative to the existing leather chairs. The cost of this option may be reduced by working with the existing supplier to get a trade-in. Or it may be less costly to sell the existing chairs. The problem with this option is the time it will take to choose another supplier and the potential cost.

Question 2:

What is the best course of action now?

Comment:

The firm should procure another set of chairs. This will ensure a quality chair installed properly. The disadvantages of this option are the time it will take and the cost. Unfortunately, over the long term, there is simply no less costly alternative to consider. The time it will take to accomplish this alternative may be significant. Given the hurry that the executives are in, it may be necessary to use the existing installation contractor to temporarily install the existing chairs as needs dictate.

Question 3:

Who is responsible for the present situation?

Comment:

Top management at Builders' Bank failed to appoint a project coordinator and must bear ultimate responsibility for this all-too-common fiasco. It appears that many organizations are responsible for their niche, but no one has overall responsibility.

Question 4:

What should Tom have done to avoid the present situation?

Comment:

The professional buyer recognizes that he or she is the "court of last resort." The buyer must look at all procurements from a systems perspective to minimize having things "fall through the cracks." A professional would have anticipated and avoided these problems.

BRANSON ELECTRONICS (PART A)

This is a highly versatile case with the possibility of discussing the following in the case:

1. price and cost analysis
2. learning curves and their application
3. transfer pricing—Stockbridge
4. negotiations versus bidding
5. coordination between purchasing and engineering
6. government data requirements from prime and sub contractors
7. overhead and indirect cost allocation techniques
8. pricing too low to *buy the business*
9. ratio analysis for the three suppliers
10. ethics on the plant visit issue
11. the use of the Census of Manufactures to get industry-wide material to labor ratios

It is also possible to role play with this case by a mock negotiation between Shawnee and Branson. There are 14 negotiation points in the case including:

1. unit price
2. delivery
3. payment terms
4. design rights
5. FOB point
6. quality and reliability testing
7. price redetermination
8. retention for warranty: percentage and time held
9. value of the learning curve
10. providing data in acceptable form
11. validity of individual cost elements
12. inventory carrying costs
13. contract cancellation
14. redesign costs and time

The case itself requires the student to make a number of assumptions. The main ones are:

1. the learning curve is applicable to only the direct labor portion of price.
2. the labor cost quoted in the case is labor cost based on a cumulative average of the 500,000 units. It is then possible to "back track up the curve" using the formula:

at 500,000 units, the labor cost is \$1.05, at 250,000, the labor cost = \$1.05 $(1/.98)$ or $1/$Learning curve percent. At 125,000 units, the labor cost = \$1.05 $(1/.98)^2$. At 62,500, the labor cost = \$1.05 $(1/.98)^3$. This is the labor cost for Shawnee. If Crow and Stockbridge were analyzed in the same manner, the formulas would be the unit labor cost divided by $[1/L.C.]$

This computation as pictured in the attached graph shows the decline in labor costs as a function of units produced for Shawnee. This is a cumulative average learning curve. A smart supplier picks these "check points along the curve" to see that costs are tracking and are on the curve. If they are too high, the labor portion will raise the price. The data to accompany the graph is attached also. This can also be done for Stockbridge and Crow.

The students should start the case with a financial analysis of the suppliers, looking at:

1. current ratio
2. quick ratio
3. collection period
4. profitability of each

All three turn out to be losers in the financial sense. By taking the values in the financial statements, it is possible to restructure the price based on past performance. Notice the bid prices include healthy profit levels. Notice also that Stockbridge is buying inventory from itself.

Next consider the impact of advancing money to the suppliers as requested. This cost of capital must be added to the price. Also have them measure the impact of getting the order on each supplier's sales volume and profit levels.

Discuss the issue of custom made versus off-the-shelf in the case of the designs. Have the students consider the question of design rights versus early supplier involvement. Was Branson guilty of soliciting "free engineering" from suppliers on the "promise of a chance to compete"? What is the difference between ESI and having the supplier engineer it for you in the bid process?

Discuss the issue of price structure. The government has a powerful set of tools in the price/cost area and the legislation to back it up. On the basis of the information provided, it is possible to construct the price structure of each supplier, setting sales as 100 percent and computing COGS as a percent of sales, S, G & A as a percent of sales and operating income. Have the students run this analysis and compare it to the annual report data. The discrepancy between the two for each supplier is wide.

Discuss the issue of warranty retention and the liability of the contractor for the performance of his subcontractors.

Discuss all the "red herrings" included in the letter offers for possible negotiation, including:

1. redesign costs
2. cancellation costs
3. inventory carrying costs
4. reliability testing with samples

The case is loaded with those giveaways. Consider the real issue:

1. reality of price
2. design rights and how much they cost *per unit of product* [hint]: they add about $0.50 per unit. This brings the Shawnee price up to $11.04 per unit.
3. meeting the schedule in a JIT posture
4. terms and conditions
5. physical proximity of the supplier
6. getting a production schedule from your supplier and monitoring it.
7. monitoring techniques on price
8. price redetermination.
9. who owns the tooling?

Analytical Data

There are millions of scenarios that could be used, thus the following data in an example of how the analysis could be carried out. Good students will set this up on a spreadsheet and iterate it.

Tables 1 and 2 reveal some interesting points to consider. Look at this data and compare suppliers from the perspective of cost components. Have your students compare these numbers to the financial data of each company. Have them look at:

1. the proposed profit in the bids versus actual profit experience of each company. This can be done by taking the selected financial data in the case, converting it to percentages and comparing the bids to the "normal" way of doing business to find where the bids have been front end loaded.

2. Is Branson better off buying the tooling for the winning bidder and having ownership? Have students consider the benefits of leasing the tooling, if possible.

3. How do the material to labor ratios of the bid compare to the industry as a whole? Have the students go to the library and look up the Census of Manufactures for the most recent five years on the SIC code and graph the material to labor ratio as a time series.

4. How does the COGS of each supplier compare to the bid data?

5. Ask the students about the Shawnee price. Is it too low? Are they buying in with a low price or is the learning curve too high? Remember a 98 percent curve would indicate an automated manufacturing process. The curve shows the cost going from about $1.24 per unit at almost 2000 units to $1.05 at 500,000 units. What if their learning curve was 95 percent. You have the raw data from the graph of the learning curve. Start at the 1,953 unit level and a $1.24 per unit price and simply follow the unit column down and multiply the $1.24 by .95, then $.95^2$, then $.95^3$ as seen on the graph table and in the graph. Compare the prices now with new labor costs.

6. Consider the cost impact of custom made versus off-the-shelf.

7. In the process of selecting a bidder, remember this is a government contract. If the low bidder is *not* selected, there is paperwork to fill out. The contract that Branson has is subject to government audit. Also, Shawnee had the best technical approach. Your engineers said so.

Part B of this case is predicated on Shawnee getting the bid. Shawnee has underestimated its costs and now finds itself in a hole. They will ask for a price redetermination as indicated in part A of the case (see Shawnee letter). You may wish to set up Part B as a mock negotiation. If you elect not to use part B, you may wish to set up part A as a mock negotiation. In using this case over seven years, I have found it is best to divide the class into five teams. Teams 1, 2 and 3 are analysts employed by Branson. They are each given a supplier to analyze and they make their reports. Teams 4 and 5 are out of the room when these reports are made. They come in after the reports and negotiate as Branson and Shawnee to come to best and final offer.

This translates to preparing an agenda and positions on agenda items. Normally the ground rules are that Branson supplies Shawnee with an agenda at least three weeks prior to the negotiation. Each of the teams prepares their positions on the agenda items and just before the negotiation begins, the remaining students (teams 1, 2 and 3) get a copy of each team's position. These students then become "umpires and score keepers" for the negotiation. About half the time, they can't reach agreement. Sometimes they get very emotional and cannot get past the passions of the process. Watch out for anger and frustration.

BRANSON ELECTRONICS (PART B)

In this part of the case, the supplier, Shawnee, has come back with the sad story of underestimation of price and wants to renegotiate. Suppliers available have been reduced to Shawnee and Stockbridge. Stockbridge appears too anxious and Crow is far too high in price. Branson needs Shawnee, but does not need the 11.25 percent price increase. Look at the new data compared to the old. The increases come in three areas:

1. labor cost up 45 cents
2. overhead up 48 cents
3. tooling up 45 cents

The tooling figure is perhaps justified as it appeared low in the A part of the case. The labor rate also was low in the first part of the case and can be measured. Two issues are left to the students to resolve. They are:

1. allowing overhead to rise penny for penny with labor and
2. S, G & A and profit came down only 20 cents when it was a high number to start the case.

Students working on this part of the case should focus attention on the possible use of incentives as well as allowing the contractor some relief in areas where there exists sufficient documentation to really verify costs. The negotiation of the new price should have the supplier making more concessions in the S, G & A and profit areas and in the factory overhead area. In addition, let us see some increase in productivity and improvement in the learning rate to say 95 percent from 98 percent. Others can do it, why not Shawnee?

Students should measure the impact of the learning process by assuming the curve is still 98 percent and working backwards again using $1.50 as the cumulative average for 500,000 units and the formula of (1/L.C.) to move back up the curve to get to the 1,953 unit figure for cost, then move to 500,000 at the 95 percent rate.

This data is shown as table B–1.

This would be a good negotiation opportunity. The agenda is price and its components. See if the students can develop a "win-win" environment from an essentially "win-lose" or "lose-lose" situation. This is a chance to see if they are creative and can craft ways to satisfy both parties. Remember also the design rights issue. This could elevate the cost to $12.22 per unit. It is a big concession and could be used to limit the increase to where Shawnee is still low bid.

Table B–1

units produced	labor cost (cum. avg.)
1,953	1.23
3,906	1.21
7,813	1.19
15,625	1.16
31,250	1.14
62,500	1.12
125,000	1.09
250,000	1.07
500,000	1.05

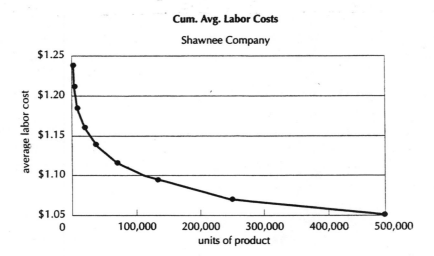

Cum. Avg. Labor Costs

Shawnee Company

BRONX BUSINESS MACHINES CORPORATION

Purpose

This case addresses the procurement of R & D services and the production of the resulting product. Also, it addresses the relationship between the supplier's risk, the type of contract, and the target amount to be paid.

Discussion

The procurement of R & D services is a most challenging area. Frequently, considerable uncertainty is involved. Uncertainty translates to risk, which translates to contingencies unless other than a firm fixed price (FFP) method of compensation is selected.

The procurement of the first production run, when cost uncertainty is present, can be equally challenging. If an FFP method of compensation is employed, the supplier will have great incentive to include a contingency in its price. If a fixed price redeterminable contract is employed, the supplier is motivated to apply a lax hand to cost control since the price of successive orders and production runs will be based on the first run. Use of a cost reimbursement contract also applies *no* incentive to control cost.

Note to the Instructor

Ron Cox's role is attached to this note so that role-playing negotiations may be employed. If the instructor chooses to use this as a discussion case only, the key elements of Mr. Cox's role should be made available to students.

Question:

If you were Ms. Oster, what action would you take? Why?

Comment:

Ms. Oster's actions must be directed to both the procurement of the required development work and to the probable follow-on production contract. We will address the development work first.

A good cost estimate from BBM's engineering department would be of great help to Ms. Oster. With or without such an estimate, Ms. Oster should be aware of the likely presence of a contingency in Tigertronix's proposal. Ms. Oster also should be sensitive to the possibility that the effort required to develop the new input/output (I/O) device may be of value to Tigertronix, not only for the BBM contract, but also for other applications. If such synergysm is present, Ms. Oster should investigate the possibility of paying only a share of the development costs or of having Tigertronix pay a royalty for any products resulting from the development effort. Ms. Oster will want to conduct some discussions with her engineers—and possibly an outside consultant familiar with these two technical aspects of the procurement—before proceeding.

Once she is prepared, Ms. Oster should meet with Mr. Cox. If appropriate, she should put the discussions into the framework of potential long-term relations. She then should gain insight into the Tigertronix proposal. What, for example, is the range of likely engineering hours? What is the number of hours at which there is equal likelihood of actual hours being greater or lesser? Are the hourly rates actual or projections? What are the bases of: overhead, G & A, and profit? Will Tigertronix gain other benefits from the proposed development effort?

For the sake of discussion, let us assume that Ms. Oster determines that:

a. Tigertronix does not anticipate gaining any other benefits from the development effort.

b. Tigertronix estimates its engineering hours to range from 2,500 to 4,200 and its engineering supervisory hours to range from 375 to 630. The point at which there is equal likelihood of hours going above or below (also known as the target) are 3,000 and 3450, respectively.

c. The overhead, G & A, and profit rates are based on historic data and projections for the coming 12 months. The profit rate of 15 percent, while higher than Ms. Oster would like, is normal for this industry. Ms. Oster is satisfied with the supporting data and concludes that the rates are acceptable.

d. A quick and dirty analysis indicates that Tigertronix's proposal (based on 4,000 hours of engineering work) is approximately one-third higher than the most likely costs established in "b" above. Noting that all costs are driven by engineering hours, Ms. Oster estimates a direct engineering hour in the proposal would cost BBM $155.25 ($621,000 ÷ 4,000); the difference between the fixed price proposal (based on 4,000 hours) and the most likely outcome of 3,000 hours ("b" above) is 1,000 hours at $155.25/hour, or $155,250. If Ms. Oster is unsuccessful at getting Tigertronix to reduce its fixed-price proposal significantly, then she should consider developing a fixed-price incentive fee contract along the following lines:

Engineering	Hours	Cost	Fee	Total Paid
Minimum	2,500	337,500	77,625*	415,125
Maximum	4,200	567,000	0	567,000
Target	3,000	405,000	60,750	465,750

* The fee when total hours are less than target hours has two components: the target fee plus (in this hypothetical example) 25 percent of the cost savings below target.

The following graph portrays the above information:

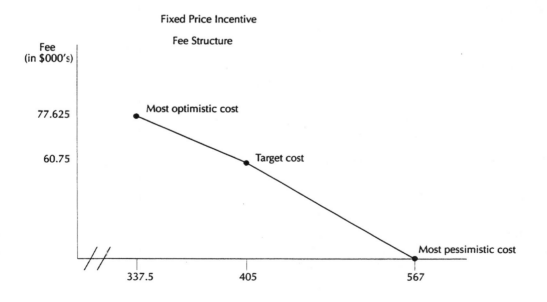

Fixed Price Incentive
Fee Structure

In this scenario, Ms. Oster should protect BBM's investment by agreeing with Tigertronix for a royalty to be paid to BBM for sales of any I/O's based on the development work.

Ms. Oster's second task is to agree on a price or a pricing mechanism for the production option. As noted in the Discussion, pricing of the first production run can be very challenging. Tigertronix proposes a cost reimbursement production option of $100 per unit for the first 10,000 units.

Again, a good estimate from BBM engineering (or even manufacturing) would be a great assistance! Along with a good cost estimate and skill in the use of the learning curve, Ms. Oster may be able to negotiate a satisfactory fixed-price production option. However, if she feels that the supplier's risk results in an unacceptable contingency, she should attempt to negotiate a fixed-price incentive contract for the first production run.

Note that the way in which BBM plans to enter into the procurement of the development and the production option is quite sound. *Now* is the time to obtain the price for the production option! And breaking the procurement into its two components is good procurement!

By purchasing the development work and all supporting documentation, BBM is able to obtain competition for the first production run if it is not comfortable with the price of the production option.

Role for Ron Cox
President, Tigertronix

Tigertronix is a dynamic, high-tech organization doing $50 million a year. It has an excellent R & D staff and facilities, plus very modern production facilities. The firm employs 450 people, including 10 engineers and 2 engineering supervisors.

Tigertronix's current bread and butter is the T–101 I/O device, which accounts for 65 percent of the firm's sales. The T–101 is one year old. Management at Tigertronix has been discussing the development of a successor to the T–101. The successor, if development were to proceed smoothly, would be available in 16 to 24 months.

Recently, Freddie Ready, vice president of marketing, met with you and discussed a conversation he recently had with June Oster, a procurement person at Bronx Business Machines Corporation (BBM). Tigertronix had been attempting to crack Bronx Business Machines for some time. Mr. Ready indicated that BBM was interested in out sourcing the development of a smart I/O device. He stated that BBM wanted to pay for the development so that it would own any patents and data rights, including procurement specifications. Ms. Oster had said that she planned to enter into an R & D contract with an FPI option for production. BBM would retain the right to complete the production work. But, as Mr. Ready pointed out, the developer would have considerable insight into the costs and nuances of production.

Your engineering staff estimated that design and development would require from 2,500 to 4,200 hours, with 3,000 hours the most likely result. Supervisory hours are at the rate of 6 hours of supervision for every 40 hours of engineering.

The overhead and G & A rates are based on last year's ratios. These rates have proven to be pretty much on target so far this year. Your profit objective on a job with this much risk is 15 percent.

The average production cost for the first 10,000 units of the T–101 has been $75. The costs are as follows:

Material	$30.00
Direct Labor	10.00
Overhead (250%)	25.00
G & A (10%)	1.00
	$66.00
Profit	9.00
	$75.00

Your design and manufacturing engineers have reviewed BBM's new I/O requirement and estimate that production costs will be approximately 30 to 50 percent higher than the present T–101.

The executive committee—consisting of Messrs. Cox and Ready; Frank James, vice president/finance; and Carl Andersen, vice president/operations—met for 45 minutes and agreed that Tigertronix should go after the business.

BROTHERS MOWERS

Purpose

This case addresses both the benefits of standardization and some of the obstacles encountered in implementing a standardization program.

Discussion

Many firms do not fully appreciate the benefits to be gained through standardization and its corollary, simplification. Standardization should aid a manufacturer in its efforts to compete successfully in the global marketplace.

Note to the Instructor

As a variation in your normal case discussion format, consider dividing your class into 2 groups or several subgroups with each group receiving one set of copies of the following instructions. After 20 minutes or so of discussion, have Rod(s) make his (their) presentation(s) and have the department heads react.

Role for Rod

Prepare to discuss the department heads on the following:

1. What benefits would your suggestion yield in regard to the following:
    a. number of parts ordered
    b. inventory
    c. production runs
    d. cost of production
    e. rework
    f. inspection costs
    g. clerical and handling costs
2. What are the benefits of simplification?
3. How would you go about organizing a new standardization program?
4. Why is procurement a required major input to the program?

Role for Department Heads

Each group member should pretend he or she is a departmental head as described in the case. Listen to Rod's presentation.

1. What factors do you see that work against Rod's suggestions?
2. Address the importance of the relationship between Brothers and its suppliers in regard to this decision.

3. Is a redesign necessary to use standardization and simplification techniques? Why?

4. What other ways could you go about solving Brothers Mowers's problems in procurement?

Question 1:

How can Rod suggest solutions to problems when the people whose cooperation he needs don't realize that the problems exist?

Comment:

Rod Stanton, the new procurement director, needs to review corporate and department objectives and identify specific advantages that each department would obtain by using standard parts. Addressing each department head individually, he can point out current potential problems and possible alternatives to solve these problems. His desire is to use standardized parts to minimize costs and keep the corporation competitive. Therefore the advantages of lower product costs, lower administrative processing costs, reduced inventory carrying costs, and fewer quality defects should be emphasized to the manufacturing, repair, administration, and inventory control heads of marketing and finance. After building a base of support, he can address the group of department heads with the proposed design modifications and supporting reasons.

Question 2:

How can Rod get engineers to redesign a whole line of products when sales are healthy?

Comment:

Redesign of the product lines is not desirable. Such action would delay the overall objective of standardizing parts because engineering would have to review every model or design a new set of models. Marketing and sales can work with engineering to identify the consumer desires and expectations of slight design modifications, but repair and service will continue to work on older models, and storage of parts could remain a problem. Instead, Rod should work with the various departments (repair and servicing, engineering, marketing) to phase in selected design changes (body frames, engine size, handles, wheels, for instance), pointing out the advantages of product availability and quality resulting from the use of standard parts. A major change in product style might not be easily accepted by the employees (who feel comfortable with the family atmosphere and the way things are managed), the consumers (who would be cautious of major changes that were made quickly), or the management (who would dislike a major change in a profitable product). By working with suppliers and emphasizing to the management that standard products would aid in the engineering design and assembly of products, Rod would ease the apprehension over creating another new design.

Question 3:

How can Rod propose changing from trusted suppliers of ten to twenty years to new suppliers of standardization products?

Comment:

The use of standard products would not require dropping trusted old suppliers and searching for new suppliers if handled correctly by Brothers Mowers. While some of the old suppliers would lose Brothers as a customer, other trusted suppliers could benefit. The purchasing and engineering departments should work with the various suppliers to outline performance and fit objectives. Such action will allow suppliers to help design the standard parts in a way which would reduce their costs. If the parts are standard and produced in large quantity, then both Brothers Mowers and the suppliers can benefit by increased demand (as compared to the smaller quantity of special parts which were produced previously) and reduced product price. Realizing that some parts may be obtained from new suppliers, the old suppliers may be motivated to provide a suitable product with equal quality at a lower price. The old suppliers have the advantages of prior service and reputation in delivery and quality when Brothers is considering the sourcing issue.

CAMPBELL TYPEWRITER CORPORATION

Purpose

The purpose of this case is to permit the student to determine how best to negotiate with a sole source under most interesting circumstances and also to determine what type of contract would best assure both prompt delivery and a fair price.

Discussion

In presenting the case, the instructor may wish to employ the role-playing method. If so, he should assign the role of Smith to one student or team of students and Ingborg to another. This is an excellent role-playing case.

Information which would be available only to the buyer (Jim Smith) or to the potential supplier (Nils Ingborg) is contained on the following pages. If the role-playing mode is employed, these roles should be reproduced and made available to the appropriate class members during class. A mock set of results is contained in the addendum to these notes. These results describe the variety of approaches which are encountered when using role playing.

If the conventional case discussion is employed, the instructor should make available to the students the information contained in the two roles.

Question 1:

What is your opinion of Ingborg's two proposals? Which, if either, could you accept, and why?

Comment:

Neither solution presented seems sound. By using the straight 2,600 man-hour figure, Smith may be either giving Ingborg a windfall profit, or conversely, causing him to lose money. A straight per-hour charge based on actual hours is the same as writing a blank check. It would be to Ingborg's advantage to start slowly and then use the higher overtime allowance to finish the job on time.

Question 2:

Are there any other choices open to Smith for arriving at an equitable agreement?

Comment:

A solution utilizing a combination of the two alternatives might be best. The fact that Campbell does manufacture its own key tops should make the estimated hours on this job somewhat realistic. Since Smith has to use Ingborg in any case, he is in a poor negotiating position. His best strategy may be to tell Ingborg he will give him the job for $95,000 (2,600 hours × $33 + $10,000) and let Ingborg make the next move. If he accepts, Smith has contracted for his requirement at a very attractive price. In any event, this is a sound base from which to negotiate. The ultimate solution might be a profit formula whereby the $95,000 figure is a target figure allowing Ingborg X percent profit. For every dollar that Ingborg's actual costs are under this figure, he would receive an additional $.20 profit. For every dollar his actual costs exceeded this target, his profit would be reduced by $.20. An upper ceiling of $109,000, for example, could be set. If Smith and Ingborg agree that some overtime will be required, the target and ceiling price should be increased accordingly.

Comment:

Smith is in a very difficult position since he must use Ingborg for his source. Ingborg's surprise offer to let Smith set the price was a brilliant piece of strategy for Ingborg, as it was completely unexpected.

Question 3:

How would you have handled the procurement if you were Smith?

Comment:

Smith could have prepared better for his meeting with Ingborg. By figuring exactly what the internal costs were for producing similar items, Smith could have made an immediate counteroffer, thus putting Ingborg on the defense. When negotiating with a sole source, the negotiator must be informed as much as is possible on the costs of alternative solutions. If a higher cost must now be paid to Ingborg, it must be understood that this is a make-buy cost directly related to the company's decision to make most of its own keys.

Question 4:

What should Campbell do to get better competition?

Comment:

Adequate purchasing agreements with manufacturers of keys probably would have prevented this problem from occurring in the first place. Also, value analysis may identify suitable substitutes which could have been procured competitively.

Role for Jim Smith

Manufacturing engineering at Campbell estimated the hours required to produce the molds and then the 120,000 required sets of keys at 2,600 hours, but this style of letter had never been produced. Further, the estimate was based on the use of internal facilities, and could be either much above or much below what actually might be experienced. It was, at best, a "guesstimate," and Jim Smith knew from experience how unrealistic such "guesstimates" could be. Campbell's fully burdened rates are $35 per hour and $45 for an hour of overtime. If the job were produced in-house by Campbell (assuming that some other job now being done by Campbell could be done by a subcontractor), the estimated cost would be $101,000 (including $10,000 for materials and supplies). If the job were done in-house on an overtime basis, the estimated cost would be $127,000.

You have one other problem: the first shipment of 10,000 sets of keys must be available in thirty days, with 10,000 sets to arrive in eleven successive monthly increments. The president of Campbell may have been joking—or maybe he was serious—when he said, "I want those keys to start arriving in thirty days or I will want a new purchasing manager."

Role for Nils Ingborg

Your firm currently is operating at 90 percent of capacity. Your hourly costs are as follows:

direct labor	$13.00
overhead (130%)	16.90
	$29.90
profit (10.4%)	3.10
total	$33.00
overtime direct labor	$19.50
overhead (130% of regular hourly rate)	16.90
	$36.40
profit (10.4%)	3.78
total	$40.18 (round to $40.00)

Although time did not permit the development of a detailed cost estimate, you believe that development of the molds and production of the 120,000 sets of required keys will require between 2,200 and 3,200 hours. Material and supply costs will be about $10,000.

Addendum

Typical Results

Team	Meet Delivery	Objectives			Outcome
		Minimum	**Target**	**Maximum**	
1	0	$100 K	110	120	$112 K
2	+	2300 hours	2600 hours	2900 hours	2800 hours @ $33 + $10,000
3	+	$82,600	95,800	109,000	FPR: month 1 at $10,500
4	+	$91 K	101	111	FPI (target: 2600 hours at $33 plus $10,000; 80/20 share of savings or cost growth)
5	0	$94 K	101 K	107 K	Make 3,000 buy 7,000 per month at $1.00 per set

CAPITAL EQUIPMENT PURCHASING

Purpose

This case is designed to give students an opportunity to think through the details of a specific capital equipment purchase.

Question 1:

Outline in step-by-step fashion the actions you suggest James Sampson take in handling this matter. Discuss the significance of each.

Comment:

General Procedure

The general steps Sampson should take in handling the purchase from this point forward are identified and discussed briefly below.

1. Make a preliminary evaluation of the proposals as they now exist. Sampson should do this himself, based on the information now available, with any required assistance from engineering and operating personnel.
2. Conduct an economic analysis of each supplier's proposed equipment, probably utilizing the life cycle costing approach.
3. At this point, Sampson now has a general idea about the strengths and weaknesses of each supplier's proposal. Before going further, it would be a good idea to talk with several randomly selected customers (buyers of similar equipment) of each of the suppliers to get a reading on their perceptions of the suppliers' respective performances.
4. If not already done, Sampson should establish and organize a selection team. He must ensure that it includes adequate technical expertise with respect to product design and operation and also manufacturing and quality control activities.
5. As chairman of the team, Sampson should arrange for individual discussions with each of the potential suppliers. The purpose of these discussions is for the team to determine with reasonable certainty the extent to which each supplier understands the technical and business requirements of the undertaking—and has the capability to handle them satisfactorily. Emphasis should be placed on the technical evaluation of the proposed equipment's operating characteristics and engineering features.
6. At this point, the team should eliminate the suppliers it thinks cannot handle the job. For those that remain, Sampson should arrange a team visit to each supplier's manufacturing facility to assess firsthand the firm's production, quality control, and production control capabilities.
7. The final step in the process is to draft a comprehensive Statement Of Work and contract document that contains appropriate operating and protective provisions.

Preliminary Analysis of Proposals

The advantages and disadvantages of each proposal are summarized briefly below.

1. Rayard Air Products

    Advantages: Rayard's proposal is the most technically complete and appears to be the lowest-risk system. The short pump-down time is an attractive feature of Rayard's vacuum chamber and should reduce operating costs.

    Disadvantages: Rayard has quoted the highest initial price of the four bidders. Rayard is 4.8 percent above the MRT bid, 9.3 percent above the Wiston bid, and 96.1 percent above the Houston Chambers bid.

2. MRT Engineering, Inc.

    Advantages: MRT's technical proposal is satisfactory and shows that the firm has a reasonable grasp of the technical issues surrounding the vacuum chamber. However, it appears that the project risk of selecting MRT would be moderate or somewhat less.

    Disadvantages: MRT's past performance and its unilateral attitude toward late deliveries suggests that MRT may not be able to meet the fourteen-month delivery schedule, and that it may not be very cooperative in working with Celebrity in this regard.

3. Houston Chambers

    Advantages: Houston's proposal is the lowest-cost alternative for the vacuum chamber itself. Houston also has offered the best delivery schedule for the unit, twelve months.

    Disadvantages: The incomplete technical proposal, however, indicates that Houston probably does not fully understand the procurement requirements. Due to its extremely low selling price, shorter delivery quotation, and incomplete technical proposal, one might well conclude that Houston is out of the competitive range. However, these points must be explored in depth during the team's conversations with Houston personnel.

4. The Wiston Group

    Advantages: Wiston's proposed price is the lowest within the "competitive range." Like the other four potential suppliers, Wiston has reportedly already produced a vacuum chamber similar to that of the subject procurement.

    Disadvantages: Wiston's cost and technical proposals were submitted late and the technical data was less detailed than Rayard's. Missing the response date suggests that Wiston already may be operating at or near capacity, or that the firm otherwise may be unable to focus attention on the Celebrity vacuum chamber project.

Statement of Work and the Contract

On-time delivery and installation of the vacuum chamber is critical to the efficient construction of the test facility. Therefore, Celebrity must develop a strict Statement of Work for inclusion in the contract to govern the following activities:

1. Performance and insurance bonds.
2. Schedule monitoring and reporting.
3. Supplier points of contact.
4. Extent of technical support provided by the supplier.
5. Coordination of the interface between the vacuum chamber and the test cell at the new facility.

Tentative Recommendation

The work to be done during the discussions with potential suppliers, and visits to their respective facilities, may well turn up a great deal of information that will add to and condition Sampson's preliminary analysis of the proposals. Likewise, his life cycle cost analysis should provide additional useful information that will assist the team in making its recommendation. Hence, without this information it is impossible to make a firm recommendation with respect to the most attractive supplier. Based on the information known at the present time, however, the strongest case can probably be made for recommending that Celebrity purchase the Rayard vacuum chamber.

Rayard's product represents the lowest technical/business risk to complete the new production test facility. In considering the total cost of ownership, two points should be kept in mind. First, while Rayard's vacuum chamber is the highest-cost product initially, Celebrity's primary end objective is timely availability of the test facility. Given the high cost of construction delays, it is reasonable to buy the vacuum chamber with which Celebrity has the greatest technical confidence. Second, the lower operating costs of the Rayard chamber may very well justify the higher initial cost. Sampson's life cycle cost analysis will determine the importance of this factor.

THE CASE OF THE COSTLY ACCOMMODATION

Purpose

This case involves a difficult management decision, compliance with the Americans with Disabilities Act, and several potential ethical considerations—in the context of a public purchasing operation. It is an excellent case that can be used to evoke analysis and discussion of ethical priorities that are intertwined with practical operating and management considerations.

Analysis

A select group of experienced public purchasing professionals were asked to study the case. Their analyses are summarized below.

Hire the Best Candidate!

Unless your affirmative action officer is asleep at the switch, he or she is going to want to be very involved in a possible decision to disqualify the best candidate because the accommodations to meet her special needs are too costly.

The ADA specifically prohibits discrimination against qualified disabled individuals in hiring decisions and mandates that "reasonable accommodation" be made to the disabled's special needs. Such a clear violation of those mandates would likely subject the institution to fines far exceeding the cost of the initial accommodations.

Moreover, the inevitable adverse publicity that would accompany a court challenge of your university's unlawful discrimination would damage the institution's image of a "politically correct public citizen." The ripple effect could pour over into your admissions and fund raising activities and could damage your ability to obtain state and federal funding.

While the cost of your accommodations seems unusually high to me, I think you have an obligation to go over your boss' head on this one—straight to your affirmative action officer. If you can demonstrate a solid case for this individual based on her skills, you are bound to find administrative support for hiring this person. It "looks good" to have diversity on the staff and it's likely that a discretionary fund can be found to cover the cost.

So, hire the best candidate! If she's as good as you think, she'll ultimately save the university many times her initial accommodation cost—and then some!

Purchasing Manager
Mid-Sized Private College

Budget Cuts, No Raises, and a Hiring Freeze—What's New?

We should explore all possible ways to hire the disabled woman. Some of the needed changes are probably necessary to comply with the basic terms of the Americans with Disabilities Act (ADA) anyway, and will make the department accessible to other disabled employees later. Changes in building layout or parking design should be the responsibility of the institution instead of any individual department.

We suggest the matter be brought to the attention of upper administration at the university. Failing to hire this woman—if she is, indeed, the best candidate—is not only not in the best interests of the department, but it could lead to an expensive lawsuit. In that event, the university would be forced to find the money somewhere, not to mention the time the various university personnel would have to spend resolving the case. Why not do the right thing now and prevent all that?

If it really came down to a choice between long-awaited raises for the staff and hiring the woman, we would suggest giving the raises first. The staff has had additional responsibilities while the position was vacant and they should not be disadvantaged in order to hire a replacement. However, we would also stress the fact that other avenues of funding should be analyzed. Accommodating the disabled should be a priority for the university as well as the entire community.

Two Buyers
Large Public University

A Look At Possible Alternatives

The best solution would be to consider contacting an outside agency, if one is available, to assist with funding ADA compliance. Thus, the needs of the department would be met by hiring the best candidate, and the raise money would still be available for that purpose.

If we can assume that the job hasn't been offered to the disabled candidate yet, another alternative would be to delay the recruitment until the raises were announced, thereby being loyal to the present employees, and try again at a later date. But in choosing this alternative, the risk is that the candidate would no longer be available then.

Another alternative, based on advice we received from the personnel director at a local college, would be to make an argument for one of the other candidates, basing the argument on the fact that the $15,000 needed for accommodations would create an undue hardship on the college by not allowing the other employees to get their raises. Of course, the college, if charged with discrimination, would have to prove that there really was a hardship.

Local Purchasing
Management Association

THE CASE OF THE ROTATING BIDS

Purpose

This case provides an interesting vehicle to use in discussing the various possibilities for collusion to develop among suppliers in unique purchasing situations.

Analysis

A "seasoned veteran" who serves as director of purchasing for a major U.S. university was asked to study this case. His analysis is presented below.

The Imperative For Evidence

There is not sufficient information to corroborate Sprat's claim. If he has any real evidence that the "big three" are price fixing and "taking turns" with winning the bid, he should present it. The U.S. Department of Justice, Antitrust Division, should be notified and asked to investigate. Until such time, the award would have to stand.

Rockwell's duty to his employer is to get the "best buy" while avoiding any participation in shady or illegal transactions. His duty to the "big three" is to allow them the opportunity to bid competitively unless there is evidence that would warrant taking them off the bidders list. His duty to Sprat's firm is to include it in future competitions, and to rebid the present job only if sufficient evidence exists to support the price-fixing allegation.

A good way to check the authenticity of "suspected" bids is to expand the bidders list to provide a broader comparison—or to perform a cost analysis of the "suspected" bids.

—University Purchasing Officer
The Pennsylvania State University

THE CASE OF THE SECRET DISCOUNT

Purpose

This is a good case to use to discuss the various ramifications of commercial bribery that can be manifested in different forms.

Analysis

A select group of purchasing professionals was asked to study this case. their analyses are summarized below.

Sleazeball Sales Techniques

The ethical problem is on the part of the supplier. Buylow and Smith have done nothing wrong up to this point. Smith should evaluate the bids received. If Alternate Technologies is substantially higher than bids for the specified equipment, I would think Dr. Smith would have no problem with the evaluation and award. If a second software package is needed, it should be bid separately. If Alternate Technologies wanted to offer it at no charge then that would be their opinion.

Knowing what Buylow now knows about Alternate Technologies' sleazeball sales techniques, I would certainly think he would want to take some action with their management. A letter to the president would be in order, saying that this was an insult to the integrity of the university, a highly unethical practice, not the way we do business, and that the university will consider removing Alternate Technologies from the bid list unless the president can assure Buylow that this will not happen again. Also Buylow must request removal of the offending salesman from the university's account. (If the president and the salesman are the same person, Buylow has another problem!)

Director of Purchasing
State-related Medical Center

Nothing Is Ever Free

Mr. Buylow's problem really involves two issues; the comparative quality and value of the machines, and the intent with which the additional merchandise was offered. We as buyers must remember that we deal with individuals as well as companies, and that the integrity of the individuals we choose to do business with will ultimately be a reflection of our own integrity and the integrity of the institutions we serve.

Buylow must first determine if As Specified and Alternate Technologies are apples-to-apples machines. If both machines meet the specs, then the lower bid must be honored.

The issue of the bribe, to me, holds far greater implications than the issue of cost. Many times, a manufacturer will offer additional products as an incentive to buy. In this case the offer must be disregarded. Nothing is ever free. A good buyer cannot allow these incentives to become a relevant factor in the decision making process. The fact that the sales rep was not willing to disclose this offer to purchasing definitely suggests that he was approaching the transaction underhandedly. This alone would make me cautious in my dealings with the company. In the unlikely event that the alternate was, indeed, a better value, I would proceed with the purchase but only after exhaustive research into the whole picture.

Purchasing Manager
Private Institution

Kudos to Dr. Smith

Any time there is acceptance of other than the lowest bid meeting specifications there could be ethical problems. In this case, since it was stated in the letter that the offer for additional software would not be on the bid sent to purchasing, it is reasonable to assume that Alternate Technologies was trying to subvert the bid process (and kudos to Dr. Smith for exposing he "fraud").

The "bid" delivered to purchasing via Smith should not be considered. Since the lowest bid meeting specifications was from As Specified, they should receive the award. Had Smith withheld knowledge of the offer and recommended acceptance of the alternate bid, then he would be guilty of unethical practices. it would be hard to justify using As Specified as an acceptable model and then reject their low bid.

I would encourage Mr. Buylow to contact Alternate Technologies immediately and expose the arrangement made by their representative. Buylow should clearly state that Swampland University demands ethical consideration from salespersons, and should corrections not be made, Alternate Technologies would be removed from the bidders list and not be permitted to do business with the university.

Director of Purchasing
Community College

Legal Action May be Required

This case presents a very serious ethical problem Fortunately, the problem is not the purchasing department's or the researcher's. The visit by Alternate Technologies to the researcher while the bid was on the street was totally inappropriate and obviously an effort to influence the award. It was further compounded by the "secret" offer. Both, taken separately or together, amount to an effort to improperly influence the award. Dr. Smith acted appropriately by immediately reporting the bid he received. It would have been helpful if he had reported the *visit* when it occurred. Then, Buylow would have been able to warn Alternate Technologies that such actions and contacts were improper.

The bids must be evaluated and awarded solely on the basis of what was contained in the solicitation and the formal responses. I would further recommend that Buylow meet with the sales rep and his manager to discuss their actions. this meeting should be confirmed in writing stating the university's policies and procedures on bidding, gratuities, and ethics. Finally, Buylow would forward a copy of the "secret offer" to the legal department for further action that may be required in some jurisdictions where there is thought to be attempted bribery.

Director of Procurement
Public University

No Problem Unless We Make One

Look for ethical problems and you will find them. If you let your imagination manage good business practices, you will find problems with ethics. Our bid specifications are—and must be—the guiding force by which we work. Since the bid specifications don't include free software, we can't consider such an offer.

The letter Alternate Technologies sent to Dr. Smith should be returned to the bidder with the explanation that this is not part of the original specifications. Then Mr. Buylow and Dr. Smith must carefully evaluate the bids and establish the lowest and most responsible bidder. A "most responsible" bidder can win over a "lowest" bidder and still remain within the bounds of the bid specifications.

In my state, during the bidding process, the law says that neither purchasing nor user department representatives can make or accept visits, letters, or calls regarding a pending bid from a potential supplier without public notice of that communication to all actual and potential bidders. The only alternative would be to reject all bids and start over. Failure to follow these rules would result in a written reprimand to all involved.

Director of Purchasing
Community College

THE CASE OF THE SLEEPING DOGS

Purpose

This case is a good vehicle to use in discussing the impact of environmental considerations on purchasing decisions. Specifically, what is a buyer's responsibility when there is a conflict between the employer's policy and sound environmental practice? What role should a buyer play in initiating change?

Analysis

A select group of practicing managers and purchasing professionals were asked to study this case. Their analyses are summarized below.

Managers Need To Make Hard Choices

Personal accountability has been grist for the philosopher's mill for a very long time. How does the honest person reconcile differences between personal beliefs and official policy?

Environmental issues seem to require tough choices based on inconclusive information. But solving problems by making hard choices is what managers do. For example, should waste paper be burned, recycled, or composted? If the incinerator were to be built across from your home, would it affect your choice? How about if the new de-inking plant were sited along the banks of your favorite trout stream? If half of your constituents lived near either the proposed incinerator or de-inking plant and you were up for reelection, how would you decide then?

On the rare occasions that there are irreconcilable differences between strongly held personal beliefs and company policy, separation might be the most ethical approach.

But Wrightman's problems don't seem to be the sort that would qualify for quitting. If he sets reasonable goals for himself he can probably lower his frustration to an acceptable level and then work to bring about changes within the organization. It could be argued that it would be immoral to quit and turn the job over to a less committed person. In the end, it will be those who stay engaged who have the most effect on the direction any organization takes.

Vice President,
Non-For-Profit Organization

Wrightman Is a Lazy Bum!

This isn't about environmental issues, it's about a purchasing director who is trying to avoid facing the music. The ethical problem isn't about whether or not Wrightman agrees with users who have environmental opinions or even whether or not his personal opinions conflict with his customers' views and/or the institution's policies. It's about a guy who buries problems (or tries to make them sleeping dogs) just because he's overworked and underpaid. At best, he's terribly frustrated by his present situation. At worst, he's a lazy bum.

It's unethical for a buyer to avoid taking care of his customer's legitimate needs just because he's short of help and resources. The solution is for Wrightman to work up action plans to accomplish each project and begin to work the plans as he can. He should also explain his workload and budgetary problems to his customers and try to negotiate acceptable time frames with them. If he gets completely bogged down he *must* approach the administration for help. Simply hoping that these jobs will go away is a breach of his duty to his employer, and avoiding work is an ethical problem of the first order.

Purchasing Director,
Large Public University

The Sleeping Dog Will Not Sleep For Long

A major question should be raised at the very beginning regarding the definition of "environmentally safe." Some products that have been declared environmentally safe by one group at one time have, after testing and analysis, been declared a bigger threat to the environment than the product they replaced. Current contracts should not be canceled just because environmentally safe or recycled products are not part of them. If the item in question has been declared illegal, then the contract can be canceled or modified. If state law mandates the use of recycled products, the contracts may need to be modified. Otherwise, information should be gathered for the next bidding opportunity, allowing a fair comparison between virgin and recycled products.

A buyer's responsibility is to his or her employer. If the buyer presents both sides of the environmental issue to management or to users, the buyer's ethical concerns and responsibility to society have been discharged, whatever the outcome is. If a buyer knowingly does not present both sides of the issue, an ethical problem would exist. Buyers of all products would be aware of how important being environmentally responsible can be to their institution. At a minimum, the director in this example should begin to gather information on environmentally safe options to existing programs. The "sleeping dog" will not sleep for long.

Ethics Panel,
Large Public University

Divided Loyalty Not Inevitable

There does not need to be divided loyalty between the university and society. In response to other social concerns, such as civil rights or worker safety, universities typically spare no expense in creating an equitable and safe workspace. In recent years, the environment has joined these pressing questions that require both social and institutional reform.

The trick is in creating the change. It does not have to be done all at once, so with some creativity, Mr. Wrightman should be able to develop a successful five- or ten-year plan. Looking at the bottom line, Wrightman could encourage departments to reduce paper use by 5 percent or 10 percent (by making double-sided copies and avoiding waste, for example). After a year of reduced consumption, the savings could offset the cost of purchasing recycled paper. The same idea could work with plasticware in the dining service.

And despite being short of staff, he could join hundreds of administrators around the country and call upon the student environmental group for help in developing specific proposals. Not only would he get free labor, or pay reduced work-study wages, but he would provide valuable organizing experiences for the students. Working with a coalition of administrators, faculty, and students, Wrightman could lead the university community toward environmental responsibility.

Manager,
National Wildlife Federation

Buyers Should Offer Recommendations

The panel concluded that an individual buyer cannot be responsible to change environmental buying practices for their institution. Policies and support are needed to sway an organization. If policies do not exist, the buyer can begin actions to develop such policies. Although one buyer cannot establish policy, they are in a perfect position to offer recommendations based on their commodity knowledge and supplier contacts.

As a personal ethics issue, buyers should investigate policies within their organization to determine if they have the ability to enforce environmentally sound buying actions within their own buying responsibilities.

For example, in the short term, they might be able to involve management to direct influence on using departments, use cooperating departments as volunteers to test new products and ideas, and approach major users to interest them in environmentally sound purchasing.

Over the long term, they might persuade management to solicit support from the top administration, provide options, and get the institution to buy into results obtained from test purchases.

Ethics Panel,
Large Public University

CHAPTER 22
PRODUCTION PLANNING

1. One of the major responsibilities of the production planning group is the determination of timing and volume requirements for materials used in the manufacturing operation.

    T F

2. An effective production planning and control operation must accomplish five general activities: (1) verifying sales forecasts, (2) aggregate scheduling, (3) detailed production scheduling, (4) release and dispatching of orders, and (5) progress surveillance and correction.

    T F

3. In the vast majority of manufacturing firms today production planning and control is largely a clerically oriented function that typically has little impact on the ultimate success of the firm.

    T F

4. In progressive manufacturing firms today, the aggregate scheduling activity often is done in such a sophisticated manner that very little follow-up detail production scheduling work has to be done prior to releasing orders for production.

    T F

5. The most commonly used production forecasting approach is time series analysis.

    T F

6. Forecasting activities typically are conducted or coordinated by a specialized staff group and generally are handled as a responsibility separate from the computerized production planning system activities.

    T F

7. Material requirements planning (MRP) is a technique used to determine the quantity and timing requirements of independent demand materials used in the manufacturing operation.

    T F

8. Production planning personnel are responsible for structuring and formatting the product bills of material eventually contained in computer memory and used in the production scheduling process.

    T F

9. Orders within an MRP system fall into two categories: (1) open orders which have been released but have not yet arrived, and (2) planned orders which are developed in anticipation of future releases.

    T F

10. An MRP system produces both purchase orders and shop orders.

    T F

11. The development of a material planning record is based on three fundamental concepts which form the essence of the MRP-based approach to materials planning and control. They are: (1) dependent demand, (2) inventory/open-order netting, (3) time phasing.

T F

12. The inventory/open-order-netting concept is used to develop the "on-hand" balance row of a material's MRP planning record.

T F

13. The function of the capacity requirements planning (CRP) segment of the production planning process is to convert the shop orders produced by the MRP system into scheduled work loads for the various factory work centers.

T F

14. The only variables that the CRP activities can manipulate to achieve a reasonable production system balance are (1) alternate routings, (2) personnel reallocation, and (3) use of overtime.

T F

15. When a shop order is released, typically it is accompanied by a packet of materials and instructions required to complete the job. Included are such things as engineering drawings, bills of materials, route sheets, move tickets, material requisitions, and labor charge forms.

T F

16. The dispatch list, containing a series of shop order releases, is prepared by the planner. If daily dispatch lists are used, the operating foreman generally has little discretion in scheduling the jobs in the work center.

T F

17. Overall responsibility for shop floor control of operations usually is vested with the production planning and control manager or the materials manager.

T F

18. It is the responsibility of the foremen to do the micro work-center scheduling and to run each production operation so that planned completion dates are met. It is the responsibility of production planning and control to keep work flowing through the shop at a steady rate, focusing on order priority control and capacity control.

T F

19. The aggregate planning and the master scheduling activities are top-management and staff responsibilities. Most activities associated with material-requirements-planning and capacity-requirements-planning activities are primarily the responsibility of production planning and control personnel.

T F

20. A closed-loop MRP system typically includes: (1) aggregate planning, (2) master production scheduling, (3) material requirements planning, (4) capacity requirements planning, and (5) production operations controls.

T F

21. An MRP II system is essentially a closed-loop MRP system to which the capabilities of financial planning and control and simulation analysis have been added.

T   F

22. Expanded use of the buyer-planner or supplier-scheduler concept and expanded use of contract buying are two typical results of MRP system use.

T   F

23. Effective use of an MRP system usually requires greater supplier flexibility and reliability than would otherwise be the case.

T   F

24. For all practical purposes, a buyer-planner's job is essentially the same as a senior buyer's job.

T   F

25. When using the supplier-scheduler concept, the production planner has the responsibility for dealing directly with suppliers and releasing and following up materials orders.

T   F

26. The JIT concept holds that inventory is evil because it hides quality problems and it hides production inefficiencies and productivity problems.

T   F

27. In a JIT operation, purchasing is geared as closely as practical to key suppliers' production operations.

T   F

28. In a JIT operation, the characteristic of small-lot flow can be traced through the entire system from a supplier's plant through the buyer's plant, out into the finished-goods distribution system.

T   F

29. The following elements tend to characterize most successful JIT operations:
    1. Product demand must be reasonably predictable and requirements must be generated accurately.
    2. Production operation setup requirements must be able to be reduced to relatively short times.
    3. Suppliers must be able to be flexible to meet the buying firm's stringent short-fused material requirements—and they must be reliable to the nth degree.

T   F

30. It is not practical to procure all materials on a JIT basis. Most successful JIT purchasing departments buy from 5 to 10 percent of their individual materials in a JIT mode.

T   F

CHAPTER 23
INVENTORY MANAGEMENT

1. Most manufacturing operations carry four types of inventories: (1) raw materials inventories, (2) MRO inventories, (3) production inventories, and (4) finished goods inventories.

                                                                                                    T   F

2. If one looks at all types of business in the United States, four types of inventory control systems are found in use:
   1. The MRP-type system
   2. The order-point system
   3. The JIT-type system
   4. The fixed order interval system

                                                                                                    T   F

3. Studies made by consultants and manufacturing firms reveal that a typical manufacturer incurs inventory carrying costs of _____% of average inventory value.
   a. 5–10
   b. 12–18
   c. 20–40
   d. 25–50

                                                                                                  a b c d

4. Inventory control is a vital element in the management of materials. One reason is that a firm's inventory commonly constitutes from 15–30 precent of a firm's invested capital.

                                                                                                    T   F

5. Maintaining an inventory catalog is essential to sound inventory management. An inventory catalog serves as a medium of communication and:
   a. eliminates the possibility of undetected duplicate orders.
   b. reduces duplicate records for identical parts.
   c. reduces operating flexibility.
   d. none of the above.

                                                                                                  a b c d

6. In typical firms, a small percentage of the total number of items carried in the inventory constitutes the bulk of inventory investment.

                                                                                                    T   F

7. Classifying inventory items on the basis of annual dollar usage of each item is commonly known as:
   a. flow control.
   b. dependent and independent demand analysis.
   c. economic order quantity (EOQ).
   d. ABC analysis.

                                                                                                  a b c d

8. The cyclical ordering system is well suited for materials whose purchase must be planned months in advance because of established and infrequent production schedules of suppliers, or for those materials which exhibit irregular or seasonal usage.

                                                                                        T F

9. The two-bin system, a variation of the basic order point system, is widely used in handling high-value hardware and supplies whose usage is recorded on a perpetual record.

                                                                                        T F

10. In a Material Requirements Planning (MRP) system:
    a. materials needed for a given period of production are determined precisely.
    b. requirements for a part used in several products can be summed to obtain the total requirements for a specific part during a specified period of production.
    c. there is an attempt to minimize material inventories and gear purchasing activities to the timing and production demands of the final product assembly schedule.
    d. all of the above.

                                                                                      a b c d

11. MRP can be used most advantageously when a material's usage is discontinuous or unstable, or when demand for material is directly dependent on the production of other specific inventory items or other products.

                                                                                        T F

12. All of the following are *major* elements that make up inventory carrying costs *except*:
    a. interest charges on investment.
    b. insurance cost and property taxes.
    c. marketing costs.
    d. storage costs.

                                                                                      a b c d

13. Acquisition costs are related to inventory size and vary directly with the size of the order quantity.

                                                                                        T F

14. The lowest annual total cost associated with inventory occurs at the order quantity where carrying costs and acquisition costs are approximately equal.

                                                                                        T F

15. Safety stocks are carried primarily as a protection against price increases.

                                                                                        T F

16. Sound inventory control policies seek to:
    a. minimize capital investment in inventory.
    b. maintain continuous production operations.
    c. purchase the optimal quantity of needed materials.
    d. all of the above.

                                                                                      a b c d

17. The average total inventory usually is designated as (order quantity/2) − (safety stock).

                                                                                        T F

18. A major practical problem in utilizing the economic order quantity concept is obtaining appropriate cost data for computing the incremental acquisition cost and the annual incremental inventory carrying cost (I & A).

                                                                                                        T   F

19. A recommended solution to the problem encountered in applying the economic order quantity concept in practice is to:
    a. use "typical" industry figures to approximate costs.
    b. group inventory items in classes and determine a set of realistic acquisition and inventory cost factors for each class of items in the inventory.
    c. use C (delivered unit cost of material) and U (expected annual usage of the material) in the computations rather than using I and A.
    d. none of the above.

                                                                                  ∘   a b c d

20. The use of the EOQ approach in managing inventories usually results in all of the following *except*:
    a. the minimization of indirect costs associated with inventory.
    b. the placing of frequent orders for small quantities of high-cost materials.
    c. fewer orders for large quantities of low-cost items.
    d. less frequent orders of high-usage materials and more frequent orders of low-usage materials.

                                                                                                        a b c d

21. A major limitation in applying the EOQ concept occurs when:
    a. unit prices vary only slightly.
    b. usage cannot be predicted reliably.
    c. lead times are predictable.
    d. material is not flow-controlled throughout the production operation.

                                                                                                        a b c d

22. ABC analysis and the 80–20 concept are two names for the same phenomenon utilized in inventory management.

                                                                                                        T   F

23. The order-point inventory management system is most effective when utilized with inventory materials that exhibit dependent demand characteristics.

                                                                                                        T   F

24. If one were to observe a JIT operation strictly from an inventory point of view, it would look very much like a flow-control operation, with material flowing into and through the plant operation in continuous streams.

                                                                                                        T   F

25. Some managers who have tried to implement the EOQ concept of inventory management have experienced dismal results. EOQ concepts are not suitable for items when:
    a. unit prices vary widely.
    b. usage cannot be reliably predicted.
    c. lead times are unpredictable.
    d. all of the above.

                                                                                                        a b c d

26. An MRP system is designed to function effectively in intermittent manufacturing operations with production items that have independent demand usage.

T F

27. An objective of the MRP system is to maintain virtually no inventory, yet to meet the timing requirements of the production schedule.

T F

28. MRP is best suited for the control of purchased materials that exhibit all of the following characteristics, *except*:
    a. raw materials or "standard" items for which lead-time requirements are relatively short and seldom vary widely.
    b. materials that are purchased repetitively and do not require new purchasing analysis, and those for which value analysis and supplier studies have been completed previously.
    c. materials that are delivered infrequently in large quantities.
    d. materials that can be purchased on long-term contracts.

a b c d

29. Many firms find the primary advantage of MRP to be in the planning and control areas, regardless of its impact on inventory levels.

T F

30. The importance of sound inventory control is not always apparent to top management because:
    a. the routine nature of the daily operation often camouflages its importance.
    b. the effects of poor inventory management are not directly visible on operating statements.
    c. decisions which should be made by an analytically minded manager often are made by clerical personnel; therefore the significance of such decisions is not noted by management.
    d. all of the above.

a b c d

CHAPTER 24
WAREHOUSE AND STORES MANAGEMENT

1. In most manufacturing firms, the stores and warehouse operation is placed under the production manager or the factory superintendent for managerial and control purposes.

   T F

2. Most accounting managers would say that receiving and stores disbursement activities should not be supervised by the department that buys and authorizes payment for the same materials. Collusion and embezzlement would be too easy.

   T F

3. Only at the receiving desk do the purchasing control documents meet the physical materials themselves.

   T F

4. The most commonly used material identification system in international business is:
   a. The Export Commodity Control Number System
   b. The ISO 9000 International Material Standards System
   c. The Harmonized Commodity Description and Coding System
   d. none of the above

   a b c d

5. In disbursing materials for use by the operating units, most warehouses use the last-in first-out system.

   T F

6. In its briefest form, a bar code label is simply a unique license plate. This license plate accesses a data file containing information about the labeled object.

   T F

7. The Universal Product Code is the most commonly used bar coding symbology in industrial stores and inventory operations.

   T F

8. The receiving and stores functions of a firm are important in materials management because:
   a. of their service to production.
   b. they are responsible for a substantial portion of a firm's current assets.
   c. of their contribution to potential increased profitability.
   d. all of the above.

   a b c d

9. The cost of rectifying a problem associated with an incorrect shipment is minimized when the mistake is discovered during the receiving inspection operation.

   T F

10. The stores operation exerts an influence on:
    a. direct labor costs.
    b. finished product costs.
    c. inventory carrying costs.
    d. all of the above.

                                                                           a b c d

11. When a shipment of materials appears to be damaged, the receiving clerk should always refuse to accept the shipment.

                                                                           T F

12. A basic objective of an efficient stores operation is to develop an order filling and delivery system which satisfies production requirements.

                                                                           T F

13. The complete receiving procedure may be thought of in terms of all the following operations *except*:
    a. checking the number of containers against the bill of lading.
    b. unpacking and inspecting the material.
    c. notifying the requesting department that the material has arrived.
    d. selecting the carrier for the next shipment.

                                                                           a b c d

14. Many firms omit the quantities ordered from the receiver's copy of the purchase order to prevent collusion between the receiver and the carrier's delivery man.

                                                                           T F

15. A primary responsibility of an industrial stores manager is:
    a. to develop a system for effective identification of materials.
    b. to unload and check the incoming shipment.
    c. to prevent pilferage.
    d. to inspect incoming materials.

                                                                           a b c d

16. All of the following are *basic* approaches used in developing an identification system *except*:
    a. symbolic approach.
    b. arbitrary approach.
    c. nonsequential digit approach.
    d. engineering drawing numbers approach.

                                                                           a b c d

17. The identification system most used in American industry is the one in which inventory items are assigned arbitrary numbers in sequence as they are received by the stores department.

                                                                           T F

18. Mnemonic systems of identification are effective where there is a large number of items involved, because visual identification is more descriptive.

                                                                           T F

19. Two basic types of systems to *control* stores materials are:
    a. computerized and noncomputerized stores systems.
    b. open and closed stores systems.
    c. physical and symbolic stores systems.
    d. numerical or mnemonic stores systems.

    a b c d

20. Because discrepancies occur between inventory records and actual stock on hand, every inventory item should be physically counted and checked at least once a year.

    T F

21. Which of the following is *not* a recognized method to use in conducting a physical inventory?
    a. fixed annual inventory
    b. arbitrary inventory
    c. continuous inventory
    d. low-point inventory

    a b c d

22. An advantage of the fixed annual inventory method is that it can be planned and worked into scheduled activities without a production shutdown.

    T F

23. From a managerial perspective, the main advantage of a centralized storage facility is that:
    a. it reduces manufacturing costs.
    b. materials are stored as close as possible to their point of use.
    c. it facilitates control of the total stores operation.
    d. all of the above.

    a b c d

24. The random-access storage system is best suited and used most for small operations.

    T F

25. A straight-line flow of activity through a storeroom with minimum backtracking for personnel is desirable, but it is not a major objective of good storeroom layout.

    T F

CHAPTER 25
TRAFFIC

1. From both a strategic and a tactical point of view, transportation services should be purchased much as any material is purchased.

T F

2. The railroads have continually lost ground to the motor freight industry since World War II—today they haul only approximately one-third of the country's freight.

T F

3. The term F.O.B. literally means "free on board;" it has nothing to do with who owns the material.

T F

4. Which of the following modes of shipment is most likely to offer the lowest published freight rate?
   a. rail CL
   b. motor LTL
   c. motor TL
   d. water carrier

a b c d

5. "Incoterms" are rules dealing with the international transportation of materials and are published by the International Chamber of Commerce.

T F

6. Among other things, "incoterms" define the responsibilities that a buyer and a supplier must assume in the transportation of a good.

T F

7. As a result of the deregulation legislation that occurred between 1977 and 1984, carriers in all four modes possess substantially increased flexibility to modify freight rates and services without regulatory intervention.

T F

8. An interesting provision of the "Motor Carrier Act of 1980" permits a contract carrier also to hold a common carrier certificate, and visa versa.

T F

9. Transportation costs usually are not a significant consideration when planning purchases.

T F

10. As a general rule, the costs of transportation are equally important when buying virtually all production materials.

T F

11. Frequently, service and quality are as critical as cost in planning transportation activities.

T F

12. Shipping terms, including who has the right to specify the carrier and the route, are specified in:
    a. the invoice.
    b. the bid.
    c. the purchase order.
    d. none of the above.

    a b c d

13. The shipping terms and conditions agreed to in the purchase contract define precisely:
    a. who is responsible for paying freight charges.
    b. the point at which the buyer takes legal title to the goods.
    c. who is legally responsible for filing loss or damage claims, if necessary.
    d. all of the above.

    a b c d

14. When a purchase is made F.O.B. seller's plant, legal title to the material passes from seller to buyer when the carrier unloads the material on the buyer's receiving dock.

    T F

15. Approximately 90 percent of all shipments are purchased under C.I.F. contracts.

    T F

16. The terms of shipment most often used in international trade, where the contract price includes costs of materials, insurance, and delivery service are:
    a. F.O.B. buyer's plant.
    b. F.O.B. seller's plant.
    c. F.O.B. seller's plant, freight allowed to buyer's plant.
    d. C.I.F. contracts.

    a b c d

17. Since World War II, the intercity freight tonnage hauled by the railroads has increased only slightly.

    T F

18. Which transportation mode do firms most often use for small packages to nearby airports?
    a. air parcel service
    b. privately operated parcel delivery service
    c. freight forwarders
    d. none of the above

    a b c d

19. Air cargo rates are usually approximately ten times greater than motor freight rates.

    T F

20. A railroad's major advantage over its competitors usually is in the area of:
    a. intracity transportation.
    b. intercity transportation.
    c. delivery time.
    d. service and quality.

    a b c d

21. All of the following are types of carriers recognized by the federal government *except*:
    a. contract carriers.
    b. private carriers.
    c. full-service carriers.
    d. common carriers.

    a b c d

22. The bulk of industrial freight moves by private carriers.

    T F

23. Regulatory agencies in the transportation field prescribe a body of operating regulations and exercise stringent control over all freight rates.

    T F

24. The process of following a shipment after its departure in order to obtain a record of the various steps of its movement is called:
    a. expediting.
    b. follow-up.
    c. tracing.
    d. routing.

    a b c d

25. Regulatory agencies have much tighter control over carriers today then they did during the 1950s and 1960s.

    T F

CHAPTER 26
INVESTMENT RECOVERY: THE MANAGEMENT OF
SURPLUS MATERIALS AND ENVIRONMENTAL CONSIDERATIONS

1. A well-managed operation for recycling surplus, obsolete, and scrap material is important whether the incentive for recovery is additional profit, the conservation of natural resources, or the recycling of used materials. All three objectives can be achieved simultaneously.

    T F

2. The Investment Recovery Department in most cases is simply a refined name for the old Scrap and Salvage Department.

    T F

3. As a general rule today, purchased scrap in the United States includes approximately 80 percent of the steel produced in this country, 40 percent of the copper, and 30 percent of the aluminum.

    T F

4. The United States is dependent on foreign sources for twenty-two of the thirty-six strategic minerals it uses in its manufacturing industries. For which of the following minerals does the United States import more than 90 percent of its requirements?
    a. chromium
    b. manganese
    c. cobalt
    d. all of the above
    e. none of the above

    a b c d e

5. More often than not, the Purchasing and Supply Department is assigned the responsibility for managing the disposal of the firm's hazardous waste.

    T F

6. Hazardous materials are identified by OSHA as:
    a. a "hazardous substance"
    b. an "extremely hazardous substance"
    c. a "hazardous waste"
    d. none of the above
    e. all of the above

    a b c d e

7. Recycling significantly reduces gaseous and solid pollutants, and it conserves raw materials; but recycling reduces energy requirements only slightly.

    T F

8. Materials managers have a direct responsibility for:
   a. balancing the cost of environmental health and safety against the nation's need for critical materials.
   b. recovering idle investment capital surpluses and recycling surplus materials into economic channels.
   c. weighing the benefits of atomic energy against its possible dangers.
   d. none of the above.

   a b c d

9. Scrap metal is the largest single category of saleable surplus.

   T F

10. Competent materials managers can eliminate the generation of surpluses that result during the production process.

    T F

11. Surpluses resulting from inefficient use of production machinery are called:
    a. scrap.
    b. damaged stock.
    c. obsolete.
    d. waste.

    a b c d

12. The "efficiency curve" describes the relationship between:
    a. production time and indirect labor costs.
    b. scrap rates and time.
    c. time and money.
    d. production time and scrap rates.

    a b c d

13. Surplus materials result from:
    a. inaccurate sales forecasting and planning.
    b. inefficient use of production machinery.
    c. obsolescence.
    d. all of the above.

    a b c d

14. Most small firms do not have an adequate volume of surplus to justify having a salvage and reclamation plan.

    T F

15. The most profitable form of surplus disposal is to:
    a. return it to the supplier.
    b. donate it to a nonprofit institution.
    c. sell it to a broker or dealer.
    d. use it within the firm.

    a b c d

16. Surplus equipment is best disposed of by:
    a. contracting, on a long-term basis, with a local scrap dealer.
    b. selling to jobbers or second-hand dealers.
    c. soliciting competitive bids from dealers.
    d. selling it to employees.

                                                                    a b c d

17. Immediate availability can be as important as price when purchasing surplus materials, especially equipment.

                                                                           T F

18. Progressive supply management departments do not passively wait for materials to be declared surplus. Rather, such departments ferret out surpluses within their firms and take timely action to obtain the best return on the surplus items.

                                                                           T F

19. The efficient disposal and utilization of surplus and scrap metal can help reduce our nation's dependence on foreign sources of scarce metals.

                                                                           T F

20. Advantages of purchasing surplus materials include: reduced transportation, processing, and energy costs; and reduced environmental pollution.

                                                                           T F

CHAPTER 27
DEVELOPING AND MANAGING THE BUYING PLAN

1. In a broad sense, a buyer can utilize one of two basic buying approaches: (1) purchase according to current known requirements, or (2) purchase primarily according to supply market conditions.

        T F

2. Progressive purchasing departments are proactive—that is, they make things happen. They prepare a flexible game plan before specific material needs arise.

        T F

3. Historically, purchasing or materials management departments have played an important role in a firm's strategic planning process.

        T F

4. Although purchasing and materials management publications frequently carry articles about the virtues of long-term contract buying, in reality this strategy is not extensively used today.

        T F

5. The most important characteristic of strategic materials planning is its focus on the impact that changes in the external environment might have on a firm's material needs and procurement policy.

        T F

6. A perfect hedge is based on two assumptions:
    1. The selling price of a buyer's finished product will move exactly parallel to the cash market price of its major raw material.
    2. Futures prices will move exactly parallel to cash market prices.

        T F

7. In manufacturing, a firm's "annual operating plan" includes a production forecast which is based on a sales forecast.

        T F

8. A formal purchasing research program typically includes which major function?
    a. procurement planning
    b. strategic materials planning
    c. research on the purchasing system and special projects
    d. all of the above

        a b c d

9. Strategic materials planning could result in a decision to make the item in-house to eliminate dependence on suppliers and various external conditions which are difficult to control.

        T F

10. Strategic materials planning could result in:
   a. greater profitability.
   b. the avoidance of shortages.
   c. a decision to make rather than to buy certain items.
   d. all of the above.

   a b c d

11. Purchase timing has become increasingly important because there has been an increase in the number of products whose price and supply fluctuate substantially.

   T F

12. Unstable markets exhibit substantial fluctuation in terms of availability and price. Products falling into this category generally are:
   a. standard, off-the-shelf industrial products.
   b. raw materials, such as copper, tin, zinc, wool, cotton, etc.
   c. hardware, pumps, valves, chemicals, tools, etc.
   d. all of the above.

   a b c d

13. The actions of an individual buyer tend to have a significant effect on the equilibrium price in unstable markets.

   T F

14. Purchase timing is *most* important in a market where there is:
   a. price and supply instability.
   b. a reasonably stable supply, but prices fluctuate substantially.
   c. market stability.
   d. unstable supply, but prices are predictable.

   a b c d

15. In a majority of cases, purchasers can control, to some extent, the prices they pay.

   T F

16. Forward buying is:
   a. buying materials in a quantity exceeding foreseeable requirements.
   b. buying materials in excess of foreseeable requirements, in anticipation such a need will arise.
   c. buying materials in a quantity exceeding current scheduled requirements but within foreseeable future needs.
   d. none of the above.

   a b c d

17. Hand-to-mouth buying is an appropriate purchasing method in stable markets when prices are about to rise.

   T F

18. The best definition of "hand-to-mouth" is:
   a. buying sufficient materials to satisfy current production schedules.
   b. purchasing frequently when prices are rising.
   c. the practice of buying material to satisfy current operating requirements in quantities smaller than those normally considered economical.
   d. an approach to reduce direct expenses incurred in carrying inventory.

   a b c d

19. Buying to current requirements is the policy most firms follow in the purchase of their important production materials.

                                                                                                    T F

20. Fluctuations in the market can be used to advantage by purchasers by:
    a. using forward buying when market prices are on the upswing and using hand-to-mouth buying when prices are on a downward trend.
    b. using hand-to-mouth buying when prices are rising and speculative buying when prices are falling.
    c. hedging and time budgeting of purchases.
    d. none of the above.

                                                                                                    a b c d

21. Buying plans should be constructed for most materials, but it is particularly important that plans for the top 20 percent or so of the materials be developed using careful, detailed analyses.

                                                                                                    T F

22. In constructing a firm's annual buying plan for its more important materials, three types of detailed analyses typically are utilized: (1) demand analysis, (2) market analysis, and (3) supplier analysis.

                                                                                                    T F

23. In developing an annual buying plan for a given material, buying plan objectives and target modes of operation should be established in each of the following areas:
    1. the use and development of effective suppliers.
    2. pricing and buying competitively.
    3. optimal material availability and investment.
    4. buying quality effectively.

                                                                                                    T F

24. In many otherwise well-managed purchasing departments, small orders account for a disproportionately high percentage of the purchase orders placed. It is not uncommon to find half of the orders issued to be for purchases of less than $250.

                                                                                                    T F

25. Hedging is a sophisticated purchasing technique that can be used in reducing market risk in the acquisition of the vast majority of the materials a firm buys.

                                                                                                    T F

CHAPTER 28
VALUE ANALYSIS/ENGINEERING

1. Harry Erlicher generally is credited with being the father of value analysis.

   T F

2. Among firms with the most successful VA/VE programs, three basic organizational approaches are most common: (1) the specialized staff approach, (2) the cross-functional team approach, and (3) the staff training approach.

   T F

3. The quality circle concept is a natural vehicle to use in implementing the staff training approach to value analysis.

   T F

4. In firms that use cross-functional teams to conduct the value analysis studies, a cross-functional management committee is usually used to select the products to be analyzed and to administer the VA program.

   T F

5. Companies subscribing to the staff training approach to value analysis, believe that VA yields maximum benefits only when it is practiced by specialized experts in all departments.

   T F

6. Suppliers are often invited to participate in selected VA studies of the buying firm.

   T F

7. The fundamental objective of all value-analysis activities is to find the lowest-priced materials available.

   T F

8. Operationally, a value-analysis program deals with two basic concepts:
   a. price and design analysis of required materials.
   b. production and marketing of required materials.
   c. design and cost analysis of required materials.
   d. research and development of required materials.

   a b c d

9. Most firms use their own specialized VA/VE checklists to systematize and stimulate a value analyst's creativity.

   T F

10. In value-analysis activity, each part is analyzed primarily in terms of the specific function it serves and its cost.

   T F

11. Often, design analysis can lead to the substitution of standard production operations for nonstandard production operations.

   T F

12. Through experience, value analysts should be able to determine "benchmark costs." This term refers to:
   a. an estimated cost of performing the function of a particular part.
   b. a supplier's cost, before profit.
   c. the cost level at which it is more economical to buy, rather than make, the part.
   d. none of the above.

   a b c d

13. A typical value-analysis study does *not* include one of the following phases of activity:
   a. the information phase.
   b. the speculation phase.
   c. the analysis phase.
   d. the feedback phase.

   a b c d

14. An important feature of the functional-cost approach is that:
   a. the value of the function itself must be equal to the cost of performing that function.
   b. the cost of performing a function should not exceed the value of the function itself.
   c. the cost of performing a function should exceed the value of the function itself.
   d. the value of the function is irrelevant in functional-cost analysis.

   a b c d

15. Enthusiasm for value analysis increases in periods of material shortages and fluctuating prices.

   T F

16. A technique in design analysis that is used to stimulate creative thinking is called:
   a. free-wheeling.
   b. evaluation period.
   c. brainstorming.
   d. feasibility study.

   a b c d

17. Suppliers generally are compensated for their assistance in value analysis programs by sharing in cost savings they helped generate or by receiving additional business.

   T F

18. In a value-analysis program, cost analysis:
   a. is conducted for currently purchased items whose costs appear excessive.
   b. serves to locate high-cost parts that could later be subjected to design analysis.
   c. provides the buyer with a negotiating tool.
   d. all of the above.

   a b c d

19. Value analysis provides more cost-reduction potential for some firms than for others. The greatest advantages can be achieved under all of the following conditions *except*:
   a. when a firm produces, on a recurring basis, a large number of different products having complex components.
   b. when the availability or opportunity to use alternative production materials decreases.
   c. when a material is used in large quantities.
   d. when material specifications can be changed.

   a b c d

20. Buyers find cost analysis most effective when dealing with standard materials and in markets where there is strong price competition among suppliers.

T F

21. The organizational approach most widely used by large companies when implementing a value-analysis program is the:
    a. committee approach.
    b. middle-management approach.
    c. staff-training approach.
    d. specialized-staff approach.

a b c d

22. Design analysis attempts to answer the following:
    a. can the part be eliminated?
    b. can the part's design be simplified to permit the use of less costly production methods?
    c. can the part's design be changed to use less expensive material?
    d. none of the above
    e. all of the above

a b c d e

23. Value-engineering and value-analysis programs are quite different and, in fact, are based on opposite assumptions and concepts.

T F

24. When firms first started using value analysis, the original emphasis was almost entirely on applications to parts and subassemblies in manufacturing operations. Fundamentally, however, the value-analysis concept really defines a creative, systematic thought process that can be applied to problem solving in a wide variety of areas.

T F

25. As a general rule, the basic concepts of value analysis are not particularly applicable to the study and analysis of systems-type problems.

T F

CHAPTER 29
APPRAISAL, CONTROL, AND REPORTS

1. Preaction control is essentially a problem prevention approach, whereas post-action control is largely a problem detection and rectification approach.

    T F

2. In developing a system to monitor and control supply performance, a logical starting point is to review the objectives of the department, and then develop a system of measurements that show how well they are being met.

    T F

3. For any but the smallest of companies, it is imperative that a large number of effectiveness measures be utilized in each of the following areas: (1) delivery, (2) inventory levels, (3) material cost, (4) material quality, and (5) supplier reliability and relationships.

    T F

4. When possible, it is sound practice for a firm to tie its performance measurement and control program to its annual purchasing/supply plan.

    T F

5. The performance measurement most frequently used by the CAPS Roundtable Fortune 500 participants is:
    a. number of long-term contracts in place
    b. average supplier lead time, by material and supplier
    c. material quality defect rate classified by material and supplier
    d. all of the above
    e. none of the above

    a b c d e

6. Although the specific measurements differ, "purchasing efficiency" and "buying effectiveness" fundamentally reflect the same concept—how well purchasing utilizes its resources in doing its job.

    T F

7. Based on operating experience, growing numbers of firms are developing precise workload models for buyers with different types of responsibilities. The objective is to develop a series of models that establish a *standard work load* for each type of buyer in the organization.

    T F

8. Control systems enable managers to appraise performance of subordinates in order to detect and rectify unsatisfactory performance.

    T F

9. Preaction control techniques seldom provide completely satisfactory control and are always subject to human error.

    T F

10. Preaction control is accomplished by:
    a. personal supervision.
    b. control checks built into the operating procedure of a given task.
    c. policies that require certain preventative measures.
    d. all of the above.

                                                                        a b c d

11. The most difficult part of any control process is comparing actual performance to the established standards.

                                                                        T F

12. When a manager delegates a particular job to a subordinate, the manager must take personal responsibility for the effective performance of that job. Therefore, to protect himself and the organization in the event that performance is unsatisfactory, the manager must establish a system of:
    a. penalties.
    b. reports.
    c. incentives.
    d. control.

                                                                        a b c d

13. In controlling an organization, a manager should design the external control system in such a way as to engender a high level of self-control among his subordinates. This may be achieved by:
    a. establishing a specific and realistic level of desired performance.
    b. measuring performance in terms of the standard of performance.
    c. creating a favorable work environment and reward system.
    d. all of the above.

                                                                        a b c d

14. The postaction control process consists of all of the following activities *except*:
    a. establishing a workable standard of performance.
    b. developing procedures for feeding back actual performance.
    c. comparing actual performance to standard.
    d. adjusting the standard to the actual.

                                                                        a b c d

15. In some cases the cost of control may exceed the benefits of control.

                                                                        T F

16. Controlling purchasing performance is especially difficult because:
    a. buyers by nature resist controls.
    b. buyers can exert little influence on established prices.
    c. each buyer's responsibilities cover a wide range of variable activities that are difficult to measure in quantitative terms.
    d. no two procurements are exactly alike, and many deal with suppliers in different industries.

                                                                        a b c d

17. One extremely effective control procedure a manager can implement is to set a standard time (or cost) that a buyer should expend in processing purchasing requisitions.

                                                                        T F

18. When direct measurement of performance is impossible, a combination of several indirect indicators may be used together to give a reasonably reliable indication of performance.

T F

19. Measuring purchasing efficiency and measuring purchasing effectiveness is essentially the same thing and can be accomplished with just about the same measuring instruments.

T F

20. A "management review" of the purchasing operation is, by nature, quite subjective; nevertheless, this appraisal activity can identify operating weaknesses and needed improvements.

T F

21. In a broad appraisal of managerial effort, management consultants typically evaluate:
    a. purchasing managerial personnel and their subordinates.
    b. policies and procedures.
    c. records and reports.
    d. all of the above.

a b c d

22. A common method used to evaluate supplier relations is a periodic supplier survey.

T F

23. Buying efficiency can be evaluated by measuring:
    a. the number of purchase orders issued per period.
    b. department operating costs.
    c. the average time it takes to process purchase orders.
    d. all of the above.

a b c d

24. A purchasing manager's report to top management normally should include detailed data regarding day-to-day operations of the purchasing department.

T F

25. Effective control of the procurement process has become increasingly important due to:
    a. competition, the cost of materials, and shortages of materials.
    b. shortages of qualified personnel and high turnover rates.
    c. the increasing use of CAD/CAM in manufacturing firms.
    d. all of the above.
    e. none of the above.

a b c d e

CHAPTER 30
LEGAL CONSIDERATIONS

1. The CISG is:
   a. a set of regulations developed by the United Nations to supplement the laws of countries involved in international trade
   b. a uniform body of law that is designed to govern the international sale and purchase of commercial items
   c. the U.S. version of the UCC, as applied to the purchase of materials in international commerce
   d. none of the above

   a b c d

2. Unless a contract specifically provides for the application of another body of law, the CISG will automatically apply if both the buyer's and the seller's countries have adopted it.

   T F

3. The CISG and the UCC have many more similarities than differences. However, one major difference deals with:
   a. the contracting parties' right to arbitration
   b. warranties available to buyers
   c. requirements for acceptance of an offer
   d. all of the above
   e. none of the above

   a b c d e

4. The Foreign Corrupt Practices Act was enacted to prohibit bribery of foreign officials by American firms selling their products in foreign countries. As such, it has little if any effect on purchasing professionals.

   T F

5. The Foreign Corrupt Practices Act does allow some forms of bribery, primarily those that are considered to be minor and inconsequential in influencing important government decisions.

   T F

6. Product liability is the responsibility held by manufacturers and downstream sales organizations to pay for injuries to users caused by defective or unreasonably hazardous products.

   T F

7. Because JIT purchasing requires a completely different relationship between the buying and selling firms, a new body of legislation has been developed to govern the performance of JIT contracts.

   T F

8. To avoid the possibility of future litigation on important contracts, buyers sometimes include in the purchase order an arbitration clause. Such a clause provides that any dispute arising out of the contract will be settled out of court by arbitration and that both parties will be bound by the decision of the arbitrator.

   T F

9. In professional life most purchasing executives seldom, if ever, become involved in legal actions.

T F

10. Purchasing executives are subject to both the law of agency and the law of contracts. Nevertheless, their taking a highly legalistic approach to contracting is both unnecessary and unprofitable because:
   a. the outcome of a court case is never certain.
   b. litigation is costly in money and executive time.
   c. the total costs are seldom recovered from damage awards.
   d. all of the above.

a b c d

11. Because an employer contracts with a purchasing manager for his services, the law permits the employer to hold the purchasing manager personally liable for:
   a. the contracts he signs.
   b. any secret personal advantages gained.
   c. errors of judgment.
   d. none of the above.

a b c d

12. Under the law, a buyer operates under:
   a. apparent authority.
   b. actual authority.
   c. both of the above.
   d. neither of the above.

a b c d

13. Purchasing managers hold the legal status of buying agents for their firms; similarly, sales representatives hold the status of selling agents for their firms. In most cases, however, unlike the purchasing manager, a salesperson cannot legally bind his or her firm to a contract because usually a sales representative only has authority to solicit orders.

T F

14. When a buyer requests a quotation from a supplier, the quotation usually constitutes an offer. The offer is accepted only when the buyer communicates his or her acceptance of the quotation in terms identical with the terms of the offer.

T F

15. Under the Uniform Commercial Code, suppliers' standard confirmation forms and acknowledgment forms generally can satisfy the requirement for valid acceptance, even if the terms stated thereon are different from the terms of the offer.

T F

16. Prompt supplier performance of a proposed contract constitutes acceptance of the offer.

T F

17. If both parties to a contract are not bound, in the eyes of the law, neither is bound.

T F

18. If the purchasing firm receives an overshipment, it cannot accept just the quantity ordered. It must either accept or reject the entire shipment.

                                                                                          T   F

19. There are two kinds of warranty, express or implied. An express warranty nullifies an implied warranty to the extent that it conflicts with the implied warranty.

                                                                                          T   F

20. When a supplier breaches a contract, the buyer usually has the right to cancel that contract and be compensated for any higher price he must pay for goods or services to fulfill the terms of the original contract.

                                                                                          T   F

21. A mistake by one party to a contract makes the contract void:
    a. when the other party is or should be aware of it.
    b. when the mistake affects the contract significantly.
    c. a and b.
    d. none of the above.

                                                                                      a b c d

22. The Robinson-Patman Act is a federal statute designed to prevent:
    a. price discrimination that reduces competition in intrastate commerce.
    b. any action that reduces competition.
    c. price discrimination that reduces competition in interstate commerce.
    d. all of the above.
    e. none of the above.

                                                                                    a b c d e

23. Under the Robinson-Patman Act a buyer who knowingly induces a supplier to allow him a discriminatory price violates the law to the same extent as the supplier.

                                                                                          T   F

24. The Uniform Commercial Code specifically states that a contract must be in writing to be enforceable when the selling price is or exceeds:
    a. $5.
    b. $50.
    c. $500.
    d. $5,000.

                                                                                      a b c d

25. A supplier who, under the terms of a valid written contract, delivers material that fails to conform to a warranty previously given orally by the supplier's representative, but which is not included in the written contract, may not be prosecuted for failing to perform the contract because:
    a. a sales representative is not the supplier's agent.
    b. a written contract supersedes all previous oral contracts.
    c. warranties must be written down.
    d. none of the above.

                                                                                      a b c d

CHAPTER 31
ETHICAL AND PROFESSIONAL STANDARDS

1. In most cases, the perception of an impropriety is just as damaging to a professional purchaser and his or her firm as is actual impropriety.

    T   F

2. Many firms have made personal purchases for their employees for years. In some cases this may not be good business practice, but there is no ethical problem associated with it.

    T   F

3. Proprietary information should be treated confidentially. An example of proprietary information is:
    a. bid or quotation information
    b. a supplier's design information
    c. customer lists
    d. a and b
    e all of the above

    a b c d e

4. If a buyer requests a bid from a supplier, he or she should be willing to do business with that supplier.

    T   F

5. If a bidder is allowed to revise its bid, all bidders should be invited to review and perhaps revise their bids.

    T   F

6. Professional purchasers have direct ethical obligations to three groups of people:
    1. The employer
    2. Their suppliers
    3. The general public

    T   F

7. Buyers should be cautious in accepting luncheon invitations from sales representatives, because:
    a. some observers may think the buyer is favoring a particular supplier
    b. such lunches frequently involve nonbusiness related discussions
    c. such social interaction may affect the buyer's objectivity in making supplier decisions
    d. none of the above
    e. all of the above

    a b c d e

8. When a supplier is operating in a depressed market, it is ethically acceptable for a buyer to negotiate with that supplier for a price reduction from the normal published price, as long as the purchase makes some contribution to the supplier's overhead and profit.

    T   F

9. Ethics are the guidelines or rules of conduct by which firms as well as individuals aim to live.

    T   F

10. In the long run, companies which adhere to a set of ethical standards are healthier than they would be should they act otherwise.

T F

11. Costs of unethical activity can manifest themselves in which of the following ways?
    a. fines and penalties
    b. increased government regulations
    c. damage to public image
    d. all of the above

a b c d

12. To influence a seller by leaving copies of bids or other confidential correspondence where a supplier can see them is an example of:
    a. sharp practice
    b. ethical behavior
    c. accepted industry practice
    d. all of the above

a b c d

13. If a buyer anticipates the possibility of awarding an order to a firm other than the lowest bidder, he or she should notify prospective bidders that factors other than price will be considered.

T F

14. Although professional buyers strive to negotiate terms which are fair to both parties concerned, they do take advantage of mistakes that have been made in a supplier's proposal.

T F

15. Purchasing goods for company officials and employees falls under the category of:
    a. samples
    b. trade discounts
    c. personal purchases
    d. none of the above

a b c d

16. If the cost of an engineering study that appears to be especially desirable exceeds normal industry practice, then _____ should be responsible for the additional costs of the study.
    a. the supplier
    b. the purchasing firm
    c. both a and b
    d. none of the above

a b c d

17. When a sample is accepted, professional buyers ensure that appropriate tests are conducted in a timely manner. The results of such tests and the suitability of the item in meeting the buyer's need are considered proprietary, and disclosure of this information would be considered unethical.

T F

18. People engaged in purchasing should not accept from any supplier or prospective supplier significant gifts or favors.

        T   F

19. It is generally the best policy to decline any sort of favor, hospitality, or entertainment in order to ensure that all relationships are above reproach at all times.

        T   F

20. Which of the following is included under the term *gifts, gratuities, and favors?*
    a. monies
    b. seasonal or special-occasion presents
    c. discounts
    d. all of the above

        a   b   c   d

21. When the return of a gift is impracticable because of its perishability, disposition should be made to:
    a. a charitable institution
    b. company employees
    c. supplier affiliates
    d. none of the above

        a   b   c   d

22. Sales representatives usually speak with real respect of the buyer who pays his or her share of entertainment expenses.

        T   F

23. Although in international business cultural customs may require the exchange of gifts, buyers should maintain U.S. standards of ethics regardless of the consequences.

        T   F

24. An employee's lifestyle and outside interests are no business of the firm and have little to do with an individual's ethical practices.

        T   F

25. Which of the following is an acceptable means of detecting possible ethics infractions?
    a. observation of employee lifestyle
    b. monitoring visitor logs
    c. investigation of the relationship with frequently used suppliers
    d. all of the above

        a   b   c   d

CHAPTER 32
PURCHASING FOR INSTITUTIONS
AND GOVERNMENTAL ORGANIZATIONS

1. The focus of operations in an institution or government must be on making a difference for people, and buyers must operate with that goal in mind. Hence, service is primary.

                                                                                    T F

2. In most governmental organizations, an important purchasing guideline is: "purchasing and politics don't mix—and they must never be allowed to do so."

                                                                                    T F

3. Purchasing in not-for-profit institutions differs from purchasing in industrial organizations because:
   a. institutions are subject to innumerable laws, rules, regulations, and administrative decisions
   b. they purchase a much broader range of items
   c. institutions must support a wider spectrum of services, agencies, and operating units
   d. all of the above
   e. none of the above

                                                                                    a b cd e

4. As a general rule, institutions and governments experience more emergencies and rush orders than industrial organizations, simply because many personnel in the operating departments do not pay careful attention to the planning and scheduling of their procurement needs.

                                                                                    T F

5. Value Analysis work is seldom done in institutions and governmental organizations.

                                                                                    T F

6. The Model Procurement Code provides for five principal methods of source selection: (1) competitive sealed bidding, (2) competitive sealed proposals, (3) small purchases, (4) sole-source procurement, and (5) emergency procurement.

                                                                                    T F

7. As used in not-for-profit institutions, the terms "responsive bidder" and "responsible bidder" mean essentially the same thing.

                                                                                    T F

8. Like their industrial colleagues, most institutional purchasing managers set a high priority on reducing and managing their supplier base.

                                                                                    T F

9. As a general rule, contract administration is delegated to the operating units in institutional and governmental purchasing.

                                                                                    T F

10. Historically, state and municipal governments have been heavy users of performance incentive contracts.

T   F

11. Some institutions rotate their bidders lists for particular goods or services to offset the tendency for buyers to rely consistently on the same suppliers.

T   F

12. The purchasing manager in most colleges and universities typically reports to a materials manager or to a vice president responsible for administration.

T   F

13. In general, industry is more motivated to control purchasing costs than are public and nonprofit institutions.

T   F

14. The potential for conflicts of interest are considerably less in institutional purchasing than in industrial purchasing.

T   F

15. Certain purchasing activities are inherently more difficult to perform in institutions than in industry, such as:
    a. inspection of incoming materials and controlling sales personnel.
    b. describing specifications
    c. negotiation and competitive bidding
    d. all of the above

a b c d

16. While profit is a primary objective of industrial purchasing, the purchasing departments of most public and private institutions seek as a primary objective:
    a. autonomy
    b. purchasing savings
    c. reciprocity agreements
    d. relief from government regulation

a b c d

17. Theoretically, reciprocity should be easier to control in schools and hospitals than it is in industry. In practice, however, this often is not the case.

T   F

18. Private institutions are required by law to purchase without favoritism.

T   F

19. One way large educational institutions can achieve significant savings in their purchasing activities is to:
    a. totally centralize the purchasing activities.
    b. centralize purchasing to the extent it is practical to do so.
    c. decentralize purchasing activities.
    d. centralize administrative purchasing activities and decentralize academic and research purchasing.

a b c d

20. To obtain the "right" prices in the institutional marketplace, institutions must:
    a. request the school discount that the law provides.
    b. make price comparisons with other institutions.
    c. hire competent buyers who can negotiate effectively.
    d. seek high-dollar-return reciprocity agreements.

    a b c d

21. There are vast functional differences between institutional and industrial organizations. As a result, most of the general purchasing concepts, especially those describing pricing methods, are not applicable to institutions.

    T F

22. Savings can often be achieved when the purchasing department contracts for:
    a. interior furnishings including desks, shelving, carpets, etc.
    b. routine construction repairs and minor alterations.
    c. construction insurance.
    d. all of the above.

    a b c d

23. Hospitals must carry excessively large inventories of patient-care supplies due to the emergency nature of patient care.

    T F

24. The importance of the receiving function in institutions is often underestimated because there are no production schedules to meet.

    T F

25. Purchasing savings available to industry are also available to institutions. Institutions can obtain these savings by all of the following methods *except*:
    a. hire an adequate number of competent purchasing personnel.
    b. provide a stimulating environment that motivates purchasing personnel.
    c. totally centralize all purchasing activities and decentralize auxiliary functions.
    d. ensure adequate training and advanced education.

    a b c d

ANSWERS

Chapter 1

1. T	6. c	11. d
2. b	7. T	12. F
3. F	8. F	13. c
4. b	9. e	14. F
5. T	10. T	

Chapter 2

1. T	6. b	11. e	16. T	21. T	26. T
2. a, c, d	7. F	12. T	17. F	22. T	27. d
3. T	8. F	13. F	18. T	23. d	28. T
4. d	9. F	14. c	19. T	24. F	29. F
5. F	10. T	15. T	20. c	25. c	30. a

Chapter 3

1. F	6. F	11. T	16. T	21. T
2. c	7. b	12. F	17. F	22. T
3. T	8. F	13. T	18. b	23. d
4. F	9. a	14. c	19. F	24. F
5. T	10. b	15. d	20. T	25. a

Chapter 4

1. F	6. c	11. b	16. F	21. b
2. T	7. T	12. F	17. d	22. d
3. T	8. T	13. c	18. T	23. F
4. F	9. a	14. F	19. T	24. T
5. b	10. T	15. T	20. d	25. a

Chapter 5

1. T	6. F	11. T	16. T	21. T
2. F	7. b	12. F	17. T	22. T
3. T	8. T	13. F	18. F	23. d
4. b	9. d	14. F	19. a	24. F
5. c	10. F	15. a	20. F	25. F

Chapter 6

1. F	6. F	11. a	16. d	21. F
2. T	7. F	12. d	17. d	22. F
3. F	8. c	13. T	18. F	23. F
4. T	9. b	14. b	19. T	24. T
5. d	10. F	15. T	20. T	25. T

Chapter 7

1. T	6. F	11. T	16. c
2. b	7. T	12. F	17. T
3. c	8. T	13. T	
4. F	9. c	14. a	
5. c	10. e	15. F	

Chapter 8

1. F	6. T	11. F	16. c	21. F
2. T	7. d	12. e	17. d	22. a
3. F	8. e	13. F	18. F	23. F
4. T	9. T	14. T	19. e	24. F
5. T	10. d	15. F	20. b	

Chapter 9

1. F	6. T	11. T	16. T	21. d
2. T	7. F	12. T	17. a	22. c
3. T	8. F	13. d	18. d	
4. T	9. F	14. c	19. T	
5. a	10. a	15. F	20. F	

Chapter 10

1. T	6. d	11. b	16. d
2. F	7. T	12. F	17. T
3. F	8. b	13. d	18. b
4. T	9. c	14. T	19. F
5. T	10. d	15. T	20. F

Chapter 11

1. T	6. T	11. c	16. F	21. e	26. T
2. d	7. d	12. F	17. c	22. T	
3. T	8. d	13. T	18. T	23. F	
4. e	9. F	14. b	19. F	24. F	
5. c	10. T	15. F	20. e	25. b	

Chapter 12

1. F	6. b	11. a	16. T	21. c
2. F	7. T	12. T	17. d	22. T
3. d	8. F	13. F	18. F	23. c
4. F	9. d	14. d	19. T	24. F
5. F	10. F	15. c	20. T	

Chapter 13

1. F	6. F	11. e	16. a	21. b	26. T
2. F	7. T	12. T	17. T	22. F	27. a
3. d	8. b	13. F	18. F	23. T	
4. T	9. T	14. F	19. T	24. T	
5. d	10. d	15. e	20. c	25. c	

Chapter 14

1. F	6. F	11. a	16. e
2. T	7. T	12. b	17. F
3. F	8. a	13. T	18. F
4. c	9. c	14. T	19. d
5. b	10. F	15. a	20. d

Chapter 15

1. d	6. d	11. b	16. F	21. c
2. T	7. T	12. F	17. d	
3. T	8. T	13. F	18. F	
4. T	9. T	14. b	19. T	
5. F	10. e	15. a	20. a	

Chapter 16

1. T	6. e	11. F	16. F
2. d	7. T	12. b	17. d
3. a	8. F	13. F	
4. F	9. T	14. d	
5. T	10. b	15. T	

Chapter 17

1. c	6. F	11. d	16. T	21. c
2. F	7. d	12. T	17. F	22. c
3. d	8. T	13. c	18. T	23. F
4. T	9. e	14. F	19. b	24. T
5. d	10. F	15. a	20. T	25. a

Chapter 18

1. c	6. c	11. d	16. F	21. b
2. T	7. F	12. d	17. d	22. d
3. T	8. T	13. d	18. d	23. F
4. T	9. F	14. F	19. d	24. T
5. T	10. b	15. T	20. T	25. T

Chapter 19

1. F	6. T	11. T	16. T	21. T
2. d	7. F	12. F	17. b	
3. F	8. T	13. c	18. T	
4. d	9. e	14. a	19. c	
5. d	10. F	15. F	20. b	

Chapter 20

1. T	6. c	11. e	16. e
2. F	7. T	12. T	17. T
3. F	8. T	13. T	18. T
4. T	9. F	14. d	19. c
5. b	10. a	15. F	20. d

Chapter 21

1. T	6. F	11. T	16. F	21. T	26. T
2. F	7. a	12. b	17. F	22. F	27. F
3. d	8. T	13. d	18. F	23. c	28. F
4. d	9. F	14. T	19. T	24. T	29. c
5. F	10. b	15. T	20. F	25. T	30. F

Chapter 22

1. T	6. F	11. T	16. T	21. T	26. T
2. F	7. F	12. T	17. T	22. T	27. T
3. F	8. T	13. T	18. T	23. T	28. T
4. F	9. T	14. F	19. T	24. F	29. T
5. F	10. T	15. T	20. F	25. T	30. T

Chapter 23

1. F	6. T	11. T	16. d	21. b	26. F
2. T	7. d	12. c	17. F	22. T	27. T
3. c	8. T	13. F	18. T	23. F	28. c
4. T	9. F	14. T	19. d	24. T	29. T
5. b	10. d	15. F	20. d	25. d	30. d

Chapter 24

1. F	6. T	11. F	16. c	21. b
2. T	7. F	12. T	17. F	22. F
3. T	8. d	13. d	18. F	23. c
4. c	9. T	14. F	19. b	24. F
5. F	10. d	15. a	20. T	25. F

Chapter 25

1. T	6. T	11. T	16. d	21. c
2. T	7. T	12. c	17. T	22. F
3. F	8. T	13. d	18. b	23. F
4. d	9. F	14. F	19. F	24. c
5. T	10. F	15. F	20. b	25. F

Chapter 26

1. T	6. e	11. d	16. c
2. F	7. F	12. b	17. T
3. F	8. b	13. d	18. T
4. d	9. T	14. F	19. T
5. T	10. F	15. d	20. T

Chapter 27

1. T	6. T	11. T	16. c	21. T
2. T	7. T	12. b	17. F	22. T
3. F	8. d	13. F	18. c	23. T
4. F	9. T	14. a	19. T	24. T
5. T	10. d	15. T	20. a	25. F

Chapter 28

1. F	6. T	11. T	16. c	21. d
2. T	7. F	12. a	17. T	22. e
3. T	8. c	13. d	18. d	23. F
4. T	9. T	14. b	19. b	24. T
5. F	10. T	15. T	20. F	25. F

Chapter 29

1. T	6. F	11. F	16. c	21. d
2. T	7. T	12. d	17. F	22. T
3. F	8. T	13. d	18. T	23. d
4. T	9. T	14. d	19. F	24. F
5. e	10. d	15. T	20. T	25. a

Chapter 30

1. b	6. T	11. b	16. T	21. c
2. T	7. F	12. c	17. T	22. c
3. c	8. T	13. T	18. F	23. T
4. F	9. T	14. F	19. T	24. c
5. T	10. d	15. T	20. T	25. b

Chapter 31

1. T	6. F	11. d	16. b	21. a
2. F	7. e	12. a	17. F	22. T
3. e	8. T	13. T	18. T	23. F
4. T	9. T	14. F	19. T	24. F
5. T	10. T	15. c	20. d	25. d

Chapter 32

1. T	6. T	11. T	16. b	21. F
2. F	7. F	12. T	17. T	22. d
3. d	8. F	13. T	18. F	23. T
4. T	9. F	14. F	19. b	24. T
5. F	10. F	15. a	20. c	25. c

CHAPTER 3
OBJECTIVES AND POLICIES

1. Policies serve two functions. They state broadly the intended course of action and set down a series of explicit steps to be followed in performing tasks.

    T F

2. From an operating point of view, all of the following statements are sound purchasing and supply management objectives *except*:
    a. to keep inventory investment and inventory losses at a practical minimum
    b. to achieve maximum integration with other departments of the firm
    c. to buy at the lowest prices available
    d. to work with suppliers to help reduce their costs

    a b c d

3. The most fundamental of all purchasing and materials management objectives is to support company operations with an uninterrupted flow of materials and services.

    T F

4. One of the advantages of decentralized purchasing is that it tends to minimize the small order problem.

    T F

5. Sound competitive bidding practice requires that a buyer be willing to do business with every supplier from whom he or she solicits a bid.

    T F

6. "To buy competitively" and "to buy wisely" are described in the text as important purchasing objectives. Although they are discussed separately in the text, both focus on essentially the same basic concept.

    T F

7. Purchasing is said to be centralized when:
    a. purchasing personnel are located in one particular location of the organization.
    b. a single person is responsible for the entire purchasing function.
    c. a single person is responsible for supervising the purchasing function, even though personnel from functional areas routinely negotiate with suppliers.
    d. top management performs the major functions of purchasing.

    a b c d

8. Research has shown that the existence of formal written policies dealing with ethical issues has little effect on the behavior of purchasing personnel in the area of ethics.

    T F

9. Situations that may justify decentralized purchasing activities include:
    a. companies that process a single natural raw material.
    b. technically oriented firms that are not involved in research.
    c. single-plant manufacturing operations.
    d. all of the above.

    a b c d

10. Decentralization is said to be excessive when the purchasing department performs less than approximately _____% of the purchasing function.
    a. 100%
    b. 95%
    c. 90%
    d. 85%

                                                                                                    a b c d

11. An important objective of any purchasing department is to achieve maximum integration with the other departments of the firm.

                                                                                                    T F

12. The major objectives of a purchasing operation in a manufacturing organization are vastly different from those of purchasing departments in governmental units or schools or hospitals.

                                                                                                    T F

13. In most well-run organizations, the purchasing department should have both the responsibility and the authority to request the user to reconsider the specifications of materials requisitioned if, in the opinion of the buyer, the interest of the firm may be better served.

                                                                                                    T F

14. The purchase of certain technical items requires a potential supplier to conduct a presale study of the buyer's specific applications of the proposed purchase. When such a study must be conducted, the buyer should:
    a. have his or her technical experts work with the supplier and conduct the study jointly
    b. accept as much free presale technical service as the supplier is willing to provide
    c. estimate the amount of money involved in doing the study, and pay for any part of the study that exceeds normal industry practice
    d. have more than one supplier make the study to ensure that it is in accordance with industry standards

                                                                                                    a b c d

15. Which of the following operating groups has a major impact on the way the "outside world" perceives the ethical posture of a firm?
    a. the service department
    b. the purchasing department
    c. the sales department
    d. all of the above

                                                                                                    a b c d

16. Most progressive firms believe that their buyers are obligated to strive for an equitable settlement of business dealings for both firms—the buyer's firm and the supplier's firm.

                                                                                                    T F

17. All bid data must be treated confidentially during the competitive bidding process; however, once the contract is awarded, all bidders should be informed of the price of the successful bid.

                                                                                                    T F

18. Presale technical service from suppliers:
    a. should never be accepted unless paid for.
    b. can place a firm under obligation to a particular supplier.
    c. is not a policy matter.
    d. all of the above.

                                                                                                    a b c d

19. Many firms make certain types of personal purchases for their employees. Aside from ethical considerations, this practice generally benefits both suppliers and a firm's employees.

                                                                                                    T F

20. A current federal law requires all firms that receive federal contracts in excess of $500,000 to award a certain percentage of their materials and service purchases to minority-owned businesses.

                                                                                                    T F

21. The National Minority Supplier Development Council was formed voluntarily to accelerate the acceptance of minority suppliers into the mainstream of business activity through improved communications between majority and minority firms.

                                                                                                    T F

22. Although in private industry there is no legal or ethical requirement compelling the buyer to award an order to the low bidder, the competitive bidding process itself implies that the low bidder will receive the order.

                                                                                                    T F

23. Purchasing policies:
    a. establish ground rules for purchasing's relationship with other departments.
    b. inform purchasing personnel about the expected conduct of department activities.
    c. are commonly used devices in business.
    d. all of the above.

                                                                                                    a b c d

24. Despite what some "do-gooders" say, a supplier's perceptions about a buying firm are not particularly important as long as the firm's business is profitable to the supplier.

                                                                                                    T F

25. Nothing offers more potential danger to a firm's reputation for fair dealing than a poorly handled competitive bid purchase. Hence:
    a. whenever the lowest bidder does not receive the order, the buyer should explain his or her decision.
    b. there is no need to notify unsuccessful bidders that the order has been placed because they will know this anyhow after the award date has passed.
    c. although bid prices in general should not be revealed, revealing the price of the lowest bidder is good practice as this is the best method of informing unsuccessful bidders of the target prices they must strive for in future purchases.
    d. all of the above.

                                                                                                    a b c d

CHAPTER 4
OPERATING PROCEDURES

1. Because policies and procedures are usually very similar, they are often combined in a "policy and procedure manual".

                                                                              T F

2. Procurement procedures provide the framework and direction for accomplishing the materials management activities, and they provide the means for processing information inputs from outside the department to produce output communications needed by other departments.

                                                                              T F

3. Policies are implemented by means of operating procedures which outline in detail specific actions to be taken.

                                                                              T F

4. In a well run organization, "rush orders" from operating departments are a rarity.

                                                                              T F

5. All of the following documents typically are used to communicate a purchase "need" to the buyer *except*:
   a. purchase requisitions.
   b. stores requisitions.
   c. bills of materials.
   d. traveling requisitions.

                                                                          a b c d

6. A bill of materials, which is a list of all materials and the quantities needed for a particular job or assembly, is usually prepared initially by the:
   a. buyer.
   b. production manager.
   c. design engineer.
   d. supplier.

                                                                          a b c d

7. Systems contracting, in reality, is simply an extension and more sophisticated development of the blanket order purchasing concept.

                                                                              T F

8. Although "request for quotation" forms vary widely among firms, typically they contain essentially the same information that subsequently will be included on the purchase order.

                                                                              T F

9. Before being sent to the purchasing department, purchase requisitions should be approved by the designated departmental supervisors to ensure that:
   a. requisitions are reviewed by qualified individuals with budget authority.
   b. a reliable source of supply has been specified.
   c. the best price has been obtained.
   d. all of the above.

                                                                          a b c d

10. The terms and conditions of purchase which are printed on the back of a firm's purchase order are important because they can assist in precluding legal difficulties, and they may protect the buyer in case legal difficulties arise.

                                                                                             T   F

11. Use of the "purchase credit card" typically generates all of the following benefits *except*:
    a. improves purchasing relations with the operating departments.
    b. eliminates the control problem for the accounting department.
    c. provides much faster payment to suppliers.
    d. reduces the purchasing cycle time.

                                                                                         a b c d

12. The purchasing department's responsibility for an order terminates once a satisfactory contract has been negotiated.

                                                                                             T   F

13. All of the following basic records are essential for the effective operation of most purchasing departments *except*:
    a. files of open and closed orders.
    b. purchase order log.
    c. invoice auditing records.
    d. commodity record.

                                                                                         a b c d

14. Since the closed-order file provides a historical record of all completed purchases, these records all should be kept for at least seven years.

                                                                                             T   F

15. A commodity record is an especially useful record for maintaining information on past requirements and orders for major materials and services that are purchased.

                                                                                             T   F

16. The single *most* effective method for reducing the number of small orders in a typical firm is to implement an electronic ordering system.

                                                                                             T   F

17. Considering the different types of contracts, which of the following is likely to be a long-term contract?
    a. definite delivery type contract
    b. evergreen contract
    c. requirements contract
    d. all of the above

                                                                                         a b c d

18. When a seller uses its own order acknowledgment form, in cases where some of the seller's acceptance terms are in direct conflict with those contained in the buyer's order, the law omits such terms from the resulting contract.

                                                                                             T   F

19. Purchasing bears full responsibility for an order until the material is received, inspected, accepted, and ready for use.

                                                                                             T   F

20. Small orders can cause serious problems for a purchasing department; methods to minimize these problems include:
    a. centralized stores.
    b. blanket or open-end ordering systems.
    c. electronic ordering systems.
    d. all of the above.

                                                                                                    a b c d

21. Specific purchasing procedures employed by a firm should:
    a. be devised in accordance with current purchasing standards as established by the National Purchasing Board.
    b. meet the unique needs of the particular firm.
    c. be clearly and precisely stated in the firm's policy manual.
    d. all of the above.

                                                                                                    a b c d

22. Small, one-time purchases often are handled best by a:
    a. blanket system.
    b. term contracting system.
    c. electronic ordering system.
    d. petty cash system.

                                                                                                    a b c d

23. In a well-run purchasing department, small orders usually constitute a very small percentage of the total number of purchase orders issued each year.

                                                                                                    T F

24. If properly used, blanket orders can help a firm reduce its small-order problem, if it has one.

                                                                                                    T F

25. To ensure that a firm pays only for the materials it has in fact ordered and received, it audits all supplier invoices. The most desirable audit procedure is to:
    a. have purchasing or accounts payable simultaneously compare the purchase order, the receiving report, and the supplier's invoice and reconcile among themselves any existing differences before payment is made.
    b. have the department requesting the material acknowledge its receipt by so indicating on the invoice before accounts payable pays it.
    c. use the "by exception" procedure—accounts payable pays all invoices a stipulated number of days after applicable copies of supplier's invoices have been distributed to the requisitioning departments provided that during this time period they offer no objection to such charges being made to their budgets.
    d. none of the above.

                                                                                                    a b c d

CHAPTER 5
COMPUTER-BASED SYSTEMS/EDI

1. When a system is computerized, the basic activities of the procurement process remain essentially the same as when the system was operated manually.

T   F

2. To function effectively in a computer-based purchasing operation, most buyers need a significantly higher level of computer skill than is the case in a purchasing department that is not computerized.

T   F

3. Most managers agree that the primary advantage a computer offers a buyer or a materials planner is the immediate availability of much more complete data for use in making cost-effective materials-related decisions.

T   F

4. One of the *first* requirements in developing a computerized purchasing or materials management system is to:
   a. develop an effective inventory control procedure.
   b. prepare an operational flow chart of the entire system.
   c. convince employees that the new system will benefit purchasing activities.
   d. none of the above.

a b c d

5. Which of the following is *not* an advantage of a computerized materials management system?
   a. reduction of clerical work
   b. immediate availability of complete data for use in decision making
   c. reduction of materials prices
   d. more effective and economical purchasing

a b c d

6. A computer-based purchasing system offers its users a wide range of benefits; one disadvantage, however, is that the records maintained in a manual system usually must be changed completely to adapt to the requirements of an automated system.

T   F

7. Common output reports generated by computer-based systems include performance reports dealing with all of the following *except:*
   a. buyers
   b. expediters
   c. commodities
   d. suppliers

a b c d

8. The basic materials activities which can be performed well by a computer-based system are similar from firm to firm.

T   F

9. The failure of many otherwise sound computer-based systems may be traced primarily to:
   a. personnel who do not know in sufficient detail how to handle routine transactions.
   b. insufficient manpower available during the training period immediately following implementation.
   c. insufficient funding of hardware and software maintenance.
   d. none of the above.

   a b c d

10. Additional clerks and expediters are usually required in an automated purchasing department; consequently the buyer's duties properly focus more on analytical work and purchasing research and less on clerically oriented activities.

    T F

11. Although the specific format and data contents vary among systems, the purchasing records most commonly available in a computerized system are an open order file, a parts behind schedule file, a supplier record file, a commodity record file, and an inventory record file.

    T F

12. Advanced computerized systems routinely can determine the urgency of a firm's need for a particular part.

    T F

13. A third-party network firm typically is used to network a firm's central computer system with the computer systems used at its various plants and other operating locations.

    T F

14. The only inventory control system that can be computerized efficiently is the "order point" system.

    T F

15. A computerized materials management system is most beneficial to a company that:
    a. carries a large number of diversified materials in inventory.
    b. processes a small number of purchase orders.
    c. deals with a relatively small number of different suppliers.
    d. processes a large number of blanket orders and term contracts.

    a b c d

16. Three types of microcomputer applications are found most frequently in a materials management department—analytical applications, database applications, and communications applications.

    T F

17. Electronic data interchange is the direct electronic transmission, computer to computer, of standard business forms such as purchase orders, shipping notices, invoices, and the like, between two organizations.

    T F

18. To use EDI effectively, both the sending and the receiving firms must use standard procedures with respect to three things—communication standards, message standards, and timing standards.

    T F

19. Although EDI produces a number of benefits for its users, the most important benefit is thought to be:
    a. the reduction of purchasing lead time
    b. the reduction in purchasing paperwork
    c. the accuracy of data transmission
    d. the simplification of the ordering activity

    a b c d

20. Inventory items whose usage fluctuates rapidly and extensively can be controlled more effectively by a computerized inventory system.

    T F

21. Computer software is available to provide periodic purchasing reports of each supplier's and carrier's performance with respect to such things as volume of business, late deliveries, rejected shipments, transit damage, and price trends.

    T F

22. The relationship between purchasing and other materials activities, particularly production control, is usually integrated more effectively under a computer-based system than under a conventional manual purchasing operation.

    T F

23. Typically, when computerization is introduced:
    a. fewer clerks are required.
    b. departmental operating costs may or may not decline.
    c. buyers are freed of a vast amount of routine work.
    d. all of the above.

    a b c d

24. Most firms using computerized systems report that 100 percent of their purchase requisitions are prepared by the computer.

    T F

25. For a small firm, the benefits of computerization usually do not compensate for the cost.

    T F

CHAPTER 6
ORGANIZATION

1. Although we read a great deal about the use of cross-functional teams in purchasing activities today, in reality very few companies utilize the concept to a significant extent.

   T F

2. Key areas in which purchasing-related cross-functional teams are utilized are new product development, commodity procurement strategy, sourcing, and supplier performance evaluation.

   T F

3. The importance of purchasing in any manufacturing organization is determined largely by three factors—(1) the availability of materials, (2) the degree of automation of the manufacturing process, and (3) the absolute-dollar-volume of purchases.

   T F

4. The purpose of organization is to facilitate cooperation among the firm's variously skilled people and to channel their efforts toward a common goal.

   T F

5. As functionalization increases:
   a. it can become counterproductive.
   b. people tend to feel insignificant.
   c. jobs tend to become boring and monotonous to some people.
   d. all of the above.

   a b c d

6. The major classifications of work found in a typical purchasing operation are (1) buying, (2) expediting, and (3) contract administration.

   T F

7. A "purchasing council" is often used when working jointly with suppliers to develop cost reduction programs.

   T F

8. The process that involves dividing the work of the total enterprise into its most basic components and then grouping similar components together into specific jobs is called:
   a. coordination.
   b. systems design.
   c. functionalization.
   d. staffing.

   a b c d

9. Purchasing's location within a firm's organizational structure usually is determined by all of the following *except*:
   a. dollar volume of purchases.
   b. competency of purchasing personnel.
   c. types of material purchased.
   d. availability of materials.

   a b c d

10. Firms which use a small number of standard production and supply materials benefit most as a result of creative purchasing performance.

                                                                                                    T F

11. The functionalization concept can be used effectively in purchasing because:
    a. the activities of purchasing naturally divide into distinct classifications which each involve a wide range of activities.
    b. control of these activities is not as important as in some other areas.
    c. there is only a narrow range of purchasing activities which are very similar.
    d. purchasing does not involve a significant amount of specialization.

                                                                                                    a b c d

12. The precise manner in which purchasing work is subdivided and grouped depends on:
    a. the skills of available personnel.
    b. the size of the department and the firm.
    c. the firm's philosophy concerning specialization and human needs.
    d. all of the above.

                                                                                                    a b c d

13. As the size of a purchasing department increases, buyers tend to specialize in increasingly narrower commodity classifications.

                                                                                                    T F

14. In a typical purchasing operation, for buying purposes materials are grouped in two ways:
    a. cost and availability of materials.
    b. materials whose purchase requires similar buying skill and knowledge, and materials used in the same finished product.
    c. standard materials and those that require special ordering.
    d. the frequency with which orders are placed and the lead time required.

                                                                                                    a b c d

15. In multi-plant firms, perhaps the greatest benefit of centralizing the purchasing function is that it permits greater technical specialization among a firm's buyers. Buyers then become more knowledgeable and more highly skilled.

                                                                                                    T F

16. Multi-plant firms may elect to decentralize purchasing in order to:
    a. respond more quickly to users' needs.
    b. utilize local sources more effectively.
    c. facilitate coordination of purchasing activities with the activities of using departments within each plant.
    d. all of the above.

                                                                                                    a b c d

17. The major disadvantage(s) of a decentralized purchasing organization in a multi-plant firm is:
    a. the failure to consolidate material requirements when different divisions use the same materials
    b. inefficiencies resulting from the duplication of buying efforts at different plants
    c. the lack of strong policy guidance and coordination at the central management level
    d. all of the above

                                                                                                    a b c d

18. Centralization of purchasing in a multi-plant firm offers maximum benefits when the firm's various plants use entirely different materials.

T   F

19. Less than 25 percent of the manufacturing firms in the United States utilize a completely centralized or a completely decentralized purchasing operation. The majority use a combination of the two.

T   F

20. Large progressive purchasing organizations frequently use a "commodity procurement strategy team" comprised of members from various operating divisions such as research and development, manufacturing, quality assurance, and purchasing.

T   F

21. The buyer-planner concept and the supplier-management concept both focus on one primary objective—more effective management of supplier performance.

T   F

22. In some industries, the need for strategic materials planning has resulted in expansion of centralized purchasing efforts.

T   F

23. The functions most commonly grouped together in a materials management department are purchasing, inventory control, physical distribution, traffic, and stores.

T   F

24. Materials management provides an integrated systems approach to the coordination of materials activities and control of total materials cost.

T   F

25. The location of the purchasing department in a firm's organizational hierarchy is determined by management's perception of the importance of the function.

T   F

CHAPTER 7
PURCHASING'S ROLE IN NEW PRODUCT DEVELOPMENT

1. Failure to consider supply base implications can severely impact a firm's profitability.

   T F

2. The new global market place and advanced communication systems have placed increased emphasis on which of the following:
   a. brand name
   b. time to market
   c. latest technology
   d. lowest price

   a b c d

3. In which stage of product development must desired levels of quality and reliability be engineered into the product?
   a. production stage
   b. manufacturing stage
   c. design stage
   d. purchasing stage

   a b c d

4. In progressive firms, early purchasing involvement in the product development cycle is viewed as a good way to increase the membership on their cross-functional teams.

   T F

5. An envelope of performance specifications:
   a. allows suppliers to add and delete certain specifications
   b. indicates that the supplier should mail back a bid
   c. allows engineers at the buying firm to concentrate on core technologies
   d. contains detailed descriptions on how to build a component

   a b c d

6. Allowing suppliers to participate in the design of a new product is taking an unnecessary risk.

   T F

7. New product design includes both completely new products as well as improvements to existing products.

   T F

8. A key responsibility of a buyer is to acquire, assimilate, digest, and share information concerning new developments in the supply markets for which he or she is responsible.

   T F

9. When developing a statement of objectives, it is important to:
   a. make sure everyone on the development team agrees to it
   b. be as concise as possible
   c. balance it against the company's objectives
   d. include financial analysis

   a b c d

10. Which of the following is a consideration when alternative design approaches are being developed?
    a. suitability
    b. producibility
    c. component availability
    d. customer acceptability
    e. all of the above

                                                                    a b c d e

11. Early supplier involvement is but one of the components which comprise early purchasing involvement.

                                                                    T F

12. The selection of components is greatly facilitated by the availability of an internal current catalog of *all* items and sources available to the firm.

                                                                    T F

13. The most successful stress tests fail.

                                                                    T F

14. Building a second generation prototype in manufacturing is a good way to:
    a. test the documentation of the first generation prototype
    b. test the manufacturing facility
    c. test the initial design
    d. waste time

                                                                    a b c d

15. When manufacturing problems arise, it is a better idea to adjust the process rather than the design.

                                                                    T F

16. It is crucial that purchasing and the function responsible for material control be involved in the review of proposed engineering changes in order to:
    a. negotiate favorable prices
    b. minimize inventory buildup
    c. discuss the timing of changes in order to minimize costs
    d. interfere with the engineering process

                                                                    a b c d

17. Purchasing personnel who have gained technical credibility with engineering are very important to the product development process.

                                                                    T F

CHAPTER 8
PURCHASE DESCRIPTIONS AND SPECIFICATIONS

1. Early purchasing and supplier involvement can reduce material costs and compress development time, but rarely does it improve product quality.

   T F

2. It is essential that suppliers are carefully selected when using performance specifications. The main reason for this is to ensure product quality.

   T F

3. Performance specifications should describe in words what the item is required to do and the materials to be used when making it.

   T F

4. Unnecessarily high tolerances result in high production costs and prices for purchased materials.

   T F

5. When specifications are fixed, the product's profit potential also is fixed.

   T F

6. Costs can be reduced more easily in the design process than in any other area.

   T F

7. Attention to specifications and standardization provides the greatest cost saving during the:
   a. procurement stage.
   b. marketing stage.
   c. production stage.
   d. design stage.

   a b c d

8. Which of the following is *not* a consideration of the product specification?
   a. design consideration of function
   b. marketing consideration of consumer acceptance
   c. procurement considerations of the market
   d. manufacturing considerations of economical production
   e. none of the above

   a b c d e

9. A design capable of solving the functional problem may introduce some production problems.

   T F

10. A person-to-person communication between buyers and designers is an aspect of which approach to specification quality/cost balance?
    a. early purchasing involvement
    b. the formal committee
    c. the purchasing coordination
    d. the informal approach

                                                                                    a b c d

11. In the formal committee approach, suppliers are provided a rough function-fit specification of the required product.

                                                                                    T F

12. What is the role of a materials engineer in the purchasing coordination approach?
    a. liaison between purchasing and design departments
    b. reviewing design work
    c. inspecting and testing raw materials
    d. all of the above
    e. both a and b

                                                                                    a b c d e

13. Specifications normally should be written around a specific product so as to limit competition.

                                                                                    T F

14. An effective method of cost reduction is the utilization of standard specifications.

                                                                                    T F

15. A commercial standard is nothing more than a loose description of the item standardized.

                                                                                    T F

16. The commercial standard description does *not* include:
    a. the quality of materials.
    b. the method for testing materials and workmanship.
    c. a listing of approved suppliers.
    d. quality of workmanship.
    e. all are included.

                                                                                    a b c d e

17. Commercial standards are applicable to:
    a. raw materials
    b. subassemblies
    c. fabricated materials
    d. all of the above
    e. both a and c

                                                                                    a b c d e

18. Because of a general lack of quality, commercial standard items should be used as little as possible.

                                                                                    T F

19. The use of commercial standard items results in:
   a. a simplification of design
   b. a limited choice of suppliers
   c. increased cost
   d. reduced acquisition and inventory costs
   e. both a and d

   a b c d e

20. If a company prepares its own specifications, it should attempt to make them:
   a. different from other standards.
   b. as close as possible to industry standards.
   c. as close as possible to competing firms' standards.
   d. different from industry standards.
   e. none of the above.

   a b c d e

21. Inspection costs can be significantly reduced when a firm prepares its own specifications.

   T F

22. The primary reason most manufacturers brand their products is:
   a. to obtain repeat sales.
   b. standardization.
   c. none of the above.
   d. both a and b.

   a b c d

23. In situations where tight quality control is essential, multiple sources of production should be sought whenever possible.

   T F

24. Utilization of samples is the cheapest and most satisfactory method of purchasing and should be used as the primary method of product description.

   T F

CHAPTER 9
STANDARDIZATION

1. A systematic method of measuring and quantifying standardization efforts exists within many manufacturing firms.

                                                                                                         T F

2. In the global market place, many overseas customers are reluctant to accept inch-based products.

                                                                                                         T F

3. A uniform identification that is agreed upon is called a standard.

                                                                                                         T F

4. Standardization is the prerequisite to mass production.

                                                                                                         T F

5. Job-shop production and process production are two of the three basic systems of production. The third is:
   a. mass production.
   b. custom production.
   c. engineering production.
   d. synthetic production.

                                                                                                    a b c d

6. In order to gain the benefits of mass production, specialized machines should be designed from standardized parts which are mass-produced.

                                                                                                         T F

7. To aid in standardization, production processes should digress from highly technologically sophisticated systems to less sophisticated ones.

                                                                                                         T F

8. Mass production is the production of many diverse products from specialized components.

                                                                                                         T F

9. Standardization after the fact is usually easier than during the design of new products.

                                                                                                         T F

10. International standards facilitate:
    a. increased international trade and prosperity.
    b. free economic zones.
    c. socialization of the free enterprise system.
    d. latent hostilities of underdeveloped nations.

                                                                                                    a b c d

11. The use of standards can permit the firm to purchase fewer items, in larger quantities, and at lower prices.

                                                                                                         T F

12. Company standards are used when industry or national standards are unavailable.

    T F

13. The two basic kinds of materials standards used in industry are:
    a. low standards and high standards.
    b. cost standards and procurement standards.
    c. safety standards and national standards.
    d. industry standards and company standards.

    a b c d

14. The use of standards permits a firm to purchase fewer items, in larger quantities, and at lower prices. Thus the use of standards decreases:
    a. quality.
    b. component availability.
    c. inventory.
    d. all of the above.

    a b c d

15. Simplification savings result primarily from the trivialization of a production effort.

    T F

16. The absence of a simplification program can affect the cost of goods sold in a negative fashion.

    T F

17. Standardization methods that gave birth to techniques of mass production were mainly the result of accomplishments of:
    a. Eli Whitney.
    b. Henry Ford.
    c. the cotton gin.
    d. the Industrial Revolution.

    a b c d

18. The benefits of standardization include:
    a. decreased processing costs.
    b. lower prices.
    c. reduced inventory costs.
    d. all of the above.

    a b c d

19. Conversion to the metric system will lead to an increase in the exports of the United States.

    T F

20. A standards committee can assist the firm by eliminating creative product development.

    T F

21. Simplification and standardization are both closely allied methods of cost reduction. Simplification means:
    a. using components manufactured by specialized suppliers whenever possible.
    b. not using different part numbers for identical items.
    c. adopting standard costing techniques.
    d. reducing the number of standard items in inventory.

    a b c d

22. Simplification can increase profit by:
    a. preventing materials shortages.
    b. coordinating the activities of procurement.
    c. reducing inventory investment and handling costs.
    d. increasing sales.

    a b c d

CHAPTER 10
OUTSOURCING AND MAKE-OR-BUY DECISIONS

1. The "outsourcing decision" and the "make-or-buy decision" require essentially the same type of analysis.

   T F

2. As a general rule, the operational considerations are the most important ones in analyzing a potential make-or-buy situation.

   T F

3. A firm's core competencies are determined largely by the types of specialized equipment it has and the degree of automation it has achieved.

   T F

4. When a firm considers which components it should make and which it should buy, it should always analyze the issue at two levels—the strategic and the operational

   T F

5. Today "manufacturing focus" means learning how not to make things—how not to make the parts that divert a company from cultivating its skills—parts its suppliers could make more efficiently.

   T F

6. Make-or-buy investigations are appropriate during periods of:
   a. new product development.
   b. declining or increasing sales.
   c. unsatisfactory supplier performance.
   d. all of the above.

   a b c d

7. Supply managers most commonly encounter make-or-buy decisions when only a nominal capital investment is necessary to make the product being investigated.

   T F

8. The two *most* important factors to consider when investigating the make-or-buy question are:
   a. supply and demand.
   b. cost and availability of production capacity.
   c. environmental impact and price.
   d. inventory carrying cost and acquisition cost.

   a b c d

9. Considerations which make it desirable to "make the part" include all of the following *except*:
   a. desire to integrate plant operations.
   b. need to exert direct control over production and/or quality.
   c. small volume requirements.
   d. desire to maintain a stable work force in periods of declining sales.

   a b c d

10. Considerations which favor "buying the part" include all of the following *except*:
    a. supplier's research and specialized know how.
    b. limited production facilities.
    c. desire to maintain a multiple-source policy.
    d. design secrecy is required.

    a b c d

11. The one factor in make-or-buy decisions that is subject to the most varied interpretation and misunderstanding is:
    a. availability of materials.
    b. cost.
    c. production capability.
    d. reliability of suppliers.

    a b c d

12. Since it is impossible to predict future cost levels accurately, it is best to make cost estimates on a short–term basis when computing costs for make-or-buy decisions.

    T F

13. Firms often elect to "make" critical parts in order to:
    a. guard against production shutdowns due to supplier labor problems.
    b. make productive use of excess plant capacity.
    c. save money.
    d. all of the above.

    a b c d

14. Although make-or-buy investigations begin with the quantitative factors of a cost analysis, various qualitative factors frequently have more far-reaching make-or-buy consequences than the quantitative factors.

    T F

15. Make-or-buy decisions should be made, or at least periodically reviewed, at the managerial level.

    T F

16. If a firm that has previously made a part, later decides to buy that part, it must exercise great care in interpreting the bids received from prospective suppliers because:
    a. some may carelessly bid unrealistically low prices thinking the buyer really does not intend to buy the part.
    b. some may purposely bid too low in an attempt to induce the buyer to discontinue making the part in favor of buying it.
    c. suppliers may later increase prices.
    d. all of the above.

    a b c d

17. Research studies have indicated that surprisingly few firms (large or small) give adequate objective study to their make-or-buy problems.

    T F

18. Firms sometimes buy and make the same part for the purpose of:
   a. economies of scale.
   b. developing managerial control data.
   c. developing a new production process.
   d. none of the above.

   a b c d

19. Most overhead costs typically are incremental costs; therefore, they should nearly always be included in the cost to "make" an item.

   T F

20. Many firms use the committee approach to analyze their make-or-buy alternatives. However, the firms most successful in solving make-or-buy problems delegate decision making for such problems to their production departments.

   T F

CHAPTER 11
SOURCES OF SUPPLY: PART I

1. A firm should consider itself as a source of supply.

   T F

2. Good buyer-seller relations facilitate the buyer's efforts to gain:
   a. superior performance.
   b. extra service.
   c. cooperation and cost reduction programs.
   d. all of the above.

   a b c d

3. Typically, a good supplier assists a customer with product development, value analysis, and timely delivery of the desired level of quality.

   T F

4. An adequate supplier base is especially critical in:
   a. an industry with a potential occurrence of material shortages.
   b. high-tech industries.
   c. industries where scarcity of materials is present.
   d. all of the above.
   e. none of the above.

   a b c d e

5. Reducing a firm's supply base:
   a. occurs only at small companies
   b. is no longer practiced
   c. requires the ability to substitute good supplier management for the effects of marketplace competition
   d. indicates poor financial health

   a b c d

6. Supplier information files are important because many purchasing operations are repetitive.

   T F

7. Trade exhibits provide a good opportunity for suppliers to present:
   a. a comparison of concurrently similar products of different manufacturers.
   b. their current line of products.
   c. modifications of old products.
   d. all of the above.
   e. both b and c.

   a b c d e

8. Which of the following is not a good source of information regarding industrial suppliers?
   a. supplier catalogs
   b. yellow pages
   c. sales personnel
   d. the Better Business Bureau
   e. trade journals

   a b c d e

9. Members of purchasing associations frequently exchange pricing information.

   T F

10. Supplier goodwill is carried as an asset in many companies' balance sheets.

    T F

11. The end result of good supplier relations is:
    a. increased competition.
    b. better inventory control.
    c. a meshing of operations of both companies.
    d. none of the above.

    a b c d

12. As the relation between buyer and supplier develops, the supplier must increase its direct selling efforts.

    T F

13. Opportunistic buyers can be detrimental to the firm they're buying for.

    T F

14. When entering into a partnership with a supplier, a firm should be prepared to:
    a. protect forecasted demand and cost data
    b. recognize a degree of dependence on the supplier
    c. make this partner a single source
    d. none of the above
    e. a and c

    a b c d e

15. There is very little risk associated with partnering.

    T F

16. The use of the Early Supplier Involvement (ESI) approach normally results in the selection of multiple sources of supply.

    T F

17. Purchases from a single supplier, as opposed to multiple sources, are *not* justified when:
    a. total system inventory will be reduced.
    b. time to market is critical.
    c. there is a strong need to be protected during shortages, strikes, and other emergencies.
    d. the buyer obtains more influence with the supplier.

    a b c d

18. As a general rule, firms should try not to be more than 15–25 percent of any one supplier's business.

                                                                                                T F

19. If high tooling costs are involved, many buyers prefer to have at least two suppliers for high-volume items.

                                                                                                T F

20. When deciding to buy locally or nationally, buyers should use local sources when:
    a. price differentials are small.
    b. actions are necessary to keep the materials physically available.
    c. supplier technical assistance is important.
    d. all of the above.
    e. both a and b.

                                                                                        a b c d e

21. In deciding whether to buy from a manufacturer or a distributor, buyers should focus on the distributor's:
    a. location.
    b. capabilities.
    c. services.
    d. none of the above.
    e. both b and c.

                                                                                        a b c d e

22. Sometimes a buying firm may need to enter into a long term contract in order to allow the supplier an assurance that it will be able to recoup the investment required to use recycled materials.

                                                                                                T F

23. The most significant motivator for firms to buy from MWBE's is corporate social consciousness.

                                                                                                T F

24. Companies manufacturing high-volume standard products are less susceptible to reciprocal pressures than those manufacturing highly differentiated products.

                                                                                                T F

25. Reciprocity is _____ problem.
    a. marketing's
    b. management's
    c. design's
    d. procurement's

                                                                                        a b c d

26. The free enterprise system should protect buying firms from receiving substandard work from MWBE's.

                                                                                                T F

CHAPTER 12
SOURCES OF SUPPLY: PART II

1. Commodity teams generally disband after an assignment.

   T F

2. Utilizing suppliers that have been ISO certified guarantees high quality products.

   T F

3. Requests for proposal, (RFP's) generally contain:
   a. required delivery schedules
   b. a purchase description
   c. standard and special terms and conditions
   d. all of the above

   a b c d

4. The weighted-factor rating system is rarely used because its results tend to be subjective.

   T F

5. A supplier's financial stability is not essential to assure continuity of supply and reliability of product quality.

   T F

6. The list of potential suppliers should be comprehensive enough to bring all the following types of competition to bear *except*:
   a. price competition.
   b. trade relations competition.
   c. technological competition.
   d. service competition.

   a b c d

7. For an extremely difficult purchase, a supplier evaluation conference frequently is held at the buyer's plant.

   T F

8. When demand for a product is inelastic, price raises are highly unlikely.

   T F

9. Plant visits are helpful in assessing a supplier's capacity and motivation. The buyer's appraisal should include:
   a. production, quality, and cost control.
   b. the appropriateness of the equipment.
   c. employee morale.
   d. all of the above.
   e. none of the above.

   a b c d e

10. Plant visits should focus primarily on an assessment of potential supplier's manufacturing facilities.

    T F

11. Firms having ample fixed-asset resources and access to raw materials:
    a. are highly desirable suppliers.
    b. probably will increase their prices frequently.
    c. usually will provide financial backing to the buyer's firm.
    d. usually lease their buildings and equipment.

    a b c d

12. In the long run, production results can depend more on people than on the physical plant.

    T F

13. Technical competence assures that a firm will be a good supplier.

    T F

14. Good service usually means:
    a. delivering on time.
    b. treating special orders specially.
    c. filling back orders promptly.
    d. all of the above.
    e. none of the above.

    a b c d e

15. The four stages of a supplier's typical progression into a JIT program are:
    a. evaluation, testing, quality control, implementation.
    b. evaluation, acceptance, delivery, quality.
    c. exploration, acceptance, pilot project, full implementation.
    d. none of the above.

    a b c d

16. A properly implemented JIT system results in benefits throughout the entire supply chain.

    T F

17. Analysis of a supplier's balance sheet and operating statement is helpful to a buyer in that he or she can:
    a. identify that because of a deteriorating financial condition it may be time to search for another source of supply.
    b. advise that it would be wise to reduce the size of orders being given to the financially deteriorating firm.
    c. advise that if profit margins of a supplier are rising, it may be possible to negotiate lower prices.
    d. all of the above.
    e. none of the above.

    a b c d e

18. JIT can tolerate defect levels for incoming materials of approximately 1 percent.

    T F

19. A firm which is considering the adoption of JIT manufacturing must focus on its supplier's abilities and willingness to meet the stringent quality and schedule demands imposed by the system.

    T F

20. Normally, a buyer's first contact with a potential supplier is with the sales representative.

T F

21. Which of the following is not a prerequisite condition for proper use of competitive bidding?
    a. The product's specifications are explicitly clear.
    b. The dollar value of the purchase is large enough to justify the expense which accompanies this method of selection.
    c. Situations in which price is not the only variable.
    d. There is sufficient time available for using this method.
    e. All of the above are prerequisites.

a b c d e

22. Purchasing judgment and analytical planning should normally be exercised before competitive bids are requested.

T F

23. It is inappropriate to use competitive bidding when:
    a. price is important.
    b. highly standardized products are needed.
    c. it is impossible to estimate costs with a high degree of certainty.
    d. purchases involve complex engineering techniques.
    e. none of the above.

a b c d e

24. Two-step bidding can be used only when adequate technical specifications are available.

T F

CHAPTER 13
INTERNATIONAL/GLOBAL SOURCING

1. One weakness of International Purchasing Offices is their tendency to represent the buyer's interest more than the sellers.

    T F

2. One good indication of a potential international supplier's credit worthiness is the ability of its key personnel to speak English fluently.

    T F

3. "Cultural understanding," in terms of international negotiations, could include which of the following:
    a. studying the history and the customs of a foreign culture
    b. becoming acquainted on a social basis with negotiating partners
    c. being flexible with the time allocated to international negotiations
    d. all of the above
    e. a and c

    a b c d e

4. U.S. buyers' unfamiliarity in dealing with foreign currencies can lead to higher costs for the buying firm.

    T F

5. Hedging can be achieved by which of the following means:
    a. forward contracts
    b. waiting for current forecasts
    c. currency options
    d. a and c

    a b c d

6. Statistics show that choosing a hedging strategy, as opposed to paying in the supplier's currency, will most likely cost the buying firm around 4 percent.

    T F

7. One main advantage of the European Single Market is the creation of European standards which will simplify the quality and performance comparisons buyers have to make.

    T F

8. Which of the following is a disadvantage of countertrade:
    a. increased plant capacity
    b. uncertainty in assigning worth to particular products
    c. increased options for buyers
    d. none of the above

    a b c d

9. One of the complexities of buying goods and services of foreign origin is the wide variability in characteristics such as quality, service, and dependability, among the producing countries.

    T F

10. _____ is the number one reason for international sourcing.
    a. Timeliness
    b. Cost
    c. New technology
    d. Quality
    e. None of the above

                                                                    a b c d e

11. International sourcing normally is desirable when:
    a. short-term currency fluctuations favor the buyer.
    b. the buyer's innovative products could be substituted.
    c. all-in-costs can be lowered significantly.
    d. domestic sources are within 0–20 percent of the cost of foreign suppliers.
    e. none of the above.

                                                                    a b c d e

12. In order to compete and win orders in many countries, it increasingly is necessary to
    enter into agreements to purchase items made in those countries.

                                                                         T F

13. The nature, customs, and ethics of individuals and business organizations from two
    different cultures generally have no impact on successful business relations.

                                                                         T F

14. The absence of fixed exchange rates greatly reduces the chance of either buyer or seller
    unduly gaining an advantage due to currency fluctuations.

                                                                         T F

15. Which of the following presents a major obstacle when developing business relations
    with foreign sources of supply?
    a. communications
    b. exchange-rate fluctuations
    c. cultural differences
    d. long lead times
    e. all of the above

                                                                    a b c d e

16. An assessed rate based on a percentage of the appraised value of the merchandise is an
    example of which import duty?
    a. ad valorem
    b. specific
    c. compound
    d. conjunctive
    e. none of the above

                                                                    a b c d e

17. Occasionally, when a U.S. industry is producing at full capacity, it is possible to get both
    faster delivery and lower prices from foreign sources.

                                                                         T F

18. Since the U.S. Customs Office is objective and fair in its rate assessments, the country of
    origin has nothing to do with the duty charged upon merchandise.

                                                                         T F

19. A bill of lading is a receipt issued by a carrier for merchandise to be delivered to a party at some named destination.

    T F

20. A document certifying the country from which merchandise originated as distinct from the country from which it was immediately exported is a(n):
    a. bill of lading.
    b. inspection certificate.
    c. certificate of origin.
    d. customs invoice.
    e. none of the above.

    a b c d e

21. Which of the following intermediaries typically assume financial responsibility?
    a. commission houses
    b. import merchants
    c. agents
    d. import brokers
    e. both b and d

    a b c d e

22. Agents are firms or individuals representing foreign sellers and their primary interests are those of the domestic importer.

    T F

23. Commission houses usually act for exporters abroad, selling in the United States and receiving a commission from the foreign exporter.

    T F

24. The use of an intermediary, though more costly than direct purchases from the foreign manufacturer, may allow the buyer to avoid many unforeseen problems.

    T F

25. Virtually all purchases from foreign suppliers are the result of:
    a. countertrading.
    b. bartering.
    c. negotiations.
    d. all of the above.
    e. none of the above.

    a b c d e

26. The organization of most non-American businesses and their mode of operation usually requires considerably more time to negotiate than is the case with American firms.

    T F

27. Which form of transaction has as its focus the creation of future goods for new market niches?
    a. creative countertrade
    b. counterpurchase
    c. barter
    d. offset
    e. none of the above

    a b c d e

CHAPTER 14
PRICING PRINCIPLES

1. Quantity discounts are becoming increasingly popular as flexible manufacturing systems continue to improve.

                                                                                    T F

2. Under conditions of pure competition, supply and demand alone determine prices.

                                                                                    T F

3. Foreign competitors have no influence in the pricing strategies of an oligopolistic firm.

                                                                                    T F

4. Economists of the classical school speak of a competitive scale that includes three fundamental types of competition. There are:
   a. practical, pure, and fair.
   b. synthetic, oligopolistic, and monopolistic.
   c. pure, imperfect, and monopoly.
   d. economic, pluralistic, monopolistic.
   e. none of the above.

                                                                              a b c d e

5. Pure competition exists when buyers act rationally, when sellers are free to enter and leave the market at will, and when:
   a. the market contains more buyers than sellers, homogeneous products are traded, and buyers and sellers have full knowledge of the market.
   b. the market contains a large number of equally important buyers and sellers trading homogeneous products with full knowledge of the market.
   c. the actions of sellers are completely ethical and full disclosure is practiced.
   d. sellers of equal importance offer a wide product mix.
   e. none of the above.

                                                                              a b c d e

6. A variable-margin pricing policy precludes competition on individual products.

                                                                                    T F

7. Optimal pricing comes to buyers who understand the pricing processes for complete product lines in all firms from which they buy.

                                                                                    T F

8. A market characterized as "oligopolistic" contains:
   a. only a few sellers.
   b. many buyers and sellers.
   c. either too few or too many sellers.
   d. none of the above.

                                                                                 a b c d

9. Which industries are typically thought of as being oligopolies?
   a. cosmetic, grocery, pet food
   b. small and large appliances
   c. steel, automobile, cigarette
   d. all of the above

                                                                                        a b c d

10. When suppliers' costs are the same, competitive positions and prices are also likely to be the same.

                                                                                           T F

11. Variable margin pricing is:
    a. a pricing method that aims to generate a suitable profit on a firm's entire product line, rather than on each product in the line.
    b. a range of prices on a given product wherein the quantity ordered determines the price.
    c. the preferred method of pricing for heavy machinery.
    d. the essence of the competitive bidding trap.

                                                                                        a b c d

12. In evaluating or justifying what constitutes a "fair" profit, skillful buyers:
    a. do not allow higher profits on new products.
    b. consider technical assistance, reliability, and service in addition to cost.
    c. should be willing to allow higher unit profits for large orders.
    d. should allow higher profits when the buying firm has developed the item being purchased.

                                                                                        a b c d

13. Price analysis is defined as the examination of a seller's price proposal by comparison with reasonable price objectives.

                                                                                           T F

14. The professional buyer recognizes that price is only a component of "all-in-cost."

                                                                                           T F

15. According to a consensus of economists, in approximately 70 percent of the U.S. economy, prices are determined by:
    a. supply and demand.
    b. costs, plus a percentage of profit.
    c. suppliers.
    d. competitive bidding.
    e. none of the above.

                                                                                      a b c d e

16. Buyers should understand how types of costs influence prices in order to effectively utilize:
    a. the purchase order.
    b. competitive bidding.
    c. price simulation.
    d. all of the above.
    e. none of the above.

                                                                                      a b c d e

17. For large-dollar-value, repetitive purchases, buyers should always seek a seasonal discount.

T   F

18. A 2/10 discount translates into an annual discount rate of 20.0 percent.

T   F

19. Up to a certain level of plant utilization, as the volume of production increases, total costs increase and:
    a. fixed costs decrease.
    b. semivariable costs double.
    c. variable costs remain constant.
    d. the cost to produce one additional unit of product decreases.

a b c d

20. The lowest price at which a firm can rationally accept an order is:
    a. total direct cost plus some overhead.
    b. total direct cost plus normal overhead.
    c. cost, plus a percentage of cost.
    d. total direct (variable) cost.
    e. none of the above.

a b c d e

CHAPTER 15
COST ANALYSIS

1. Cost models should be developed and used:
   a. when it is not possible to obtain cost data from suppliers
   b. whenever possible
   c. when the cost data obtained seems unrealistic
   d. a and c

   a b c d

2. Activity-Based Management allows management to identify and implement cost savings opportunities.

   T F

3. Price driven costing means starting out with what the market is willing to pay and designing to that price requirement.

   T F

4. Cost analysis is a review and an evaluation of actual or anticipated cost data.

   T F

5. Cost analysis should not be used when purchasing nonstandard items or services.

   T F

6. Cost analysis involves the application of which of the following when attempting to project reasonable estimated contract costs?
   a. experience
   b. knowledge
   c. judgment
   d. all of the above
   e. none of the above

   a b c d e

7. A plant's overhead costs are directly influenced by its size. Thus, a buyer must be alert to detect firms whose operations are adversely affected by size.

   T F

8. Competition can be a buyer's key to locating the desired low-cost producer.

   T F

9. Effective purchasing by the firm's suppliers will reduce the defect rates of incoming materials.

   T F

10. An important element which affects cost is:
    a. the capabilities of management.
    b. the amount and quality of subcontracting.
    c. the efficiency of labor.
    d. the plant capacity and the continuity of output.
    e. all of the above.

    a b c d e

11. The Prime Contractor is:
    a. the negotiator between buyer and seller.
    b. the supplier.
    c. an alternate supplier.
    d. the subcontractor's agent.

    a b c d

12. The learning curve is defined as an empirical relationship between the number of units sold from inventory and the number of labor hours required to produce them.

    T F

13. Intelligent use of learning curves demands that learning rates be uniform throughout the relevant industry.

    T F

14. Suppliers frequently subcontract some of their production work. Subcontracting decisions are important to the buyer because:
    a. subcontractors are often more efficient than the supplier.
    b. subcontracting decisions may involve a large percentage of the contract money.
    c. prime contractors often second-guess production schedules.
    d. knowledge of subcontractor habits aids in forecasting.

    a b c d

15. Allowance for rework, geographic variations, and variations in skills all must be considered when the buyer is analyzing:
    a. direct manufacturing labor estimates.
    b. subcontractor purchasing involvement.
    c. research on the purchasing system.
    d. materials needed for production.

    a b c d

16. When profits are based on capital investment, it is impossible for an inefficient producer to have higher profits than an efficient producer.

    T F

17. The learning curve is used by buyers in developing:
    a. target costs for new products.
    b. make-or-buy information.
    c. delivery schedules.
    d. all of the above.

    a b c d

18. Profit is the basic reward for risk aversion.

    T F

19. In a capitalistic society, profit generally implies the reward over costs that a firm receives for the measure of efficiency it attains and the degree of risk it assumes.

T F

20. A learning rate of 90 percent implies that the labor requirement for all units declines by _____ percent each time production doubles.
    a. 10
    b. 20
    c. 50
    d. 90

a b c d

21. Most procurement authorities advocate that the buyer pay for and take title to special tooling equipment because:
    a. it demonstrates to the supplier the nature of the buyer's commitment.
    b. such an investment would reduce the supplier's general and administrative (G & A) expenses.
    c. such an approach allows the buyer maximum control.
    d. it lessens the material overhead of the supplier.

a b c d

CHAPTER 16
DEALING WITH COST UNCERTAINTY –
TYPES OF COMPENSATION AGREEMENTS

1. The "cost" of uncertainty is often transferred to the buyer in the form of higher prices.

   T F

2. Compensation arrangements:
   a. exist in a continuum of varying risk assumptions
   b. can motivate suppliers to control costs
   c. reflect the sharing of cost responsibility
   d. all of the above

   a b c d

3. Cost risk is best described as:
   a. a function of technical and contract schedule risk
   b. the risk associated with the nature of the item being purchased
   c. the affect of inflation of forward-priced goods
   d. none of the above.

   a b c d

4. Commodity-type contracts are a good example of high technical risk.

   T F

5. There are three broad types of compensation arrangements: fixed-price, incentive, and cost-reimbursement contracts.

   T F

6. Cost-type arrangements are used:
   a. to motivate the supplier to control costs
   b. when product specifications are incomplete
   c. when cost risk is relatively low
   d. to procure R&D
   e. b and d

   a b c d e

7. The contracting parties of a firm-fixed-price contract establish a firm price either through competitive bidding or negotiation.

   T F

8. The supplier has no incentive to control costs under a firm-fixed-price contract.

   T F

9. Under a fixed-price with economic price adjustments contract, the supplier is hurt if the changes exceed its estimate, and the buyer will overpay if the input unit cost increases do not materialize.

   T F

10. When using a fixed-price with economic price adjustments contract, the cost element to adjust is:
    a. depreciation
    b. direct labor
    c. development
    d. all of the above

                                                                              a b c d

11. Incentive type contracts place a majority of the cost responsibility on the supplier.

                                                                                 T F

12. Under an incentive-type contract, the potential cost decrease:
    a. is also known as the MPPr point
    b. is the difference between the target and the most optimistic point.
    c. provides an estimate of the cost risk to the supplier.
    d. none of the above.

                                                                              a b c d

13. Because the supplier has no cost risk under a cost-plus-fixed-fee contract, the profit potential is relatively high.

                                                                                 T F

14. Cost-plus-fixed-fee-type contracts:
    a. limit the fee paid to the supplier, but not the total obligation
    b. is designed for use in research and/or exploratory development
    c. is appropriate when dealing with cost risk to large to assume
    d. all of the above

                                                                              a b c d

15. Cost-plus-award-fee contracts award suppliers for nonquantitative aspects of the performance.

                                                                                 T F

16. Cost-sharing contracts provide for price adjustments that can be made upward or downward; however, an upward limit of 10 percent is usually imposed.

                                                                                 T F

17. A buyer considers many factors when determining the best contract for a specific purchase. The type of contract ultimately selected depends on:
    a. price considerations
    b. market conditions
    c. the nature of supplies or services to be purchased
    d. all of the above

                                                                              a b c d

CHAPTER 17
NEGOTIATION

1. Sometimes a buyer will need to evaluate prices in terms of the quality provided. This should be done:
   a. within the context of obtaining the lowest "all-in" or total cost
   b. with the support of an advanced and accurate management information system
   c. by the VP of Engineering
   d. a and b

   a b c d

2. When negotiating, the buying and selling representatives should disclose their positions rather than their interests.

   T F

3. Recommended techniques for collaborative negotiations include:
   a. invent options for mutual gain
   b. separate the people from the problem
   c. insist on using objective criteria
   d. all of the above

   a b c d

4. In the case of preferred supplier or strategic supply relationships, a detailed analysis of the supplier's cost partially replaces the role of competition in the marketplace.

   T F

5. In its broadest context, negotiation is a process of _____ used by a buyer and seller to reach acceptable agreements.
   a. planning
   b. reviewing
   c. analyzing
   d. all of the above

   a b c d

6. Negotiation agreements and compromises revolve solely on the issue of price.

   T F

7. Which of the following are *not* objectives common to negotiations?
   a. developing sound relationships with suppliers
   b. assurance of a timely performance of contracts
   c. obtaining fair prices
   d. All of the above are objectives of negotiation

   a b c d

8. Inability to meet delivery schedules for the quality and quantity specified is the single greatest supplier failure encountered in purchasing operations.

   T F

9. Negotiation is the appropriate method of purchasing when:
   a. the five prerequisites for competitive bidding are met.
   b. early supplier involvement is employed.
   c. tooling and set-up costs represent a large percentage of the supplier's total costs.
   d. all of the above.
   e. both b and c.

   a b c d e

10. Negotiation should be used when the business risk and costs involved can be accurately predetermined.

    T F

11. Negotiation is the appropriate method of purchasing when:
    a. production is interrupted frequently because of numerous change orders.
    b. a long period of time is required to produce the items purchased.
    c. the products of a specific supplier are desired to the exclusion of others.
    d. all of the above.
    e. none of the above.

    a b c d e

12. When free to make its own decision, the seller often makes the easiest decision in terms of production scheduling.

    T F

13. Typically, a buyer will be the sole representative for the firm's negotiations when:
    a. the purchase involves technologically sophisticated items.
    b. capital equipment of a high dollar value is being purchased.
    c. recurring purchases of standard items are involved.
    d. the purchases are for research purposes.

    a b c d

14. In team negotiations, the design engineer usually serves as the team leader and coordinates the various specialists into an integrated whole.

    T F

15. Which of the following is *not* a major phase of the negotiation process?
    a. contract bidding
    b. preparation
    c. face-to-face discussions
    d. establishment of objectives
    e. All of the above are major phases of negotiation.

    a b c d e

16. For follow-on contracts, and for contracts for common commercial items, price analysis is usually sufficient to assure the buyer that prices are reasonable.

    T F

17. The less a seller needs or wants a contract, the weaker its bargaining position becomes.

    T F

18. Most prenegotiation leaks that give sellers a feeling of confidence about getting a contract occur in the technical departments of a firm and can not only be costly, but a continuing source of profit loss as well.

T   F

19. The most important step in successful negotiations is:
    a. price analysis.
    b. proper planning.
    c. face-to-face discussions.
    d. none of the above.

a b c d

20. In some sole-source negotiations, the seller's objective is to maximize its position at the expense of the buyer.

T   F

21. In a successful negotiation process:
    a. on both sides, the wins and gains are equally divided.
    b. one side is the clear winner while the other is the loser.
    c. both sides win something, but one wins more than the other.
    d. both sides meet all objectives.

a b c d

22. A buyer's position is strengthened when there are a number of other competent sellers available and when:
    a. a short lead time is required.
    b. the engineering department negotiates prices on technical purchases.
    c. the buyer possesses a comprehensive knowledge of cost and price analysis information pertaining to the purchase.
    d. the industry is in a boom.

a b c d

23. Generally, the negotiator who exercises hard bargaining at the initial meeting gains the upper hand in the negotiating process and can proceed with minimum difficulty.

T   F

24. In negotiated purchasing, requests for contract proposals usually request not only total price, but also a complete breakdown of all attendant costs.

T   F

25. Which of the following is *not* an advantage of price analysis negotiation?
    a. Precise and accurate estimates of direct labor costs are provided.
    b. Negotiation time is shorter.
    c. Support of technical specialists is seldom needed.
    d. Pricing data are relatively easy to acquire.
    e. None of the above.

a b c d e

CHAPTER 18
PURCHASING CAPITAL EQUIPMENT

1. The purchase of capital equipment differs significantly from the purchase of production materials mainly because:
   a. capital equipment generally does not affect profitability
   b. supplier reliability is much less important
   c. the using department plays a more active role
   d. more emphasis is placed on price

   a   b   c   d

2. A unique feature of most capital equipment purchases is the lead-time requirement.

   T   F

3. The most influential factor in selecting the supplier for a capital equipment purchase is the package of operating characteristics the supplier's equipment offers.

   T   F

4. Life-cycle cost analysis is used in the purchase of capital equipment to show clearly a machine's total cost over its life, including such cost factors as those associated with installation, ongoing adjustment and calibration, energy and labor for operation, routine maintenance, major overhauls, and eventual disposition of the machine.

   T   F

5. It is possible to generate profit by the purchase of capital equipment.

   T   F

6. Which of the following is not usually a significant consideration in source selection when purchasing capital equipment?
   a. operating characteristics of the equipment
   b. total economic analysis
   c. location of supplier
   d. engineering features of the equipment

   a   b   c   d

7. Purchasing departments usually find a wider variety of available sources when purchasing capital equipment as compared with buying production materials.

   T   F

8. The two most influential factors in selecting a capital equipment item are operating characteristics and design features.

   T   F

9. Unlike purchasing production materials, when purchasing capital equipment, supplier location, supplier's financial health, and supplier's willingness to render special services are not meaningful considerations.

   T   F

10. Typically, the finance department participates in the purchase of capital equipment. The primary reason for this is:
    a. the price of the equipment.
    b. capital budgeting responsibilities.
    c. the long-term performance of the equipment.
    d. none of the above.

                                                                                    a b c d

11. Discussions must always take place between the using department and the capital equipment manufacturer's representatives. Although such discussions may be highly technical, the buyers should be present to:
    a. try to learn more about the significance of the technical considerations.
    b. serve as a reference source in case questions arise concerning purchasing and cost matters.
    c. ensure that no premature commitment is made by personnel from the operating departments.
    d. all of the above.

                                                                                    a b c d

12. Selecting capital equipment solely on the basis of price is unwise because:
    a. maintenance costs may differ widely, especially if compatible equipment has already been installed.
    b. operating costs per unit of production may vary.
    c. price is only one of many elements of cost.
    d. all of the above.

                                                                                    a b c d

13. The purchasing department's main responsibility in the purchase of capital equipment includes:
    a. gathering information.
    b. assessing supplier capability and willingness to provide service.
    c. assessing supplier reliability.
    d. all of the above.

                                                                                    a b c d

14. The various discounted cash flow techniques are not very useful in analyzing the potential profitability of several alternative capital equipment purchases. That is why the payback method is so widely used.

                                                                                    T F

15. For the purpose of economic analysis, net investment can be defined as the out-of-pocket cost for a piece of equipment. It is computed as the difference between the installed cost and the realizable disposal value of the equipment being replaced.

                                                                                    T F

16. Although payback analysis reveals total profitability, it is seldom used because it is a complicated model.

                                                                                    T F

17. Why would a purchasing manager consider buying used equipment?
    a. cost savings
    b. immediate availability
    c. to have stand-by equipment
    d. all of the above

                                                                                    a b c d

18. The majority of used equipment purchases are made from:
    a. owners of the equipment.
    b. brokers.
    c. auctions.
    d. used equipment dealers.

                                                                                      a b c d

19. Machines available in the used equipment market typically are sold:
    a. as "reconditioned" machines
    b. "as is"
    c. as "rebuilt" machines
    d. all of the above

                                                                                      a b c d

20. Cash flow and technological considerations often make the leasing of capital equipment
    the most desirable acquisition alternative.

                                                                                      T F

21. A major advantage of leasing capital equipment is that:
    a. no interest is paid by the lessee.
    b. leasing frees working capital for other uses.
    c. leasing provides greater depreciation allowances than when equipment is owned.
    d. all of the above.

                                                                                      a b c d

22. Leasing capital equipment has some disadvantages. Among them:
    a. the lessor retains control of the equipment.
    b. high costs, as a rule.
    c. purchasing prerogatives are constrained.
    d. all of the above.

                                                                                      a b c d

23. The role of the purchasing department is quite similar in the acquisition of both capital
    equipment and production materials.

                                                                                      T F

24. An advantage of leasing is that the risk of equipment obsolescence is substantially
    reduced.

                                                                                      T F

25. As a rough rule of thumb, in industry today the delivered price of a piece of productive
    equipment seldom exceed 50 percent of the eventual total cost of ownership of the asset.

                                                                                      T F

CHAPTER 19
PURCHASING SERVICES

1. Organizations should always outsource to service providers whenever they can do so at a lower total cost than they could by performing it in-house.

   T F

2. The ideal service provider:
   a. designs service products to solve customer problems
   b. gives large discounts to new customers
   c. invests to increase customer satisfaction and employee productivity
   d. a and c

   a b c d

3. What distinguishes the procurement of services from the procurement of production-related goods is that purchasing personnel are involved much later in the procurement process with services than is the case with production items.

   T F

4. The Statement of Work (S.O.W.) identifies:
   a. what the contractor is to accomplish.
   b. the primary objective so both the buyer and seller know where and how to place their emphasis.
   c. the future price of the contract.
   d. both a and b.
   e. all of the above.

   a b c d e

5. To a large degree, successful completion of the objectives of a service contract depend upon which attributes of the S.O.W.?
   a. clarity
   b. accuracy
   c. completeness
   d. all of the above
   e. none of the above

   a b c d e

6. The S.O.W. must maintain a delicate balance between protecting the buyer's interests and encouraging the contractor's creativity during both proposal preparation and contract performance.

   T F

7. Selecting the correct source of supply is much more of an art when purchasing materials than when purchasing services.

   T F

8. Unless the potential supplier possesses some truly unique skill or reputation, competition should usually be employed.

   T F

9. During the evaluation of a service contractor, emphasis should be placed on:
   a. quantitative benefits
   b. marginal costs
   c. total risks
   d. all of the above
   e. none of the above

                                                                        a b c d e

10. Due to the highly evolved and efficient competitive process within the service markets, buyers generally can forgo negotiations and concentrate on selecting the lowest-price supplier.

                                                                        T F

11. Cost-type contracts should be considered when there is considerable uncertainty concerning the amount of effort which will be required or when there is insufficient time to develop a realistic S.O.W.

                                                                        T F

12. For lower dollar amounts, labor-hour contracts do not require close monitoring because the quality of labor is obviously apparent.

                                                                        T F

13. For small professional services, _____ contracts are the most practical to administer.
    a. cost-type
    b. cost plus incentive fee
    c. fixed-price
    d. cost plus award fee
    e. none of the above

                                                                        a b c d e

14. The most costly approach to buying building construction services has been found to be:
    a. conventional method.
    b. design and build, firm-agreed-price method.
    c. the building-team method.
    d. the owner-as-contractor method.
    e. design and build, cost-reimbursable method.

                                                                        a b c d e

15. The design-and-build, cost-reimbursable method employs separate contracts for both the design and construction phase of operations.

                                                                        T F

16. When the owner acts as his own contractor it is possible for construction to proceed prior to completion of the total design phase.

                                                                        T F

17. Janitorial and cafeteria operations are typical of:
    a. contract administration.
    b. operating services.
    c. technical services.
    d. professional services.
    e. none of the above.

                                                                        a b c d e

18. Insurance services should be sourced and priced through the use of competition of carefully prequalified suppliers.

T F

19. With the _____ method, the owner contracts directly for the various work elements and performs the functions of integrating and controlling that would otherwise be accomplished by a general contractor.
    a. design and build, firm-agreed-price
    b. conventional
    c. owner-as-contractor
    d. building-team
    e. none of the above

a b c d e

20. In which service industry must the buyer pay particularly close attention to the insurance coverage of the organization?
    a. research and development
    b. construction
    c. landscaping
    d. none of the above

a b c d

21. Research and development services normally are purchased through a fixed price for a level of effort or a cost-plus-fixed-fee contract.

T F

CHAPTER 20
POST-AWARD ACTIVITIES AND THE
MANAGEMENT OF SUPPLIER RELATIONS

1. A cost-based supplier performance evaluation system takes into account supplier nonperformance.

   T   F

2. It is common for a buying firm to support a supplier in meeting productivity, cost, and quality goals when the two firms have formed an arms-length relationship.

   T   F

3. Under JIT manufacturing, large inventories are essential in order to ensure prompt delivery of products to customers.

   T   F

4. The preaward conference is the vehicle the professional buyer and his or her team uses to ensure that the provisions outlined under the request for proposal and the proposed contract are fully understood and implemented.

   T   F

5. An article which shows the time required to perform the production cycle is known as a:
   a. request for proposal.
   b. phased production cycle.
   c. Gantt chart.
   d. categorical plan.
   e. none of the above.

   a b c d e

6. JIT manufacturing involves all of the following *except*:
   a. inventory depletion.
   b. strong supplier management.
   c. WIP buildup.
   d. tight schedule integration between buyer and supplier.

   a b c d

7. Under the categorical plan, personnel from various departments of the buyer's firm maintain informal evaluation records on a supplier's performance.

   T   F

8. A limitation of the Gantt chart is that it fails to provide the full impact of an element's being behind or ahead of schedule.

   T   F

9. Critical-path scheduling is a relatively low-cost tool which is best applied to simple projects of a repetitive nature.

   T   F

10. To monitor and control the progress of a supplier, buyers have a number of techniques available to assist them in their evaluations. Which of the following would be the best method for focusing on information relating to the *activities* which must be performed?
    a. Gantt
    b. CPM
    c. PERT
    d. additive synthesis

    a b c d

11. Which of the following items are addressed, if appropriate, during the preaward conference?
    a. delivery or operations schedule
    b. staffing and supervision
    c. site conditions, work rules, and safety
    d. permits
    e. all of the above

    a b c d e

12. The most successful supplier management results when the buyer and the supplier view their relationship as a partnership.

    T F

13. CPM and PERT are both planning and control tools which utilize network diagrams to show time dependency relationships between factors contributing to developing a system, project or task.

    T F

14. In critical-path scheduling, the path of the longest duration is called:
    a. the completion path.
    b. the terminal path.
    c. the slack path.
    d. the critical path.

    a b c d

15. In contrast to the categorical plan, which is largely objective, the weighted-point plan has the advantage of being somewhat more subjective.

    T F

16. Which of the three plans presented by the National Association of Purchasing Management (to aid in supplier evaluation) involves informal and largely nonquantitative evaluation techniques?
    a. PERT and CPM
    b. the weighted-point plan
    c. the cost-ratio plan
    d. the five-point plan
    e. none of the above

    a b c d e

17. An often-overlooked aspect of successful supplier management is the solicitation of supplier feedback.

    T F

18. The procurement system review (PSR) provides a framework which a customer firm may follow when reviewing and assisting its key suppliers to upgrade their procurement systems.

    T F

19. When using the cost-ratio plan, the buying firm's costs uniquely associated with quality, delivery, and _____ are determined for each supplier.
    a. fixed overhead
    b. inventory
    c. service
    d. control

                                                                                                            a b c d

20. Two common approaches to motivating suppliers to perform satisfactorily are:
    a. greed and avarice.
    b. supply and demand.
    c. competition and incentive.
    d. punishment and reward.

                                                                                                            a b c d

CHAPTER 21
MANAGING FOR QUALITY

1. A majority of the problems associated with a firm's product quality are caused by the quality level and variability of incoming materials used in the manufacturing process.

    T F

2. Total quality management (TQM) is an approach that utilizes specialized quality experts to design the quality assurance system and manage the firm's total product quality.

    T F

3. Basically, quality can be defined:
    a. in absolute terms.
    b. relative to a perceived need.
    c. as conformance with stated requirements.
    d. all of the above.

    a b c d

4. Quality has no meaning in purchasing *except* as it relates to:
    a. specifications and standardization.
    b. price and availability.
    c. cost and availability.
    d. function and ultimate cost.

    a b c d

5. Purchasing departments usually have the authority to change quality requirements for economic reasons.

    T F

6. The objective of most firms is to develop products that have the best possible technical design, and therefore, the highest quality.

    T F

7. Quality determinations include all of the following considerations *except*:
    a. intrinsic value of the materials requested.
    b. availability of materials.
    c. potential substitute materials.
    d. standardization.

    a b c d

8. Suppliers often are qualified to suggest quality changes that can reduce production costs without reducing a material's suitability.

    T F

9. Engineering design is a more important factor in quality control than are production methods and the performance of external suppliers.

    T F

10. A quality assurance program impacts all the following *except*:
    a. competitiveness.
    b. suitability.
    c. total cost of products' "quality."
    d. reliability.

    a b c d

11. In progressive firms today purchasing and supply management is the key unit responsible for managing supplier quality.

    T F

12. A primary responsibility of the purchasing department is to ensure that:
    a. quality is "built into" a firm's products.
    b. suppliers possess the ability, motivation, and information necessary to produce the desired materials and components.
    c. quality standards are defined during the design stage.
    d. none of the above.

    a b c d

13. The long-run quality level of a firm's purchased material is determined by:
    a. selection of suppliers having the technical and production capabilities needed by the firm.
    b. creation of complete and proper specifications for quality requirements.
    c. development of a realistic understanding with suppliers of quality requirements and motivating them to perform accordingly.
    d. all of the above.

    a b c d

14. In preparing a specification, it is desirable to consider the requirements of the design, purchasing, production, and marketing departments.

    T F

15. A primary responsibility of each buyer is to develop a list of suppliers who can deliver an acceptable product that meets the buyer's quality requirements.

    T F

16. The purchasing department is usually solely responsible for setting up and conducting tests to ensure quality levels.

    T F

17. While a buyer can monitor the quality of materials received, there is really no way a buyer can determine in advance how a supplier plans to maintain a certain quality level.

    T F

18. "Use tests" are sometimes conducted by buyers to compare the products of different suppliers. Since this type of experimental testing is not scientific, commercial testing firms normally should be used.

    T F

19. Purchase contracts should include provisions for handling defective materials, including defect classification and material disposition.

T F

20. Every process possesses some natural variability caused by both mechanical and human variation in performance. Over time, this natural variability in the output of a process produces a distribution of outputs which, because of the statistical "central limit theorem," is always a normal distribution.

T F

21. When a buyer's required quality range is narrower than the natural capability range of a supplier's process, the supplier will always produce some unacceptable parts.

T F

22. A process capability index expresses a process's capability relative to the $\overline{X}$ control limits.

T F

23. Cp and Cpk are both process capability index measures. Cpk is the more useful index for a buyer to apply when:
    a. the manufacturing process average is aligned with the buyer's target specification value.
    b. the manufacturing process average exhibits significant fluctuation.
    c. the manufacturing process average is not aligned with the buyer's target specification value.
    d. none of the above

a b c d

24. A process capability index of greater than 1.0 indicates that the quality capability of a process exceeds the buyer's requirement.

T F

25. $\overline{X}$ and R charts are commonly used in SPC applications. When SPC sampling measurements fall outside the $\overline{X}$ and R control limits, this is an indication that the process is being affected by nonrandom variations.

T F

26. The major objective of a supplier certification program is twofold: (1) to maintain desired quality levels, and (2) to reduce duplicate efforts in inspection.

T F

27. Statistical acceptance sampling to determine the quality characteristics of a lot of material should be utilized when it is necessary to locate defective materials with complete accuracy.

T F

28. Buyers, with careful planning and advance contractual arrangements, can pass along inspection costs to the supplier.

T F

29. Occasionally, shipments of satisfactory quality are rejected by a statistical inspection plan; therefore, it is advisable:
    a. not to inform suppliers in advance when sampling inspection is to be used.
    b. not to use sampling inspection.
    c. to inform suppliers when shipments are to be subjected to sampling inspection.
    d. none of the above.

    a b c d

30. The ISO 9000 series of standards is one of the most rigorous international product-quality standards in existence today.

    T F

A CASE OF TOO MUCH HELP

Purpose

Early purchasing involvement is every bit as important at schools, hospitals, universities, government agencies, zoos, and banks as it is at manufacturing firms.

Discussion

This case was developed by one of the authors when he was asked to address 160 school purchasing agents. The majority of the participants acknowledged that their role was to process paperwork. Others (teachers, department heads, administrators, etc.) made the sourcing and pricing decisions. Such an attitude costs our school districts uncounted billions of dollars. A proactive buyer or purchasing agent makes most of his or her contribution up front!

Questions 1 & 2:

What courses of action are open to Nancy? What are the advantages and disadvantages of each?

Comment:

1. She can proceed with the procurement from the Twinsburg Chair Company.
   + Nancy creates no waves.
   - Nancy has *not* added *any* value. She is functioning as a clerk. She is *not* helping the school district stay within budget. (Approximately $80,000 will be wasted.)

2. Nancy can buy the lowest-cost chair which meets the functional requirement.
   + Nancy saves the district $80,000.
   - Nancy may be looking for a new job. (But she probably does so with a sense of satisfaction.)

3. Nancy obtains all appropriate data (costs, specs, etc.) including sample chairs and requests that the superintendent (or his or her cabinet) review the requirement and all data and then select the appropriate chair.
   + This is the most politically astute approach.
   + Purchasing has the right (requirement) to challenge, but not to change specifications.
   - There are no obvious disadvantages.

Question 3:

Write a policy statement for the school focusing on early purchasing involvement.

Comment:

Students should be asked to present their policy statement. These statements should call for all school administrators and other personnel who may originate requirements for non-standard supplies, services, or equipment to contact purchasing for assistance in refining their requirements. When appropriate, purchasing should obtain information from prospective suppliers and provide the information to the internal customer.

THE CASE OF THE UNRULY SPIDER

Purpose

The purpose of this case is: (1) to point out the direct relationship between the specifications the buyer provides and the quality the supplier delivers, (2) to suggest means of settling disputes when they arise over such difference, and (3) to discuss the importance of selecting properly qualified suppliers.

Discussion

If there are any engineering students in the class or students with a machine shop background, this case will usually create a lively discussion about specifications. The students who have had practical experience with machined parts usually will take the position that Speedy produced exactly what was desired (by the specifications)—a 0.0004-inch tolerance. Therefore, it may take effort on the instructor's part to get some students to defend the position that the supplier should have known that this was a bearing seat that should have had a ground finish. However, a lively class discussion is possible if the instructor will ask such questions as, "Shouldn't a good supplier know what is really wanted" or "Shouldn't he know what the part is to be used for?"

If this case is used as a written assignment, some students may check with machine shops to obtain help with the answer. This activity should not be discouraged, as this case is a practical one to be solved in as practical a way as possible.

The concept of value analysis can be applied to this case. It may very well be that the gears are overdesigned and could be used as they are. The case only gives the engineer's word for the need for a ground finish.

The instructor may want to use this case to discuss the wisdom of using a supplier who has performed well in one type of work to supply an entirely different type of work. The class can be asked to discuss the probability of a company that is highly efficient at building tooling, but has not had much experience at production, also being successful in production work. An experienced production company almost positively would have based its bid on a firsthand knowledge of the tooling that was to be buyer-supplied. Speedy, lacking production experience, did not look at the tooling prior to making its bid and thus incurred $25,000 in rebuilding costs.

The importance of good relations with the engineering department should be stressed. When the relationship is not one of mutual confidence, as was the case in this situation, problems are inevitable. In its discussion, the class should not overlook the fact that the final responsibility for specifications lies with the design function (engineering).

Good long-range relations with the supplier also are essential. This case is a typical situation where the possibility of pushing a company's own mistakes or oversights on a supplier is possible. A small monetary gain today must be balanced against supplier goodwill tomorrow.

Question 1:

What are the sources of the problem?

Comment:

Several factors may have contributed to the present situation: unrealistically tight toler-ances, an inflexible and possibly unreasonable engineer, inadequate specifications, and poor source selection.

Question 2:

What do you think would be an equitable solution to this problem?

Comment:

A fair solution might be for Alex to assume the cost of chroming the 32 spiders, pay Speedy $25 per unit to rebore these and future units, and also pay the additional $2,000 fixture cost.

Any fair solution must be influenced by the size of the order and the significance of the total additional cost per unit to Alex. If the order is substantial, Speedy may be negotiated into a no-cost settlement. However, by absorbing these costs, Alex can make future dealings with Speedy more friendly and therefore more mutually advantageous and profitable.

The legibility of the magnaflux marking can be increased by either applying the marking to a flat surface (if available) or by providing Speedy with a curved marking stamp. If the unsatisfactory stamp is the same stamp which was used satisfactorily by previous suppliers, in-struction in its use might be all that is required.

Alex and Speedy have had a long relationship which has apparently been satisfactory to both parties. In settling this dispute, it must be remembered that this is just one problem in a long, continuing relationship. Therefore, it is impossible to settle this problem solely on what Alex believes to be the "merits of the case," unless Speedy also agrees on these same points, which it does not. Compromise is mandatory. In searching for a compromise, the following specific facts should be discussed:

1. The parts are unsatisfactory in their present condition, but will be acceptable if chrome plated and rebored.
2. Speedy must invest in a new $2,000 fixture to bore the holes to the tolerance wanted. This additional boring operation will increase its cost per unit by $25.
3. Speedy has been forced to invest over $25,000 to repair Alex-supplied tooling to make it usable on this job.
4. The magnaflux marking stamp is also owner-supplied and will not print legibly on a curved surface.

THE CENTENNIAL COMPANY

Purpose

The purpose of this case is twofold:

1. To illustrate the financial impact purchasing decisions and material costs can have on company profitability, and to explore purchasing's role in corporate strategy decisions.
2. To consider purchasing's responsibility to provide top management with various types of operations and materials information that are useful in making top-level strategy decisions.

Discussion

It is clear in this case that top management is being pressed to achieve cost reductions wherever possible within the organization's operation. It is in the purchasing manager's best interest to have a top management group that is knowledgeable about and understands in depth the details and subtleties of the purchasing operation. A management so informed should thus understand what purchasing realistically is in a position to "bring to the table" in the proposed cost reduction effort. They should understand whether purchasing realistically can be expected to reduce material costs much further and, if so, what trade-offs will likely be involved. Similarly, if an across-the-board staff reduction is in the offing, management must again understand what the trade-offs in purchasing likely will involve. By the same token, management should be cognizant of the additional profitability purchasing may be able to generate if its staff size is increased.

An astute purchasing manager understands this situation and should assume the responsibility for orienting and educating his or her top management people. Consequently, the necessary information should flow to management from the purchasing department in a regular, systematic fashion.

Question 1:

As a purchasing manager, what is your responsibility concerning top management's knowledge and expectation of the purchasing operation?

    a. What performance data should management have been receiving?
    b. What information is necessary to control material costs?

Comment:

Purchasing management's responsibility is to "condition" top management so that it can see clearly the possible alternative courses of action for purchasing in this situation. In order to do this effectively, management should have been receiving the following data:

a. Ongoing information about:

- Specific material price and market data for key materials—and the possibility for control and further price reductions.
- Specific cost reduction achievements for given materials, the techniques utilized, and the likelihood of further cost reductions.

- The efficiency of utilization of purchasing personnel, including buying work loads, cost reduction activity work loads, supplier relationship work loads, etc.
- The complimentary and trade-off relationships between buying efficiency and buying effectiveness. In other words, if buying work loads are increased, what impact does this have on buying effectiveness for key materials?
- Specific information regarding existing contractual agreements and other unique supplier arrangements for key materials—and any expected near-term buying strategy changes.

b. Knowledge about the purchasing/sales leverage factor, and what it is possible for purchasing to accomplish, given the existing market conditions and supplier arrangements. For example, in this organization at the present time the firm's profit position can be equally improved by a 5 percent reduction in material costs or by a 65 percent increase in sales. *This situation produces a purchasing/sales leverage factor of approximately 13 to 1.* This factor will vary from time to time as the percentage of material cost changes and as the percent profit margin changes. It increases as the percentage of material costs increases, and it decreases as the profit margin increases.

The important thing to note in the Centennial case is the existence of an unusually high purchasing/sales leverage factor—13 to 1. (In a firm whose material costs are 50 percent of sales and whose profit margin before taxes is 10 percent, the purchasing/sales leverage factor is 5 to 1.) Consequently, the purchasing operation in the Centennial Company is in an unusually strong position to generate profit improvement for the firm, as compared with Centennial's sales organization. This factor obviously should be weighted heavily in management's final strategy decision.

Question 2:

What types of suggestions might the purchasing manager make in his report that would be worth exploring? Making several reasonable operating assumptions, quantify the estimated results from a profitability point of view.

Comment:

As a starting point for the analysis, the purchasing manager should point out the unusually high purchasing/sales leverage factor that exists in Centennial's operation. He should make a strong case for the fact that purchasing staff should *not* be cut, but rather that it should be expanded modestly to exploit the department's high potential for profit improvement, relative to the alternative of increasing sales. This approach assumes that the purchasing manager is reasonably confident that the addition of one or two buyers to the purchasing operation could reduce material costs noticeably through the use of better market exploration, more effective long-term contracts, and working jointly with key suppliers to reduce their costs through operations and value analysis activities.

To support this general position, the purchasing manager would probably develop several scenarios utilizing quantitative assumptions about material cost reductions, price increases, etc. Two such scenarios are developed here for illustrative purposes.

Scenario A

- Assume that the purchasing department adds two buyers at a cost increase of approximately $70,000 per year.
- Assume that these buyers are dedicated to cost reduction activities, and that they can reduce the shaver's annual material costs by approximately 10 percent.
- Assume that sales volume and shaver price remain unchanged.

Scenario B

- Assume that the shaver's selling price is increased 5 percent.
- Assume that the price increase produces a 2 percent reduction in annual shaver sales.
- Assume that all other factors remain constant.

The results of Scenario A and Scenario B are shown quantitatively in the accompanying flow diagrams. Note in these cases that Scenario A produced a profit margin increase from 5 percent to 11.24 percent, and that Scenario B produced a profit margin increase from 5 percent to 9.52 percent. In making a final analysis of such a presentation, the weights attached to the quantitative data would obviously be conditioned by a number of subjective managerial and marketing considerations. However, if the purchasing department can actually deliver a 10 percent material cost reduction, this alternative does look very attractive.

A large number of different scenarios ("what if" alternatives) could be developed for consideration in the decision-making process. The purpose of this question simply is to illustrate the significant impact that purchasing performance can have on the final outcome. It illustrates further that the purchasing manager should be a key player in the analytical process that leads to the final strategy decision. This requires a reasonably aggressive attitude and proactive posture on the part of purchasing management personnel.

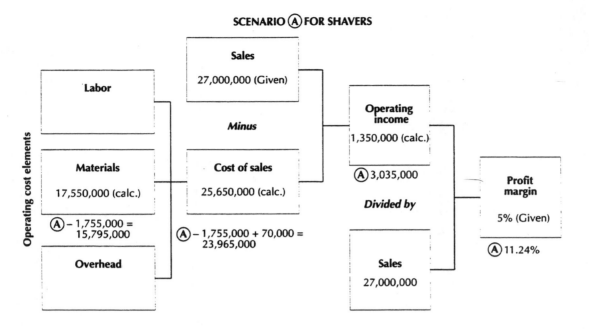

SCENARIO Ⓐ FOR SHAVERS

Operating cost elements

Labor

Materials
17,550,000 (calc.)

Ⓐ – 1,755,000 =
15,795,000

Overhead

Sales
27,000,000 (Given)

Minus

Cost of sales
25,650,000 (calc.)

Ⓐ – 1,755,000 + 70,000 =
23,965,000

Operating income
1,350,000 (calc.)

Ⓐ 3,035,000

Divided by

Sales
27,000,000

Profit margin

5% (Given)

Ⓐ 11.24%

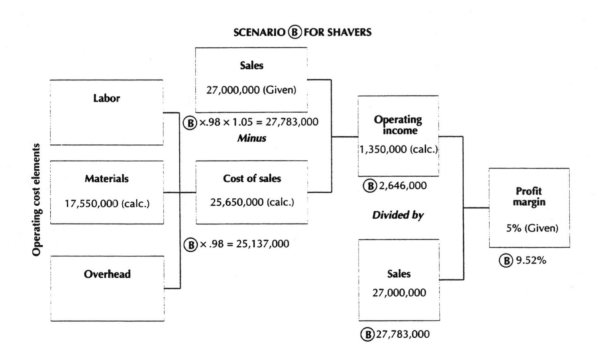

SCENARIO Ⓑ FOR SHAVERS

Operating cost elements

Labor

Materials
17,550,000 (calc.)

Overhead

Sales
27,000,000 (Given)

Ⓑ ×.98 × 1.05 = 27,783,000

Minus

Cost of sales
25,650,000 (calc.)

Ⓑ × .98 = 25,137,000

Operating income
1,350,000 (calc.)

Ⓑ 2,646,000

Divided by

Sales
27,000,000

Ⓑ 27,783,000

Profit margin

5% (Given)

Ⓑ 9.52%

CHEAPER BY THE DOZEN

Purpose

This case gives the student an opportunity to gain actual experience in determining the optimal order size. It also provides the student an opportunity to develop a common-sense or intuitive approach to solving inventory and EOQ problems without resorting to the use of mathematical models. Classroom experience indicates that many students who "black out" when confronted with the EOQ model are able to identify an optimal order quantity through the use of the tabular approach.

Question 1:

What items should be considered when determining the optimal order size?

Comment:

When the unit price for an item is a function of the quantity ordered, the following items should be considered in determining the optimal order quantity:

1. the item's cost for different order quantities
2. the item's transportation cost for different order quantities
3. inventory carrying costs associated with different quantities
4. variable order processing costs (including the solicitation of prices, preparation of the purchase order, receiving and inspection costs, and accounts payable costs)

Question 2:

What is the optimal order quantity (Q) for Coal Dust's shores?

Comment:

This problem lends itself to the development and use of a table which portrays the total annual cost of purchasing the annual requirement of shores.

Annual Demand: 16,000/year
Purchase Order Processing Cost: $60.00
Inventory Carrying Cost (ICC): 30%

Purchase Order Size (Q)	200	400	600	800	900	1000
Average Inventory (I)	100	200	300	400	450	500
Cost/Unit including Transportation	$8.75	8.00	7.75	7.75	7.75	7.75
Acquisition Cost (16,000 units)	$140,000.00	128,000.00	124,000.00	124,000.00	124,000.00	124,000.00
Cost of Carrying Inventory	$262.50	480.00	697.50	930.00	1,046.00	1,162.50
Purchase Order Processing $\left(60 \cdot \dfrac{16,000}{Q}\right)$	$4,800.00	2,400.00	1,600.00	1,200.00	1,667.00	960.00
Total	$145,062.50	130,880.00	126,297.50	126,130.00	126,113.00	126,122.50

The instructor should recommend selection of various possible purchase order quantities based on the price breaks. For example, if 399 shores are purchased, the unit price (including transportation) is $8.75. However, if 400 units are ordered, the delivered unit price drops to $8.00. Thus, the annual costs associated with purchase orders of 400 and 600 should be computed. Costs associated with a small order size of 100 or 200 should be determined. Some order quantities larger than 600 should be used as the basis of annual costs. Order size should increase until total annual costs reach a minimum and begin to climb.

Some students may not see the relationship between purchase quantity and average inventory. Use of the following diagram will prove helpful:

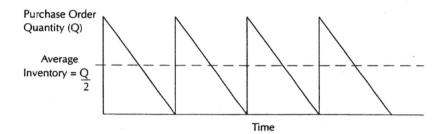

From the table, it is seen that the optimal purchase order quantity (Q) is closest to 900 units. Use of the EOQ model with a delivered price of $7.75 indicates that Q is approximately 908.

$$Q = \sqrt{\frac{2(16,000)60}{2 \times 325}} = 908$$

COLLIER COMPANY I

Purpose

The purpose of this case is to discuss various techniques, advantages, and disadvantages of securing prices by means of bid solicitation. The case also points out some of the implications of the use of this method of pricing—things such as the effect on supplier relations, business ethics involved, and the value of established procedures and sound communications. This matter of fair price determination, particularly in a depressed market, is also a major consideration.

Discussion

This is an excellent case for bringing out a full discussion of all the principles of competitive bidding.

Question 1:

What suggestions could you make regarding possible improvement in the purchasing manager's handling of this matter?

Comment:

Suggestions for possible improvement in the way the purchasing manager handled this bid situation:

a. Requests for *firm* bids would probably have averted most of the difficulties the purchasing manager encountered. There is always the possibility that firm bids might not yield as low a final price as was obtained in this case; however, in a competitive market, if suppliers know they have only one bid, they will usually offer their best price on that bid. Furthermore, a request for firm bids avoids any possibility of the subsequent charges of favoritism or sharp practice and is probably the fairest and most efficient method of handling bids.

b. It is best in such a situation to give out no information on the bids before the award decision is made. Doing so only encourages haggling and unethical practices on the part of the bidders.

c. The purchasing manager probably should have had engineering make a cost estimate on the stools before the bid closing date to give him some guide to use in evaluating the reasonableness of the bids (particularly since he knew he was dealing in a depressed market). Thus he would have been in a position to make his decision quickly after the closing date, or else to throw out all bids and request rebids.

d. Since the purchasing manager accepted revised bids from some bidders and extended the time of bidding, he was ethically obligated to notify all bidders that revised bids were being accepted and the bid time was being extended.

Question 2:

What would you recommend that he do now?

Comment:

The purchasing manager handled the supplier relations aspect of this situation very badly and has probably done irreparable damage. In the first place, he was obligated to notify Vendor C that new bids were being accepted. Even though Vendor C was remiss in his follow-up duties, the purchasing manager should never have attempted to use this fact as a scapegoat for his own errors. The contract has now been awarded (at a good price), and this decision should stand. The least the purchasing manager can do, however, is to write a letter of apology to Vendor C, admitting his error and assuring C of entirely fair treatment in future negotiations. Perhaps this will repair some of the damage that has been done.

Even though the purchasing manager was right regarding final supplier selection prerogatives, his tactless retort to Vendor F was wholly uncalled for. Generally speaking, the purchasing manager should solicit bids from only qualified suppliers with whom he is willing to do business. Thus, in the absence of restrictive quotation qualifications, it is normally expected that the low bidder will get the job. Consequently, if the purchasing manager does not award the contract to the low bidder, he must be able to justify his action. In this case Vendor F has every right to know why his bid was not satisfactory, and the purchasing manager should have explained to him specifically on what grounds it was rejected. Again, about all the purchasing manager can do now is to write a letter of apology to F explaining what he should have explained at their previous meeting.

If the purchasing manager thinks C or F really will carry out their threat of writing nasty letters to his superior, in his own interests he had probably better explain the situation to his boss first and break the ice for the rough barrage that is to follow.

For the sake of supplier relations and consistency of action, it would probably behoove the purchasing manager to set down a definite policy and procedure to be followed in future bidding situations. At this point, he appears to be playing each situation "by ear."

Questions 3:

To what extent would you concur in the purchasing manager's belief that suppliers should at least be allowed to recover direct costs?

Comment:

Price is only one of several factors which should receive purchasing consideration. In a normal business situation a producer must cover its variable and its fixed costs and also make a certain amount of profit if it wants to stay in business and develop into an established, reliable producer. During a temporary slack period, a producer may not be able to make a profit, but it must cover variable expenses. Any sale which makes a contribution to fixed costs tends to minimize the firm's short-term losses.

Thus, in a highly competitive and temporarily depressed industry, the producer is often willing to sell a product below total cost as long as it makes some contribution to fixed costs; in this way the firm is able to sustain the operation until normal conditions again prevail.

Purchasing's interest in this situation is simply this: in order to operate at optimum efficiency, any purchasing department (and the firm it represents) must develop a group of reliable suppliers who are willing to take an interest in the firm and offer various additional services which are advantageous to the firm. Such lasting cooperative supplier relations can come about only in a stable business situation in which all firms concerned prosper reasonably.

While the purchase in question may be somewhat of a "one-shot" affair, the underlying philosophy still applies. The selected supplier must receive enough to cover its variable costs and, depending upon the condition of the industry, should perhaps even receive enough to cover total costs.

Question 4:

Who do you feel should have received the order?

Comment:

Without knowing the full details of each quotation (i.e., delivery schedules, terms, adjustment provisions, and other qualifications) it is difficult to select one supplier. All things being equal, the low bidder, Vendor F, should have been awarded the contract. The total contract difference between Vendor F and Vendor D, however, is small (0.6%) and could easily be overshadowed by service or other considerations. The point is that the purchasing manager must be able to logically justify selection of any supplier other than the low bidder.

COLLIER COMPANY II

Purpose

The purpose of this case is to discuss some of the fundamental considerations of pricing using costs analysis and negotiation.

Discussion

The instructor can use this case to illustrate many of the basic principles of negotiated purchasing. Additionally, the authors have found it to be an excellent case for discussing variable, fixed, and partly variable costs. To start such a discussion, it can be pointed out that in the cost breakdowns, submitted by companies C and G, the labor and material costs are variable, while the overhead is made up of both fixed and variable costs. It can further be pointed out that in a short-run pricing situation, the fixed costs of companies C and G can be ignored. These costs would be incurred whether or not either of the companies produced the stools. A contract for the stools will increase either company's profits or decrease either company's losses to the extent that it absorbs any fixed overhead costs. These are the basic pricing facts that the purchasing manager for the Collier Company must keep in mind as he evaluates the cost breakdowns submitted by companies C and G.

Question 1:

What are some of the most important factors that will influence the cost to both C and G of the stools that are being purchased?

Comment:

The cost of a particular product to an individual manufacturer is influenced by a number of factors. While these factors themselves can be readily identified, their effect on the cost of a specific product is often difficult to assess. For purposes of this case, the most significant factors that should be considered are:

    a. Plant volume and present rate of output.
    b. Prices for material and labor.
    c. Degree of automation.
    d. Size and nature of the overhead structure.

Question 2:

How can the purchasing manager (PM) use the cost breakdown information that he has available to help him negotiate the price he wants?

Comment:

As a first step, the PM should add another column, i.e., a percentage of cost column, i.e., a percentage of cost column, to the cost breakdown information he has obtained from companies

C and G and his own engineering department. After doing this, the cost breakdown data would appear as follows:

	Company C		Company G		Collier Company Estimate	
	Cost	% of Cost	Cost	% of Cost	Cost	% of Cost
Labor	$13.20	33%	$ 9.00	23%	$13.20	29%
Material	13.08	33%	12.00	31%	13.62	31%
Overhead	13.20	33%	18.00	46%	18.00	40%
	$39.48		$39.00		$44.82	

These percentage figures suggest a number of things. For example, they disclose that G has lower labor and material costs than C, but G's overhead rate is much higher—200 percent of direct labor as contrasted to only 100 percent of direct labor for C. Labor and materials costs are variable, and they increase in direct proportion to increases in quantity; therefore, they represent actual cash outlays to the manufacturer. The PM knows that this is not true with the fixed portion of the overhead charges.

Because of the variances among C, G, and Collier's own estimated costs—particularly labor and overhead, the PM may wish to ask C and G for more breakdown information concerning labor costs and how overhead rates were developed. He may even consider the $1.08 difference in materials cost worth pursuing; if so he could ask C and G for priced bills of materials.

The PM notes, however, that in the case of C that the labor and material estimates are quite close to those made by his own production department. The relationship between the higher overhead and the lower labor and materials charges for G are logically consistent. The higher overhead rate suggests that G has more highly automated equipment than C. This permits G to perform the same operations as C, but at a lower labor and material cost. All in all, the figures suggest that competition in this purchase is good.

Question 3:

What principal negotiation arguments should the PM present to the two low bidders before requesting their final quotations?

Comment:

The PM knows from the great interest in this purchase and his knowledge of current depressed conditions that idle capacity exists. In such a situation, the buyer is in the driver's seat. He knows G really wants the order. Hence, he can point out to G that it is better for him to cover all of his variable costs, ignoring fixed costs, than it is to lose this large order. With competition as keen as it is, this is probably the only suggestion he needs to make. He can keep C interested by questioning all three of the cost elements.

Question 4:

Approximately what dollar profit do you believe the successful supplier will most likely receive from this order?

Comment:

If G accurately sensed the competition he faced from C, the final quotations could well look something like this:

	C	G
Labor	$12.60	$ 9.00
Material	12.90	12.00
Overhead	6.60	9.00
	$32.10	$30.00

At the price of $30.00, G would cover all of his direct costs of labor and material and apply $9.00 per unit to the recovery of his overhead costs. If we assume that $3.50 per unit represents the variable portion of the overhead costs and that his plant is operating at less than full capacity, then the value of this order to G is:

Fixed overhead recovery = $5.50 per unit.
Contribution from the order then is $5.50 × 850 = $4,675.00.

THE COUNTY WATER WORKS

Purpose

This case is a good vehicle to use for a general discussion of:

- The purchase of capital equipment
- The differences between capital equipment purchasing and production purchasing
- The pros and cons of standardization
- Various approaches to implementation
- The desirability and development of a centralized purchasing operation in a small organization

Analysis

Facts

The general manager wants to use the same software and hardware in all departments.

CWW does not utilize a list of pre-approved suppliers.

Concern has been expressed by the department heads over the high price of the recommended machines and the appropriateness of the chosen software to their particular department.

The department heads do not see a need for standardization of the computers and software.

CWW has a distributed purchasing system (no central purchasing department).

CWW anticipates purchasing a significant number of personal computers over the next two to four years.

CWW has a potential need for sharing information between departments in the future.

The computer committee established a set of standards, consulted suppliers for guidance in equipment selection, and recommended hardware and software to management.

Current procurement rules specify a bid process where the lowest bidder is usually awarded the contract, without regard to other procurement issues.

CWW departments anticipated buying different types of hardware and software from different suppliers.

Problem Statement

How can the County Water Works meet its current and anticipated computer needs at a reasonable cost while taking advantage of the benefits of standardization?

Alternatives

1. Instead of selecting personal computers, use a mini-computer system

   Advantages: All of the data and programs used would be compatible; all personnel would be trained on the same equipment and software; sharing of data is optimized; a common warranty and service agreement would be obtained; the per unit computer cost for a user is less; and there would be less hardware to support.

   Disadvantages: There will be a delay in the use of the system due to installation; the system may not be supported by the manufacturer in the future; a system malfunction affects all users; the system may be limited in processing ability; the system may be difficult to expand (number of terminals); and there may be a limited number of software suppliers for an integrated system.

2. Buy the least expensive computer model that fits the needs of CWW.

    Advantages: The price will stay within initial department budgets and will be justified if an outside organization audits the CWW purchase records; personal computers will meet the future needs of the departments; they will be compatible with other models; other machines can be used if one computer becomes inoperative; a common service and warranty contract can be obtained; there could be a discount for multiple orders; and there will be ease in training of personnel on one model of computer. Additionally, the purchasing department can be given the responsibility of negotiating the contract.

    Disadvantages: The computer chosen may not have the best system reliability; the warranty and service offered on that model may not compare favorably with other models; if the manufacturer is small, it may go out of business; and the selected model may be discontinued in the future.

3. Allow the departments to choose from the committee's list of recommended products.

    Advantages: this will allow the departments to choose the computer which they feel best suits their needs; it will allow the departments to stay within their approved budgets; it will allow compatible units within each department; and will allow the use of computers which have been chosen by the committee as meeting the company's needs.

    Disadvantages: This removes the purchasing department from picking the best product for the company; the products may not be compatible between departments and sharing of data will be complicated; the optimum operating platform for a department may not be available on the list or it may not be chosen; the training between departments will differ; different service contracts will have to be negotiated with suppliers; and there may be less of a discount for multiple orders.

4. Buy the hardware and software recommended by the committee.

    Advantages: The company will obtain computers which meet most of the needs of the departments; there will be compatibility among machines; other machines can be used if one computer becomes inoperative; there will be a common warranty and service contract; and there could be a discount available for multiple orders. Additionally, the purchasing department can be given the responsibility of negotiating the contract. The CWW will have software which is compatible between departments and which will allow seamless data transfer; training personnel will be easier; the group learning curve will be higher; and there may be discounts for multiple orders.

    Disadvantages: The high price of the recommended machines will need to be fully justified for any future audits; the price is above the initially approved budgets for some departments; some departments feel that they do not need such a powerful or expensive machine; and the model may not be supported by the manufacturer in the future. Some departments feel that the software does not fully meet their needs.

Recommendations

The products recommended by the committee should be selected for use by all departments in CWW. One type of software should be chosen and all departments should use it during a trial period; after the trial period, the departments desiring different software should justify the need for the additional software. After management has decided the quantity desired, bids for the items should be obtained from all potentially qualified suppliers in the local area. Additionally, pre-qualifying conditions should be established to determine which suppliers are financially stable and will be able to satisfactorily supply the desired machines and service. CWW should then establish a partnership relationship with the chosen supplier. This supplier should be chosen based on price, financial stability, service contract and warranty agreement, and its ability to meet the current and anticipated needs of the CWW.

It is additionally recommended that a centralized purchasing department be established and given the responsibility for sourcing, obtaining bids, writing contracts, and monitoring the service of contracts. This will need management support, require more personnel in purchasing, and require training and guidance on appropriate government procedures.

Question 1:

What additional information should Rick obtain or develop in preparation for the meeting?

Comment:

a. A list of advantages to CWW from standardizing the purchase
b. A list of the capabilities of the software, and a comparison with the functions required by each department to show how their needs would be met
c. Plans to show how the machines will be funded
d. A comparison of services and warranties offered by suppliers for the products
e. A list of local suppliers and general market prices

Question 2:

Identify improvements and/or additions to the procurement system that need to be implemented.

Comment:

A centralized purchasing department needs to be established and given full management support. This may require additional personnel.

Purchasing should be performing the functions of prequalifying the suppliers, sourcing materials, requesting bids, negotiating contracts, and managing the contracts.

Question 3:

How important is the issue of computer standardization?

Comment:

To the general manager, it is important because of required training of personnel on the equipment, reduction in the number of different types of software programs, ease of data transfer between departments, and the potential benefits of quantity discounts. To the department heads, standardization within their respective departments is important, but they do not identify with the requirements of other departments and therefore standardization is not perceived as an important issue. If a problem develops in one of the machines, others will be available to use with no loss in capabilities.

Question 4:

Rick feels unqualified to fully address the questions of the department heads. Who might be able to help?

Comment:

Rick should bring some of the suppliers or consultants who helped to determine which type of hardware and software would best meet the needs of CWW. They should be able to inform the department heads why a particular model type was specified, its potential future advantages, and why the particular brands were chosen. Also, members of the committee can further explain how department tasks were identified. Finance can assist with explaining the impact on budgeted allotments.

Question 5:

How can the water works enter into a long term relationship with a supplier and continue to fulfill the prerequisite of choosing the supplier with the lowest bid?

Comment:

Technically, they could not since suppliers would not be willing to guarantee that they will provide the lowest cost in the future. However, a preferred supplier can be chosen. For this situation, a memorandum of understanding can address the concerns between CWW and the supplier. As deemed appropriate, CWW will rebid the product list to ensure that the lowest priced supplier is chosen. If the preferred supplier has provided excellent service in the past, proven to be reliable, and maintains a competitive price (for example, within 5 percent of lowest price), then selection of this supplier could continue.

CWW must carefully pre-qualify all suppliers invited to bid on contracts. Items to be considered might include financial stability, ability to meet the contract, services, and warranty offered. Items to be bid on must be specified as completely as possible to prevent suppliers form bidding an inadequate product.

CWW will need to identify specific reasons why a particular model type is chosen, and these reasons should be written down to justify their decision should any audits be conducted in the future. This should also be done when they decide upon a supplier, identifying reasons why a specific supplier was chosen over others.

When discussing the contract, fluctuating market prices must be addressed (market prices drop below contract price, or supplier costs rise above contract price). The service agreement should also include a list of services rendered to CWW (training, cleaning, maintenance), and it should specify which services are not provided.

What Actually Happened

Rick asked the two suppliers to attend the meeting, ready to answer the concerns of the department heads. The meeting went well; by the end of it, the department heads agreed to all of the recommendations made by the committee. The general manager included funds in a revision to the budget to cover the additional expenses, and as he predicted, the Board was more interested in buying a reputable name than in the savings through the use of less established manufacturers.

A software supplier was chosen as the preferred supplier. No contract was signed but CWW did negotiate competitive corporate rates. The supplier is kept "honest" by comparing prices to other suppliers randomly and without notice. A similar arrangement was reached with the hardware supplier.

Standardizing the software and hardware has saved countless dollars in terms of saved work, training, and backup hardware. In terms of saved work, once information is entered into one application in one department, it never has to be entered again by anyone else. CWW also received group training discounts. CWW employees share knowledge about the hardware and software with their co-workers, which greatly accelerates the learning curve. Having the same hardware available in another department to use when needed has proven useful in keeping the workload flowing.

Procurement issues are beginning to be addressed. A plan is underway to centralize purchasing. Currently, one person in each of four departments acts as a buyer. CWW is looking at the possibility of grouping these workers together, hiring a manager and creating a separate procurement function.

CROSSING THE BORDER

Purpose

This case illustrates some of the issues and problems that exist when part of the manufacturing process is in another country. Japan happens to be a small, more or less culturally uniform country where creating a just-in-time environment is easier than in this case. Including two additional countries in the manufacturing process makes a JIT system more difficult to operate.

Suggested Student Assignment

You are the TAI plant manager. You need to develop and implement a Just-in-Time system. What team of individuals do you assemble and what process/system do you request the team to develop? Create a flow chart of the process.

Possible Discussion Questions

1. Is Just-in-Time manufacturing possible at the maquiladora? Why or why not?
2. Should bribes be used in the regular course of TAI business with the Mexican maquiladora? Under what circumstances, if any, might this type of bribe be acceptable?
3. If the process at the Mexican maquiladora is critical, should Tokisan continue to use the Mexican operation as part of its JIT production system? Discuss.

Analysis

Immediate Issue:

1. The immediate issue clearly is: "What should Katie do that will insure continued production at the maquiladora?"

Basic Issues:

1. How can TAI decrease and stabilize the time required to supply the maquiladora with material?
2. How can TAI install a JIT operation, given the problems that appear to be outside the control of TAI?

Comment:

Often, when an established system that has operated well receives an external shock, such as the strike in this case, the traumatic event reveals the weaknesses of the system. And management must be empowered and able to make quick decisions effectively.

1. Can major purchases from TAI suppliers be scheduled on a JIT basis to develop a smoothly functioning JIT operation at the U.S. Tai operation? How long will it take to develop such an operation.
2. After number 1 is accomplished and stabilized (if possible) can the TAI production schedule be coupled with the maquiladora's production schedule to provide a flow type

operation? Can this be done with a minimal part and component inventory being maintained at the Mexican maquiladora operation?

3. Identify precisely the normal potential time requirements in the material flow system from TAI to the maquiladora operation. How much inventory must be held at the maquiladora to provide coverage for *normal* and anticipated *maximum* time requirements?

4. Investigate each major activity or time delay and attempt to minimize the probability of the delay occurring, as well as the length of the delay itself.

5. Can a long-term arrangement be worked out with the Mexican Customs officials to minimize the time required for clearance at the border? If not, should TAI seriously consider paying the minor transaction bribes requested?

- How many dollars would be involved in this action?
- What legal issues are involved?
- What ethical issues are involved?

What Actually Happened

TAI was successful in developing a JIT production and purchasing operation in its own facility. It was able to work with most of its key suppliers to ship several times a week, permitting the maintenance of low inventories at TAI's plant. It did not attempt to JIT its MRO and low value materials.

TAI increased its shipment volume to the maquiladora, but not enough to cover all system delays. The strike did occur, and production continued until raw material was exhausted. Production was stopped for only one day.

After the strike was over, the company stocked roughly one week of supply at the maquiladora. Although this was not a true JIT operation, it was thought to be the best possible solution, given the circumstances. However, management was still not satisfied with the process, and the possibility of further modifications were being explored.

THE DEAR JOHN MOWER COMPANY

Tom has his work cut out! One of purchasing and supply management's most challenging tasks is to get its internal customers, whether in design engineering, plant engineering, administration, etc. to recognize and accept the advantages of early purchasing and supplier involvement in the development of materials, equipment, and services to be provided by outside suppliers. The keys are: (1) the presence of professionals in purchasing who will add value through their and their suppliers' early involvement, and (2) the use of marketing skills by these professionals to convince their customers—and, perhaps—management of the necessity of early involvement. (It is interesting to note that marketing skills are as essential to purchasing professionals as they are to sales personnel!)

1. Prepare a list of advantages of the inclusion of purchasing and pre-qualified suppliers.

    The advantages of including purchasing and pre-qualified suppliers include:

    *   reduced time to market
    *   improved quality
    *   reduced costs

2. Prepare a list of disadvantages of excluding purchasing and suppliers from the new product development process.

    *   quality problems resulting in redesign, rework, retrofit, and field failures
    *   cost overruns
    *   foregone cost savings
    *   major scheduling problems
    *   new products which are late to market
    *   failure to recognize problems in a timely manner

3. Assuming that the three executives agree on early involvement of purchasing and suppliers, develop a plan to implement this new way of doing business.

Rather than going from no involvement to involvement on all projects all at once, many supply professionals would begin with a sample or showcase project. A member of the purchasing staff who can "add value": one who can read prints, knows his or her suppliers, and can speak "engineeringese" and one who has exemplary people and team skills should be invited by Mr. Steel and the new product project manager/engineer to participate in a key project. This individual, in turn, should invite a carefully pre-qualified supplier (and one acceptable to engineering) to participate in the project at the appropriate point.

Another approach which we have seen work with good success is to invite a key procurement professional and the senior engineer who will become involved on a new project to attend (together) a course on value engineering/value analysis and/or a high quality procurement/supply management conference such as ones conducted by the National Association of Purchasing Management, the Conference Board, or the University of San Diego.

DELTA STEEL COMPANY

Purpose

The purpose of this case is to discuss three important sources of supply questions: (1) should a single supplier or multiple supplier be used? (2) how much weight, if any, should be given to trade relations considerations? and (3) under what circumstances, if any, should local suppliers be given economic preference over suppliers located some distance away?

Question 1:

If you were the president of the Delta Steel Company, what decision would you make regarding this controversy? Explain why.

Comment:

The president should decide in favor of the director of purchasing because:

a. Trade relations have great value to both buyer and seller.
b. Eureka has not asked to be released from its contractual obligations.
c. The ninety-day termination clause will provide a safety factor if Delta must eventually establish other sources of supply.
d. The loss of Eureka as a supplier to Delta because of a fire, or for any other reason, would not have the disastrous effect on Delta that the loss of its Hydro-Matic transmission plant (discussed in the text) had on G.M. Sulphuric acid is a standard commodity manufactured by many producers; hence, the loss of any single producer would not materially reduce total supply. Supply would be available at a price. Since Delta is saving $225,000 to $340,000 per year because of the Eureka contract (15%–20% of $1,700,000), plus gaining other benefits, a reasonable risk is justified of having temporarily to pay higher prices should getting new sources of supply ever become necessary.

Question 2:

With respect to sulphuric acid or any other item of major importance, what are the advantages and disadvantages of concentrating purchases with a single supplier?

Comment:

There is a great difference between materials with standard specifications, which are manufactured in many factories and have wide geographic distribution (such as sulphuric acid) and high-technology or costly proprietary products (such as G.M. Hydro-Matic transmissions). Keeping these difference in mind, the advantages and disadvantages of using a single supplier are:

Advantages

a. better trade relations—easier adjustments of commitments even to the point of cancellation of a current schedule of shipments
b. greater purchasing power—better terms, larger discounts
c. better service and deliveries

d. easier inspection at supplier plant

e. more uniform and consistent quality

f. less inventory investments and less storage space—supplier frequently maintains stock or guarantees a schedule of deliveries

g. lower shipping costs with carload shipments

h. opportunity for and greater likelihood of cooperative research and development by supplier and purchaser

i. less purchasing time and attention—also, contract buying ordinarily involves less clerical effort in the purchasing office

Disadvantages

j. the hazard of interrupted supply owing to strikes, fire, or other unforeseen difficulties

k. inability to take advantage of price fluctuations, unless contract includes an escalator provision

l. difficulty of comparing quality and service on a continuous basis

m. inability to obtain the reciprocal business of many suppliers

n. great difficulty of dropping a supplier in favor of new and different source of supply

o. problem of selecting the best single supplier from a group of qualified sources and insuring that the one supplier continues to be the best

Question 3:

What are your reactions to the proposition of patronizing home industries as advanced by the salesmen of the local acid manufacturers?

Comment:

Local industries do not have to have pricing identical with more distant industries because of the inherent advantages of a close local source. These advantages include a potential for carrying smaller inventories, lower transportation costs, and ease in integrating buyer and seller operations. However, the local supplier must be competitive when *all* considerations are weighed. In this case the local price level would seem to be excessive.

Question 4:

The director of purchasing in the Delta Steel Company reported to the president. Under what circumstances do you think the purchasing function should enjoy equal organizational status with such other functions as engineering, production, sales, and finance?

Comment:

The circumstances under which the purchasing function should enjoy equal organizational status with engineering, production, sales, and finance are the following:

a. when materials cost constitutes a large proportion of total cost

b. when consumption of materials and suppliers is widely dispersed and where sources are worldwide in location

   c. when forward buying or even extensive market buying is practiced. Here the advanced commitment of substantial funds is involved, and responsibility cannot or should not be delegated through subordinate echelons or levels

   d. when a large volume of purchases is for resale

   e. when reciprocal buying contributes importantly to profit

   f. when the operating organization pattern of a company is on a product-division, a regional-division, or a subsidiary-company basis, and where corporatewide purchasing policies and practices need to be established and made uniform, and where major or common needs of the divisions can best be purchased centrally

   g. when certain other important functions, i.e., overall inventory control, warehousing, and traffic, etc., are combined with purchasing and are headed up by the chief purchasing executive—such departments are in reality materials management departments, but many are still called purchasing departments

   h. when production and sales are conducted on a highly decentralized basis but are directed centrally by functional executives. Here it is necessary to coordinate purchasing with production, sales, and finance at headquarters

   i. when production is carried on in many locations but at a volume which locally could not justify purchasing service

   j. when a very large volume of subcontracting is done; the importance of the purchasing function in this situation is measured not alone by the amount of money involved, but also by the technical and other relationships of the purchasing company with the suppliers

DIATECH VERSUS RPM

Purpose

The purpose of this case is to illustrate the importance of cohesive contract and subcontract management. A contract management system integrates procurement, quality control, and materials engineering to monitor contracts and resolve problems.

Discussion

This case illustrates a problem of subcontract management at Diatech. Paula Green, a senior buyer, did not assume a proactive role in administering the RPM contract. The specifics of the contract were outlined by the manager of materials engineering. The contract failed to specify provisions for quality control approval, a milestone plan, and reporting requirements. There was even a dispute regarding ownership of the tools. Paula received the contract and approved it without alteration. Further, she did not investigate the progress at RPM until the schedule had slipped to the point that the introduction of Spectrum II was in doubt.

Facts

The major facts of the case are as follows:

1. RPM had originally committed to a mold fabrication time of ten to twelve weeks.
2. Three months have passed and RPM claims to be half complete. Thus RPM has taken more time than estimated.
3. Two major contract disputes have arisen:
   a. RPM has stopped production, demanding a second payment of $14,734. Diatech will not pay the second installment because specifications have not been met.
   b. There is a dispute over ownership and definition of the tools. The contract is not explicit in either of these matters.
4. Contract management responsibilities are not clearly defined at Diatech.
5. Diatech suspects financial problems at RPM.

Question 1:

What alternatives are available to Diatech at this stage?

Comment:

1. Diatech can make the second payment of $14,734 in order to continue the relationship with RPM. This would be a gesture of good faith that could move RPM to action. On the other hand, RPM may accept payment and never meet the schedule or specifications. If this alternative is taken, Diatech should negotiate with RPM on the issues of a milestones plan and quality requirements before the check is issued. Once the agreement is made, RPM could be paid and, hopefully, the work will continue.
2. Diatech could refuse the second payment until the first mold has been reworked to meet the specifications. The advantage of this alternative is that specifications would be met

without payment. But this could also lead to more schedule delays, or RPM may not be able to continue work, necessitating a search for another supplier.

3. Diatech could attempt to obtain the tools in their incomplete state and contract with a new supplier for the completion of the tools. While it may be possible to find a supplier with whom Diatech may enjoy a better working relationship, there may be a legal dispute over the contract and the tools. Besides, there is a good chance that Diatech would be forced to sacrifice the initial payment, and it may have to put up with increased costs and further delays.

4. Legally terminate the relationship with RPM. The advantages and drawbacks of this alternative are the same as the previous one without the potential suits.

5. Assess the financial status of RPM. This may lead to some conclusions about the corporate behavior of RPM.

Question 2:

Which alternative should Paula choose?

Comment:

The best solution to this problem of poor subcontract management and a standoff situation is to choose the first alternative. This alternative is the least costly, and less time will be lost putting the Spectrum II in the marketplace. Paula should arrange to make the second payment only after:

1. establishing production schedule milestones
2. instituting contractual quality control approval procedures
3. instituting delay penalties
4. developing reporting requirements and a monitoring system. In addition, she should correct the monitoring situation at Diatech. Specifically, Paula should organize a contract management team and system to include all responsible functional organizations to monitor and manage contracts and subcontracts.

Conclusion

Contract and subcontract management cannot be delegated to third parties or left to the responsibility of the contractor. Specifications in a contract must be explicit. The proactive buyer must assure that the terms of a contract mean the same to both parties. In summation, both parties must develop a good working relationship to resolve any problems that arise.

DONLEY BROTHERS

Purpose

The purpose of this case is to explore the question of make versus buy—focusing particularly on the contribution to overhead that is involved in a make-buy decision.

Discussion

This is an excellent case for discussing the question of who is responsible for make-buy decisions and what role purchasing should play in these decisions. Some students may believe that decisions on making or buying should be left solely to top management. Others may believe so strongly in the purchasing function that they would have this decision left to purchasing. The instructor should explain to the class that Purchasing certainly should participate actively all make-buy decisions, but that the final choice must remain with top management.

The case states that the reason for considering buying rather than making is the present 12 percent defective rate. Many students will fail to recognize the important fact that all defects must be part of *any* price paid. It may indeed be that a supplier that machines its own castings could have a lower rate of defects than Donley Brothers has; thus, the firm could quote a lower price. However, it is entirely possible that the supplier might have a higher defect rate.

The prospective supplier is a foundry. The class should discuss the wisdom of using a supplier for work in which it is not expert. Purchasing history is replete with buyers who learned, to their sorrow, that just because a company excels in one line of work, no guarantee exists for its excelling in a different line. One of the primary reasons for buying instead of making is to take advantage of the specialty supplier and its proven ability in a specialized field.

Many students will presume that Donley Brothers can only buy or make. Actually, many companies make part *and* buy part of their requirements for the same item. In such cases, the outside supplier becomes an accurate cost barometer for the firm's internal manufacturing operation. The answer to the sole-source question in this case could easily be that the second source could be Donley's itself. With present production at 90 percent of capacity, partial use of an outside source might be a very practical solution.

Question 1:

Should Bob Donley contract with Akron Foundry for finished castings?

Comment:

Before Bob decides whether or not to contract with Akron, he should first investigate the cause of the defective castings. It may be that by means of new manufacturing and inspection methods, Donley Brothers can stop or at least reduce the rejection rate. If Donley Brothers finds ways to lower the rejection rate, it will stand to gain.

Donley Brothers, in cooperation with its supplier, should call in specialists to examine the existing patterns, the methods of pouring, inspection methods employed, ability to detect failures, and so forth. In short, a full-scale study should be made to be sure that all of the recent developments in casting technology are being applied to this problem. If this full-scale study discloses that advanced casting technology is being fully exploited, then it is proper for Bob Donley to start his consideration of the make or buy question.

The make or buy consideration should start with the most elementary computations. The cost of making 1,000 good castings is based on three principle elements of cost: materials, labor, and overhead. One thousand and one hundred forty (1,140) raw castings must be purchased and machined in order to provide the 1,000 good finished castings required by Donley Brothers each year.

Annual Cost to Make 1,000 Finished Castings

Materials (raw castings)	$600 × 1,140 =	$ 684,000
Labor	$156 × 1,140 =	$ 177,840
Overhead	$156 × 1,140 =	$ 177,840
		$1,039,680

The cost to purchase 1,000 good finished castings is $1,000 × 1,000 = $1,000,000.

On the face of things, it *appears* that purchasing the annual requirement of 1,000 finished castings is less expensive ($1,000,000) than making the finished castings ($1,039,680). But such a conclusion overlooks the contribution to overhead resulting from making the castings. Overhead at Donley Brothers currently is 100 percent of direct labor or $156 per casting. Fifty percent of this overhead is fixed and 50 percent is variable. Thus, the true variable (out-of-pocket) cost of making 1,000 good castings is:

Annual *Variable* Cost to Make

Materials	$600 × 1,140 =	$ 684,000
Labor	$156 × 1,140 =	$ 177,840
Variable Overhead	$ 78 × 1,140 =	$ 88,920
		$ 950,760

Thus, the variable cost of making is less ($950,760) than buying ($1,000,000). A contribution of $49,240 to fixed overhead results if Donley Brothers makes the castings—provided that the firm is operating below capacity.

This analysis ignores any real costs of production disruptions and lost sales. Investigations must be conducted into whether such "costs" are emotional or real. If real, then estimates should be made as to their size. The investigation should also determine if any such costs could be avoided by maintaining a buffer stock of finished castings.

Question 2:

Would there be any dollar savings by contracting with Akron if Donley Brothers's machine shop were operating at full capacity?

Comment:

This is a difficult question whose answer is "It depends." If Donley Brothers were operating at full capacity but *not* turning down potentially profitable work, then making the castings would still provide a contribution to fixed overhead. Under these conditions, if Donley were to buy the finished castings, total fixed overhead would remain the same, resulting in other production items being assessed a higher fixed overhead rate. This in turn would result in each of these items becoming less profitable.

However, if as a result of buying the finished castings Donley Brothers can apply its productive resources (plant, equipment, labor, and management) to items which yield a higher contribution to fixed overhead and, hopefully, to profit, then it is in the firm's best interest to buy finished castings.

Question 3:

What are the dangers involved if Akron becomes the sole source for Donley Brothers?

Comment:

If Akron becomes the sole source for the castings, there are two major problem areas the class should discuss.

1. Donley Brothers is tied to Akron. They are "locked in." If Akron fails to perform, then Donley Brothers is in trouble.
2. Donley Brothers will have an obligation to Akron that may be difficult to break. Akron may tie its future to Donley Brothers, and loss of Donley Brothers's business may financially bankrupt Akron.

As mentioned in the discussion section, a possible second source could be Donley Brothers itself.

Question 4:

Who is responsible for the make-or-buy decision?

Comment:

The make-or-buy decision is principally a management decision. The chief executive officer (CEO) of a small or medium-size firm normally would make the decision. In larger firms, in some industries, the decision is sometimes made at a level below the CEO yet at an organizational level high enough to insure that the financial well-being of the firm is properly considered. The decision maker should have reliable input from production, finance (on the true cost of making), and purchasing.

Question 5:

What other suggestions can you make for improving the situation at Donley Brothers?

Comment:

1. It is possible that the terms and conditions of the purchase order under which the raw castings presently are purchased are deficient. Quality standards, the right of source inspection (monitoring of the supplier's production and quality control processes), provision for damages, etc., all need to be covered in the purchase order.
2. Donley Brothers may find it cost effective to have a casting engineer review the present supplier's production process. Perhaps the number of holes and cracks can be reduced.

Frequently, an industrial customer will find it to be in its best interests to provide technical assistance to its suppliers.

3. Some of Donley's present problems in the area of production disruptions could be reduced or avoided were an adequate buffer stock of finished castings available.

4. The perceptive student may ask: "Why select a *casting* shop to *machine* the castings?" It appears possible that Bob Donley, the purchasing manager, may not have done an adequate job of sourcing.

5. The machined casting appears to be an excellent candidate for value analysis. What does the finished casting do? What else would do the job? What would be the alternative cost? Are the tolerances realistic? Are commercially available substitutes available? Etc., etc.

DRIVE SHAFT DECISION: CASE A

Purpose

1. This case can be used to illustrate the interrelationship of supplier selection by the purchasing function with many of the other functional areas and the ultimate end product. It illustrates that supplier quality and reliability are vital to the success of the firm.

2. This case can be used so that the class can get a feel for the many decisions that need to be made very quickly when a major quality problem occurs with a purchased part.

3. This case can be used to discuss the importance of good communication and quality assurance whenever a new part, or an existing part from a different source, is being procured. It illustrates that even a very reliable source may have problems with a new and different item.

4. This case also illustrates that it is important not to "burn bridges" with past suppliers; they may be an important resource in the future.

Immediate Issue

1. What actions must Robert Hardin take to minimize the damages/loss from the defective drive shaft?

Basic Issues

1. How should initial shipments from a new supplier be inspected?
2. How should samples of an item from a new source be treated when determining acceptability?
3. How do decisions made by the purchasing function in supplier selection affect the firm's overall image, quality, and product availability?

Suggested Student Assignments

1. If you were Robert Hardin, what steps would you take?
2. List all the decisions that need to be made.
3. Develop alternatives for each decision.
4. Make a decision and justify that decision.

Possible Discussion Questions

1. What is the first thing that Robert should do? Why?
2. What do you see as the cause of this problem?
3. Could this problem have been prevented? How?
4. Who, if anyone, is responsible for the current situation?
5. Should the previous supplier be approached at this point? If not, why not? If so, what should Robert say to him?

Analysis

This is a complex case for a number of reasons. There are many issues which Robert Hardin needs to address:

1. Contact BPT. Have them stop production, if production is occurring, and figure out what went wrong.
2. Stop production using this part at DMW.
3. Determine if the first batch was also defective.
4. If first batch was defective, locate and replace all parts used in production. This may mean pulling the parts out of machines that have been assembled.
5. Find replacement parts either from BPT or alternative source.
6. Determine whether they should allow BPT to supply this part, or go immediately to another supplier for the cotton picker drive shaft.
7. Expedite a replacement shipment to prevent lost sales, down time, etc.
8. Determine the cost of replacement, and who is going to pay for the parts and labor.
9. Determine the impact this problem will have/should have on DMW's relationship with this supplier.

The most immediate concerns are items 1–3, which should all be addressed simultaneously. Based on the results of 1, a decision can be made regarding how to handle items 5 and 6. Clearly, this is going to cost the company some money to fix. More importantly, if they don't get replacement parts soon, they will miss the very seasonal selling period for the current year.

Perhaps this problem could have been prevented if DMW insisted that BPT use the proper materials in the sample, or required that a certain material supplier be used, or if the first batch had been subjected to more rigorous testing. However, there was no apparent reason to complete additional tests on the first shipment.

Much of the problem stems from miscommunication and cultural differences. The Koreans are very anxious to please American companies and to gain their business. Sometimes they will agree to or say they understand things even if they do not. Experience has taught DMW that Korean firms must demonstrate their understanding, not just say that they understand.

It is impossible to say who is to blame for this problem. It was a new experience for DMW. Focusing on fixing the problem, and learning from mistakes, is more important than placing blame.

Approaching the previous supplier is probably premature. BPT has performed well up to this point. DMW must express the urgency of the situation, and give BPT a chance to fix the problem. On the other hand, transit time from Korea is extensive. The previous supplier might be approached as a fill in, until BPT's capability with this part is established.

THE DUTZEL DIESEL CASE

Purpose

This case focuses on the nuances of doing business overseas. We live in an interdependent world. While we may prefer to buy at home in order to "protect our nation's jobs and industry," purchasing managers and buyers must be aware of two important factors: (1) Foreign industries, governments, and citizens purchase many goods, services, and foods from us. Their ability to make such purchases depends on our willingness to "buy foreign." (2) Any firm which embraces a policy of paying premium prices for goods and services purchased in America runs a higher risk of becoming less competitive and possibly going out of business than does its more cost-conscious competitors.

Question 1:

Do you believe that foreign purchasing is destined to give purchasing managers and buyers an increasing number of problems? Discuss.

Comment:

Buying in international markets introduces problems not encountered in domestic markets. The most difficult problem is that of communications. The buyer and seller must communicate in a common language, frequently one that is foreign to one of the parties. The buyer must also understand the nature and the customs of the foreign country in which he is buying. Other areas of possible problems include: standards and quality, problems of lead time, import licenses, currency differences and exchange rates, non-tariff barriers, requirements for offsets, laws, customs, business ethics, exchange restraints, documentation requirements, payment terms, government controls, and transportation facilities and practices.

In spite of all of these problems, international buying is more common than ever and probably will continue to increase. Many foreign suppliers have excellent technical skill and facilities. In most cases, they make excellent and dependable suppliers. Also, international trade increases the prosperity of all trading partners by creating a larger pie for all to share.

Question 2:

What is the easiest way for buyers to start making foreign purchases?

Comment:

For many firms, the best way to start making foreign purchases is to place their initial orders with a trading company or an import merchant. Trading companies guarantee the quality of the items they handle and they take care of all of the necessary documentation and financing, which normally is in U.S. dollars. Import merchants buy and inventory commodities for their own account. They take care of all documentation. They sell through their own outlets. Purchasing from them is like dealing with a domestic supplier.

If a large dollar value of business is involved and if the buyer has the required knowledge of foreign business practices, dealing directly with foreign suppliers generally is more economical than dealing with a trading company or import merchant.

Question 3:

If you were Jack how would you decide this issue?

Comment:

To make a correct decision, Jack must examine four aspects of this procurement: (1) technical, (2) delivery and service, (3) cost, and (4) dependability and survivability of the selected supplier. Jack can complete much of his investigation before planning a trip to Europe.

On the technical issue, it appears that the project manager is indifferent concerning the Dutzel and Great American engines. However, this issue should be explored in greater detail. What are the reliability, maintainability, and marketing implications of each engine? The program manager will want to obtain input from Dynamite's engineering and marketing departments on these issues. As a point of interest, many American firms purchase overseas due to the technical excellence of some foreign suppliers.

Timely delivery of the required engines is a major concern to the Dynamite Truck Company. The longer the supplier pipeline, the greater the possibility of disruption. Jack should discuss with Dutzel Diesel the plans Dutzel has to comply with Dynamite's requirements for engines and for any extraordinary service that might be required. Late delivery of engines can mean lost sales. After seeing Dutzel's plans to comply with Dynamite's needs, Jack should check with other U.S. Dutzel customers and other purchasers of similar West German equipment to learn if delivery and service are problems. As a point of interest, many U.S. firms which purchase overseas indicate that once the initial bugs are removed from the applicable procedures, overseas suppliers can be as or more dependable than their U.S. counterparts.

In addition to the obvious difference in purchase price of $2,024 per unit, Jack should investigate other less obvious costs. Would selection of the foreign supplier require larger inventories of engines and spare parts? Will additional administrative costs be involved in dealing with the West German firm? (For example, a pre-award survey involving 3 to 4 people could cost well over $10,000). Again, other purchasing personnel with relevant international experience should be contacted for information on such costs.

Some of the required information on the dependability and survivability of Dutzel Diesel can be obtained in the United States. Other firms doing business with Dutzel and a member of the economic mission at the Embassy of the Federal Republic of Germany in Washington may be able to provide information on Dutzel's financial status.

If after conducting the above investigations, Dutzel appears to be the most attractive potential supplier, then Jack should develop a pre-award survey team. The team should visit Galisdorf to determine if Dutzel will be a willing, capable, and dependable supplier who is still likely to be an efficient producer in five, ten, or more years.

THE DYNAFLIGHT CASE

Purpose

The purpose of this case is to demonstrate the difficulties which may be experienced in attempting to apply ethical procurement practices.

Discussion

This case suggests that standards of ethical conduct must have the clear and unqualified support of the majority of employees in order to be effective. In order to gain and measure this support, training and other means of instilling ethical standards must have a built-in proactive feedback mechanism and not rely on reactive feedback.

Question 1:

What are the options that Williamson faces in writing up the electrical contract?

Comment:

a. Williamson can write up the contract for Shining Light and submit it to her department head for approval.
b. She can write up the contract for Eveready.
c. She can include the facilities manager in the decision-making process by soliciting cost quotations and pointing out the cost differences between the two companies.

Question 2:

What are the principle sources of conflict that Williamson faces in preparing contracts?

Comment:

The principle sources are the entrenched ways the department heads do business with suppliers, coupled with a weak purchasing department.

Question 3:

What resources are available to Williamson to support her desires to reach a fair and equitable contract for electrical maintenance?

Comment:

The primary resource is the company rulebook. In the environment at the division, this resource does not appear to have a lot of value. It is up to Williamson to establish its value for the company. In order to achieve her objective, Williamson may have to educate the department heads on both company policy *and* the reasons for the policy being the way it is, especially the ethical reasons.

Question 4:

What is the prevailing atmosphere at the division regarding procurement?

Comment:

The prevailing atmosphere is an "old boy" operation that can get things done in a quicker and more effective manner than if operations were run by the book. It is ironic to note that the biggest obstacle to efficient by-the-book operations is the old boy network.

Question 5:

Do you think the department heads at the division would view their actions to circumvent company policy regarding procurement as unethical?

Comment:

This depends on the amount of exposure to the ethics program that they have received and the company emphasis on adhering to the ethics policy. It is entirely probable that they do not think they are behaving unethically and, in fact, believe that they are serving the best interests of the company by cutting through a lot of red tape.

Question 6:

What breakdown in the ethics policy occurred at the division?

Comment:

Probably the biggest breakdown came from the procurement department head. He knows the score and should have brought conditions at the plant into line with company policy.

Another breakdown is that the ethics policy does not appear to have an effective feedback mechanism on how it is received throughout the company. At the California Division, there seems to be little concern about the ethics program.

Question 7:

Do you think the corporate ethics department is aware of the goings-on at the California Division?

If so, why have no actions been taken?

If not, why not?

Comment:

The corporate ethics department probably is not aware of the goings-on. It appears likely that no one has ever bought the issue to the attention of the ethics department. The turnover rate in the purchasing department is over 25 percent. Professional buyers who are frustrated with conditions are simply leaving. Those remaining are the ones who have adapted to the unwritten rule of not making waves.

Relying on "informants and whistle-blowers" is the most common way that ethics departments receive indications of conditions gone awry. Unfortunately, this is probably the least effective way of nurturing employee behavior in favor of ethical policies. Especially in the area of procurement, a company ethics program must have some means of proactively seeking to get into the act; the rare individual that ethics departments rely on to stand up to questionable actions may be motivated by a personal set of values, and not by any perceived conflict with company policies.

Ethics policies, in order to have more impact on day-to-day activities, must have an ongoing training program that looks at recent cases for lessons learned. The attitude that must be fostered is not that an ethics department sits in judgment of those who have done wrong, but rather that the ethics department is a reference source that should be turned to frequently for guidance and suggestions in the day-to-day activities of employees.

Question 8:

How can the company change the existing atmosphere at the Long Sand Division?

Comment:

First the ethics department must be made aware of what's going on. After that, the quickest way, and probably the least effective way in the long run, is to go in kicking rears and taking names. A more effective means, but one that would take longer, is to consider that if there are problems at the California Division in complying with the company ethics policy, there must be something wrong with the way the policy is being communicated to the employees.

DYNAMIC AIRCRAFT

Purpose

The purpose of this case is to explore the important question of modifications in specifications suggested by members of the purchasing department.

Discussion

The extent to which buyers should question specifications submitted by engineers is one that calls forth a wide range of opinions. No buyer would argue that final determination is his responsibility; that responsibility would require a degree of technical knowledge most buyers simply do not possess. On the other hand, a conscientious buyer, such as Mr. Marshall in this case, might feel that his experience and his knowledge of the commodities he is buying entitle him at least to *challenge* specifications. The right of purchasing to challenge specifications is directly provided for or implicitly allowed in the purchasing policy manuals of most progressive companies. Some of the reasons for giving purchasing this right, and some of the problems that are raised because of this right, are the subjects for examination in the discussion of this case. The right becomes more tenuous in situations involving high risks such as the risk of human life, the risk of big law suits, etc.

Question 1:

If you were Mr. Marshall, what action would you take now?

Comment:

There are at least six courses of action open to Mr. Marshall at this point. He can (a) award the contract to Advanced; (b) refer the case to his boss, the purchasing manager; (c) continue to press his case with the engineering department; (d) negotiate a better price with Advanced; (e) split the order; (f) work directly with the engineer in question.

Some members of the class may argue that Mr. Marshall should simply award the business to Advanced. After all, he has questioned the engineer's judgement in the matter and has been told that despite the availability of other sources that can meet the specifications at a lower price, the engineers still want Advanced's wire. Since final determination of specifications rests with engineering, perhaps Mr. Marshall should give in at this point and award the business to Advanced. Mr. Marshall feels that engineering has been "sold a bill of goods" with respect to Advanced's wire, but it must be remembered that this is simply an interpretation on Mr. Marshall's part and not necessarily the fact of the situation. The engineers may very well have sound technical reasons in mind for specifying Advanced—reasons about which Mr. Marshall may know very little.

Other members of the class may argue that the problem which has arisen in this case is too important a one to drop before reaching some sort of conclusion which harmonizes the interests and the prerogatives of both purchasing and engineering and which properly balances technical and economic considerations. The wires submitted by the other sources, it should be remembered, meet the governing specifications. There is no question of purchasing attempting to substitute new specifications. Since the wires submitted by the other companies meet the governing specifications, it can be argued that purchasing should be free to decide which of the several sources it should deal with. Since the current problem involves engineering and is representative of problems which have occurred in the past, Mr. Marshall might bring it to the attention of his boss, the purchasing manager, rather than attempt to solve it on his own.

The purchasing manager could, if he wished, make an issue of the case. If he decided that this was a wise policy to pursue, he could get together with the head of engineering and thrash out with him, on an informal basis, the respective responsibilities of the two departments. Such a meeting need not lead to anger and should be conducted on a friendly basis. Nevertheless, the purchasing manager should be forthright in defending his prerogatives. Essentially, he would argue that his department has been given the right to challenge specifications but not to change them or make a final determination on specifications. The reason why top management has given purchasing the right to challenge specifications is to increase profits by reducing costs and make available to engineering any useful information the purchasing department may possess or acquire. If engineering does not pay attention to the suggestions which purchasing offers, there is no point in giving purchasing the right to challenge.

If the purchasing manager gets nowhere in his discussions with the head of engineering, he probably has no immediate alternative other than to go along with engineering and buy Advanced's wire. However, in this eventuality, the buyer should keep a record of why the award was made to Advanced. Over a period of time, situations like this may accumulate, and each time one occurs the purchasing manager or the materials manager should be informed. If a number of such situations have accumulated, the problem may merit the attention of top management. In raising the issue with top management, the materials manager should, as in the case of any informal discussion with the head of engineering, present his case and defend his prerogative in a forthright manner. He should indicate that the company may be losing substantial amounts of money in failing to utilize sources other than those called out by engineering. The results of such a meeting might be a clarification or a restatement of the prerogative of the two departments with respect to both specifications and mandatory sources.

Finally, some members of the class might argue in favor of the third alternative. After all, they may point out, Mr. Marshall has initiated the action, and he should follow it through to a conclusion that is acceptable to him. In the actual case, this is what was done. Mr. Marshall went back to the engineering department and said, in effect, that because the wire submitted by the other suppliers met the governing specifications, he should be permitted to deal with any one of the companies he wished. Accordingly, Mr. Marshall asked the engineering department to run tests, in cooperation with the purchasing department, to determine if the wire submitted by the other suppliers met the governing specifications. The engineering department agreed to this request, ran the tests, and found, as the production development laboratory had found earlier, that the other wires were acceptable. In view of the evidence produced by these tests, the engineering department agreed with Mr. Marshall's position and permitted him to award the business to any one of the suppliers whose wire met the specifications. Mr. Marshall placed the order with the Easternhouse Electric Company, who met the contractual requirements successfully.

Question 2:

Should Mr. Marshall have challenged the engineering department's specification of Advanced's wire?

Comment:

The second question is general in nature, and in discussing the immediate action problem posed by question 1, members of the class will undoubtedly discuss also Mr. Marshall's right to challenge the specifications in the first place. This right has ben discussed briefly in the comments above, and the following information is an expansion of points already made.

The buyer, although he does not initiate specifications or have the final determination of them, is nevertheless importantly concerned with them. Essentially, his concern arises from two factors: (1) his role as the liaison between his company and commercial suppliers, and (2) his knowledge of the commodities which he is responsible for buying. Because of the first factor, the buyer can often bring to the attention of technical personnel information from commercial suppliers which may be useful in reappraising the quantities requested, the quality specified, or, indeed, the item or the materials themselves. Because of the second factor, the buyer is in a position to appraise the quantities requested or the specifications stated and in so doing contribute to more effective procurement and lower ultimate costs. For example, by questioning quantities that are either so small as to be uneconomic to produce or so large as to overload a company, the buyer may be able to reduce the cost of the procurement. Or by determining the intended use of the material, the buyer may find that a lower quality than specified may be adequate. In other cases, a more suitable material than the one specified may be suggested by the buyer.

In appraising the above illustrations as well as the question of whether Mr. Marshall should have challenged engineering in this case, it should be emphasized that the final determination in matters of this kind rests unequivocally with engineering. An airplane is too complex an item and the substitution of materials is too important a matter to permit questions of specifications to be decided by other than technically qualified personnel. Having agreed to this position, however, there are still important contributions that the purchasing department can make as suggestions to engineering personnel which may lead to lower costs and more effective procurement.

EAGLE MACHINE COMPANY

Purpose

This case examines ways to reduce inventory investment and the possible dangers of such reductions. It then explores ways to reduce the cost of goods purchased. It raises the question: "Should the purchasing staff be reduced when a firm is attempting to reduce its costs?" Lastly, the case examines the desirability of the introduction of the materials management concept in a small firm.

Question 1:

What actions should Sally take to reduce inventories by 10 percent?

Comment:

The company's purchases and inventories probably follow the "ABC" pattern, with 20 percent of the items comprising approximately 80 percent of the dollar value. The crash cost-cutting program should concentrate on these high dollar value items.

Close cooperation will be needed between marketing and manufacturing people to pinpoint inventory categories where levels are too high. Some commitments may be stopped entirely, others bought on a hand-to-mouth basis. Possibilities are sales of surplus material, trimming safety stocks to a minimum, and holding reorders to items needed for confirmed sales requirements.

Purchasing should attempt to get suppliers to carry more items needed in locations near Eagles's plant. If this effort is unsuccessful, then purchasing should attempt to obtain suppliers who will provide the desired level of service.

Question 2:

What dangers, if any, are there in reducing inventories?

Comment:

Reductions in inventory may result in material being unavailable when required by manufacturing. The cost of the resulting production disruptions in the form of set-up costs and lost learning can more than offset the savings in inventory carrying costs.

Such reductions in inventories also may require the use of premium transportation to avoid production disruptions. The total cost to the firm *may* be lower. But management must recognize that transportation expenses may increase when inventory levels are reduced.

Question 3:

In what ways could the cost of goods purchased be reduced?

Comment:

The application of good purchasing principles in the areas of sourcing, competition, pricing, and negotiations can all lead to significant savings. Supplier suggestions under a value analysis/value engineering program can significantly reduce the cost of goods purchased.

Question 4:

What position should Sally take on the president's plan to reduce the purchasing payroll by 10 percent?

Comment:

Some chief executives relish debate and disagreement. But under most circumstances, Sally would not want to confront the president head-on on this or any other issue. She should study the areas of possible reductions in purchasing expenditures. If these reductions will require the current level of staffing, or even an increase, Sally has her work cut out. She must identify the effect of varying levels of staffing on the cost of goods purchased. In effect, Sally must do a cost benefit study at different levels of staffing. Then, if the current level of staffing (or an increase) appears to be a good investment, Sally must put her marketing hat on and sell the president on the benefits of such staffing action.

Question 5:

Develop a list of arguments in support of and another in opposition to the introduction of a materials management organization at Eagle.

Comment:

Arguments in favor:

All material responsibility will be focused on one individual
Better cooperation, especially between purchasing and production control
Lower inventories
Fewer production disruptions
Better purchasing lead time and lower cost of goods purchased
Lower costs in materials area

Arguments in opposition:

Manufacturing loses some authority and responsibility
Assuming that a new position (director of materials management) is created,
    overhead will increase $30,000 to $60,000 per year

ELITE ELECTRONICS

Purpose

This case provides the student with insight into the expanding role of purchasing and materials management in a modern, high-technology firm. Purchasing is seen as an identifier of solutions to technological problems and as a source of information on future materials. Purchasing is seen as the activity within the firm most concerned with dependable *and* economic sources of supply.

The case allows the student to apply logic and reasoning to a relatively simple situation. It is the authors' experience that many students who quickly grasp the concepts and excitement of purchasing have convinced themselves that they cannot cope with anything quantitative. This case provides an opportunity to coax such individuals to get their feet wet in the magic of simple quantitative reasoning. If the instructor goes through the reasoning portrayed in the answer to question 1, he or she then may want to change the numbers slightly and use the case as a quiz or examination question—with the objective of increasing the student's confidence in his or her ability!

It is our experience that it is very desirable to post all of the facts on a blackboard before proceeding with the analysis. Such a posting should include the following:

Total market @ $1,000: 10,000/year
Current Model EE2201 selling price: $1,485
Purchased cost of Gamma ADC: $90
Gamma ADC capacity: 1,000 units/month
Variable production cost with Gamma ADC: $675
Test, rework, and assembly cost included in $675: $200
Probability of problem with new unit incorporating Gamma ADC: .4 (2 of 5)
Test, rework, and assembly cost, if problems: $800
Variable production cost, if problems: $1,275

Variable production cost if Elite waits one year: $630

	Projected Sales		
	Incorporating New ADC		Wait One Year for Alternative to ADC
	No Problems	Problems	
Year 1	10,000	4,000	—
Year 2	6,000	4,000	6,000
Year 3	6,000	4,000	6,000
Year 4	6,000	4,000	6,000
Year 5	6,000	4,000	6,000

Note: The analysis *must* focus on *contributions*, remembering that the fixed costs of $200 per unit will be incurred regardless of the action taken.

Question 1:

Should Elite proceed with the new low cost oscilloscope incorporating the new analog-to-digital converter (ADC)? Explain your reasoning.

Comment:

A good way to get a discussion going is to poll the class on this question and then request members supporting each position for their reasoning.

If Elite proceeds with the low-cost oscilloscope incorporating the new ADC, the likely contribution of the new unit to overhead and profit will be: Expected contribution = (probability of no problems × contribution with no problems) + (probability of problems × contribution with problems).

Contriburion with no problems:

Year 1: sales = 10,000 units	
Gross income: (10,000 × $1,000)	$ 10,000,000
Less cost of goods sold: (10,000 × $675)	6,750,000
Anticipated contribution:	3,250,000
Years 2–5: sales (6,000 per yr × 4 yr)	24,000,000
Less cost of goods sold: (24,000 × $675)	16,200,000
Anticipated contribution: (years 2–5)	7,800,000
Total contribution: (years 1–5)	$ 11,050,000

Contribution with problems:

Year 1: sales = 4,000 units	
Gross income: (4,000 × $1,000)	$ 4,000,000
Less cost of goods sold: (4,000 × $1,275*)	5,100,000
Anticipated contribution: (loss)	(1,100,000)
Years 2–5: sales = 16,000 units (4,000 per yr × 4 yr)	
Gross income: (16,000 × $1,000)	16,000,000
Less cost of goods sold: (16,000 × $675**)	10,800,000
Anticipated contribution: (years 2–5)	5,200,000

The expected contribution (years 1–5) if Elite proceeds now are:	$ 4,100,000

Expected contribution = .6(11,050,000) + .4(4,100,000)

$$= \$6,630,000 + \$1,640,000$$
$$= \$8,270,000$$

*Includes $800 for test and rework cost as per text.

**Assumes possible defects in ADC have been corrected.

If Elite waits one year and alternatives to the ADC are available at a cost of $45 per unit, production costs will drop to approximately $630 per unit. Expected contributions will be:

Sales = 24,000 units (6,000 units per yr × 4 yr)	
Gross income:	$ 24,000,000
Less cost of goods sold: (Manufacturing cost – 24,000 × $630)	15,120,000
Anticipated contribution:	$ 8,880,000

Elite's expected contributions increase from $8,270,000 to $8,880,000 if it waits for a less risky, less costly alternative to the new ADC.

Question 2:

Who should be involved in the decision-making process? Who has the final responsibility for the decision?

Comment:

Historically, marketing, engineering, finance, and production were involved in developing recommendations on such issues. But with the increasing cost, criticality, and scarcity of purchased materials, purchasing or materials management has become a key member of the team recommending such production decisions. One of the many benefits of the materials management concept is the organizational status of the materials manager. In a situation like that at Elite Electronics, the purchasing manager frequently is at an organizational disadvantage in attempting to provide input and influence such analysis and the resulting recommendations. Whether such should or should not be the case is not the issue. All too frequently, purchasing is at too low an organizational level to make such input.

The chief of materials management, on the other hand, is much more strategically located and in a much better position to influence such analyses and the resulting recommendations. The materials management organizational approach aids purchasing in reaching its full profit-making potential.

The final responsibility for such decisions rests with the firm's chief operating officer.

Question 3:

What other issues concerning this problem should be of concern to purchasing and materials management?

Comment:

In addition to providing insight into the scope of purchasing and materials management, this question allows the instructor to telegraph the issues that he or she wants to emphasize that are to be discussed later in the course, such as the role of the learning curve on production costs, the benefits and dangers of long-term contracts, the dangers of a sole source of supply, value analysis/engineering, etc. The question also allows the instructor to discuss the effect of such new products on sales of the entire oscilloscope product line. And finally, the instructor may choose to perform a present value analysis on the two alternatives.

ERIE MACHINE SHOP

Purpose

The purpose of this case is to discuss surplus disposal problems.

Discussion

Initially, surplus disposal is not a problem in small companies. But as they grow it can become one if it is not formalized. It's amazing how much surplus even companies as small as Erie can generate. As the company grows and ages, surplus capital equipment is certain to become available as well as surplus production materials. If there are not policies for disposal, surpluses are often sold at ridiculous prices. For example, while serving as a consultant to Erie, one of the authors observed a machine conservatively valued at $5000 sold for $250, and a used truck conservatively valued at $3500 sold for $900. Even though the money value may not be significant, policy laxness in one phase of operations can lead to laxness in other areas on the part of employees. Hence, in controlling small operations, management can have more at stake than current money value alone.

Question 1:

Would a small quantity of metal be worth the trouble of setting up a good procedure to handle it?

Comment:

Yes, small quantities always seem to grow. Even twelve tons of scrap, the amount involved in this case, would probably return over $7500 per year. Also, the procedure established for metal surplus disposal could be extended to include other surplus and salvage items which could total equally as much or more than the $7500 for scrap. Additionally, as strategic minerals and materials become scarcer from increased usage throughout the world, the prices of surplus materials will increase.

Question 2:

If so, who would be responsible for managing such surplus materials?

Comment:

The section making the purchases also should control the disposal of scrap metal or any other items to be disposed. The president should be requested to make this company policy. The purchasing department, under this policy, should develop procedures that will insure adequate controls. All metal should be sold as a lot on a bid basis for a period of a year. This would save Erie the expense of having to pay a trash collector to haul away these items plus provide revenue.

FAUQUIER GAS COMPANY

Question 1:

What are the key facts?

1. The current procurement system does not include early purchasing involvement.
2. Purchasing, design, and construction are not working as a team to complete the project.
3. The design engineer works autonomously in determining material specifications.
4. No purchase request has been completed for the project.
5. Construction is scheduled to begin in 6 weeks.
6. Pipes needed for project completion require substantial lead time.

Question 2:

What is the problem?

What should Fauquier do to obtain a cost/quality effective procurement of pipes in a timely manner?

Question 3:

List and discuss three alternative solutions.

1. In the design stage, the construction and design engineers should be developing alternative technical approaches to complete the project. Developing alternatives allows purchasing more options. More options gives purchasing the opportunity to make better decisions on price, quality, and timely delivery. Different designs also encourage the use of various tolerance levels—possibly ones more appropriate for the job at hand.

   This solution will require more time in the design stage. Another problem may be the inability of the engineers to develop alternative solutions. They may prefer focusing on the "best" design only. Or the design and construction project engineers may not want to work together since they have always worked independently.

2. Another possibility is to develop a requirements/procurement team. This team must include people from design, construction, and purchasing to ensure cost/quality effective specifications are established. Mr. Murphy can contribute his insight on market availability, cost, quality, and lead time needed for materials. This approach also lets each functional group learn about the needs of the others. The range of specifications used narrows, increasing the timeliness of the procurement process. More time allows purchasing to get the best price for materials requested.

   While this group effort may have prevented the current situation, the time pressure may keep the three representatives from cooperating fully. It also becomes easier to blame each other for cost overruns or quality and scheduling problems that may occur. The engineers may not feel that purchasing personnel are able to understand their needs.

3. Purchasing should develop a material catalog for the design engineer. The catalog must include information regarding previously purchased pipe and wrapper specifi-

cations, market availability, quality, and supplier lead time. This catalog would make it easier for the designer to provide specifications. Costs would be controlled by minimizing the use of unique pipe sizes. Also, Murphy would not be required to meet frequently with the design engineer. A lot of the engineer's questions could be answered with the catalog.

Developing an effective catalog is a costly procedure requiring a lot of time. This is also a method of effectively standardizing materials, an effort some engineers may perceive to hinder their creativity. Thus, the engineers may not use the catalog. Or the engineers may resent using a catalog put together by purchasing, a department which has been told what is needed.

4. Early supplier involvement could be pursued. This would prevent having the engineer design in a vacuum. Supplier knowledge would provide information regarding the newest materials or processes available. This makes the job easier for the designer. Proper specifications can be established quickly, resulting in both direct and indirect cost savings.

    ESI requires finding reputable and qualified suppliers. This information gathering requires time. Another problem is the possibility Murphy will resist investigating new suppliers. He may find it easier to rely on the familiar. The engineers must also be flexible enough to open up to new ideas the suppliers offer.

Solution:

Improved communication and coordination between the design, construction, and purchasing groups must occur. Personnel from each must start working together immediately to solve the pipe specification problem quickly. By discussing the problems each is facing, alternatives can be discussed until the proper specification is established. To prevent this problem from occurring again, this team approach should be consistently used from the design stage through completion of the project. Alternatives in design, a materials catalog, and ESI are all key elements that need to be incorporated into the system to make it an effective one.

FLORIDA RETAIL COMPANY

Purpose

The purpose of the Florida Retail Company case is to discuss issues involved in procuring software systems.

Discussion

Issues include: procuring a newly developed service product, Statements of Work, performance considerations, administration of contracts, types of contract, quality, and the role of purchasing.

Question 1:

Do you feel that the fixed price contract agreed to by FRC was the best way to procure ACME's computer system?

Comment:

A fixed-price contract is appropriate in this case. Since the software costs are prorated over an indeterminate number of potential customers, any type of "cost plus" contract with ACME would be subsidizing the development cost for other customers. However, the execution of the contract did not include any provision for FRC to monitor progress against the supplier's schedule. Furthermore, the contract did not motivate ACME to deliver a quality product on time.

A fixed-price contract paid out in milestone payments with an amount reserved for bonus payments would be the preferred agreement. The critical nature of the computer system makes delivery on schedule vital. In order to motivate ACME to perform in a timely and quality manner and for FRC to closely monitor progress on the contract, milestone payments should be based on the delivery of system functionality (accounts payable, accounts receivable, general ledger, purchasing functions, inventory control, sales analysis) in a specified period of time. The milestones should be clearly spelled out in the contract along with a detailed description of how ACME would be evaluated against these milestones. ACME will not get paid unless certain functionality of the software system is completed and evaluated by FRC. In addition, bonus payments should be used to further motivate ACME. The bonus payments would be awarded if the milestone was completed on time and had satisfactory quality based upon the evaluation agreed to in the contract. These bonus payments would be determined for each milestone.

The dollar amount for the contract should be a combination of a fixed price plus the potential bonus payments. There should be appropriate incentive built into the contract to reward good performance and punish poor performance. As an example, assume the following: the value of the fixed-price payments paid out in milestones total $325,000, the total bonus payments are potentially worth $50,000. If ACME meets all the contractual obligations, the potential contract value is $375,000. This is $50,000 extra for ACME and FRC receives a quality software system *on time.* However, if ACME does not perform satisfactorily, the bonus will not be awarded and only those milestones completed satisfactorily will be paid.

Question 2.

Where did FRC go wrong in purchasing the software system?

Comment:

Listed below are some of the major errors that FRC made in purchasing the software system:

- Purchasing was not involved in the procurement of the software.
- There wasn't any early supplier involvement between ACME and FRC.
  Helen Cooley, the systems manager, and Jack Murphy, the owner of FRC, should have been involved in the meetings.
- The Statement of Work was not well-written or administered properly.
- FRC didn't make any inquiries about ACME's quality assurance procedures.
- The option of either hiring an outside consultant or contacting faculty members of a university that offer consulting services was never considered. This would have been very valuable since nobody at FRC knew much about developing computer software.
- The progress of ACME was not monitored.

Question 3:

Was the Statement of Work sufficient?

Comment:

The Statement of Work was not sufficient; the only objectives that FRC identified were:

- Obtain a new software system capable of all functions of the old system, plus integrating a customized point-of-sale system.
- New computer system must have an optical bar code reading capability to facilitate the cash transactions.
- Hardware to be in place one month before opening day.
- Software to be in place two weeks before opening day.

Listed below is what *should* have been included in the Statement of Work:

Primary Objectives

- SCHEDULE—Software delivery was not scheduled far enough in advance to solve any of the problems that are inherent in developing a new software system.
- ACCEPTANCE TEST—Require that ACME run FRC's actual data successfully through the system.
- SUPPORT—Guarantee that support and services for the system be available for at least a year, even if ACME goes out of business.
- RESPONSE TIME—Require that an acceptable response time of the computer be identified, for example under 2 seconds.
- IDENTIFICATION OF KEY PERSONNEL—Identify in the contract the individuals at ACME who will be working on the project. Many times more experienced individuals or consultants make the sale to a company, but once an agreement is reached, the project is handed over to less experienced personnel.

Subordinate Objectives

- GUARANTEE—Guarantee of functionality of the software system should be identified and obtained through the use of milestone payments.
- BINDING ARBITRATION—Stipulates that FRC can elect to have disputes resolved by an outside arbitrator.
- TRAINING—A training program for FRC's employees shall be developed by ACME and included in the timetable.

Question 4:

What are the problems encountered in purchasing a high-technology software system?

Comment:

There is a great deal of risk involved from the buyers' perspective concerning the quality of the finished product or service, since it is not proven out with other customers. Unknown technology problems usually will adversely affect the schedule and final delivery of the service.

Question 5:

How could the problems on opening day have been avoided?

Comment:

If FRC had monitored the progress of ACME (with milestones), it could have anticipated possible problems and prepared a back-up plan. A manual procedure should have been developed in the event that the software system failed or the system crashed. The delivery schedule of an unproven software system was too tight. The delivery date should have allowed enough time to test the system and to properly train the personnel at FRC.

FOUR SQUARE LUMBER MILL

Purpose

The purpose of this case is to illustrate that although challenging specifications and making value analysis studies are purchasing responsibilities, these responsibilities cannot be effectively executed unless purchasing establishes a cooperative working relationship with those who use the materials which purchasing buys. Many of the possible ways of gaining such a working relationship are discussed in this case.

Discussion

The case discusses the purchasing concept of quality, i.e., that "economic quality" embraces the elements of technical quality, functional requirements, and cost. Also, the case discusses the importance of having specific quality descriptions incorporated as a provision of the purchase order.

Question 1:

What could Jon have done to avoid this situation?

Comment:

Jon should have done the following:

a. He should have determined specifically why Sam did not think the Dipson blade would work and then investigated these objections thoroughly before ordering it. Perhaps Sam had valid reasons (from the operating point of view) for preferring the Swiss blade.

b. If the case for the American blade still looked good, John should have tried hard to work out with Sam a testing program whereby the Dipson blade's performance could be objectively evaluated on the job. This sort of thing must be a mutual endeavor, however, and he must obtain Sam's sincere cooperation. Jon could have applied a little basic psychology at this point by letting Sam be the "kingpin" in setting up and directing the testing operation.

The important point in this overall situation is that the purchasing department should not attempt to force unwanted materials down the using department's throat. The value analysis function must be jointly borne by the purchasing department and using department. Only by close cooperation between the interested departments can purchasing effectively spearhead a good value analysis program.

Question 2:

What should Jon do now?

Comment:

Jon should:

a. determine the cause for the blades' poor performance. Were Four Square yard men responsible, or did the blades simply fail to maintain performance after they received a little wear? Jon should probably first attempt to hash the situation out with Sam. Throughout his efforts in this regard it is mandatory that he make every attempt possible to cooperate with Sam, to understand his operating problems, and to gain Sam's confidence and cooperation. If he creates animosity among the yard personnel, he only reduces his chances of success for future material substitutions and value analysis projects.

    If Jon fails to uncover the facts in his talk with Sam, the implications of the situation are serious enough that Jon's boss should probably try to get things straightened out through Sam's boss. Again, the spirit of cooperation should set the tone for the investigation.

b. If the blades' failure was intentionally caused by Four Square personnel, it is evident that much work needs to be done in improving purchasing-yard personnel relations, and in promoting understanding of procedures for value analysis work in general. In this case it is the purchasing manager's responsibility to spearhead the development of such a program. The specific objectives, policies, and procedures, however, must be worked out jointly by the purchasing manager, yard manager, and probably the operations manager.

FRICH TURBO ENGINE COMPANY

Purpose

The purpose of this case is to outline and discuss some of the typical problems and difficulties of cost and price analysis. It is not the intent of the case to supply answers to all the questions raised, but rather to suggest possibilities and indicate the lines of investigation to be followed in analyzing costs.

Discussion

Cost and price analysis are not precise pricing techniques. However, they are useful techniques for which in many situations there are no substitutes. The more that is known concerning costs, the more precise are the techniques. Their overall value is attested to by the fact that they are used extensively by leading industrial companies and major government procurement agencies.

Question 1:

What factors might have caused the variance between Bayfleet's quotation and Mr. Fingold's estimate? Between Bayfleet's quotation and Union's quotation?

Comment:

Mr. Fingold's estimate was drawn up for comparative purposes, in order that he might more closely appraise the reasonable cost of the new valves. An examination of Mr. Fingold's estimate may supply some reasons for the variance that has occurred between the low quotations and his own estimate of costs.

In the first place, three of Mr. Fingold's cost items were rather loosely established assumptions. His overhead estimate was a rough guess. Here Mr. Fingold, using his knowledge of the pipe and fitting industry as a whole, had pegged the manufacturing overhead costs at 150 percent of direct labor. But it is quite possible that the overhead of certain bidders would not agree with this cost projection. General and administrative expenses and profit were also assumptions of Mr. Fingold, with no factual data given in support of his figures. The very nature of this method of estimation is such that averages of the many companies in the industry must be used leaving unaccounted the diversity that may exist among various companies.

On the other hand, Mr. Fingold's estimate of material, direct labor, and tooling costs was based on historical data and on Mr. Fingold's knowledge of the production processes involved; consequently, these figures were likely to prove more dependable than overhead and G & A costs. Here again, however, Mr. Fingold's estimates would necessarily have been based on average or normal conditions for the industry as a whole and would have left out of account the special circumstances that may affect the industry or individual producers in the industry. An examination of Bayfleet's and Union's bids may suggest a number of possible explanations for their variance with each other and with Mr. Fingold's estimate.

The direct material cost as quoted by Bayfleet is .344 per unit, while Union Stamping's quotation is .408 per unit. Some of this difference is reduced when the portion Bayfleet intends to subcontract is added to direct material cost. The cost of these subcontracted parts increases Bayfleet's bid by .080, which when combined with Bayfleet's direct material cost, raises its material quotation to a higher figure than that quoted by Union Stamping. Some of this cost variance may occur because Union Stamping can manufacture the parts which Bayfleet intends to subcontract at a lower cost than the subcontracted price to Bayfleet. Such a situation often arises when a company does not have the necessary equipment to convert the raw material to a semifinished component. In this case the comparison between costs submitted by two contractors must involve the sum of material and direct labor costs.

It is not at all certain here, however, that subcontracting fully explains the difference. Union's bid may be lower than Bayfleet's because Union's purchasing position is such that it can obtain material at a lower cost than Bayfleet. Again, perhaps Union Stamping purchased the needed raw material in the past at a lower price than that obtainable at present, whereas Bayfleet may have to purchase the raw material at present market prices.

Direct labor cost as quoted by Bayfleet is .288, while Union's bid is .400 per unit. The difference of 11.2 cents per unit again may be due to several different factors. One of these has already been noted: the difference in the labor necessary for Bayfleet's product because one or more of the components is subcontracted. This is not likely to be the whole explanation, however, because the sum of material and direct labor costs for Bayfleet is .712 as against .808 for Union. The simplest reason for the discrepancy would be that Bayfleet's labor force is highly skilled and is more efficient than Union's. It should be pointed out, however, that efficient *use* of labor is not always correlated exactly with labor rates. It is possible that both companies have equally skilled labor but that Bayfleet's labor is being paid at a lower figure. In this case the possibility of a wage increase should be taken into account in contract pricing. The factor of efficiency, of course, should not be excluded. It may be that Union's labor force is actually receiving a lower average rate of pay than Bayfleet's but takes considerably longer to complete the work, and so generates a larger total labor cost. Perhaps Union Stamping includes some supervisory labor in its direct labor quotations, such as foremen or floor supervisors, although this does not seem likely in view of the extremely low overhead rate. Perhaps either one or both companies have poor cost collection methods which affect their estimate of the time necessary to complete the job. It is always possible that both companies have made errors in their understanding of the specifications and have attributed less labor to the job than is actually necessary.

Finally, the facilities used by the two companies will affect labor costs. If Bayfleet has new and more fully automatic machinery than that owned by Union, then it will be able to produce the item at a much lower unit labor cost. Similarly, the arrangement of Bayfleet's plant may be such that materials move along much more smoothly, and this would be reflected in a labor savings.

Manufacturing overhead, in dollars, shows little difference between the two concerns, though in both cases it is considerably lower than that proposed by Mr. Fingold's estimate. Percentagewise, however, Bayfleet's quotation is some 35 percent higher than Union Stamping's percentage overhead cost. This indicates that if labor rates change, Bayfleet's cost may increase in greater proportion than Union's.

While the dollar overhead is nearly the same for both companies, it may have been arrived at by different methods. Bayfleet may have charged off engineering items that Union considered to be tooling labor. Rent, heat, light, and power may have been segregated departmentally or on an overall basis, which may have changed the final amount of overhead chargeable to the contract. Union Stamping may have charged off some supervisory personnel in the overhead, while Bayfleet may not have, preferring to collect such costs under general and administrative expenses. Accounting practices may present overhead at a lesser or greater charge according to the differing reduction of the total contract price to the contractor's total volume of yearly business.

Even if the companies' accounting methods are comparable, the overhead in both cases may not reflect actual costs. Both companies may be suffering from an industry-wide shortage of business; perhaps some new plastic or synthetic item has replaced many of their former products. In depressed periods many companies are willing to accept a contract at a lower-than-actual overhead figure, in order that they may continue in business until such time as they can obtain other work to replace that lost to new products. It may be suggested that such a reduction is more likely to show up in overhead than in other costs, and the reason for this may be discussed.

Tooling cost as quoted by Bayfleet is .104 per unit, while Union Stamping's quotation is .232 per unit. Perhaps Bayfleet has manufactured an item of a somewhat similar nature before and, unlike Union Stamping, does not need to fabricate new tooling to produce on this contract. It is possible that Union has the necessary tooling also, but wishes to charge it off to this particular contract. Then again, perhaps Union has the necessary tooling but estimates that it will be necessary to replace it before the contract is completed. It may be that Bayfleet feels it will be unnecessary to fabricate expensive tooling and intends to use cheap tooling, which will be practically useless at the completion of the contract. It may be that some of the difference between the tooling quotations of the two concerns appears in some other account, such as overhead.

General and administrative expenses as quoted by Bayfleet are much higher than Union Stamping's quotation—by some 167 percent. Both, however, are lower than Mr. Fingold's estimate, and the same considerations apply as in the case of manufacturing overhead.

Union Stamping's profit, considered on a dollar basis, is more than twice as large as Bayfleet's. Many charges which Union feels justified may appear here, for lack of a better place to put them. Another thought is that Union Stamping may feel that its low quotation should receive a higher profit because of the efficiency it expects to realize in producing under the contract. Bayfleet, on the other hand, may feel that a low profit figure may obtain the contract for it, and its true profit may actually be hidden in some other cost.

Many other reasons may be offered by the class to suggest why one contractor's figures are higher or lower than the others or why both bidders appears to be out of line with Mr. Fingold's estimate. The instructor should endeavor to point out that the possible reasons for the variance in costs are in the hundreds, depending upon innumerable unknowns. Not until the buyer who examines the cost elements has pinned down the "whys" of these costs can he make reasonable assumptions as to what the proper cost should be.

Question 2:

In the light of your previous answer to the above questions, what conclusions can you draw concerning: (a) the reliability and usefulness of cost estimates made by the buyer, and (b) the value to be gained from comparison of one supplier's quotation with that of another?

Comment:

Perhaps before an accurate answer can be given to the above question, a decision should be made as to whether or not a supplier's quoted price reflects "true" costs. Industry-wide conditions may so affect the bidding on a contract that quoted costs may be much lower than actual costs. For example, the cotton industry may be suffering because of increased consumer acceptance of synthetic fibers. A contract in the cotton industry may result in lower than actual prices, for the several cotton manufacturers may now bid low prices in order to obtain a contract, with the thought that, while they will sustain some losses at such a low price, at least the loss will not be as great as if they had no contract at all. If, as time passes, the industry receives the necessary "shot in the arm" and volume increases serve to boost their businesses, the contractors may bid higher than actual prices in order to recover their losses on previous contacts. In either situation, it is apparent that the cost breakdown does not reflect true cost.

All in all, it would appear that the buyer must bear in mind the fact that costs as portrayed in a cost breakdown may or may not bear resemblance to actual costs of production. To this extent, then, the buyer must realize that each cost breakdown needs careful analytical scrutiny and that costs as presented by a contractor are not always reliable and, therefore, they are ever open to question and negotiation.

What, then about the reliability of cost estimates as initiated by a buyer; are they reliable and useful?

Any cost estimate must make a variety of assumptions. The buyer compiling such a list of costs may be fully aware of the techniques and methods of manufacture in the industry in question; yet he must make several assumptions in every cost category. The presumed production facilities, for instance, will govern his estimate of the amount of direct labor necessary to complete the job, as well as the estimate of the amount of direct material scrap generated. Overhead, also, being a percentage of direct labor and a collection of costs subject to the various methods of accountants or supervisory personnel, will be difficult for the buyer to forecast accurately. General and administrative expenses will present much the same problem as overhead. Profit will fluctuate within an industry and from contractor to contractor. By their very nature, estimates are generalizations of costs. Cost estimates are a useful tool, however, even with the generalizations found in them.

Cost estimates will give an indication, at least, of the fair value of an item of production and may show that even when prices appear competitive, reductions can still be achieved.

A comparison of quoted prices is another method available to the negotiator in attempting to "peg" the most realistic price. From the foregoing discussion, however, it is clear that even this method of comparison is subject to severe limitations. Industry-wide fluctuations in volume, the availability of raw materials, the cost of direct labor and the resulting overhead costs, constantly changing techniques of production, new automatic machinery, the cost of living—all of these and hundreds of other factors operate to change a contractor's costs. The buyer, already overloaded with many other problems, must examine each of the several constantly shifting cost factors, asking himself the reasons why such costs are what they are. Such an examination many times calls for attention to minute detail and complex accounting techniques. Only through such an overall costing, however, can the buyer obtain the proper quality and quantity of goods and services needed at fair and reasonable prices.

FUTRONICS, INC.

Purpose

The purpose of this case is to involve the student in three different but related activities:

- To consider the activities and costs associated with the procurement and storage of office and MRO supplies.
- To think through the development of a blanket/systems contracting type of purchase.
- To introduce the student to an outsourcing situation that involves the purchase of a service, as well as material.

Question 1:

Assume you are Steve Hastell. Prepare an analysis and report on this issue for presentation for the next program meeting.

Comment:

Advantages of purchasing outside stores services:

1. A purchase price saving of approximately 6 percent can be realized on approximately 90 percent of the items purchased. Assuming that this 90 percent includes a proportionate number of high-value items, minimum purchase savings should approximate $48,000 to $50,000 per year ($900,000 × .90 × .06 = $48,600).
2. If the stores operation is abolished, inventory carrying costs of approximately $42,000 per year can be eliminated ($140,000 × .30 = $42,000 per year).
3. If the stores operation is discontinued, personnel and facilities operating costs can be reduced approximately $200,000 per year. (This assumes that the four individuals can be absorbed on an attrition basis elsewhere in the organization, and that the freed-up space can be used for other productive purposes.)
4. If Futronics is able to enter into a systems contracting type of agreement for three years with one of the supply houses, the incremental supply ordering costs in purchasing will decline markedly. This is a very significant operating efficiency which will free a buyer up to engage in additional analytical purchasing work.
5. Discontinuance of the stores operation will virtually eliminate the time requirements for supervision of the operation. Similar to item number 4, this additional time can be used by purchasing personnel to do a more productive and professional job of purchasing.
6. Futronics now has 42 operating sites. As the organization continues to grow, delivery of materials to these sites will become more costly and more troublesome to manage. Generally speaking, one would expect the supply houses to be better equipped to handle material delivery operations effectively.

Note: In analyzing the potential cost savings noted above, Steve will have to review each situation carefully to ensure that the expected cost savings will actually materialize—that is, that the cost savings are in fact incremental in nature. Any cost savings that are not incremental must be adjusted accordingly for purposes of analysis.

Potential disadvantages of purchasing outside store services:

1. By far the major disadvantage of discontinuing the stores operation is the potential loss of control with regard to service offered the Futronic users. The delivery system now in operation is integrated with the firm's mail delivery service and, by and large, it works well. Delegating the responsibility for providing this service to a supply house may also work well if the right source is selected. Nevertheless, the buyer moves one step farther away from direct control in such an operation.

2. What is in one sense an advantage, can also be a significant disadvantage—namely, the fact that Futronics would be locked into a three-year agreement with the supplier. If the new operation "bumps along" at a mediocre level, three years is a long time to be stuck with it. Hence, it is vital that the right supplier be selected and that a contract be carefully and thoroughly developed to provide necessary remedies in the case of less-than-satisfactory performance.

3. Discontinuing the stores operation is a major decision from an operating point of view. Once the stores activity is discontinued, it would require a major effort to reestablish the operation (organization, space, storage racks, systems, and management). Hence, although the decision is not irreversible, it is a major step that would require significant effort and budget to reverse.

4. When each individual operating unit is issuing supply releases against a master contract, it is not uncommon to experience a growth in the "unofficial inventories" maintained at each office site. Hence, there may be some dilution of the original inventory saving by this decentralized self-sufficiency phenomenon. Consequently, Futronics management would likely have to establish some type of periodic monitoring and control system simply to ensure that unofficial inventory levels at the various sites are maintained reasonably.

Managerial considerations:

1. Steve and his boss must attempt to anticipate any significant changes in Futronics's operation, during the next five to seven years, that might impact this decision. They must look ahead to determine if any significant new or modified storage requirements are on the horizon. Clearly, the decision made now should fit future operating requirements as effectively as possible.

2. Both the materials specifications and the Statement of Work defining the service aspects of the purchase must be drawn up carefully and completely prior to the request for a proposal from any of the supply houses. The suppliers must know precisely what elements of performance are expected if they are to respond intelligently and responsibly. Subsequently, material specs and the Statement of Work must be refined and included as an integral part of the purchase contract.

3. If Futronics enters into a three-year agreement with one of the supply houses, operating details and performance remedies must be carefully thought through in advance and included in the contract. Various release provisions in the event of unsatisfactory performance should be included. A price escalation/de-escalation clause should also be included in the contract, detailing specifically the documentation that will be used to justify price changes. For office supplies, various Producer Price Indexes frequently can be used for this purpose.

4. A major decision Steve must make is whether he is going to negotiate the contract or use the competitive bidding process. The two major alternatives are (1) to use two-step bidding, or (2) to request operations proposals from the potential suppliers, followed by negotiation with the top one or two firms submitting the most attractive operating proposals. While one might make a case for the utilization of either approach, the authors' preference is for the proposal/negotiation approach. Utilizing this approach in this competitive market, Steve may well be able to negotiate improved service performance and also improved price performance (particularly for the 10 percent of the items that was originally less attractively priced than the others).

5. With regard to the receiving operations at the various sites, a standard blanket order receiving/invoicing procedure might be used. Upon receipt of the material, the secretary could simply initial a priced sales or delivery slip, and the supplier could batch these slips and submit them monthly in support of its invoice. Operationally, this procedure could work well and create the desired audit trail. However, since the same secretary is issuing releases against the contract and subsequently receiving the material, there is some possibility for collusion to develop between the secretary and the supplier's shipping clerk. Futronic's internal audit staff probably would want to monitor this situation on a periodic basis.

6. If the stores operation is discontinued and management does not want to lay off the four displaced individuals, it must be able to absorb them elsewhere in the organization as attrition occurs. This may take some planning and a bit of time to accomplish.

Concluding Comment:

Steve's report for the next program meeting should contain an analysis and evaluation of the advantages, potential disadvantages, and managerial considerations discussed above. In the absence of any overriding negative factors that emerge from an analysis of future operations, Steve will probably recommend to management that Futronics purchase its stores services from one of the external supply houses.

Generally speaking, if properly designed and implemented, this type of arrangement typically produces excellent results for the buying organization. It helps the buying firm solve its small-order problem and permits the utilization of purchasing personnel for much more productive activities. If properly conceived, this type of arrangement has the potential to improve stores and delivery services to Futronics's users. Finally, the buying organization should experience a significant reduction in direct material costs because of the volume capabilities of the supply house.

Two factors are vital in the development of an effective long-term contracting operation. First, the "right" supplier must be selected. This requires thorough preliminary investigation of the supplier's operating, financial, and management capabilities, along with an assessment of the supplier's attitudes and motivation to join the buyer in a partnering type of operation. The second factor is the preparation of a comprehensive contract that protects the buyer against poor performance and, at the same time, provides the supplier enough latitude to use its resources and creativity to do a good job and also to keep costs down.

In all likelihood, Steve will want to identify three or four customers of the leading supply house, and then discuss with them their experiences with the supplier in such an operation. This type of investigation can do a great deal to confirm or contradict Steve's tentative conclusions about the supplier.

Finally, if Futronics is still undecided about the best course of action to take, it may want to consider the possibility of experimenting with the concept for a selected group of items. The firm may decide to retain its stores operation for the next six to twelve months, but simultaneously enter into an experimental term contract with one of the supply houses for a modest sample of representative supply items. In this way, the firm can gain some experience with the concept and defer its decision for six to twelve months.

G.A.R. MANUFACTURING COMPANY

Purpose

The purpose of this case is to develop a discussion concerning the possible merging of the purchasing and supply management functions after the merger of two firms.

Discussion

Mergers are very common these days; hence, almost all businessmen face merger problems sometime in their careers. When the two merging firms are physically located within 100 miles of each other (as the two firms are in this case), traditionally some form of purchasing or materials management merger is profitable. The greater the similarity of the product mix between the two firms, the greater the opportunity for profitable merger. However, even with a dissimilar product mix (as is the case in this merger) many purchased materials and services can still be common to both firms, and thus lend themselves to profitable combination. For example, among the many common items that probably could be purchased at lower prices if combined are office supplies and office equipment, automotive and materials handling equipment, hand tools, small power and cutting tools, plant and office cleaning materials (or service contracts for janitorial work), lubricants for plant machinery, etc.

Question 1:

If you were Ralph Foster, what facets of the situation would you explore in order to make an intelligent report?

Comment:

The following steps are recommended to develop an intelligent report:

a. The director of purchasing for the acquiring company must first establish what his company has planned for the overall merging of corporate structure, top management, offices, and so forth. It is suggested that he get this information from his company president and other operating department managers.

b. Foster should establish communications with the purchasing manager at the other company after first briefing himself as completely as possible on the industry, the company's finances, and production processes. Then Foster should begin a detailed examination of the operational aspects of purchasing's job—what is bought, major suppliers, relevant cost figures, facilities, methods, procedures, policies, stores, inventory, surplus materials, make or buy, shipping, receiving, how purchasing relates to other departments, and all similar purchasing and materials management problems which could bear on this case.

c. Foster should look into the managerial aspects of the operation, including a pinpointing of responsibilities for buying decisions in and out of purchasing, capabilities of the purchasing manager and his staff, and an assessment of their potential in the merged company.

d. Foster should investigate possible opportunities for integrating the materials function, if such opportunities appear to exist.

Question 2:

What recommendations would you put into a formal report to your president?

Comment:

The G.A.R. purchasing director should make the following recommendations to his president:

a. Investigate and consolidate areas of purchasing in the two companies that can immediately be combined at a cost savings. Not all of the specific items need be mentioned, but an estimate of possible total annual savings would be desirable.

b. A broad, five-year plan for integrating the two functions should be considered. In the interval, policy control should be vested in G.A.R.'s purchasing director.

c. The possibility of combining purchasing research operations in the two companies, accomplished by acquiring a capable analyst that neither company can now afford, might be recommended.

d. A frank appraisal of Wonder's purchasing staff including the purchasing manager would be valuable information for Foster's president.

e. The feasibility of a materials management department, combining both companies' purchasing, inventory, traffic and other appropriate materials functions, should be outlined. The combined companies are large enough to have a materials management department, and if inventories are large, a materials manager could be a most profitable investment.

GAS TURBINES INCORPORATED

Purpose

The purpose of this case is to discuss the economic and non-economic issues which are involved in making a decision on whether or not to implement a value analysis proposal.

Discussion

This case presents several issues which are involved in value analysis decisions: economic issues, technical considerations, supplier responsiveness, purchasing's role in the process, and the difficulties which can be encountered in "selling" a cost reduction idea to design personnel.

Analysis

Question 1:

What other information would be useful for Bill to take with him to the meeting?

Comment:

Information on the quality and schedule performance of both Smith Controls and Valient is available from the GTI supplier rating system and should be presented at the meeting. In addition, information on the reliability of both the Smith Controls and the Valient valve, in their current applications, would be very valuable. This information could be obtained from the suppliers and verified by GTI's field service personnel.

The impact of requiring a different connector on the electrical harness should also be investigated. If the harness has not yet been placed on order, the cost of the connector change would be limited to the engineering effort to change the drawing.

Question 2:

Who should Bill invite to the meeting?

Comment:

The decision on which valve to procure will likely be made by first level management. Because of the technical nature of this decision and the necessary interaction of several disciplines, the meeting will have a number of participants. Bill should invite his manager for support of his position. Another key person is the principal project engineer or program manager who has over-all technical (and preferably business) responsibility. In addition, persons from manufacturing engineering, quality engineering, reliability engineering, pricing and field service engineering should attend.

Question 3:

What economic factors should be considered in arriving at the procurement decision?

Comment:

The total costs associated with the design, procurement, development, and qualification testing, must be considered in the cost analysis.

The Smith Controls valve has the highest per unit price, but does not have any non-recurring engineering cost or additional engineering design cost. There is, however, a procurement cost associated with an inconsistent quality level and a poor on-time delivery record which must be considered. The cost-ratio plan approach can be used in the cost analysis. Development and qualification testing costs are not known, but should be estimated based on field experience of the similar valve on the A320 aircraft.

The Valient Engineering Corporation valve is one-third less expensive than the Smith Controls valve, but requires design changes. Based on the sale quantities estimated by marketing, the program savings are $361.00 per valve for 100 valves per year for 10 years, or $361,000.000. A large number of design changes can be made for this amount. Since valve reliability, quality, and on-time delivery are likely to be as good or better than Smith's, this is a fairly conservative estimate.

Question 4:

Discuss the non-economic factors involved in this case.

Comment:

One of the main non-economic factors involved in this case is Linda Mitchell's relationship with Julio Lopez. Linda has had a professional relationship with Julio for many years. During the development of the design, she presumably worked closely with Julio to gain information on such items as weight, size, connectors, functional characteristics, etc. It is probable that through this interchange, Linda ended up specifying a valve that Julio's company could readily supply. The problem with this approach is that GTI is likely to be tied into a single source situation. This type of problem is very common in American industry and is contrary to the concept of early supplier involvement.

Other factors involved are: how much influence does engineering have in the company, how cost conscious is the project engineer or program manager, does any type of formal value engineering program exist, and how much support and respect is given to the purchasing department?

Question 5:

What organizational changes could be made at GTI to give greater emphasis to value analysis or value engineering?

Comment:

A value analysis program should be introduced to help meet the needs of the new market which GTI is pursuing. The committee approach to value analysis is probably the best for this particular case. An executive committee could oversee this activity. A steering committee would be formed and charged with establishing and maintaining a company-wide value analysis/value engineering program. A consultant could be hired or an in-house value engineering department established to train value analysis teams.

Six to eight teams could be established for the APS 2000 program. Each one would address a different module within the engine (turbine, compressor, combustor, gearbox, electronic controls, hydro-mechanical controls, etc.). Each team would be made up of a purchasing representative (chair), manufacturing engineer, design engineer, quality engineer, and project engineer. Cost targets would be established and team meetings held to identify cost savings. These teams would report to the steering committee and to the executive committee. The committees would monitor team progress toward the cost targets. They would also evaluate and approve different alternatives when large expenditures are required to achieve the desired cost target.

Recommendations

It is recommended that, if the meeting attendees agree, Bill negotiate with Smith Controls to gain a price reduction and delivery guarantees. Bill must complete this negotiation within one week or else place the order with Valient. Any negotiations should include options for multiyear procurement to prevent large price increases during subsequent years.

GTI should implement a value engineering/analysis program to formalize and structure all cost reduction efforts. The program presented in the response to question number 5 is recommended.

Implementation Plan

The implementation plan presented below is the one actually used by the company.

GTI was segregated into two business segments: military and commercial. A new Vice President and General Manager was hired to head up the commercial division. He was hired from a major U.S. aircraft gas turbine engine manufacturer with extensive experience in doing business with commercial airlines. An engineering manager was hired who had spent his career designing auxiliary power units. Together they established a value engineering executive committee composed of themselves and the directors of operations, purchasing, quality assurance, finance, marketing and engineering. A steering committee was formed consisting of managers who report to the directors on the executive committee, plus two consultants who provide training and VE program management. Seven VE teams were formed within two months of the establishment of the commercial division. To date, the firm has initiated design, manufacturing, and procurement changes which are estimated to reduce the cost of the APS 2000 by over 10 percent. Other changes, in the planning stages, will reduce the cost by over 30 percent within the next year.

GENERATION DISK SYSTEMS, INC.

Purpose

The purpose of this case is to explore the ways in which procurement can affect product quality through effective motivation of suppliers. The discussion should focus on activities that purchasing managers can use to encourage active supplier participation in quality improvement.

Comment:

In today's increasingly competitive business environment, product quality is essential, replacing price as the key to profit and increased market share.

Suppliers are an extension of a company's manufacturing capability and need to share responsibility for improving the quality of their customer's products and efficiency of their operations. Suppliers are getting the message that if they want a share of the business, they must share the work. A basic tenet of the W. Edwards Deming Doctrine is that buyers must aim for nothing less than 100 percent performance in selecting new suppliers and evaluating old ones. Although perfect conformance to requirements might seem an almost impossible ideal, more purchasing managers are using this message and other techniques to motivate suppliers. Supplier quality programs are becoming an integral part of procurement strategy.

Although quality can be imposed on a supplier, it is much more desirable if the supplier recognizes that a quality program can be mutually beneficial. Such benefits to the supplier include: (1) improvement of reputation among customers and increased marketability of its products, (2) improvement in its own manufacturing processes and profits, (3) reduced rework costs, and (4) improved employee motivation from doing a good job. Of course, the primary motivation to a supplier is the expectation of a long-standing business relationship, arrived a by providing quality products, on schedule, and at a competitive price.

Analysis

Question 1:

Who should be responsible for establishing and monitoring the quality plan at GDS?

Comment:

The cost of the purchased materials that go into the manufacture of the GDS disk drives is estimated to be approximately 72 percent of the cost of the company's finished products. These procured items have a tremendous impact on the reliability of the firm's products. Because such a significant portion of GDS's expense and income comes under the control of the purchasing department, purchasing should manage the supplier quality program with quality assurance's active assistance. Other parts of the organization have a part to play, but the ultimate responsibility for management of supplier quality rests with purchasing. Norman Garvey should administer the strategy in order to achieve optimal quality from the firm's suppliers. This includes product quality, service, value, quality of delivery, and the supplier's attitude.

Question 2:

The effectiveness of GDS's supplier quality program will rely on Norman's ability to persuade GDS's suppliers to WANT to perform satisfactorily. How can he motivate the suppliers so that GDS will meet the deadline and with a high-quality product?

Comment:

First, he must consider the perceptions of the suppliers. Suppliers respond to those factors which they perceive to be of greatest importance to the purchasing manager. For example, if a buyer places emphasis on cost in negotiating a purchase, the supplier is likely to perceive cost to be of greater importance than factors such as quality, service, and delivery. Therefore, Norman must stress quality requirements as the first priority, and on-time delivery second. (After all, what good would it do to come to market on time, but with a poor-quality disk drive?!).

Peter F. Drucker once stated that we could learn only two things from Japanese management: (1) an effective program cannot be built on adversarial relations, and (2) responsible employees can be created by giving them responsibilities. These same concepts can be applied to suppliers. Collaboration, rather than antagonism, is rule number one; and, second, responsible suppliers can be "created" by delegating more responsibility to them. Again, the objective of the supplier motivation program is to get the supplier to accept the responsibility for quality.

This discussion can be enhanced by relating some real-life experiences of companies that manage successful supplier quality programs. Several of these could be implemented at GDS. Some examples are:

- *DMA Systems Corporation*—similarly competing in the computer industry—was able to hit the market with a running start with a sophisticated approach to integrating suppliers directly into its production operation. DMA's practice includes treating key suppliers like members of the company. All efforts go toward building strong relationships that have the characteristics of partnerships. The program was designed to tap the technical expertise and resources of suppliers who have years of experience in the field.

  The benefits that DMA has reaped from the program include: (1) starting far down the learning curve because of its suppliers experience; (2) a great reduction in tooling costs; (3) lower costs where suppliers have offshore facilities; (4) extended credit terms through good relationships and communication.

- At *Xerox Corporation*, the answer to improving supplier performance is in raising expectations. The vice president of materials planning believes that giving the supplier short lead times and accepting low-quality levels motivates the supplier to be a low-quality producer.

- *3M* was one of the pioneers in putting on supplier seminars that emphasize quality. These seminars are condensed versions of the company's own in-house quality training program.

- *Motorola, Inc.* regularly sends out quality engineers to supplier sites for assistance and training. It is part of Motorola's corporate commitment to "boost quality ten-fold in five years." The company broadcasted this commitment in a series of full-page newspaper ads, which was its way of communicating that it wanted a quantum jump in a short time.

- To some companies, motivation is expressed through reducing the number of suppliers. *Thermo King Corporation* consolidated its volume and order quantities to fewer suppliers, which proved advantageous to both parties. The efficiencies of supplier base reduction and sole-sourcing work to motivate suppliers toward long relationships through quality improvement.

- The *Tennant Company* of Minneapolis has developed a unique method to stimulate supplier involvement that stresses positive, ongoing communication and interaction. Its quality program includes getting top executives from supplier companies involved from the start by inviting them to the company for a full day of discussions. At the end of the meetings, the executives are asked to commit to quality goals within several weeks. This supplier pledge reads:

> "We pledge to do our job right every time. It is our personal contribution toward zero defects and a statement of our commitment. Our individual efforts, along with those of all Tennant Company employees, will enhance our mutual overall continued success. Through our teamwork, Tennant Company and its customers, employees, and suppliers will benefit from this total quality commitment."

In addition to the initial management conferences, the company holds "celebrations" to review and renew employee and supplier commitment. These events, known as "Zero Defect Days" are resulting in decreased costs and improved quality. Tennant's supplier quality program is based on the following principles:

1. Involve top supplier management.
2. Dedicate quality department people to purchased material quality improvement.
3. Establish communication channels among members of both companies' quality control departments.
4. Qualify suppliers, don't just survey them.
5. Reduce the number of suppliers.
6. Qualify parts before they're used in production.
7. Train people in problem-solving techniques.
8. Work on your biggest problems first.
9. Don't assign disposition to rejections without eliminating the cause of rejection.
10. Reduce inventories.
11. Encourage suppliers to use statistical methods for process and quality control.
12. Communicate, communicate, communicate.

Question 3:

Suppose goods received from one or more suppliers do not conform to GDS requirements. What actions can you suggest to motivate the supplier?

Comment:

This discussion should focus on reactive supplier motivation (as opposed to the proactive approaches described above). Certainly it makes better sense to involve suppliers in quality performance before the fact. But sometimes customers are forced to deal with surprise nonconformances of a product at its own receiving dock. The alternatives available to motivate the supplier in such a case include product returns, cancellation of contracts, collection of rework and scrap charges, and legal action. Non-monetary reactive means include letters to management, discrediting of quality image through press releases and ALERTS, on-site reviews, and disapproved product lists. Action taken would depend on the severity of the problem and the demonstrated attitude of the supplier to cooperate.

Question 4:

Managing an effective supplier quality program requires the allocation of substantial time and money. How can Norman Garvey justify the program's costs compared to the contributions made to company objectives and profits?

Comment:

The following graph provides a good illustration of the "cost of quality trade-off".

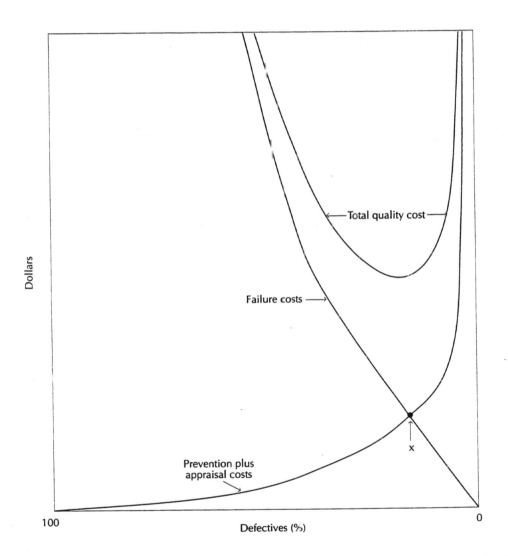

As the sum of prevention and appraisal costs increases, the number of defectives decreases. The optimum mixture of effort is indicated at the minimum point on the total cost curve.

Determining the costs that are directly related to GDS's supplier quality program is a difficult task. First, Norman must consider scenarios that could occur without the program, then quantify the costs associated with them. For instance, the costs of prevention and evaluation should be weighed against the costs of

- extra inventory due to anticipated problems;
- extra inventory due to nonconforming material held for disposition;
- rework due to supplier defective material;
- scrap due to supplier nonconforming material;
- production delays;
- thorough inspection of materials;
- evaluating new suppliers;
- frequent supplier visits to correct problems;
- lost business.

GOLDEN BUFFALO, INC.

Purpose

The primary purpose of this case is to discuss what should be reported to the president so that he or she can evaluate purchasing performance and also be aware of purchasing problems that are important to the company as a whole. A secondary purpose is to identify the types of information a purchasing manager should make available to his fellow managers.

Discussion

Purchasing and other functional managers often have difficulty in distinguishing between information that is essential to them and information that is essential to their bosses. The information needed to operate their departments efficiently and control them effectively, and the information that is essential for their bosses to control the entire company, or a group of company functions, is quite different.

Bosses are quite different in their methods of operations and, therefore, in what information they want from department heads. This being a fact, the astute department head will ascertain exactly what kinds of information his boss wants. To provide this information as rapidly, as completely, and as economically as possible, the data normally should be prepared as a by-product from the information already accumulated for the head of the purchasing department.

Question 1:

What information should Ruben Gomez gather and report to his fellow managers at the weekly meetings?

Comment:

Ruben is fortunate in that he can communicate with the general manager both individually and in association with other managers at the weekly management meetings.

At the management meetings, Ruben has the opportunity of making a continuous series of short (very short) reports that are carefully planned to integrate purchasing and his other materials responsibilities with the overall company effort. All of Ruben's reports should be on subjects reflecting company-wide problems presented with a company viewpoint. When possible, these reports should be presented graphically to facilitate interpretation and speed up the presentation. Topics suitable for presentation could include the following:

1. Data on and problems concerning inventories
2. Reports on mergers of major suppliers and other similar economic information concerning the competition moves of competitors. Purchasing should be the economic ears of a company. What these ears hear is of great interest to other departments
3. Impending changes in lead times and prices of interest to other departments
4. Information about new materials and equipment that are soon to come on the market or are already on the market
5. Suggestions for better integration of the materials functions of the company

6. Any make-or-buy suggestions that will reduce costs and require cooperation of several departments to achieve

Question 2:

What information should Ruben report directly to the general manager?

Comment:

Reports made to the general manager should include events directly affecting profits. These events would include the following:

1. Savings made from more efficient buying
   a. by value analysis
   b. by changing suppliers
   c. by purchasing research
   d. by changing types of contracts
   e by better negotiation
   f. by more thorough procurement analysis
   g. by better control of inventories
   h. miscellaneous
2. Information on future price changes or lead times that would significantly influence company operations
3. Changes in work load of such magnitude as to require increases in personnel, costly equipment, office or warehouse space, etc.

GOTHAM CITY BUYS FIRE ENGINES

Purpose

The purpose of this case is to discuss coordination between the user and the buyer in a government buying context. The basic point of dispute, however, is restrictive specifications, and this is a problem area that affects all purchasing departments, not just government purchasing departments.

Discussion

Fire chiefs, city engineers, and police chiefs all have strong opinions about specific brands of equipment needed to perform their jobs. It is not unusual to find a fire chief who insists that all brands of fire extinguishers except one are prone to failure and are not acceptable. Fire chiefs have been known to so "load" the specifications that only one manufacturer can meet them. For example, fire engines have been specified that have a 12-cylinder engine that must be "manufactured" in the same plant as the body. Only one manufacturer can meet this specification. It is not at all unusual for fire chiefs to feel so strongly about specific brands that they will state they will no longer be responsible for putting out fires if their preferred brand is not purchased.

Police chiefs have often insisted on vehicles with excessively high performance characteristics. Increasing the horsepower in a car engine can raise the price sharply (as much as $2200 per car). Yet many police departments have little or no requirement for pursuit work and operate in a highway network where speeds of 120 miles per hour are neither safe nor possible. Students may be interested to learn that a few successful purchasing executives in such situations (where there is not need for a high-powered vehicle) have even been able to sell their police departments on the concept of using low-powered compacts.

When buying for users of expensive capital equipment, in addition to the problem of specifications, there can be a problem of entertainment. If the manufacturer of an expensive piece of equipment can have his brand specified in preference to all others, it is possible for him to include in his price all costs of production and sales as well as a considerable profit. One of the costs of sales sometimes includes elaborate pleasure trips to the factory of the manufacturer. The trip includes considerable entertainment for the fire chief, police chief, city manager, and on occasion the entire city council. These costs of doing business (not to mention the ethical considerations) can only be avoided if the purchasing executive is successful in pointing out to this organization the high cost of specifications that are unduly restrictive.

Question 1:

What should Frisby tell the Mayor?

Comment:

Frisby has got himself in a cross fire by not getting Chief Clark to agree personally to the general specifications as well as to specific brands of fire engines that are acceptable. Although Chief Clark sent his representative to the specification meetings, Frisby would have been much wiser to have insisted before the requests for bids were sent out that Chief Clark agree that the specific brands being bid on met the specifications.

Frisby must now tell the mayor that purchasing erred to this extent (not getting Chief Clark to agree to brands before sending out bids). He must also tell the mayor how he plans to solve the present problem. If the low bidder does meet the specifications, and if the specifications are reasonable, the mayor must be told that any policy other than accepting the low bidder would once again cause the city and its suppliers to lose confidence in its purchasing department. Frisby must tell the mayor that the only justification for throwing out the low bidder would be failure of the equipment to meet the specifications.

Question 2:

How should the city purchasing manager help solve the fire engine dispute to the satisfaction of the fire chief and the city council?

Comment:

The problem has two parts: a short-run part involving the fire trucks, and a long-run part of establishing effective standards and procurement procedures. The purchasing manager should start on the short-run part by making a personal contact with the chief to determine his factual objections to the low bidder's equipment. The purchasing manager should try to get Chief Clark to consider extensive tests and investigations into other cities' experiences with the trucks of the low bidder. A trip to the factory to inspect manufacturing methods, competency, and so on, may prove beneficial. The purchasing manager should privately emphasize to the Chief the need to rebuild public confidence in the mayor's administration, and the political risk of opposing a "cleanup." Face-saving devices such as a call for new bids based on a revision of specifications to accommodate any real deficiencies might be used. However, in view of the thoroughness with which the specifications were prepared, the most practical face-saver seems to be letting the fire chief check out the equipment by visits to other cities using it, visiting the factory, and making extensive tests of his own.

Frisby should next discuss the problem with the mayor, pointing out that he has talked to the fFire chief. He should report what happened in their meeting and discuss strategy with the mayor. He and the mayor should reach a joint decision as to what the next step should be.

If the city council battle is inevitable, the purchasing manager and the mayor must go prepared with test reports, recommendations of fire-preventive groups, insurance companies, and other experts. Their case can be so well documented that the biases of the chief will be obvious for all to see.

The long-run solution may be to put department heads on the standardization committee, or to get top-level review and agreement from them as the acceptance of these standards for competitive bidding.

GREAT WESTERN UNIVERSITY I

Purpose

The purpose of this case is to permit discussion of the problems involved in selecting a supplier from among several potential suppliers having very different management philosophies.

Question:

What should Dan Summerfield do? Should he contract with Bumble Bee? Automated? A small supplier?

Comment:

If the cost of carrying inventory is rounded off to 30 percent per year, the following quantitative analyses can be made:

Savings over present method	Bumble Bee	Automated	Small Supplier
Invoice price savings (Purchases = $400,000 per year)	$0	$60,000	$100,000
Possible reductions in inventory (currently $240,000)	160,000	80,000	0
Possible inventory carrying cost savings (30% of inventory reduction)	$ 48,000	24,000	0
Total likely savings	$ 48,000	84,000	0

Some students and faculty may find it easier to look at the total costs associated with each supplier.

TOTAL COSTS			
Annual expenditures ($400,000 less discounts)	$400,000	340,000	300,000
Required inventory	80,000	160,000	240,000
Annual inventory carrying cost (30% of value of inventory)	24,000	48,000	72,000
Total annual cost	424,000	388,000	372,000

Thus, it is possible to conclude that Great Western could be paying $52,000 per year (the difference between Bumble Bee and a small supplier) because of an inability of the plumbers to plan. The class can then logically ask:

1. Why not hire a "plumber-planner" and take advantage of the big discounts?
2. Automated may look like the best of both worlds because there is some savings or price, and some on inventory.
3. Isn't Bumble Bee's super service worth more?

Whenever a stock-out occurs, buy the part from Bumble Bee at wholesale price, and pick it up personally, 3 percent stock-out limit.

On the evidence available most students choose Automated. But the quantitative facts and analysis support selection of the small supplier.

Most students tend to get bogged down in the quantitative aspects of this case (which are presented above). The instructor, however, may wish to direct the discussion toward the many interesting qualitative aspects of the case by asking questions such as the following:

> Do you think Automated would devote the time to assist Great Western in value analysis studies that Bumble Bee would? Do you think Automated would respond to special orders with the speed of Bumble Bee? What advantages could accrue to Great Western from Bumble Bee's very large cash position? Can any reliance be placed on Mr. Bee's system of inventory control?

Note to Instructor

Immediately following these Great Western University case comments is the Great Western University II case. This case is a sequel to the Great Western University case. However, it is not included in the textbook. It is included here in the Instructor's Manual for the confidential use of the instructor.

The authors have successfully used Great Western University II in a number of ways: (1) to extend the discussion of the Great Western University case by, at the appropriate time, advising the students what actually happened; (2) as a written report, and (3) as a handout case for discussion at the next class.

Whether or not Great Western II is used, reading it should prove helpful to the instructor in directing the discussion of the Great Western University I case.

GREAT WESTERN UNIVERSITY II
(THE CASE)

Two years ago Dan Summerfield signed an annual contract with Automated Plumbing Supply. At first, the university's plumbers were unhappy that they no longer had an excuse to go to Red City to chat and drink coffee and soft drinks at Bumble Bee. However, the 15 percent savings on prices paid, and savings on the reduction in inventory reduced Great Western's plumbing costs by about $84,000 during the first year of the contract. This was most pleasing to the university's administrators. Although deliveries were made only twice weekly, rarely was Great Western in difficulty because of a lack of plumbing supplies. Indeed, thanks to the computer, Automated's stock-outs averaged closer to 3 percent, rather than 5 percent anticipated. It appeared that Dan had made a perfect purchasing agreement for Great Western, and he was feeling quite pleased about the entire situation

One morning while eating an enjoyable breakfast, Dan read the following news item in the paper:

AUTOMATED PLUMBING BANKRUPT

Today, Automated Plumbing Supply Company, with headquarters in Field, closed its doors. The president of the company announced that the company was hopelessly insolvent and would be able to pay its bills only at the rate of 25¢ on the dollar. All past customers were thanked for their patronage. All creditors were advised to contact the law firm of Smith, Smith, and Smith who have been appointed receivers for the firm.

Mr. Summerfield's enjoyable breakfast immediately became unappealing.

1. What should Summerfield do when he gets to his office?
2. What are the lessons to be learned from this case?

GREAT WESTERN UNIVERSITY II

Purpose

The purpose of this case is to permit a discussion of what can happen when a company becomes too progressive. In the interest of time, the instructor may want to read this case to the class after discussing Great Western University I.

Question 1:

What should Summerfield do when he gets to his office?

Comment:

Dan Summerfield should immediately attempt to make a short-term contract with Bumble Bee or other suppliers who offer delivery as good as that received from Automated. If Mr. Bee refuses such a contract, Dan should immediately have the inventory control records reviewed for the purpose of increasing the stock levels of those fast-moving items which it was necessary to stock in large quantities before the Automated contract was made. Also, if Mr. Bee refuses a contract, Dan should buy from Bumble Bee as before, and immediately start a restudy of the entire problem of plumbing supplies.

Question 2:

What are the lessons to be learned from this case?

Comment:

The critical lesson to be learned from this case is that managers with advanced degrees, having the use of the latest available electronic data-processing machines, and the latest models of automated warehouses, are not per se insured achievement greater than that of cagey, experienced, long-time managers who thoroughly understand their products and industry, but do not progressively take advantage of the latest available managerial and mechanical aids.

This case permits a full discussion contrasting the thoughts and actions of the two types of management involved. First, the risks which each takes can be compared. In this case, the extremely progressive management of Automated risks the ultimate penalty of bankruptcy by pushing forward just a little too fast (too fast is often difficult to distinguish—bankruptcy came to Automated as a great surprise). Second, the extremely conservative management of Bumble Bee does not risk the ultimate penalty of bankruptcy, but it continuously and unnecessarily sacrifices the rewards of greater profit.

The instructor can proceed to compare the effects of these two differing operating philosophies on all of the functions of business management, i.e., design, finance, personnel, purchasing and materials management, production, and sales.

Finally, the instructor may point out that Great Western enjoyed two years of savings—and other sources are available.

HARDY COMPANY

Purpose

The purpose of this case is to explore (1) how development costs resulting from buyer requested proprietary specifications should be charged, and (2) how proprietary specifications can influence supplier relations, value analysis, quality, and price.

Discussion

This case centers around two questions:

1. How should bids for jobs involving engineering development services be handled?
2. What is the advisability of proprietary bids?

Cutting across both of these question areas is the overall problem of ensuring supplier relations.

Question 1:

Do you feel that the purchase of this motor was properly handled? How would you have handled it?

Comment:

Mr. Monaghan might have handled this purchase much more effectively from the standpoints of value analysis and supplier relations. There seems to be little logic in his award of the contract solely on the basis of informal discussions with various suppliers' sales representatives. The fundamental problems involved were engineering problems which most salesmen are not qualified to answer; therefore, it is entirely possible that another supplier might have been able to do the job as well as or better than Centennial had the proper engineering personnel of the various suppliers been called in on the job. It is true that a good salesman would have seen to it that this was done, as did the Centennial vice president, but it is equally true that a good buyer in the interests of economical purchasing would have facilitated this action by issuing engineering drawings and specifications along with a formal request for quotations. By doing so, he would have given every supplier an equal opportunity, and he would have forestalled any subsequent charges of favoritism. Perhaps if purchasing had been part of a product development committee, odd-size motors would not have been used.

Question 2:

Should the Hardy Company have solicited competitive bids?

Comment:

It would have been much fairer to all suppliers concerned if purchasing had issued formal bid requests, including all of the engineering data required by suppliers, for an approximate price on the job. Similarly, this procedure would have assured purchasing of a more competitive price. Where extensive development work is required before a bid can be made, reasonably close estimates can usually be made which will at least serve as a basis for further negotiation with the competitive suppliers. If the award decision cannot be made upon receipt of the initial bid, it can certainly be made after such negotiation.

The buyer might also have taken steps to avert the nebulous situation he now finds himself in regarding supplier coverage of development costs. When obtaining bids, he could have obtained prices in such a way that his firm would know specifically when all development costs were recovered. He could have requested prices in one of two ways:

a. Motor cost bid at the level which would have covered all special tooling and production costs on (and guaranteed purchase of) a specified number of units. All engineering development costs bid separately

b. Motor cost bid at a level which would have covered all special tooling, production, and development costs in a specified number of units

Thus, the buyer would not have been tied to the developing supplier for an unreasonable length of time. The supplier is treated fairly and purchasing is in a position to apply the natural pressures of competition in obtaining the best possible buy, without jeopardizing relations with loyal suppliers.

Question 3:

What would you do if you were in Mr. Monaghan's position now?

Comment:

As an immediate course of action, Hardy is justified in requesting competitive bids on the motor at this date for the following reasons:

a. The sales of 350,000 units over the two-year period certainly appears to be a reasonable volume with which Centennial should have recovered its special tooling and development costs. The fact that Centennial quoted the special motor at a standard motor price on the second order of 100,000 units particularly indicates that the majority of the special costs were probably covered on the initial order of 100,000 motors. Furthermore, inasmuch as Centennial refused to bid its development costs as a separate item, it indicated its willingness to risk selling enough units to cover these costs. It is unlikely that good business practice would allow the management to prorate the costs over a period extending beyond two years on a small, unproved product such as this.

Although the details of Centennial's cost accounting system are unknown, there is also a good possibility that it allocates its engineering expenses over the entire operation. Thus, although production of this special motor ceases, its unabsorbed development costs are still being covered by the sale of other products.

b. From both the supplier's and purchaser's points of view, two years later is more than a reasonable length of time for the purchase of these inexpensive motors to be made on a proprietary basis.

c. It is reasonable to assume that Centennial has taken adequate patent steps to protect the technical aspects of its special motor. If such is the case, it is unlikely that any other supplier would be able to underbid Centennial unless Centennial's price is out of line.

d. Mr. Monaghan should talk with the president of Centennial, commending him for his company's fine performance to date and explaining the desirability of requesting competitive bids on the motor. If done tactfully, Hardy will improve its supplier relations in total and also keep its motor suppliers competitive.

HARTINCO, INC.

Purpose

This case provides the student with an insight into the differences between direct and indirect costs. Direct costs are directly attributable to a project or process, are readily identifiable and are large enough to merit measurement. Indirect costs, on the other hand, cannot be easily identified, are not directly associated with a specific project or process or are too insignificant to merit measurement.

In this case students are required to identify direct and indirect costs and come up with an appropriate rate of allocating overhead to the three projects. Finally the full cost is calculated on a "per-hour" basis. This cost, plus a fair profit, would be the fair and reasonable price.

The instructor may want to encourage the students to first prepare a table listing the various indirect costs and then the method used to allocate these costs to the 3 projects. Tables 1 and 2 below show this information.

TABLE 1
Information Sheet

	Production		Service	
	Information Retrieval	Report Writing	Data Processing	Library Service
1. Direct labor hours	265	80		
2. Proportion of labor	77%	23%		
3. Space occupied—sq. ft.	5000	5000	1250	10,000
4. Proportion of space	23.5%	23.5%	6%	47%

TABLE 2
Allocation of Overhead

	Total	Production		Service	
		Information Retrieval	Report Writing	Data Processing	Library Service
Rent (see 4 above)	$2,000	$470	$470	$120	$940
Utilities (4)	400	94	94	24	188
Indirect					
Labor (actual)	4,930	350		3,200	1,380
Other expenses (actual)	1,100	____	____	1,000	100
Total overhead					
Before allocation	8,430	914	564	4,344	2,608
Allocation of:					
Data processing (2)		3,344	1,000	(4,344)	
Library service		2,008	600	____	(2,608)
Overhead after allocation	8,430	6,266	2,164		

Question 1:

Calculate the amount of direct costs for each project for the month of January 1989.

Solution:

Direct Costs	Project A Hrs.	A $	B Hrs	B $	C Hrs.	C $
Labor: Info. retrieval	80	560	25	175	160	1,120
Report preparation	20	140	10	70	50	350
Total	100	700	35	245	210	1,470
Direct labor cost/hr		7		7		7

Question 2:

Calculate the indirect costs for each of the production and service departments for January 1989.

Solution: (See Table 2)

Question 3:

Calculate the rates at which indirect costs should be allocated to each project for each of the two production departments.

Solution:

Overhead	Total	Project A	B	C
Labor: Info. retrieval	$6,266	$1,892	$591	$3,783
Per hour (÷ by 265)	23.65			
Report preparation	2,164	541	271	1,352
Per hour (÷ by 80)	27.05			

Question 4:

What is the full (total) cost of each of the three projects that were performed in January?

Solution:

	Project A	B	C
Total direct costs	$ 700	$ 245	$1,470
Share of overhead: IR	1,892	591	3,783
RP	541	271	1,352
Full cost	3,133	1,107	6,605
Cost per hour	31.33	31.63	31.45

Question 5:

Develop a logical pricing mechanism for Vista's contract with Hartinco.

Solution:

John Angst should consider himself fortunate that Jennifer provided him with cost data. He now has a couple of alternatives:

1. Average rate:

The average hourly rate for projects in January 1989 was $31.47 ([31.33 + 31.63 + 31.45] ÷ 3). To this may be added a fair profit of say 10 percent ($33.15). This would result in a price of $34.62 per hour.

2. Specific rates:

This would mean setting different prices for information retrieval and report writing respectively. In both cases the direct costs are $7 per hour. Overhead rates are $23.65 and $27.05 for retrieval and writing respectively. Prices (with a 10 percent profit) could be established as follows:

	Information retrieval	Report preparation
	(in $ per hour)	
Direct labor	7.00	7.00
Overhead	23.65	27.05
Profit	3.07	3.40
	33.72	37.45

Comments:

The instructor may want to emphasize the point that these rates are based on the data obtained for one month only. Perhaps a review of data covering a few more months will provide more realistic rates for allocating overhead.

Finally, if Hartinco has unused capacity, John Angst can expect price changes (reductions) in the hourly rate if new projects fill the unused capacity, thereby spreading overhead.

HOLY CROSS HEALTH CARE, INC.

Purpose

The primary purpose of this case is to discuss economic and noneconomic issues encountered when implementing standardization procedures. Other issues involve the store's operation and the management of inventory.

Discussion

This case discusses several issues involved in the analysis of a standardization program including the roles of purchasing and administration as related to supply management.

Question 1:

Identify the major issues that need to be addressed in this situation.

Comment

Supplier management problems are at the root of the current problem. The possibility of reinstating the JIT system and dissolving the warehouse would depend on future supplier relationships. If suppliers relocated back to the Pittsburgh area, the warehouse could become obsolete.

Question 2:

What additional information would be useful in developing a solution to the hospital supplies management problem at Holy Cross?

Comment:

Information on the mission and goals of Holy Cross would be helpful. A goal of quality patient care *at the lowest cost* would encourage establishment of a standardization program. Future growth plans and the current financial capability of Holy Cross would assist Joe Jones and the purchasing department in planning for the future management of medical supplies.

Knowing the supply management goals of the other area hospitals would assist planning at Holy Cross. Accurate records of the number of sales to each hospital should be kept to help determine what type of market exists in this area. Joe should be aware of other hospitals' plans for changes that would negate Holy Cross's current sales to them.

The actual incremental cost of buying, storing, shipping, and associated accounting expenses for the materials being sold to other hospitals should be developed and used as the basis of the markup to these customers.

Question 3:

Consultant's outline for a report to management:

Facts:

1. The off-site warehouse contains 6,000 items, including several duplications. Three years ago only 800 items were stocked.
2. Items are being added to the master inventory list without purchasing's knowledge or approval. The JSC is determining which items to delete from the inventory.
3. The JSC is overstaffed and incapable of decisive action. Political interests have prevented management from intervening, resulting in a lack of direction and goals.
4. Major suppliers have relocated to Philadelphia. Other hospitals in the city buy supplies from the Holy Cross warehouse on a regular basis.
5. Purchasing reports two levels below administrative services and has no ties to professional services. No feedback on item usage or patient care is given to purchasing.

Problem Statement

How can Holy Cross obtain and distribute medical supplies in a timely and cost-effective manner without adversely affecting patient care?

Alternatives

1. Do nothing.

    + The health-care system is currently operating and providing excellent patient care. Several staff personnel are quite satisfied with current operations.

    + The administration avoids alienating the professional staff by letting the current acquisition and inventory policies continue.

    − Warehouse costs are escalating out of sight. Item acquisition appears to have higher priority than cost control or quality of patient care. Items are added to inventory with very little screening in terms of cost, appropriateness, quality, or availability. Costs will have to be brought under control soon. Waiting to change the current system will continue to drain Holy Cross funds needed elsewhere.

2. Reduce the numbers of items in the system through standardization.

    + Item reduction would allow better management of the remaining inventory base.

    + Fewer items to maintain in inventory would reduce purchase, handling, and storage costs.

    + Substitutes that are less expensive may be found for some items while maintaining the necessary quality level. No search for substitutes is currently being conducted. Monitoring to determine if only one or a few physicians are using some items should also be implemented to facilitate the standardization program.

    + Establishment of a standardization policy would assist in new item review. JSC currently is operating on the winds of the moment without any criteria to evaluate items for addition or deletion.

    − Implementing an aggressive standardization program will meet with resistance. Without top administration support, special interest groups will prevent the program from achieving meaningful success.

    – Professionals will need to be reeducated when substitutes are chosen and familiar items are deleted. Doctors and nurses must be included in the standardization planning to make wise decisions in these areas.

3. Establish a subsidiary business out of the warehouse.

    + The warehouse would be free from JSC controls in item selection and could concentrate on high-volume sales and quantity discounts.

    + A larger markup than 5 percent could be charged to all customers. Additionally, lower costs should be realized through quantity discounts and possible direct purchasing from manufacturers.

    + Marketing efforts could better fulfill the needs of all area hospitals. Current suppliers have left a vacuum by moving out of the area and an opportunity exists for aggressive action.

    – Current warehouse costs are fully borne by Holy Cross. There is no guarantee that independent operation would be a financial success and the risk for further losses exists.

    – Current market information is incomplete. Other hospitals may not choose to support the Holy Cross subsidiary and continue to use it only for emergency supplies.

Recommendation

Holy Cross should immediately undertake a standardization program to reduce costs and the number of items currently held in inventory.

Implementation

The JSC should be reduced to five or so members. It should establish clear policies and guidelines for supply personnel to follow in managing the medical supplies inventory. Item consolidation should be followed up by using the stronger bargaining position of larger quantity purchases to obtain discounts on the remaining items. The purchasing department should implement the new cost-saving and value-adding features necessary. A strong relationship with administrative services will need to be maintained and the support of the hospital administration will also have to be obtained

The possible creation of a subsidiary business from the warehouse should be studied further. The opportunity created by the major suppliers' exit from the market should be explored. The market demand needs to be studied further and a profitability analysis prepared before proceeding. Such an idea could prove very successful but additional time, information, funding, and personnel are needed prior to launching the venture.

HYDROSUB'S UNFLOATABLE AMPHIBIOUS ASSAULT VEHICLE

Purpose and Objective

This subcontract management case challenges students to discover administrative problems and corrective actions. The successful administration of a contract involves preparing and controlling delivery schedules, resources, costs and the product design process.

Hydrosub's problems illustrate the interrelationship of design planning and contract preparation. If the design process had been adequate, much time and money would have been saved in the production stage. Administrative processes further complicated discovery and correction of problems. Since the contract has been awarded and production begun, management must expedite and motivate the supplier to complete the work.

Question 1:

Who is responsible for the poor performance of the Bolger contract?

Comment:

Hydrosub's chief buyer failed miserably when preparing the A.A.V. contract. Hydrosub's design problems and poor contract terms doomed the project. Hydrosub's procurement process did not properly reconcile its contract preparation with the project's goals. It failed to prepare adequate tactics for avoiding the design problems and recognize the impact of Bolger's poor cost reporting system.

Question 2:

What caused the production delays and cost miscalculations?

Comment:

Errors in Hydrosub's procurement process have caused both design and completion problems. Insufficient design review led to the eventual work stoppages, contract snafus, and high costs. Questionable source selection resulting in communication problems and cost-reporting logjams only aggravated the design problems.

Question 3:

What can Kathleen Johnson do now to ensure completion of the project and prevent further problems?

Comment:

Hydrosub's engineering staff and Bolger's production staff should jointly review the vehicle design specifications. Major design flaws should be eliminated prior to resumption of work. Completion dates and minor design alterations should be negotiated into the contract. Milestone planning and progress reporting should be used to identify areas for immediate attention.

Under Bolger's current cost control system, costs are not analyzed for up to three weeks. Consequently, problems are not quickly identified and contract negotiations are delayed. Speeding up Bolger's cost-reporting system is an important element of contract negotiations.

Supplier motivation also is lacking. The cost plus fixed fee contract terms do not motivate Bolger. After the many delays, Bolger has developed a lackadaisical attitude toward this project's completion. A completion bonus should be negotiated into the contract.

Switching suppliers and paying off Bolger is an alternative. However, the small supply of skilled aluminum welders may force Hydrosub to stay with Bolger.

Question 4:

How should Hydrosub's staff have prepared for negotiations with suppliers on this contract?

Comment:

Review of the engineering quality requirements and a consultation with a production engineer would have alleviated many of the technical problems that Bolger encountered. Contract terms should have included easier terms for changing design specifications. Allowance for some rework should have been part of the original contract.

Additionally, Bolger's cost-reporting systems should have been tested and altered. Cost estimates should have been reviewed by experienced managers for reasonableness.

HY TECH

Purpose

The purpose of this case is to discuss a difficult purchasing problem which is intensifying with the development of an ever-increasing number of new, highly technical products. The basic problem is: how can a firm's purchasing department bring new products and new product ideas to the scientific and technical divisions without wasting their time? A second objective is to recognize purchasing's responsibility to pay prompt and courteous attention to potential suppliers and their offerings.

Discussion

As products become technically more complex, the worth or potential worth of new products becomes increasingly harder for the typical purchasing department to evaluate. However, such evaluations must be made. In making an evaluation for the Hy Tech Company, the immediate problems the purchasing director must solve are:

a. What products fit into the company's long- and short-range financial, research, marketing, and production objectives?
b. What are the sources of information about likely new products? How can purchasing evaluate the products and suppliers?
c. How can purchasing efficiently direct this intelligence to appropriate groups in the company?

Question 1:

What generally happens when purchasing departments fail to pay prompt and courteous attention to potential suppliers and their offerings?

Comment:

Successful sales personnel bypass purchasing when they do not receive prompt and courteous treatment. The sales personnel will go directly to the engineering department in the case of developmental work. (The same behavior will take place for equipment, supply, and service requirements.)

In very short order, purchasing will find itself totally ignored during the development stage of the firm's new products. Yet this is the stage where purchasing can and should make its greatest profit contribution. Directors of purchasing at several multibillion-dollar manufacturing firms maintain that the profit potential of purchasing involvement during the design process is far greater than at any other point in the procurement process.

If purchasing does not satisfy its responsibility to identify new products and new sources, it may be unable to insure that the items specified for purchase are economically available, in the quantities required, and from dependable sources of supply.

Question 2:

What can Ed Williams do to develop an effective new-product screening system?

Comment:

1. Williams should start by asking Hy Tech's president for a definition of general product objectives and get detailed development plans from Dr. Schmidt and others in marketing and production. These moves could initially be informal, but final recommendations should be set up as purchasing—and company—policy.

2. Williams then must study the technical complexity of the information provided and determine whether his shop-trained buyers can handle it. Ed may find that additional technical help in the form of a purchasing research division is required, with the new man for the job coming from the research and development section. This person should be an engineer, trusted by Dr. Schmidt and other researchers and be familiar with the firm's product plans.

3. As new product ideas are brought to the attention of the buyers, they would direct them through the liaison contact for evaluation without wasting Dr. Schmidt's time or disclosing company secrets.

4. An alternate solution would be to put the same functions in the hands of a purchasing-engineering-production-finance-marketing committee, with a buyer as chairman. Williams could meet weekly with Dr. Schmidt for a two-way exchange of product information and needs, with Williams passing the information on to his buyers individually or by sections, but not necessarily to all buyers. Williams would make a brief summary of these meetings, showing subjects discussed with priorities and action points determined. The summary would be sent to Dr. Schmidt, and the president as well, if he requested it.

5. The following are guides for the type of information needed:

   a. Would this new product have any advantage to Hy Tech in present or future products?
   b. Could the product be used with possible modification? What about modifications to Hy Tech equipment? Would new facilities and manpower be needed?
   c. What volume might be required? What are probable cost and price levels? What are profits and return on investment?
   d. What are the supplier's capabilities? Can he contribute to Hy Tech's research effort?

Sources of information include salesmen, trade journals, annual reports, and so on. Salesmen would not be sent to the laboratory without authority from Dr. Schmidt. Approved sales representatives or engineers working with Dr. Schmidt would receive a research and development pass from purchasing after a check-in.

Supporting programs should include technical training for buyers to acquaint them with company needs and the latest developments in their specialties; a supplier education and evaluation plan to inform them of Hy Tech's needs and check their new idea contributions; and a topic filing system to index new ideas in order that buyers can quickly check what is new, whether it fits into company plans, and whether it had been previously considered and discarded.

THE INVENTORY OCTOPUS

Purpose

The purpose of this case is to discuss a company's inventory problems and how they can be solved.

Discussion

Without strong direction and coordination from corporate headquarters, large multi-division plants invariably generate different inventory philosophies and carry inventories that are not tightly controlled and are larger than economically justified.

Question 1:

What are the company's inventory troubles?

Comment:

Smithers' inventory problems showed deep troubles in the planning, direction, and control of company funds in the material cycle without coordination at the corporate level. Each division has specific inventory problems.

    a. Purchasing at the Mill Machinery Division has stashed away a large but unknown amount of raw stock and castings to service customer orders and spare parts requirements. Division management will have to change its parts policy.

    b. Whizzo Tool has worked itself out of a heavy stock of raw materials through a buildup of finished goods. Sales forecasting and production scheduling are on a crash seasonal basis, complicating the purchasing job.

    c. Aerlectro has only a small amount of electronic gear in stock. Its problems are standardization, subcontract administration, deliveries, and value analysis.

Question 2:

How can Tom cure these problems?

Comment:

Johnson must present a program to the president to pass on through the division vice presidents to cut the required $1,000,000 from raw stocks. Key points would be:

    a. Stop buying wherever possible.

    b. Review all outstanding orders to see if material is on order elsewhere or available in inventory that should be worked down. Reschedule or cancel if possible.

    c. Stretch out lead times, order in smaller lots, and try to get suppliers to hold material in stock for subsequent release.

    d. Transfer Mill Machinery surplus raw material into production stock and maintain a smaller reserve for frequently ordered spare parts on late-model machines.

e. Review major material accounts for surplus sale or scrap, recognizing that this may involve losses on original cost, tax write-offs, and charges against corporate earnings.

f. Mill Machinery offers the most reduction potential, but Johnson should point out that in-process and finished goods inventories at Whizzo and Aerlectro are other sources of capital, and a speedup in customer deliveries, billings, and progress payments will turn them into cash.

g. As Johnson begins to get to know the company and management, he should formulate an inventory program for all divisions, stressing basic operating procedures, standards of performance, and reports. Basic points would include:

1. Gathering information, such as actual physical inventory, carrying costs, review of existing inventory control, purchasing and production control.

2. ABC analysis of inventory and purchasing, trial applications of min-max inventory and EOQ techniques, and standardization and coordinated buying of common-use items in materials, MRO and office supplies.

3. Improved coordination with purchasing, divisional marketing, production, engineering, and financial managers.

JAY MANUFACTURING COMPANY

Purpose

The purpose of this case is to discuss conflicts of interest, particularly the ethical considerations of a buyer placing orders with his brother's company.

Discussion

Purchasing ethics and company conflict of interest *policies* are the major issues in this case, not the malfeasance or careless action of Paul Hertz. Because this case indicates that Paul's brother has made a significant contribution to Jay, the instructor should have no difficulty in obtaining vigorous class discussion on both sides of the ethical question.

On the other hand, the case is clear in stating that Hertz's brother had supplied a product that filled a definite need for the company. It can be argued that brother Harold would not have worked as hard as a supplier if there had not been the team effort of the two brothers. Indeed, it can be pointed out to the class that in large companies purchasing and research are usually part of the same team for developing new products. It may be that Harold's invention did give Jay a jump on the competition.

On the other hand, a strong case can be made for the ethical position that buyers should no buy from suppliers that could in any way reflect unfavorably on the image of the company's integrity. Many suppliers will not offer new ideas to companies they believe are "sewed up" by close personal relationships between the buyer and seller. Therefore, it can be pointed out to the class that the 35 percent profit made on Harold's invention may have been a drop in the bucket compared to other inventions that Jay was not offered because suppliers were unwilling to make such offers. It is fundamental that good supplier relations can come only when suppliers feel the company treats all suppliers impartially.

This discussion can go beyond the case questions to the general question of conflicts of interest. A conflict exists when a company executive (whether he be buyer or president) has outside business interests that adversely affect the fulfillment of his obligations to his principal employer. The following questions should provoke a lively discussion on this subject:

1. Should buyers be required to disclose all of their business interests to their employers?
2. It is wrong for a buyer to buy products from a large company listed on the New York Stock Exchange in which he or she is a stockholder?
3. Should buyers be forbidden by their employers to have any outside business interests? For example, should a buyer of MRO items be told by the manager that his or her small printing operation in the basement at home on weekends conflicts with his or her buying responsibilities?
4. Should selling firms be disqualified as potential suppliers if the buyer has a relative working for the company?

Question 1:

What should Charlie do about Paul Hertz now?

Comment:

The fact that Paul told Wilson, with pride, that he was buying from his brother's company seems to indicate he has been trying to act in the best interest of his company. Wilson must find out how long New Technology has been supplying Jay; who was the competition on the original component order; and whether New Technology is competitive in price. If he finds that Paul Hertz's actions have all been in good faith, the following action is recommended.

Wilson should talk to Paul Hertz about the problem involved with his dealing with his brother's firm. He should emphasize the fact that his actions are not being criticized. However, in order to circumvent any possible future cries of favoritism, Wilson will take over all future negotiations with New Technology. If Wilson handles this tactfully, Paul will neither be personally hurt nor "lose face."

If Wilson takes over the negotiations with New Technology, this should improve the company's image with other suppliers as well as help to ensure that nothing unethical is happening. it will also give Wilson an opportunity to ascertain if anything unethical was going on. If unethical conduct is discovered by Wilson, the only course is prompt disciplinary action. Failure to deal promptly with either the appearance of unethical conduct or unethical conduct itself not only will harm supplier relations, but it will encourage the practice to spread to other buyers.

Question 2:

What should Charlie do about this problem in the future?

Comment:

A company policy approved by top management should be the ultimate outcome of this situation. The policy should apply to all company personnel in a position to influence the decision as to supplier selection. The policy should be published to prevent any misunderstanding concerning its content.

Since this subject has come up with other members of the Jay management team, now is the time for Charlie Wilson to point out that ethics are not just a purchasing problem. Indeed, all too often it is at higher levels of management that unethical or seemingly unethical relationships are established. Charlie should try to make it clear that throughout the company all employees must assume the most ethical posture possible. Charlie can point out that in addition to the moral rightness of such a posture, it also will be good business practice, as suppliers will all know that they are at all time being judged fairly. Thus, they will be motivated to offer Jay their best price, quality, and service, including technical development assistance. Buying from relatives and owning substantial stock in a supplier's company are most frequently top management's and purchasing management's most common conflict of interest situations. Designing specifications that describe just one manufacturer's product is technical management's most common conflict of interest situation.

JULBERG, INC.

Purpose

Increasing purchasing and supply personnel's overall effectiveness, organizational efficiency, and decision-making capabilities are among the reasons cited for acquiring computer support for the materials function. But getting to this point frequently is more difficult than negotiating a complex procurement.

The purpose of this case is to:

1. Develop the student's awareness of the contributions of computer technology to the materials function, with emphasis on purchasing.
2. Develop managerial strategies to overcome the behavioral problems associated with the introduction of a computer-based management system.

A computer-based system, properly developed, can improve overall performance of the materials function. Typical applications and results include:

1. Automation of repetitive, clerical tasks such as issuing purchase orders. Administrative time is saved and accuracy is increased.
2. Reduction of paperwork and duplicate reports and files. Many departments now can have access to a variety of information via their computer terminals, thus avoiding the need for each department to maintain separate files.
3. Creation of a central supplier analysis file. Buyers can simultaneously compare the performance of several suppliers in such areas as lead time, delivery schedules, quality of shipments, and overdue shipments.
4. Facilitating sensitivity analysis. The microcomputer gives buyers the capability of answering "what if" questions. For example, the effects of different lead times and price changes can be calculated rapidly through use of the computer.
5. Simplifying record keeping. The computer will facilitate the record keeping associated with receiving and inspection activities.
6. Expediting data analysis. The computer can rapidly perform many of the time-consuming calculations associated with inventory management.

While the computer has much to offer, management should not overlook the behavioral and organizational changes required to ensure its successful implementation and utilization. The overall success in implementing and managing a computer-based management system often is determined by the personnel who will be using and relying on the system.

This case examines the behavioral aspects of such changes. The case requires students to develop strategies which minimize resistance to the required changes. The insightful student should show how to encourage acceptance of a computer system by materials personnel. The case also allows the instructor to discuss the organizational changes the computer inevitably brings.

Questions 1 and 2:

- What weaknesses are evident in the present materials system?
- How can these weaknesses be minimized or eliminated by the use of a computer-based operating system?

Comment:

The buyer's function at Julberg essentially has become one of an order placer. In fact, one buyer stated that all management had previously required them to do was to place an order and make sure the materials arrived on time. It is doubtful, under the present system, that Julberg is obtaining the best price for its purchases. Also, it appears likely that many deliveries are late.

Buyers should spend more of their time doing the creative purchasing functions of their jobs. Activities such as developing alternative sources, developing the use of commercially available material, make-or-buy analysis, "what if" analysis, and forecasting will result in better purchasing and lower costs for Julberg.

Use of a computer system could enhance the buyers' capability to make timely decisions in these areas. First, the necessary data needed for supplier analysis (ability to meet delivery dates, lead times, credit ratings, quality assurance, etc.) would be in the computer's database and would be immediately available, via the terminal. As future purchasing decisions are made, a supplier's past performance could be examined before additional orders are placed. This feature of the computerized system would be especially advantageous if additional personnel were hired. New buyers would have immediate access to objective data compiled over time, rather than relying on someone's memory for this information. Second, buyers will have additional time available to spend in the more productive areas of purchasing, including negotiations, the establishment of competition, and assisting in the requirements determination and specification development process.

Most purchases are being made using Julberg design specifications. In a well-run materials organization, the use of design specifications are frequently challenged. Suitable commercially standard material usually is less expensive for several reasons: increased competition, longer production runs, and the fact that carrying some inventory can be passed from the purchaser to the supplier.

Personnel in receiving, inspection and stores do not appear to understand the importance of their roles in the materials system. As happens altogether too often, these individuals appear to view the execution of their paperwork as an end in itself rather than as part of a materials system. ("It seems they feel that they should not have to change the way they do their jobs in order to put data into a computer for you guys in purchasing. They're happy with just filling out all the old forms.")

Question 3:

What is the basic problem confronting Robert Hanson?

Comment:

Mr. Hanson must develop a comprehensive project plan to guide both the introduction and implementation of the new computer system. (Specific stages of the plan can be developed in

Question 5.) Attention should focus on the strategies required to overcome resistance to the computer among the materials personnel as well as to encourage its acceptance.

The buyers, for example, are expressing justifiable concerns about the project. Mr. Hanson should first consider the natural resistance employees feel toward any type of change. The way a change affects an individual is an important factor in whether or not the change will be successful.

In this case, many factors contribute to employee resistance:

a. The nature and objectives of the buyer's job are changing. Management is now focusing on cost-reduction objectives rather than on the timely award and follow-up of the large number of purchase orders.

b. The skills required of the buyer to perform the job are changing. Management has indicated that the computer will give buyers more free time. They will be able to spend more of their time in negotiations and supplier analysis. Many buyers may not have any training in these areas. They are naturally reluctant to undertake such tasks without the necessary skills.

c. Personnel tend to fear that a computer has the power to put them out of a job. Computer technology has the ability to provide the materials function support in two areas: (1) automation of repetitive, clerical tasks, and (2) decision analysis support. With the automation of clerical tasks, it is likely that the need for specific personnel could be reduced. (This very real concern should be addressed in Question 5.) Even if provisions are made from the outset to transfer displaced personnel to other departments, the affected individuals will be reluctant to give up the familiarity and security of their current work group relationships.

   It is essential that the employee's perception of the computer be accurate. This issue must be addressed on a work group level. For example, the computer will enhance the buyers' knowledge and skills rather than eliminate the need for them. The buyers will perceive that their job function has been changed due to the computer's capacity to perform certain functions quicker and better. The buyers may feel that even though it is not management's intent to put them out of a job, their status within the organization will somehow be lowered.

d. The style of the personal interaction will be altered. Individuals will be required to obtain information from a computer terminal rather than through the present manual system or from associates. Interacting with a computer via a terminal and keyboard is extremely different from the present technique for obtaining information. People are comfortable with the old system even though it is tedious and does not always yield the best information.

e. Mistrust of computer-supplied information is a common reaction. Mr. Hanson must secure the support and cooperation of all the related departments which will be entering data into the computer. He needs to develop strategies that will address end-user resistance among all the departments in order to maintain an accurate and current database. Personnel can and do develop their own secret duplicate record-keeping system if they do not believe that the information entered into the computer is valid. Furthermore, if problems with inaccurate data are common, personnel often avoid responsibility. Statements like: "It was the 'computer's fault' that a delivery deadline was missed" become common. In effect, the computer becomes a scapegoat.

Question 4:

What should or could Mr. Hanson have done to improve communication with his subordinates?

Comment:

Mr. Hanson conducted the first meeting using a unilateral change approach in which the members of his department were asked to make no contribution. They went to the meeting with the knowledge that a decision had been made for them. It would have been better to have solicited their views in a formal way earlier. For example, personnel could have been advised that their parent company was considering the purchase of a computer for the materials area and wanted their professional opinions on how to proceed. Members would have been involved from the start and their research in this area could have generated some enthusiasm.

Hanson also should have planned his introductory meeting better. Through a little research and preparation he might have anticipated the buyers' concerns and been prepared with answers to their questions.

What should Hanson do to resolve his current problems given his failure to take these actions in the past?

First, he must admit that he recognizes the concerns of the employees as being valid and that he recognizes the need to develop workable solutions with their input. Hanson must be prepared to spend a substantial amount of time discussing this change and its problems with his staff. From these discussions he will be able to identify biases and reasons for resistance to the new system. Repeated, meaningful discussions provide the eventual end user with a sense of both participation and responsibility for the outcome. All departments should be asked to establish objectives describing how the computer can help them to do their jobs better. Some possible areas for input include:

a. How could a supplier analysis program be developed and computerized?
b. In what ways could the need for duplicate information be reduced?
c. What information is continually needed when preparing reports?
d. What type of information is the most time-consuming to compile under the current system?
e. Etc.

Finally, once specific areas have been identified, Hanson may want to set up teams or committees that would have responsibility for the transformation of ideas into workable procedures.

Question 5:

How could the materials personnel's resistance to using the computer be overcome?

Comment:

The implementation of any computer system needs to be managed as much in human terms as in technological terms. Very often the computer becomes the focal point for a variety of organizational changes.

Two prerequisites must be present in order to produce a successful change. First, frustration or a desire for help must have been experienced by the key individuals or group targeted for change. Because the buyers at Julberg currently are not required to obtain the most cost-effective price, the present system appears to be adequate for their needs. Thus they see little value in adopting a computer system.

Mr. Hanson is enthusiastic about the computer's abilities and has assumed that the rest of the staff would share his enthusiasm. He apparently feels that if a project reduces costs, increases decision accuracy, streamlines jobs, and eliminates tedious record keeping, all members of the purchasing department should welcome the required changes. Yet here is the fallacy. Top management benefits the most from the fulfillment of the above objectives. Accordingly, top management evaluates the project on that basis. Top management does not have to learn to operate the system in order to receive its benefits. The purchasing department as well as the other materials departments must adapt and learn to use the new system in order to accomplish top management's objectives. Any change program needs to pay attention to the needs of both the organization and the individual.

If implementation of the computer is to result in significant cost reductions for Julberg, the buyers must be able to perceive personal benefits to be gained. One approach to establishing visible personal benefits would call for all materials personnel to be rewarded with monetary bonuses upon attainment of mutually established cost objectives. Another approach would be the establishment of a profit-sharing plan.

Monetary incentives are not the only potential benefits present. For example, the possibility of planning and organizing purchasing activities with less repetitive and time-consuming paperwork should be attractive to buyers. Mr. Hanson should not underestimate his buyers' capability (especially that of the younger members with degrees in business) to understand management's cost control objective. It is quite possible that some of the buyers have been frustrated in their attempts to perform their purchasing duties under the present system. Such buyers should readily see that these objectives of timeliness, quality, and cost effectiveness could be achieved better with the assistance of the microprocessing system.

Ideally, the initiation or introduction of a change must come from a respected and prestigious influence agent. Employees being targeted for change need to have confidence that the change is valid and that the person managing the change (in this case Hanson), has the knowledge and the power to cope with the change program.

The purchasing department as well as the other materials departments should be made aware that the computer idea is not Hanson's and that cooperation will be noticed and supported at higher organizational levels. Materials personnel may be reluctant to participate in the program if they are unsure of Hanson's ability to manage such a large change.

Employees tend to be more committed to seeing self-imposed innovations succeed than those that are imposed from outside. While the requirement to convert to the microprocessing system is an imposed one, the design and implementation plan can and should involve key buying and other materials personnel. Such involvement will increase the usefulness of the resulting system. Further, the involvement will overcome resistance to the new system.

Mr. Hanson should consider the following factors and approaches:

a. Consider how previous changes were implemented in the organization. What contributed to their success or failure?

b. Directly involve personnel who will use or be affected by the computer in the design of the software program and possibly the hardware requirements. What information does the end user need in order to do the job better? Give involved personnel meaningful responsibility and control over the outcome of the project.

c. Solicit ideas on additional ways to achieve the goals of cost effectiveness, timeliness, and quality. Personnel may have valid workable suggestions on how to reduce the cost of purchases under the present system.

d. Wait to implement this major change until the business operating cycle is at a low point rather than during an upswing in activity.

e. Jointly determine realistic goals and objectives against which progress can be measured and rewarded.

f. Maintain open and effective communication between all departments involved (see Question 4).

g. Develop a training program with objectives designed to:
   (1) Familiarize personnel with computer terminals and basic computer vocabularies.
   (2) Develop newly desired skills (example: negotiation).
   (3) Enhance the interaction between all departments of the materials function.

h. Design a system that is easy to use. The current term used by design analysts is "user friendly." Technology does not have to be complicated to be workable.

i. Develop provisions for personnel who will be displaced by the computer project. Timing is a crucial factor. Voluntary transfers along with job retraining should be considered.

j. Introduce the changeover gradually. Begin with the computer performing the most repetitive tasks. Try to encourage personnel to come up with their own ideas on what the computer can do for them.

k. Design and purchase a system that is reliable and does what it is supposed to do. Things can go wrong in a computer system due to faulty hardware or software.

l. Monitor the entire project with an evaluation plan. If a certain procedure is not workable under the new system, change it. Just because an idea or method is associated with a computer does not mean that it is inherently the only way to do something.

KOCH BROTHERS

Purpose

This care presents some typical issues a small business faces in a mature market. Technology and large businesses with considerable resources are putting pressure on small firms to come up with unique organizational forms in order to survive. In particular, this case highlights the problems of purchasing small buyers face and the potential advantages and disadvantages of group buying. This case can lead to a discussion of the industry growth cycle, technological changes, small business planning, and inventory control. In addition, there are buying plan and contracting issues that are vital to the firm's strategic plan.

This case highlights the need for strategic planning for small firms in order to remain in a competitive position.

Immediate Issue

Will Koch Brothers survive without changes?

Basic Issue

What facts should Richard Koch take into consideration when making his decision?

Suggested Student Assignments

- If you were Richard Koch which plan would you select and why?
- What additional information is needed in order to make an optimal decision?
- Identify opportunities and threats which exist in the industry.

Possible Discussion Questions

1. What has caused Richard Koch to call for an action plan?
2. Is a new action plan urgent?
3. What factors should Koch take into consideration in making his decision?
4. Are there other alternatives that have not been discussed?
5. What impact might the basic-net plan have on the organization?
6. What impact might the IS plan have on the organization?
7. What is the likely reaction of Koch's wholesalers if they select either plan?
8. Might they lose sales if other larger members contract with company headquarters in their own areas that have operations in Des Moines?

Analysis

The process employed by Richard Koch to make his decision is important in both internal and external analysis. A sample process may consist of

1. External analysis
   a. identify industry structure
   b. identify driving forces in the industry
   c. identify competitor strengths

2. Internal analysis
   a. identify company mission
   b. identify present strategy
   c. identify organizational strengths
   d. identify organizational weaknesses

3. Decision process
   a. identify urgency of the time frame
   b. identify balance between internal strength and weaknesses and external opportunities and threats

Key Points

- The issue of competitiveness for a relatively small firm is exemplified in this case. The nature of planning in a small family owned company is an important application of this case.
- Establish the skills to analyze a situation with a limited amount of information and to identify missing information.
- Reinforce the necessity of staying alert to changes in the environment and making decisions before the situation reaches a crisis state.

KRAUSE COMPANY

Purpose

This case is good for presenting make or buy analysis in a real world context. It is a good case for helping the student organize information and find the relevant facts for analysis. It also demonstrates how direct monetary impacts may be overridden by other qualitative issues. It can also be used to raise the question of what is the difference between a quantitative factor and a qualitative factor.

Immediate Issue

Should Steve Rothel recommend purchasing the pipe or making it?

Basic Issues

1. Economic comparison of making an item and purchasing it.
2. Identification of the costs involved in making an item.
3. Integration of the qualitative and the quantitative factors.

Suggested Student Assignment

- How would you compare these two options on a strictly monetary basis?
- What factors beside the monetary factors are relevant to the decision?
- If you were Steve Rothel, what would be your recommendation?

Possible Questions for Discussion in Class

1. In the actual incident upon which this case is based, the option selected was to purchase the pipe prefabricated. Why do you suppose this decision was made?
2. If you knew how long it took to make a reweld and you could estimate the probability of a bad weld on a pipe fabricated in-house, would quality then be able to be treated as a quantitative issue?
3. Is it necessary to include the cost of weld gas? Weld wire?

Analysis

A good unit of comparison is cost per foot of pipe. The fact that 6,500 feet of pipe are needed does not directly enter the decision, since the fixed costs are not significant (not given here). A per-foot-of-pipe basis simplifies the analysis.
1. Purchased pipe cost: $18.10/foot
2. Fabricated pipe cost:
   - Material cost per foot:

Steel:

The circumference of a 10-inch diameter pipe is 31.4 inches, thus it is best to buy 36-inch-wide sheets of metal, 8 feet long. (Note: this leaves some scrap.) The price per sheet will be 24 sq. ft. × 2.5 lbs/sq. ft. × $1.80/lb = $108. Since this is an 8-foot length, the cost per foot is $13.50.

Weld wire:

.03 lbs per foot × (8 feet for seam + 2.6 feet for joint) × \$5.20/lb = \$1.65 per 8-foot section. This results in a cost of .21 per foot.

Weld gas:

\$.25 per seam + .10 per joint (rough estimate) = .35 per 8-foot length. This results in a cost of \$.044 per foot.

<u>Total material cost = \$13.754 per foot.</u>

- Labor cost per foot:

(Forming time + seam time + joint time) × (hourly rate) × (1 + overhead rate)

(6 min + 10 min. + 18 min) × (\$32.60 per hour) × (1 + .40) = \$25.863 per 8-foot section. This results in <u>a labor cost of \$3.233 per foot.</u>

- Total cost for fabricated pipe = \$13.754 + \$3.233 = \$16.99 per foot.

Key Points

- In-house production includes material costs, labor costs, and overhead costs. Overhead can include fixed costs.
- It is not always clear, in a real-life case, how to account for all costs in an analysis that is less than exhaustive. In this case, the decision maker decided to adjust for the fact that the purchased pipes were 20 feet long and the fabricated pipes were only eight by adding the cost of one weld to each eight-foot section. One could argue against this approach. But, to get an accurate figure would require determining the total number of joints needed for the entire project, using each of the two approaches. the energy of uncovering this data is perhaps not worth the effort.
- Quantitative and qualitative approaches must be integrated in real decision making.

Teaching Strategy

1. Hand out the case near the end of class and discuss the opening paragraph.
2. Dismiss the class and ask them to answer questions 1 through 3 of the sample questions section.
3. At the next class session use discussion questions.

LAXTEC, INC.

Purpose

This case discusses purchasing ethics, the role purchasing should take, and related issues involved when dealing with suppliers.

Discussion

This case provides an opportunity to discuss several different issues involving purchasing ethics. Ethical considerations are extremely important in the selection process and in the development of supplier relationships. The importance of fair dealing by the buyer with both his or her employer and the salesperson, how these relationships can be altered by favoritism in any form, general guidelines for ethical purchasing behavior, and a list of areas wherein there is danger of unethical practice occurring are all addressed.

Note to the Instructor

Select two of your extroverts, one to play the role of Larry Morris and one to play Peter Ferdenzi. Begin the play with: "Larry was unsure of what to do."

Question 1:

Is it ethical to:

a.   tell suppliers that there are many bidders?

Comment:

Unfortunately, this question does not have a simple answer. Most people would probably say that it is unethical to tell suppliers that there are many bidders when, in fact, there are not. The buyer is taking a chance of ruining his or her reputation. However, the buyer might think such a practice is ethical so that the firm can receive fair and reasonable bids. Telling suppliers that there are many bidders gives the buyer the opportunity to seek out the lowest bid. Is attempting to apply competitive pressure to obtain a reasonable price unethical?

b.   delay telling unsuccessful suppliers of an award?

Comment:

Yes. Suppliers awaiting a decision on the award probably have provided or reserved production for this contract. If this is the case, the odds of the supplier losing money by under-utilizing production capacity is high.

c. void a contract on the basis of dishonesty?

Comment:

When one discusses the topic of honesty, one needs to take a look at his or her own morals and standards. Honesty is the best policy! It is not unethical to void a contract on the basis of honesty. When dishonesty occurs, it creates a mold for future dishonest acts. Eventually the company loses all of its standards and its reputation becomes tarnished. As a result of this, quality of products, net profits, and reputation all suffer.

d. allow companies to bid even though they would not be considered for the contract (out-of-towners)?

Comment:

To encourage a company to bid on a contract when it is not going to be considered is unethical as well as dishonest. All the time and effort put into a bid is a costly investment. Therefore, the supplier deserves the buyer's sincerity and honesty in asking for and reviewing all potential bids before making award to the lowest responsive, responsible bidder.

e. refuse to award on the basis of personal relationships?

Comment:

The first concern of the buyer should be what is best for the company. Therefore, to disregard a potential supplier on the basis of personal relationships is unethical and poor business. Once again, the question of one's personal ethical and moral standards is the key factor. When dealing with company business, one acts in the best interest of the company.

Question 2:

How important is it to have written ethical procedures in a company?

Comment:

It is very important. When an employee acts unethically, it not only costs his or her employer money, but it also brings about government intrusion and regulation. Many companies have spent a great deal of money paying fines and penalties and also paying to rebuild their public image. Many companies are initiating ethical procedures in their organization as a result of these costs. It is extremely important to have and maintain a good ethical program in business organizations!

Question 3:

What should Larry do?

Comment:

Larry should first discuss the problems and costs of unethical purchasing practices with Peter. Ethical purchasing is good business.

The president of Laxtec (Peter) must fully support the implementation of ethical and professional standards within the company. Current practices are costing the company time and money due to inept selection of suppliers, poor supplier relationships, and reputation. The first step the president must take is to get out of the procurement business and let the procurement director do the job. If Larry is unable to take appropriate actions, the parent corporation should replace him.

Once the barrier for good procurement is removed (the president), Laxtec should contact Prextel for immediate negotiations and dump Tomos for its unethical behavior. Prextel is the most qualified supplier, according to Larry. To avoid further problems, Larry should make certain that Peter's ex-wife will not let personalities get in the way of the relationship.

Laxtec can now concentrate on developing policies to ensure ethical and professional procurement. It is management's first responsibility to develop a set of written ethical and professional standards applicable to all members of the organization. Logically, this job should fall to the ethics staff already in place at corporate headquarters. The standard procedures they establish should follow professional purchasing practices as prescribed by N.A.P.M. standards. Other companies' experiences with ethics should be studied and their additions to the N.A.P.M. standards considered. The ethics staff should provide periodic training to all relevant personnel on these ethical standards.

In addition to the above, the ethics staff should define management's personnel responsibilities in avoiding conflicts of interest. This responsibility starts at the hiring process, where the supervisors should obtain detailed information on applicants' previous performance, experience, and reputation. All possible conflicts of interest must be resolved. There are several additional managerial actions recommended in the text by Bernard Fried. These should be considered.

The standards established should be made known to all relevant employees in the parent company and the subsidiary companies. Initially, a "swat" team of corporate ethics staff members and purchasing professionals could visit all the subsidiary companies in order to provide ethics training and to evaluate the purchasing functions. This "swat" team, with the assistance of top management, could then make recommendations for improving the purchasing function and ensuring that ethical standards are followed.

LION INDUSTRIES

Purpose

This case addresses what a buying team should do when its only viable source cannot meet schedule commitments. It also discusses actions to take to minimize or avoid such situations.

Question 1:

How should the buyer approach the situation with Polytek?

Comment:

The student must recognize that Polytek is Lion's only hope, at least for the next 40 weeks, of supporting the Boeing program requirements. The emotional response is to default the supplier for nonconformance, but since it is the only supplier possessing tooling, this simply cannot be done.

Lion is in a position where it must find a way to produce acceptable parts using Polytek tooling. One possibility is to pull the tooling out of Polytek and manufacture the parts either at Lion or at another supplier's facility. However, this strategy is rarely successful due to the lack of commonality between tooling and tooling concepts.

A second possibility is to send a team of Lion employees into the Polytek plant to actually perform the manufacturing operations necessary to produce the ducts. This strategy is also rarely employed, mostly due to union agreements. In this case, temporary deployment of up to 30 Lion employees from San Diego to Grand Rapids would be necessary. In addition, Polytek's production personnel are members of the United Auto Workers, and their contract expressly prohibits outside personnel from performing duties in the Polytek plant.

The proper strategy to follow is to continue providing Polytek with key advisory personnel. Full-time engineering, tooling, quality and production personnel should be stationed at Polytek to provide direction. In addition, purchasing should be involved in monitoring the progress. Polytek's president or general manager should be involved in daily update meetings with the Lion team.

The student should recognize that acceptable results are not guaranteed. Lion is in a position of selecting the best solution from a list where all selections are marginal or unacceptable.

Question 2:

Should the company consider alternate sources of supply? Discuss.

Comment:

Yes. Polytek has not given any indication that it can support production requirements. Although the additional capital needed to develop a second source will most likely come directly out of Lion's pockets, the company must show Boeing that positive corrective action has been taken.

A make-or-buy meeting involving top company personnel should be scheduled immediately. Given the immediate need for the duct, it would probably be in Lion's best interest to make it in-house. This would achieve better control and visibility on the program. It should be stressed that sometimes costs are not the key factor. In this case, support of program requirements takes precedence over cost factors. It is also important to remember that even if Lion makes the unit, it is still dependent upon Polytek until Lion is at full production and possibly longer, considering the backlog. Another alternative to consider would be to locate new suppliers and offer both financial and technical assistance.

Question 3:

What corrective actions would you recommend to preclude another occurrence of this situation?

Comment:

It's easy to say that all major assemblies should be second-sourced. Often, however, the nonrecurring costs are prohibitive.

The key lies in (1) fully understanding the technical assumptions made on the supplier's part, and (2) closely monitoring progress through the developmental stage. In employing the team approach, review of technical knowledge is usually the responsibility of the engineering department, but purchasing should be involved as well. In retrospect, it appears that the drawings were not adequate and that perhaps performance specifications would have been more appropriate. Program review meetings involving the supplier's top management should have been scheduled regularly.

MAINE-BARNES, LTD.

Purpose

The purpose of this case is to give the student an opportunity to analyze a real-life make-or-buy situation. Like most make-or-buy situations in practice, cost and related operating data available in the case are not entirely complete; hence, the student is required to make a few realistic assumptions in order to proceed with a reasonably thorough analysis of the case.

Question 1:

What factors should Josh consider in conducting a make-or-buy analysis for this product?

Comment:

All factors discussed in the text, pages 193 through 204, are factors that should be considered in this case. The more important ones are discussed briefly below.

1. *Capacity considerations:* This case is typical of many situations in practice. Maine-Barnes has excess shop capacity that will accommodate up to approximately 75,000 units per year of the new product; this is exclusive of the recharger unit. It is estimated that Maine-Barnes could make the recharger unit in-house, if no more than approximately 70,000 calculators per year were produced. Beyond 70,000 units new equipment must be purchased if Maine-Barnes is to make the recharger in-house. Obviously, beyond the production of 70,000 to 75,000 calculators per year, Maine-Barnes will have production capacity problems. The firm may be able to squeeze out 100,000 units per year, but costs will probably go up somewhat because of less efficient use of facilities and people beyond 100 percent capacity. It is safe to assume that approximately the same situation would result for the production of recharger units in the event of a make decision.

   Disregarding the new equipment costs, if one considers only the capacity factor, it appears that the simplest (and perhaps the most logical) decision would be to buy the recharger units. The decision, however, is not an open-and-shut case. If production of the recharger unit were ultimately to stabilize at approximately 75,000 units per year (and the unit amortization cost of the new equipment is not excessive) a make decision might work very well.

2. *Manufacturing jobs and work-force stability for Maine-Barnes:* This factor also produces a "mixed-bag" group of considerations. If sales level off at 75,000 units per year or less and market demand continues to be reasonably stable, a make decision would help Maine-Barnes achieve this objective. Beyond the 75,000-unit-per-year level, the situation is not clear—but in all likelihood, work-force stability would be somewhat uncertain because of the capacity problem. If the new calculator does not sell well in this competitive market (and the unit is completely unproven at this point in time), then work-force stability probably would be adversely affected in the event of a make decision.

   In any case, Maine-Barnes must pay particular attention to this factor because of prior labor concerns generated by the firm's subcontract activity.

3. *Design secrecy:* It is difficult to asses the significance of this factor with respect to the recharger unit, although it certainly is possible that this could be a significant con-

sideration. Several design features in both the calculator and the recharger unit are innovative, yet unpatentable. If premature leaks of this information to competitors could adversely affect Maine-Barnes's marketing strategy, the inclination obviously would be to make the item in-house. Such action would tend to minimize, though certainly not eliminate, the probability of any adverse consequences from preliminary information leakage.

4. *Control of quality:* For the recharger unit, the control of quality probably is not a difficult matter to achieve. Certainly, if the item were made in-house Maine-Barnes would have full control over output quality. However, since the technology and production operations are not particularly complicated, it is reasonable to expect that the three suppliers asked to bid could do a completely satisfactory job of quality control. A good proactive purchasing operation would ensure this to be the case before selecting the supplier.

5. *Control of delivery performance:* Again, this element can be controlled most effectively when the unit is made in-house. On the other hand, good supplier selection, coupled with good contract administration and follow-up by Josh's group, would normally be expected to produce completely satisfactory results, except in the case of an unforeseen emergency in the supplier's operation.

6. *Management control of costs:* If Maine-Barnes decides to buy the recharger under a long-term, single-source contract, thorough cost analysis and negotiation prior to development of the contract is essential. A properly designed contract, however, should preclude the possibility of Maine-Barnes paying an excessive price for the recharger units. Nevertheless, many firms prefer to have more direct feedback and control of product cost and quality. Consequently, in situations such as this many firms would elect the make-and-buy alternative. Thus the firm can monitor its own internal costs and quality carefully—and compare these results with an external supplier. The control and leverage produced by this decision, from a buying point of view, is obvious.

7. *Cost to make vs. cost to buy:* In the case of Maine-Barnes's recharger unit, this may be the most important factor to review carefully because of the intense price competition Maine-Barnes faces in the calculator market. Once a thorough comparative cost analysis has been done, the results should be reviewed in the context of the analysis of the preceding six factors.

A comparative cost analysis is discussed in Question 2.

Question 2:

Prepare a comparative cost analysis of the make/buy alternatives. Which cost elements should be investigated particularly carefully?

Comment:

In refining the controller's cost estimate to make the recharger unit in-house, the following cost elements should be investigated thoroughly:

1. *The 15 percnt scrap material allowance:* This may well be a legitimate material cost inclusion. However, Josh should talk with the appropriate manufacturing engineer to determine exactly what the 15 percent scrap allowance covers—and to ensure that the percentage figure is reasonable. If the allowance simply provides for the cost of scrap materials produced by the manufacturing process, then one would not expect a com-

mensurate allowance to appear in the labor cost figure. On the other hand, if the allowance is to compensate for rejected materials that also contain a labor component, then one would expect a similar scrap allowance factor to appear in the unit labor cost.

2. *Material handling cost:* The controller's estimate includes materials at $3/unit; the $3 figure includes a 20 percent internal material handling cost. In most cost accounting systems, this handling cost would normally be picked up and included in the variable factory overhead figure. In all likelihood, that is the case in the Maine-Barnes system. Consequently, Josh must track this item through the system to ensure that no double counting is occurring.

3. *Variable overhead:* Josh should talk with the appropriate cost accounting personnel to determine exactly what cost elements are included in the variable overhead figure. Normally, the regular variable overhead cost attributable to the recharger unit would decline noticeably if new equipment has to be purchased (to produce the recharger units) and amortized separately. The controller is correct that this new equipment amortization cost should be borne by the recharger production operation, but the $.58 standard variable cost allocation should decline significantly.

4. *New equipment amortization:* This unit cost figure must be estimated based on the expected number of units of production during the equipment's life. Fur purposes of discussion, production of the recharger unit is estimated to be 50,000 units during the first year and 75,000 units/year for the following six years. Thus the $84,000 capital expenditure is amortized over 500,000 units at a rate of approximately $.17/unit. Should different sales and production rates be assumed, the new equipment amortization figure should be modified correspondingly.

In the following table, the controller's original cost estimate has been refined to reflect actual *incremental costs*, in light of the discussion of the preceding four cost elements.

In-House Unit Costs to Make the Recharger

		Modified estimates	
	Original controller's estimate	Estimate with excess capacity (50-70k units/yr)	Estimate with no excess capacity (> 70k unit/yr)
Direct labor	$1.50	$1.50	$1.50
Materials	3.00	--	--
Materials less handling cost	--	2.50	2.50
Factory overhead (110% labor)			
Fixed	1.07	0	1.07
Variable	.58	.58	.29**
New Equipment Amort.	--	0*	.17***
Factory cost	6.15	4.58	5.53
General admin. and sell. expense			
(10% factory cost)	.62	.46	.55
Total cost/unit	$6.77	$5.04	$6.08

*Assume no new equipment has to be purchased.

**This assumes that only half of the regular variable overhead rate is attributable to production of the recharager units, since new equipment is being used and amortized separately.,

***$84,000 equipment amortized over 7 years of production (50K units the first year, and an average of 75K units/year for the next 6 years).

To bring into sharp focus the correct treatment of fixed overhead costs, estimated cost figures are shown for two different levels of operation. The first level of operation, 50,000 to 70,000 units per year, probably can be accomplished with the existing facilities. In other words, production of the new calculator and recharger units can be accomplished with what is now considered to be excess capacity within Maine-Barnes's production operation. This admittedly represents an assumption with respect to the recharger unit, but until the 75,000 unit/year level is approached, this is probably a reasonable assumption. The second level of operation occurs beyond this point, where, for practical purposes, no excess capacity exists. Somewhere in the area of 70,000 to 75,000 units/year, in-house production of the recharger unit requires the purchase of the new equipment that can be used to make the units.

Now, review the factory overhead cost figures utilized in these two modified estimates. When excess capacity exists, the incremental cost to make the recharger unit should not include fixed factory overhead costs, simply because these costs will continue to be incurred by Maine-Barnes whether it produces any recharger units or not. Until other products are developed that could also utilize this excess capacity, the fixed overhead opportunity cost is zero. Even with excess capacity, however, the recharger unit should bear its full share of the variable overhead costs that are attributable to its production.

Looking at the overhead cost figures now in the estimate where no excess capacity exists, it is clear that the recharger unit operation should bear its fair share of the fixed overhead costs as well as the variable overhead costs attributable to the recharger production operation. In this case, the recharger manufacturing operation must also bear the amortization for the new equipment utilized in the manufacturing process.

Given the assumptions made, then, the *incremental cost* of production in the excess capacity situation runs approximately $5.04/unit—and at the level where no excess capacity exists, the incremental cost of production in-house is approximately $6.08/unit.

Josh must now compare these "cost-to-make" estimates with the "cost-to-buy" bids. Using Boston Electrical's low bid figures, a make decision clearly produces substantial cost savings at both levels of operation. In all probability, however, Josh would seriously consider bidding or negotiating a 3-year single-source contract, in which case bid price improvements clearly would be possible. At the 50,000 to 70,000 unit/year level, Boston Electrical would have to reduce its price at least 30 percent to become competitive with Maine-Barnes's in-house incremental cost figure. Above the 70,000 unit/year level, a 15 percent price reduction would make Boston Electrical very competitive with Maine-Barnes's in-house incremental cost figure. This latter situation would appear to represent a distinct possibility for Josh to pursue.

Question 3:

Prepare a complete report for the general manager, including the details of your analysis—and your recommendation.

Comment:

The written report should include a comparative make/buy cost analysis along with an analysis of the significance of each of the factors discussed in Question 1.

With respect to the comparative cost analysis, it is clear that at the lower level of operation, as long as excess capacity exists, a make decision would be the most economical. This course of action would have two disadvantages, however:

1. There is no guarantee that Maine-Barnes will have excess capacity for an extended period of time. Hence, this attractive cost alternative may be short-lived.
2. Until the new calculator has been on the market for a year or so, there is no way to estimate the probability that sales will exceed 70,000 units/year during the life of the unit. If sales exceed 70,000 units/year, Maine-Barnes will be forced to reconsider the issue, or perhaps move into a make-*and*-buy-type operation.

With respect to the second level of operation, production of more than 70,000 units/year, the make-buy decision appears to be roughly a toss up, from strictly a cost point of view. Using a three-year fixed-price contract (perhaps including an escalation/de-escalation clause), Josh should be able to negotiate a price with Boston Electrical (or perhaps D and A Manufacturing) that is as good or better than the Maine-Barnes in-house cost figure. In this case the factors of design secrecy, work-force stability, control of quality, and control of delivery flows may be the controlling factors in the make-buy decision.

Concluding Comment:

Based on the market uncertainty Maine-Barnes faces, coupled with the operating assumptions an analyst must make, a reasonable case can be made for recommending any of three courses of action to management—(1) buy, (2) make, or (3) make up to 60,000 or 70,000 units/year and buy requirements beyond that level of operation. The latter alternative likely would be more costly and must be justified by adequate qualitative assessments. The buy alternative is the simplest and most flexible approach from manufacturing and managerial points of view. (This assumes that a requirements/termination clause can be included in the contract to guard against disastrous effects of a second- or third-year calculator sales decline.)

Although a majority of the students and practitioners who have analyzed this case recommend the buy alternative, the specific course of action recommended is not as important as the analysis and justification that underly the recommendation. The primary instructional purpose of the case is to require a thorough and realistic analysis of all of the factors that Maine-Barnes should consider in making its decision. The importance of most of the factors depends to some extent on the assumptions made by the analyst. Hence, the analytical process and the justification one provides for the recommendation are really the focal points for the instructional use of the case.

MAZDA ELECTRONICS

Purpose

The case provides the student with an insight into the role of purchasing in a high-tech firm. Students are required to use some basic concepts of cost accounting (contribution analysis) and sensitivity analysis (expected values). Most of all, the case provides an opportunity for the instructor to gradually coax students into using simple calculations in problem solving.

The instructor should first post all the available data on the board.

Current model	ME	1001
Sales (units per year)	$200,000	
Selling price per unit	$150	
Total sales per year	$30 million	
Net margin	5%	
Net income	$1,500,000	
New Model	ME	2001
Selling price per unit	$100	
Variable cost per unit	$65	
Contribution per unit	$35	
Contribution margin	35%	
Fixed costs per year	$4.0 million	

Next, a simple table should be constructed showing the expected profit for the ME 2001 under different sales scenarios.

Sales Volume (units)	18,000	200,000	240,000
Total Revenue (× 100)	$18,000,000	$20,000,000	$24,000,000
Contribution (× .35)	6,300,000	7,000,000	8,400,000
Less: Fixed Costs	4,000,000	4,000,000	4,000,000
Profit before Taxes	2,300,000	3,000,000	4,400,000
Less: Taxes (.50)	1,150,000	1,500,000	2,200,000
Profit after Taxes	1,150,000	1,500,000	2,200,000
Expected Value (.90)	$1,035,000	$1,350,000	$1,980,000

It may be necessary to point out that there is a 10 percent probability that the cost of rework would turn the profit contribution into a loss. Assuming that the firm is able to at least break even in case of rework costs, the expected value as shown above can be used as a realistic forecast of profits under 3 sales scenarios.

Question 1:

Should Mazda electronics proceed with the low-cost ME 2001 incorporating the new frame developed by Burton, Inc.? Explain.

Comment:

The students may be polled on this question. Then ask some of them to support their positions.

With the uncertainty involved in using a new supplier and the numbers obtained in the table above, Mazda would be taking a fair amount of risk by moving to the production of ME 2001. Further, if sales should increase to above 240,000 per year, Burton would not be able to meet Mazda's requirement for the special plastic frame. Expanding capacity to meet this demand will require a further investment of capital. Other alternatives to consider include:

a. Wait a year and then introduce the new model.
b. Increase the selling price of the ME 2001 so that the expected value at 200,000 units makes it a feasible alternative.
c. Seek out other sources for the frame in case Burton fails to perform to standard.

Question 2:

Who should be involved in the decision-making process? Who is ultimately responsible for the decision?

Comment:

Historically, marketing, engineering, finance, and production were involved in developing recommendations on such issues. But with the increasing cost, criticality, and scarcity of purchased materials, purchasing or materials management has become a key member of the team recommending such production decisions. One of the many benefits of the materials management concept is the organizational status of the materials manager. In a situation like that at Mazda Electronics, the purchasing manager frequently is at an organizational disadvantage in attempting to provide input and influence such analysis and the resulting recommendations. Whether such should or should not be the case is not the issue. All to frequently, purchasing is at too low an organizational level to make such input.

The chief of materials management, on the other hand, is much more strategically located and in a much better position to influence such analysis and the resulting recommendations. The materials management organizational approach aids purchasing in reaching its full profit-making potential.

The final responsibility for such decisions rests with the firm's chief operating officer.

Question 3:

What additional information would you require if you were in Dennis Kwok's place?

Comment:

- Prices of competing products
- Impact of learning on production costs
- Trends of costs in the plastic frame industry
- Availability of other sources
- Alternative materials that are available

- Actual/realistic cost of rework in case of problems with Burton's frames
- References from companies that have used the same or similar frames from Burton
- Does Burton have a close relationship with anyone in engineering (why is engineering so keen on this frame)?

Question 4:

What other issues related to this problem are of concern to purchasing and materials management?

Comment:

In addition to providing insight into the scope of purchasing and materials management, this question allows the instructor to telegraph the issues that he or she wants to emphasize that are to be discussed later in the course, such as the effect of the learning curve on production costs, the benefits and dangers of long-term contracts, the dangers of a single course of supply, value analysis/engineering, etc. The question also allows the instructor to discuss the effect of such new products on sales of the entire oscilloscope product line. And finally, the instructor may choose to perform a present value analysis on the two alternatives.

METROPOLITAN UNIVERSITY

Purpose

This case introduces the student to the fundamental role of the purchasing function and to the basic activities involved in organizing and operating a purchasing department in an institutional setting.

Discussion

Although it is a significant issue, the absence of control is not the major problem in this case. The real problem is inadequate performance by the purchasing department; a related problem is poor communication with users and suppliers. Had purchasing performance not been so poor, the control issue may never have surfaced. This is a classical case in which purchasing is performing a "green eyeshade" order-placing function, as opposed to a professional service-oriented function for the university.

Question 1:

Assume you are a consultant called in to work with Daniel Bluestone. List and discuss the major problems you see in the present Metropolitan University purchasing operation.

Comment:

Although not much detailed operating information is provided in the case, four problem areas can easily be discerned: (1) the existence of a poor service orientation by purchasing personnel, (2) a sluggish, reactive purchasing system, (3) poor document flow and control, and (4) a poorly handled work load for departmental personnel. Each of these problem areas is discussed in detail in the following paragraphs.

1. *Poor service orientation:* Purchasing personnel must never forget that the primary reason for the department's existence is to provide an effective professional service for the organization's operating units. Any purchasing department that overlooks this important factor is destined to be circumvented by the users it is supposed to serve—precisely what has happened at Metropolitan. Three key actions the purchasing department should take are:
   a. All buyers should make a deliberate effort to develop good two-way communication with their key users. A buyer's ultimate goal should be to help users solve their materials problems. Hence, each buyer should get to know his or her key customers on a first-name basis to develop a mutual respect and a satisfactory rapport.
   b. The department should develop and implement a good "rush order" system, as described in Chapter 4 of the text. Requisitions obviously should be prioritized as they are received by the department, and those that are genuinely emergencies should be handled within several hours.
   c. Bluestone should make a study of order-processing times within the department itself. Most purchasing organizations handle regular purchase requests within a 2- to 4-day time period, on overage. If Metropolitan is taking longer than this, internal operating procedures should be analyzed and refined to correct the situation.

2. *A sluggish, reactive system:* The Metropolitan purchasing department appears to be functioning completely in a reactive mode—it simply handles purchase requisitions as they are forwarded to the department from the university's various schools and departments. It appears that no significant advance planning for purchases is being done. This type of purchasing operation is several decades out of date. The departmental focus should be proactive—that, is, buyers should be attempting to develop advance buying plans for as many items as forecasted usage throughout the entire university permits. Several analytical investigations are necessary to provide the information required to achieve this objective. These issues are discussed below.

   a. An ABC analysis of all purchases for the past several years should be conducted to determine precisely what types of materials represent given percentages of the University's total annual purchases. At the same time, a "small order" analysis, as discussed in Chapter 4 of the textbook, also should be conducted. These analyses provide the starting point for developing appropriate buying plans for specific materials. The objective, whenever possible, is to utilize annual (or longer-term) contracts for many of the A and B items. As these materials are required by operating units, releases can be issued very quickly to provide timely service to the operating units. C items and many small orders can be handled expeditiously through the use of blanket orders, systems contracting, purchase credit cards, and other similar techniques described in Chapter 4 of the text.

      Thus the objective is to design a purchasing system that permits the expeditious and timely handling of most small orders and low-value items, and at the same time permits buyers to do a careful and thorough job of selecting suppliers and preparing contracts for major dollar purchases (which are also designed to provide timely service to users).

   b. Bluestone should analyze the University's stores operation. Many low-value items purchased on a recurring basis can profitably be carried in a central stores inventory.

      The inventory control system should be automated (computerized); standard software systems for use on either micro- or mini-computer hardware are available and affordable. If properly developed, the system can easily handle the entire purchasing/inventory operation. For items carried in inventory, some type of max-min control system should be used so that orders for those materials are generated internally by the stores operation, not by the ultimate users.

   c. Bluestone also should conduct an annual user needs analysis. This information can be used to help make decisions about how to handle some of the items discussed in (a) and (b). In some cases, it may be appropriate to create small inventories of unique items in the user's operation (laboratories, printing services, etc.).

      Purchasing should also work with users to develop and implement a standards program for materials that are commonly used throughout the university. A standards catalogue should be published and distributed to all user departments.

3. *Poor document flow and control:* The following actions will help improve communication and control.

   a. All purchase orders should be prepared in the purchasing department, and purchasing should control all PO forms. This will preclude the use of purchase requisition forms to make unauthorized purchases, as is now being done by some users.

b. After a buyer analyzes an incoming purchase requisition, the corresponding purchase order should be prepared by the same computer-based system that is used to control inventory.

c. Order follow-up and completion also can be handled automatically by the system. Distribution of purchase order copies should follow approximately the same communication lines as indicated on page 63 in the text; certainly the user should receive a copy of the PO which includes all relevant technical and delivery information for the order.

d. The department also should maintain a purchasing log to summarize all purchase requisition and purchase order data. This record would permit the buyer or clerk in charge to provide feedback data in response to any user request.

e. The invoice processing operation also could be handled almost automatically by the computer-based purchasing/inventory control system.

4. *Work load:* All of the actions described above should reduce the burden of repetitive paper processing and, hence, the overall work load for departmental personnel.

Nevertheless, Bluestone should conduct a work load analysis for all personnel in the purchasing department. On average, present departmental staffing and PO volume provide approximately 25 to 35 minutes for the handling of each order. The idea of the proposed changes obviously is to handle routine purchases much more quickly and to spend much more time doing the analytical work required for the purchase of major items, capital equipment, etc.

The department clearly needs a stable, experienced staff. It should use part-time student help only for departmental support jobs in which a temporary person can perform effectively.

If most of the suggested changes can be made, it appears that Metropolitan's purchasing department is adequately staffed at the present time. If the work load actually grows at a 20 percent rate in future years, the department clearly will need additional staff at some point in time. The important thing now, however, is to develop an efficient system that utilizes appropriately trained departmental personnel efficiently and that can serve most university users in a timely and a professional manner.

MICROCOMP, INC.

Purpose

The purpose of the case is to emphasize the importance of performing a financial analysis of the potential supplier during a preaward survey. Students should be able to identify and calculate key financial ratios and make their own judgement on the stability of a potential supplier, including the ability to fulfill all conditions of the contract, not just at the beginning but during the entire duration of the proposed contract.

Discussion

Although at first glance, Wedge Computers appears to be an ideal source, this case highlights the need for performing a preaward analysis of a potential supplier. Jeff Neuber obviously had made up his mind that there would be no problems. However, after the memo from Shannon Richey, financial analyst, he has his doubts about Wedge's ability to meet the required level of quality and delivery schedules should it run into cash flow problems.

Purchasing is generally responsible for determining the need for a preaward survey and also who should participate in it. In most cases departments like engineering, production, quality assurance, finance and industrial relations are consulted. It is important for representatives from these departments to visit the potential supplier's facilities and turn in an objective report of their findings.

Question 1:

Calculate the key financial ratios and comment briefly on each one.

Comment:

There are four broad categories of ratios to be considered:

(i)   Liquidity ratios
(ii)   Activity ratios
(iii)   Debt/financial ratios
(iv)   Profitability ratios

LIQUIDITY RATIOS:

1. Current Ratio $= \dfrac{\text{Current assets}}{\text{Current liabilities}}$

This ratio indicates the ability of the firm to cover its short-term obligations (less than one year) with liquid assets (those assets that can readily be converted to cash) like cash, marketable securities, inventory and accounts receivable. The current ratio has been above the industry average almost every year and is currently 2.7 versus an average of 2.13. This indicates that the firm can presently cover its immediate obligations 2.7 times.

Wedge Computers, Inc.
Selected Financial Ratios

	1981	1982	1983	1984	1985	Industry average
Current ratio	2.13	2.48	1.97	4.30	2.70	2.13
Quick ratio	0.32	0.68	0.07	2.77	1.61	1.18
Inventory turnover	6.62	5.50	3.45	7.77	6.14	6.95
Average collection period	50.89	72.10	68.18	147.67	179.42	60.00
Fixed asset turnover	10.92	13.08	4.97	6.08	4.06	12.35
Total asset turnover	2.10	2.04	1.41	1.28	1.08	5.75
Debt ratio	0.54	0.51	0.66	0.63	0.74	0.50
Debt-equity ratio	0.93	0.63	1.38	1.55	2.34	1.00
Times interest earned	5.48	10.18	8.69	5.15	1.88	10.00
Gross profit margin	0.17	0.19	0.21	0.21	0.20	0.22
Net profit margin	0.02	0.04	0.05	0.05	0.02	0.07
Return on investment	0.05	0.03	0.07	0.06	0.02	0.09
Return on equity	0.19	0.28	0.29	0.20	0.10	0.25
Average stock price		3.81	19.48	41.41	44.37	N/A
Earnings per share		0.69	1.15	1.21	0.99	1.37
Price earnings ratio		5.52	16.94	34.22	44.82	N/A

2. $$\text{Quick Ratio} = \frac{\text{Current assets} - \text{inventory}}{\text{Current liabilities}}$$

Since it is difficult to dispose of inventory in order to meet short-term obligations, the quick ratio measures the firm's ability to meet short-term commitments without resorting to depletion of inventory levels. To this end, inventories are not included in the current assets.

The position was precarious for the first three years but seems to be above average for the years 1984 and 1985. But students should be very cautious in viewing the high current and quick ratios as a sign of liquidity. The abnormally high amount of accounts receivable tends to distort the two ratios. If Wedge is not in a position to recover all of its receivables, there will be insufficient funds to meet short-term obligations.

ACTIVITY RATIOS:

3. $$\text{Average Collection Period} = \frac{\text{Accounts receivable}}{\text{Sales per day}}$$

The ACP indicates the number of days that an average bill is left unpaid. While it is useful to compare this with the industry average, the right comparison would be with the firm's credit policy. Having an ACP above the stipulated credit period indicates that the firm needs to revise its credit policy or step up its collection of outstanding receivables.

At present this ratio indicates that the firm's customers take almost 180 days to make payments against bills. Either they are facing a severe financial crisis or there may be several disputed bills over the past two years. Wedge's credit policy could be questioned. In any case, this ratio should raise a red flag for a person analyzing the financial statements.

4. Fixed Asset Turnover = $\dfrac{\text{Sales}}{\text{Net fixed assets}}$

The ratio indicates how effectively the firm is able to use its fixed assets in generating sales. Of course, an extremely high ratio could indicate that fixed assets are being overworked, which is not in the best interest of the firm over the long run.

5. Total Asset Turnover = $\dfrac{\text{Sales}}{\text{Total assets}}$

Like the fixed asset turnover, this ratio indicates how effectively the firm uses all of its assets in generating sales. Both these ratios (4 and 5) are way below the industry average. This indicates that the sales of Wedge Computers are not proportionate to the heavy investment in assets. In other words, the firm is overcapitalized. To be on par with the rest of the industry, sales should be at least three times the present amount. If this is not possible, then many machines would be kept idle for extended periods, unnecessarily blocking funds.

DEBT/FINANCIAL RATIOS:

6. Debt Ratio = $\dfrac{\text{Long-term debt}}{\text{Total long-term funds}}$

The debt ratio measures the content of long-term funds in the capital structure of the company. In other words it indicates how much of the total long-term commitment of funds is contributed by lenders. One minus the debt ratio would indicate the percentage of long-term funds generated from the stockholders of the company.

7. Debt-Equity Ratio = $\dfrac{\text{Long-term debt}}{\text{Total equity}}$

This ratio relates the long-term borrowings to the amount put up by the stockholders through common stock issued and retained earnings. A ratio of more than one indicates that the stockholders have borrowed more from outside than they have contributed themselves, and vice versa if the ratio is less than one.

In 1985 the debt and debt/equity ratios were 0.65 and 2.34 respectively. Both ratios show that Wedge is heavily dependent on borrowed funds to finance short- and long-term investments. Being so heavily leveraged is very risky, and suppliers of funds view this factor seriously when considering further extensions of credit.

8. Times Interest Earned = $\dfrac{\text{Earnings before interest and taxes}}{\text{Interest charges}}$

This ratio indicates the ability of a company to meet its interest payments. Obviously Wedge is barely able to meet its obligations to its lenders. The industry expects firms to earn at least 10 times their respective interest charges. In 1985, Wedge earned a mere 1.88 times its interest payment. If the firm is not able to meet interest payments on time, let alone the principal amounts, banks and other lenders may exercise their right to foreclose on hypothicated (pledged) property.

PROFITABILITY RATIOS:

9. Gross Margin $= \dfrac{\text{Gross profit}}{\text{Sales}} \times 100$

10. Net Margin $= \dfrac{\text{Net income}}{\text{Sales}} \times 100$

11. Return on investment $= \dfrac{\text{Net income}}{\text{Total assets}}$

12. Return on equity $= \dfrac{\text{Net income}}{\text{Stockholders' funds}}$

The last four ratios are profitability ratios. They indicate the income earned as a percentage of sales, total assets, stockholders' funds, etc. Apart from being below the industry average, they have decreased during 1985 after showing some growth potential in the first few years.

Question 2:

Based on the information provided in the case, do you think Jeff Neuber is justifiably worried?

Comment:

From question 1 and the memo from Shannon Richey, there is no doubt that Wedge Computers, Inc. faces a precarious financial position. Jeff has cause to be worried because of the implications of a cash-out at Wedge. The poor state of the financial statements is indicative of a weak management team and the lack of strategic long-term planning. Investing heavily in the new equipment could work against the company at this rate. Perhaps it may have been wiser to concentrate on the huge accounts receivable balances than on plant expansion.

In any case if Wedge runs short of cash during the life of the contract, it may not be able to continue to maintain a high quality and also may not be in a position to supply the requirements of Microcomp. This would delay the production of the MCD86.

Question 3:

What problems would you anticipate with the Wedge contract?

Comment:

Most of the problems would naturally be associated with the firm's inability to meet its obligations to financial institutions and creditors. Some of the likely problems are:

- The firm will first try to overcome its cash shortage by cutting down on expenses, resulting in a compromise on quality.
- Creditors will stop or delay supply of raw materials until their bills are paid.
- Banks and other financial institutions may foreclose on the assets secured under the loan agreement.
- Inability to pay wages and salaries would lead to layoffs and possible labor unrest.

- Bondholders or other creditors may petition for declaring the firm insolvent, which may, in turn, force its dissolution.
- The company may become the target of a takeover.

In all these cases the activities of the firm will be disrupted and it would be reasonable to expect a delay in the delivery schedule. Even if delivery is made on time there is no guarantee that Wedge will be able to maintain its quality standard. Finally, Microcomp may have to resort to one of the other suppliers to bail it out in the event of the failure of Wedge to fulfill its commitment.

Question 4:

What additional sources could Shannon Richey use in order to assess the financial position of Wedge Computers?

Comment:

Some of the sources of industry and company data are:

- Dun and Bradstreet
- Moody's
- Standard & Poors
- Value Line
- Robert Morriss Associates
- The Federal Trade Commission's Quarterly Financial Report

These publications provide industry ratios for manufacturing firms by industry groups. Dun & Bradstreet, for example, shows the mean ratios for those firms whose performance places them in the median range, upper or lower quartile of their respective industry.

Question 5:

Are there any disadvantages to using financial ratios in a preaward survey?

Comment:

Although financial ratios are used as tools in decision making, there are a number of cautions:

- Different accounting methods can lead to substantial differences in some ratios, for example, leasing assets versus purchasing them.
- Ratios can change dramatically as a result of one, or several, transactions at year end; for example, making payments on current liabilities will reduce current assets and current liabilities by the same dollar amount, but the current ratio will improve.
- There are many seasonal factors to consider.
- It is difficult to determine whether a particular ratio is good or bad unless more information is available.
- Finally, an industry average is just that, an "average." It would be most helpful to know dispersion about the average; if most values are very close to it while our firm is way off, we would be more concerned than if there is wide dispersion.

An analysis of a firm's financial ratios is useful when used intelligently and with good judgment. However, an analysis conducted mechanically and without much thought is dangerous.

Question 6:

What specific action would you recommend? Would your recommendation be different if Wedge's price were only 1 or 2 percent lower than another supplier's?

Comment:

Quite obviously, there is no correct answer to this question. It is included to force the student to take a position. The second part of the question is included to see if differing kinds of cost savings will affect an individual's attitude toward risk.

MIDWEST OIL COMPANY

Purpose

This short case has been an extremely successful vehicle for discussing the means of obtaining upper-management support for a surplus management program, as well as outlining an action plan for the development of such a program.

It can also be used to illustrate the various categories of surplus/waste/scrap.

Immediate Issue

How to increase the number of items voluntarily placed on the surplus listing by the various divisions.

Basic Issues

1. What actions are required to obtain voluntary cooperation by the various divisions?
2. What should the elements of the action plan be?

Suggested Student Assignments

- Develop a Surplus Disposal Priority System.
- Develop a Surplus Policy Statement.

Analysis

Key Points

- The major source of surplus is generally excess equipment or idle/obsolete equipment that cannot be returned to the supplier.
- Surplus problems cross divisional lines.
- Internal advertisement and extensive communication is required.
- Transfer of surplus is a more complex activity than it at first appears to be.
- Future planning and assessment is required.

Teaching Strategy—Open Discussion

1. From reading assignment: Ask class to list the categories of surplus. Which should be included within the program?
2. Discuss under which categories specific items should be listed. Which offered to divisions? Which to the supplier? Which to employees?
3. What categories include transfer of funds? What types of actions are cost or revenue, and to whom?
4. Who should take action (and what action) to obtain voluntary participation in the program? How monitored? What rewards for participation?

Suggested Class Plan

10 min.:   Read the case and define issues.

10 min.:   Class lists major issues and subordinate issues.

10 min.:   Discuss items to be included within policy statement, topical headings for written procedures, transfer of funds, etc.

10 min.:   Develop action plan.

10 min.:   Wrap-up.

MISSISSIPPI MUTUAL LIFE INSURANCE

Purpose

This case is typical of the issues and decisions involved in establishing ethical standards in organizations. It can be used to highlight apparent awareness of a need for formal standards, along with the problems of what constitutes ethical behavior. Students can focus on several possible avenues for discussion, including the stimuli for ethical standards, the process of promulgation, issues of reinforcement and enforcement actions, and implications for applications within and outside the division. The nature of this case also underscores the need for stakeholders considerations.

Immediate Issues

What ethical standards should Frank Smithson propose?

Basic Issues

What factors should be taken into consideration in coming up with ethical standards?

Suggested Student Assignments

- If you were Frank Smithson, what standards would you propose? Outline the process Frank should use to develop the ethical standards for the division.

Possible Discussion Questions

1. Should Mississippi Mutual even attempt to address the issue of ethics?
2. What factors should Frank take into consideration?
3. What reinforcements and/or enforcement actions would you come up with, if any?
4. Would you attempt to achieve consensus among the leaders within the division prior to finalizing your standards? Is so, what strategy would you employ to gain consensus?
5. Should the same standards, reinforcements, and enforcement actions apply across the entire group?

Analysis

The process employed by Frank was important both in terms of standards content and acceptance. A simple process may consist of:
1. Input—Internal Division
   a. Identifying past questionable situations.
   b. Gathering input from division leaders.
   c. Gathering input from buyers.
   d. Identify the relevant stakeholders.
   e. Identify the alternative courses of action.
   f. Identify practical constraints.
2. Input—External Division
   a. What are acceptable purchasing practices?

       b.   What may be considered questionable purchasing practices?

       c.   What are possible reinforcement and enforcement actions?

3. Rough Draft

       a.   Prepare rough draft of standards.

       b.   Get acceptance of rough draft from Division Vice President, and selected division leaders and buyers.

       c.   Obtain necessary acceptance based on internal guidelines (legal, human resources, etc.), if applicable.

4. Consolidation

       a.   Rewrite standards based upon reviews from the draft.

       b.   Identify the alternative courses of action.

       c.   Identify practical constraints.

       d.   Review possible courses of action.

5. Finalization

       a.   Prepare guidelines for distribution to buyers.

       b.   Prepare follow-up procedures.

       c.   Prepare communications process for within and outside the division.

6. Submit the recommended guidelines and other procedures to vice president and other leaders.

Key Points

1. The issues of unethical behavior are broader than the issue of illegal behavior; thus, there are factors of individual and professional judgment, value systems, culture, and moral development to consider.

2. There are no consistent applications of ethical standards.

3. Establishing ethical standards, particularly unnecessary standards, may have an adverse impact on morale and productivity.

4. Ethical standards, like other guidelines, are more effective when they are linked with the recognition and rewards system of the organization.

5. There is considerable attention given to ethics in practically all facets of society. Major companies are especially sensitive to those actions or behavior which may possibly be considered questionable by their stakeholders.

6. It is important to recognize that this case is not intended to give the complete history and details involved in examining the issue of ethical behavior. There are a number of background and policy considerations which may alter the situation substantially. if the standards promulgated are not accepted or followed by leaders or buyers there may be other courses of action which may bring about desired results. There are a number of assumptions as well as questions that can apply in this case, and students are encouraged to surface those. The primary focus is on addressing the difficult task of establishing standards to regulate conduct in a professional organization.

MUENSTER PUMP BUYS A CAR

Purpose

This role-playing case provides a hands-on negotiating experience to which virtually everyone can relate. The case and the subsequent discussion demonstrate the importance of preparation for negotiations, the desirability of understanding one's opposite and his or her wants and needs in a negotiation, and the importance of understanding one's self and one's objectives. The presence of hidden agenda items and the relationship between discovering these hidden agenda items and the outcome of the negotiation is brought to the student's attention.

Note:

In preparing for this class, the instructor should have the required number of copies made of (1) Role for Terry Dorf, Purchasing Manager, (2) Role for Fran Fay, Salesperson, and (3) Muenster Pump Buys a Car summary sheet.

Mechanics

This case has been successfully tested on undergraduate and graduate students at the University of San Diego and on numerous members of the Purchasing Management Association of San Diego. Each play of the case has been enjoyable to the participants and to the instructor. The degree of student participation leaves a longer-lasting impression than many conventional teaching methods.

The case should be used after the students have read Chapter 11 (Negotiation). The class should be divided into pairs consisting of a buyer and a seller. If there is an odd number of students, the instructor can complete a pair by playing the role of Fran Fay, Salesperson.

Before distributing the roles, the instructor should tell the students that they will be involved in a one-on-one role-playing experience. They are to study the role given to them, analyze the facts, and be prepared to play their assigned roles. They should be encouraged to "get into the spirit of things"—to act as they think they would behave were they a buyer or a salesperson. They have the relevant facts from the roles and are free to ad-lib as appropriate. The students are requested *not* to discuss their roles with others until after they and their negotiating partners have reached agreement or have agreed not to agree. Each role has privileged information, however, neither role has facts or information which is in conflict with the "opponent's" role.

Some students may request permission to conduct their negotiations in another room. Don't let this happen! A fantastic synergy is achieved when several pairs are negotiating in the same room simultaneously. A synergism results. Interest increases.

After providing introductory guidance, the instructor should distribute the roles. Provide 10–15 minutes to allow each person to prepare for the negotiations. Remember, some people never have enough time. Fifteen minutes is more than enough.

As you sense or observe that two members of a negotiating pair have each completed their preparation, instruct the buyer (Terry Dorf) to stand up and enter the Muenster Spitbug salesroom. If necessary, advise the salesperson (Fran Fay) to get up and greet the person who just entered. (After one pair has gone through the welcoming process, all remaining pairs will duplicate it.)

Normally, most pairs will either reach agreement on a price or agree not to agree after 15–20 minutes. If any pairs are still negotiating after 15–18 minutes, give them a gentle nudge and request that they reach a conclusion in a minute or two.

The questionnaire is optional. It provides a spirited bit of discussion and keeps the pairs which have completed the negotiation occupied. The questionnaire provides a guide to be used for the most important aspect of the role-playing experience: posting results on the blackboard and drawing conclusions.

Each play involving ten or more pairs has shown a definite tendency for there to be a relationship between a realistic price objective and the results achieved. For example, a buyer who has established a target price objective of $11,500 tends to obtain a lower agreed-upon price than does a buyer whose target objective is $12,000. There is only a tendency for this to occur, since the personality and objectives of the individual playing the role of Fran Fay, the salesperson, have an impact on the outcome.

The buyer (or salesperson) who has prepared a good negotiation strategy which begins with reasoning and then, possibly, progresses to hard bargaining tends to do far better than the negotiator who plays it by ear.

The buyer (or seller) who learns of their opponent's hidden agenda ("The boss is getting married and wants a new car tomorrow; it's the last day of the month and I'm one car from meeting quota and gaining a $1,000 bonus") tends to do far better than does his or her less-informed counterpart in other negotiating pairs.

Each play is unique. Each provides an opportunity for the instructor to make negotiating a real event and to emphasize the importance of the previously discussed negotiating principles.

This case confirms our belief that learning can be fun!

Role for Terry Dorf, Purchasing Manager

It is Friday morning, the 30th of the month. Terry Dorf, purchasing manager at Muenster Pump Company of Muenster, Ohio, is finishing a purchase order for valves. Bob Dorf, Terry's cousin and president of Muenster Pump, enters Terry's office.

Terry: "Bob, I'm, surprised to see you here. Is the wedding still on?"

Bob: "Sure is. Everything's set. Well, almost everything. I'm more nervous than the first time. Last night, Sue and I were talking about our honeymoon. After we get married tomorrow morning, we plan to drive down to Kentucky for a couple of days. Well, anyhow, last night we decided that my old Continental might be a bit stuffy for our honeymoon. Terry, to make a long story short, I want you to purchase a new Spitbug 8 for the company and, as you might guess, I want it tomorrow, bright and early!"

Terry: "I've seen a couple Spitbugs—really dreamy. What acceleration. What model do you want?"

Bob: "That's no problem. There is only one model and it comes fully loaded. AM-FM, cassette player, air conditioning, five on the floor, and radials. The only choices are color and where you're going to buy the car. I want a metallic blue or a bronze one. Last week, I read an ad in the *Newburg Times* from a dealer up in Michigan, and, as you can see from the ad, he quotes a price of $11,500. Unfortunately, he cites delivery two weeks after receipt of an order accompanied with a deposit of $5,000.

"As we both know, Terry, Muenster Pump does need a new car. Maintenance is getting to be a real problem on the Continental. When we get the new car, I'm going to sell the

Continental to your Uncle Ned. He's a good mechanic and can keep it going. Also, I think that it's about time that we break out of our stuffy image. And what better time to buy one than in time for the president's honeymoon? See what you can do, cousin!"

As soon as Bob left, Terry got on the phone. The first call was to the dealer in Michigan. The salesman confirmed the price of $11,500 and indicated that delivery would be in two weeks and that both desired colors would be available.

Terry then called the local Spitbug dealer and talked with Fran Fay. Terry learned that Muenster Spitbug had three cars in stock, including a bronze one. Fran quoted a price of $12,950, but seemed very anxious to make a deal.

Terry then called the Spitbug dealer in State College, a large city some 100 miles from Muenster. A price of $11,950 was quoted with immediate delivery of any color, including metallic blue and bronze.

Armed with this information, Terry decided to visit the local dealer in an effort to negotiate a better deal. On the way to the Muenster showroom, Terry recalled something from a course in purchasing taken while attending State University. Salespersons frequently receive as much of their income from bonuses as from commissions. A classmate at State U. supported the instructor, saying that his bonus for meeting his monthly car sales quota was $1,000. And that was three years ago!

With these and other thoughts in mind, Terry enters the Muenster Spitbug showroom.

Role for Fran Fay, Salesperson

Fran Fay of Muenster Spitbug is sipping a cup of coffee. The Muenster Spitbug dealership handles only the revolutionary new Spitbug, a car which combines incredible acceleration (10–60 in 6 seconds) with great gas mileage (40 mpg combined). The Spitbug comes in only one model. Standard equipment includes AM-FM, cassette player, air conditioning, five on the floor, and steel-belted radials. A five-year, 50,000-mile warranty on the drive train is included in the purchase price. The dealership has three cars all prepared and ready to go, including a metallic blue one, a white one, and a bronze car.

Fran looks very downhearted. "Boy, oh boy, what a month this has been. Here it is the last day of the month and I'm one car short of meeting quota. I've already spent that $1,000 bonus. What am I going to do? Why in blazes did I ever get into this business?"

Stan Sherman, owner of the Spitbug dealership, interrupts Fran's reverie. "Fran, I'm leaving for the weekend. I know how anxious you are to meet quota, but don't do anything foolish. The Spitbug's really selling like hotcakes. As I told all the salespeople, I don't want any of you to undercut the market. I don't want to quote a price below $12,950."

Fran asks, "Stan, if you're unavailable, I've got to have some flexibility. I know that the car only costs us $11,000. How low can I go if I get a live one?"

Stan replies, "Fran, I guess you can go down to $12,000 if you really have to, but not a cent lower. Don't forget that your 25 percent commission is on anything over the $11,000 we pay for the car! See you Monday."

After Stan leaves, Fran drifts back into a state of deep thought. "One car from quota. I wonder if that purchasing manager from Muenster Pump whom I quoted $12,950 this morning is going to come in today. Maybe I'll call over there."

Just then Terry enters the showroom.

Muenster Pump Buys a Car

These questions are to be completed by each Negotiating Pair (Buyer and Seller)

<u>PLEZ</u> PRINT!

_____   _____
Buyer's Name .   Seller's Name

Terry, if agreement was reached on price, it was for $ _____

This portion is to be completed by the buyer (Terry):

If you had price objectives, they were:	$ _____	_____	_____
	low	target	high

Did you use any of the following negotiation techniques?	_____	_____	_____
	Reasoning (e.g., a discussion of supplier's costs and needs)	Hard Bargaining (e.g., a threat to leave)	Lying (Shame on you.)

Hidden agenda items:

Did you learn that Fran needs to sell one more car *today* to meet quota and receive a handsome bonus?	_____	_____
	Yes, and boy, oh boy, did it help!	Gosh, no!

This portion is to be completed by the seller:

Fran, if you had price objectives, they were:	$ _____	_____	_____
	low	target	high

Did you use any of the following negotiation techniques?	_____	_____	_____
	Reasoning	Hard Bargaining	Lying (A Car Salesperson?)

Hidden agenda items:

Did you learn that Terry *had* to have the car by tomorrow morning?	_____	_____
	Yes, ha, ha!	No, darn it!

THANK YOU!

THE MUENSTER PUMP COMPANY

Purpose

The purpose of this case is to discuss the economic and noneconomic issues which are involved in making a decision on whether to make or buy an item.

Discussion

This is an excellent case for discussing several issues which are involved in a make-or-buy analysis: economic issues, quality, responsiveness, purchasing's role in the process, and management's responsibility to its employees.

Question 1:

What other information would be useful in arriving at this make-or-buy decision?

Comment:

Information on the quality of potential suppliers' products would be a key input. This information could be obtained in several ways. It may be possible to obtain samples of the required item or of similar items. Discussion with some of the foundry's customers could provide additional information.

Alternative uses of the Muenster foundry should be investigated. If no alternatives appear feasible, and if there is not viable employment for the foundry workers, then retrenchment costs must be examined.

Question 2:

Who should take part in the make-or-buy decision process?

Comment:

The make-or-buy decision is principally management's responsibility. For a firm the size of Muenster Pump, Bob Dorf, the president, must ultimately make the decision. He should, however, at a minimum, have reliable input from production, finance (on the true cost of making), and purchasing.

Question 3:

What role should purchasing play?

Comment:

The purchasing manager's responsibility is to obtain accurate information on the cost, quality, reliability, and responsiveness of prospective suppliers. Purchasing inputs facts, but does not make the make-or-buy decision. Nevertheless, purchasing's part in the make-or-buy decision is a very important one.

Question 4:

How should the noneconomic factors be evaluated?

Comment:

This question is answered in comments to questions 1 and 5. Question 4 is included to ensure that the student considers the noneconomic issues as well as the economic ones.

Question 5:

Should Muenster make or buy its casting housings?

Comment:

Before a decision can be reached on this question, several issues must be addressed. The first is economic. At the present, it costs $180 to make the L-1012 housing. Of this, $96 is a variable cost ($60 for labor and materials and $36 for variable overhead) and $84 is an allocation of fixed overhead. This $84 "expense" occurs whether or not Muenster continues to make its casting housings. It includes depreciation on plant and equipment, taxes, security costs, etc. This fixed overhead should not be a consideration unless the firm is operating at full capacity and is considering adding new facilities which would result in the incurrence of new overhead expenses. The economic value to use for our analysis is $96. The value to be used for the buy cost is a bit less precise. It includes the purchase price of $90 plus any related incremental costs of purchasing and inventorying the casting housing *plus* any expenses which might result from shutting the foundry down. The related incremental costs involved in purchasing include the cost of additional purchase orders, inspection costs, and receiving costs. Inventory carrying costs would have to be determined and compared with the cost of inventorying the housing now being made. The shutdown costs would include severence pay, if any employees were to be discharged; or retraining costs, if they could be used elsewhere in the firm.

If a satisfactory level of quality and responsiveness could be obtained from outside suppliers, if a satisfactory long-term economic commitment were possible, and if shutdown costs were not a major hurdle, then the economic analysis favors buying the casting housing.

The noneconomic issues which must be included in the decision include dependability and responsiveness of outside sources of supply, quality considerations, and management's responsibility to its employees. The last issue (management's responsibility to its employees) deserves special attention. This is not a simple issue that can or should be decided on apparent moral grounds. If Muenster continues to make the housing in order to provide employment to its foundry workers, it may, in the long run, have performed a disservice to all of its employees. Such action could result in Muenster later becoming noncompetitive in the agricultural pump industry, resulting in reduced sales and reduced employment. In the extreme, such action could lead to the closing of the plant. If several decisions of this nature are made on the grounds of loyalty to "our employees" *without* due consideration to the survival of a viable economic business, several groups may pay a high price. Employees, owners, management, and suppliers alike will suffer. This does *not* mean that a decision resulting in retrenchment would automatically result. It does mean that the issue of responsibility to a firm's employees must be analyzed within its real economic context.

Question 6:

What do you think of the organizational structure at Muenster?

Comment:

Muenster Pump Company is suffering under an archaic and inefficient organization. The subordination of purchasing to manufacturing frequently is found in production-oriented firms. Such an organizational approach may facilitate day-to-day operations. But this approach may block purchasing from reaching its full profit-making potential.

In order for purchasing to make its full contribution to the efficiency and profitability of an organization, it must be able to interact with engineering, manufacturing, finance, and marketing as an equal partner. Purchasing should assist engineering in the quest for cost-effective solutions to engineering problems. Purchasing's advice on the economic and availability implications of different materials is a key (and frequently missing) prerequisite to a highly profitable organization.

Purchasing's ability to buy economically is dependent, in part, on adequate lead time. Marketing, through its responsibility for sales forecasts, has a key role in providing adequate lead time. The organizations responsible for long- and mid-range production planning (manufacturing or operations at Muenster Pump) and for inventory control (it looks like no one is responsible for inventory control at Muenster), have critical roles in providing adequate procurement lead time. When purchasing is subordinated to manufacturing, it is placed in the position of reacting to manufacturing's demands. Inadequate planning is hidden through costly emergency purchasing actions.

Under the present organizational structure, it is unlikely that purchasing is receiving adequate procurement lead times. Such a situation can increase material expenditures significantly. It also appears likely that purchasing at Muenster would be hampered in other profit-making areas such as make-or-buy analyses and value analysis.

Various solutions to this problem include:

1. Implementation of a materials management concept with production planning and inventory control, purchasing, traffic, receiving, and inspection assigned to a vice president.
2. Elevation of purchasing (with or without inventory control responsibilities) to a level comparable to engineering, manufacturing, finance, and sales.
3. A variation of 1 or 2.

NADIA DEVELOPS A COMMODITY STUDY

This case is designed to make available to the instructor some of the elements commonly addressed in a commodity study. Such studies were a part of Michigan State's undergraduate program when John Hoagland and, then, Lee Budress were on faculty. Developing the questions listed below (provided by Lee Budress) can be a very useful in-class exercise. Or the questions can be the basis of a directed research project for the advanced student.

COMMODITY STUDY GUIDELINES

Information resulting from a commodity study should:

- provide a basis for making sound procurement decisions.
- present purchasing and supply management and top management with good information concerning future supply and price of purchased items.

The completed commodity study should provide data and/or answers for each of the following points or questions (the investigation should not necessarily be limited to these items; depending on the particular commodity under consideration, additional items may be very pertinent, and some of the listed items may not be important).

I. CURRENT STATUS

1. Description of commodity
2. How and where commodity is used
3. Requirements
4. Suppliers
5. How commodity is purchased
6. Current contracts and expiration date
7. Current price, terms, and annual expenditure
8. Inventory control
9. Scheduling
10. Releasing
11. Receiving
12. Inspection
13. Expediting
14. Complaints
15. Packaging
16. Other

II. OBJECTIVES

1. Long Range
2. Short Range

III. FORECAST OF REQUIREMENTS

1. Usage, past and present
2. Forecast of future requirements
3. Plan for keeping forecasts up to date

    4. Source of forecast information

    5. Approval of forecast

    6. Lead times

IV. THE MARKET SITUATION

    1. Supply-demand relationships past, present, and future

    2. Pertinent price information

    3. Geographic considerations

    4. Forces affecting the market as a whole

        a. Political

        b. Technological

        c. Reserves

        d. Other

    5. Forces affecting our position in the market

    6. Trends

V. PRODUCTION PROCESS

    1. How is the item made?

    2. What materials are used in its manufacture?

        a. Supply/price status of these materials

    3. What labor is required?

        a. Current and future labor situation

    4. Are there alternative production processes?

    5. What changes are likely in the future?

    6. Possibility of making the item?

        a. Costs

        b. Time factor

        c. Problems

VI. USES OF THE ITEM

    1. Primary use(s)

    2. Secondary use(s)

    3. Possible substitutions

VII. PRICE EVALUATION

    1. Cost to produce including investments

    2. Incremental costs

    3. Co-product of by-product

    4. Profitability to suppliers

    5. Potential rock-bottom price

    6. Price objectives

    7. Price history

    8. Price forecast

VIII. EVALUATION OF SUPPLIERS

1. Strengths and weaknesses of each producer as a supplier
2. Potential new suppliers
3. Trade relations

IX. EVALUATION OF PROPOSALS

1. Suppliers
2. Make or buy

X. STRATEGY TO REDUCE COMMODITY COST

Considering forecasted supply, usage, prices, profitability, proposals, strengths and weaknesses of suppliers, our position in the market, etc., make plan to lower cost.

1. Make commodity or integrate backward
2. Spot purchase
3. Short term contract
4. Long term contract
5. Acquire producer
6. Find a substitute
7. Develop a new producer
8. Import
9. Exploit all methods to make maximum use of our purchasing power
10. Detailed preplanning of negotiations
11. Use of agents
12. Hedging
13. Value Engineering
14. Other

XI. OTHER INFORMATION

1. General information
   a. Specifications
   b. Quality control
   c. Freight rates and transportation costs
   d. Storage capacity
   e. Handling facilities
   f. Weather problems
   g. Raw material reserves
2. Statistics
   a. Price trends
   b. Production trends
   c. Purchase trends
   d. Etc.

NATIONAL COMPUTERS

Purpose

This case describes some of the problems involved in developing and implementing standardization and inventory management programs.

Discussion

Sound standarization and inventory management programs result in major savings. A standardization program permits a firm to purchase fewer items, in larger quantities, and at lower prices. Purchasing, receiving, inspection, storage, and payment costs all are reduced. Inventory management programs can reduce the firm's investment in inventories, frequently saving millions of dollars *plus* freeing badly needed working capital.

Question 1:

What specific techniques and methods should Tom use to convince engineering to reduce part numbers?

Comment:

The key question here has to be "What's in it for engineering?" Reduction of the part number base is a time-consuming and costly process. The benefits to engineering may not be readily apparent. Specifically, Tom must be able to convince the director of hardware engineering that his or her efforts to reduce the part number base will result in tangible benefits for both the engineering department and the firm as a whole. Tom's first task should be to estimate the reduction in both design and product development times resulting from a 40 percent reduction in part numbers. Since this reduction in part numbers would be achieved primarily through standardization efforts, the ancillary benefits of improved quality and reliability should also form a part of this initial study.

Tom should consider presenting these benefits to engineering in a meeting with his boss present. This meeting would consist of a formal presentation briefly outlining the Supply Line Management strategy and showing, in dollar terms, the important contribution which can be made through part number reduction. A major portion of the presentation would address the benefits to be gained by the engineering department in the design and development phase of new product introduction. Senior management support might be mentioned, especially if the vice president and general manager place significant value on the SLM strategy. The presentation should be followed by a discussion of concerns and questions raised by engineering.

Question 2:

What kind of evidence should he use to support his case?

Comment:

The objective here is to use evidence which supports purchasing's case and demonstrates to engineering the benefits it gains through a reduction in part number count. Trade magazines, business school texts and other divisions of the company are all sources of evidence which could be used to support Tom's case. The type of evidence that Tom's research people should look for are articles which show the dollar and time benefits which have been realized by companies who have reduced their part number base. Richard Schoenberger in *World Class Manufacturing* gives several such examples.

Another type of evidence which could be used would be a trade study using National Computers products to show specific benefits which would be realized by the San Diego division. If Tom does not have any research people, consultants are available who could conduct the required study, one tailored to the engineering department's needs. This would be a very powerful form of evidence.

Question 3:

What suggestions could he give engineering to facilitate the reduction in part numbers?

Comment:

The obvious suggestion here is to establish a catalog of standard parts which must be used for new designs. A time schedule would be agreed upon for the development of this catalog. The creation of a catalog is the prime area where purchasing help could be given. A team, or teams, could be established consisting of buyers, design engineers, procurement quality engineers and reliability engineers to develop the catalog. In order to achieve a 40 percent reduction in part numbers, it probably would be necessary to redesign existing products by replacing existing components with standardized components. This process probably would require requalification testing of the product to assure no reduction in product reliability. Because of the expense of this redesign and retest effort, such a process may be difficult to justify. But certainly a cost analysis should be made. A schedule should be developed and assignments made which will support the 4th quarter 1990 date for implementation of the 40 percent reduction in part number base.

Question 4:

Outline in general terms an overall inventory management program for National Computers.

Comment:

Assuming that all inventory items have been completely described, identified by manufacturer's part number, cross-indexed by National Computers part numbers, and classified generically for indexing purposes, an inventory catalog should be developed.

Next, the inventory manager should determine the importance and the dollar value of each item. The price, usage, lead time, and any technical or procurement nuances should be identified. An ABC or "Pareto" analysis (as described in Chapter 23) then should be conducted.

Given the nature of National Computers products, it is likely that the firm uses an MRP system for production planning and control. If so, the MRP system will determine when to order materials. The size of the order will be a judgement call based on the quantity required during the planning period—the "lot for lot" approach.

NATIONAL MACHINE AND ELECTRONICS

Purpose

This case addresses the issue of developing an international sourcing program in a decentralized environment—one with purchasing managers who are reluctant to source offshore.

Questions 1 & 2:

What choices does Mike have for starting an international sourcing program? What are the advantages and disadvantages of each?

Comment:

a. Increase central procurement activities through company-wide standardization efforts.
   + The many benefits resulting from standardization (see Chapter 7) would result.
   − There is no guarantee that cost saving-foreign sourcing would result.

b. Make wider use of Singapore's purchasing department.
   + Little or no incremental administrative cost would result.
   − Top management would have to "convince" department managers to give it a try.
   − The Singapore staff may be biased in favor of Singapore or other Asian sources.

c. Issue a corporate policy change requiring that products be considered for foreign sourcing and that orders be planned when savings exceed a standard threshold.
   + Such an approach would get the attention of the department purchasing managers.
   − In NME's environment, the department purchasing managers might ignore the policy statement. Certainly, several would resent it.

d. Establish an international procurement office (IPO) reporting to the corporate purchasing department.
   + Establishment of such an office would get the attention of all purchasing managers.
   + If properly staffed, the office would be able to develop realistic objectives and plans in concert with the division purchasing managers.
   − Some incremental cost for the IPO will result.

e. Establish cost reduction objectives for each division's purchasing department.
   + Additional cost pressure may force the purchasing managers to consider foreign sources.
   − Division chiefs may resent "outside" interference with their operation.

f. Source more assembly operations offshore.
   + Offshore assembly operations normally result in increased sourcing in proximity to the new assembly's location.
   − Such action can lead to a further hollowing of NME's domestic industrial base and a lowering of domestic employment.

Question 3:

Would NME benefit from an Asian IPO?

Comment:

The obvious answer is yes! The obvious question is: How does NME obtain maximum use of such an IPO? The following integrated plan is one approach:

- Arrange a one-day 'International Sourcing' seminar at corporate offices for the 15 division purchasing managers. This seminar would provide information on the advantages and disadvantages of international sourcing and would also give some specific examples of cost savings which can be achieved.
- A corporate purchasing directive requiring consideration of international sourcing should be written and a draft copy presented at the seminar.
- The Singapore facility should be used as the focal point for foreign procurement. A corporate purchasing function, which would be staffed by both Asian and American personnel should be established at this facility. This function would make full use of existing sources and people.
- This international procurement office should also include engineers, to help facilitate a company-wide standardization program.
- A corporate audit program should be established to assure that each division is complying with corporate buying policies and that established cost reduction goals are being pursued.
- Each division head (vice president and general manager) should have as one of his or her performance measurements a 'cost reduction through foreign sourcing' goal which is reportable to the company president.

The actual progression of events in this case are as follows:

1. All divisions were asked to submit drawings of parts which might be subjects for offshore sourcing. CAE Singapore got quotes on parts whose drawings were submitted by three divisions. Cost savings on these parts were consistent with previous CAE results.
2. Mr. Phillips had the director of purchasing from Singapore come to the head office to conduct a seminar on offshore sourcing and doing business with East Asia. All 14 other divisions were invited to send representatives. Eight divisions complied.
3. Two task forces were appointed from seminar attendees to explore other products which might be suitable subjects for offshore sourcing. These groups will report results next month.

NATIONWIDE TELEPHONE

Purpose

The purpose of this case is to discuss the alternatives and processes which can be used by a buyer to determine whether a price obtained from a supplier is "fair and reasonable."

Discussion

This case is very well suited for class discussion and individual case analysis. Many key issues are evident in the case: quality, tools used in price determination, supplier management, risks of sole sourcing, and employee relations.

Question 1:

What type of analysis tools can be used by the purchasing group in order to determine the right price?

Comment:

There are many tools the professional buyer can access and use to help him or her determine the most fair and reasonable price. However, the first thing Jan and Bill must do is develop an estimate of the supplier's cost. Jan will need the following information to accomplish this: quoted prices, the supplier's annual report, the most recent 10-K report, and some basic industry data.

After Jan and Bill have gathered this information, the next task is to determine the *best* tool for estimating a fair and reasonable price. Three tools which will help them in this situation include: price analysis, price justification from suppliers, and break-even analysis.

Price analysis offers several advantages: It could help Jan and Bill determine pricing objectives for plastics as a commodity. It can also be used as a negotiation tool for future price negotiations with ABC Plastics. By forcing the buyers to become aware of the different variables composing the price of a plastic part, Jan and Bill will be better prepared to negotiate their position. Through the analysis of market prices via the industrial indexes, both Jan and Bill will have a better understanding of plastic part pricing. They can then feel assured of which bid prices are fair and reasonable. The final advantage of price analysis is that it is a time-saver when compared to cost analysis. It allows the buyer to obtain a fair estimate without having to spend hours on a more detailed analysis.

Break-even analysis would have been a great tool for Nationwide to have used to help prevent the current situation. Bill would have seen that his part prices were already or were going to be out of line with his firm's objectives. Furthermore, break-even analysis is a quick, relatively easy and effective tool to use when a lot of supplier information is unknown. The biggest problem with this alternative is that it is only a rough approximation of ABC's true selling costs.

By having the supplier submit a detailed price analysis/justification, Jan and Bill will be able to determine where and why the prices are increasing. However, many suppliers are reluctant to divulge this sensitive information. Professional buyers use this information to further supplier partnerships rather than as a negative tool during negotiations.

A sound and open supplier partnership should have been encouraged from the start of Nationwide's relationship with ABC. A supplier partnership would have helped to increase the flow of technical as well as management information between the two companies. Nationwide would have been given the opportunity to anticipate the price increases, and maybe even offer its expertise in an effort to prevent them from occurring.

Question 2:

How could Nationwide's purchasing department have prevented the price escalation?

Comment:

There are many ways in which Nationwide could have prevented the price escalation. A few key ways are as follows:

1. A properly implemented and managed supplier development program could have been established. This program should actively require supplier involvement and cooperation in all areas of a business (i.e., quality, production, deliveries, costs, etc.).
2. Nationwide did not have a sound process for accepting or denying price increases. The current process, as demonstrated in the case, was not an effective tool for monitoring or determining a fair price.

Comments to question 2 also review the means by which price analysis tools could have prevented the price escalation from becoming an unforeseen problem.

Question 3:

How does the competitive condition of the plastics component industry impact the use of price analysis?

Comment:

The competitive nature of the industry is a key factor because it governs how free a firm is to adjust its prices. When there are many plastics suppliers offering differentiated products, the competitive position of the firm will be a dominant factor in its pricing policy. Since most suppliers will not have the same real costs of production, buyers must attribute similar bid prices to the competitive forces. This awareness allows buyers to include this important component when estimating a fair and reasonable price.

Competition in the plastics industry will have an impact on the availability of information necessary to conduct a thorough price analysis. Without any meaningful competition, industry-wide standards of production may not become established. These standards can be used to estimate basic costs of production, both variable and direct, from which reasonable price ranges can be determined and then offered to the supplier.

Question 4:

What kind of resistance might Jan encounter from Bill? How can Bill help to facilitate the pricing analysis process?

Comment:

Jan has been mandated by Nationwide's management to help Bill solve this problem. She has some very difficult problems related to her relationship with Bill to overcome before she can offer her assistance. Bill may feel that his manager does not perceive he is capable of handling the situation; therefore he may not cooperate fully with Jan. He also may feel threatened by Jan's pricing analysis expertise, a technique unfamiliar to his "old school" of knowledge. As a means of reinstating his authority, Bill may shoot down Jan's proposals for solving the situation, stating that they will not work in this type of industry.

Obviously there are a number of ways in which Bill can thwart the successful completion of this project. However, Bill's assistance is essential in the price analysis process. Bill has a lot of purchasing experience in the plastic component industry to offer, so Jan must work to gain Bill's cooperation. His knowledge of the various products, markets, costs, and competitive conditions are all critical components of pricing analysis.

This readily available information can be used to minimize the time and effort needed to perform the analysis. Rather than having to search for pricing information, the effort can be expended toward verifying Bill's data. An "old pro," Bill should be aware of the competitive position of each firm. Therefore, Bill also can help to uncover clues concerning the reasons a supplier prices the way it does.

Another important factor in pricing analysis is to gather as much relevant information as possible. Suppliers could have developed an understanding of their pricing methodology with Bill over the years. These suppliers may be more willing to divulge this data to him rather than to the unknown "new kid."

Question 5:

What are some of the costs/benefits of continuing to source from the same local suppliers?

Comment:

Some benefits of continuing to source locally include:

1. "All in costs" can be kept to a minimum. Shorter lead times are required with local sources when compared to national firms. Inventory can be maintained readily and financed by local suppliers since Nationwide is a continuing local buyer. Proximity to the supplier allows Nationwide to settle disputes without the extra costs required to deal with remote suppliers.
2. This alternative keeps the supplier base low. A tight supplier base can be attractive because of its many cost efficiencies. Lower costs of sourcing, processing, and expediting should result from continued use of current suppliers.
3. The continuing relations established with the current suppliers eliminate many costs that can result from using new sources. Currently, quality and reliability are known factors. This favorably impacts on inspection costs and manufacturing costs.

On the other hand, there are important potential costs involved in not qualifying new sources of supply. The use of competitive bidding limited to only local suppliers limits competitive pressures on prices. Since the forces of supply and demand affect bids, Nationwide may be forced to pay higher prices than the industry average when Arizona plastic suppliers face periods of high demand. Nationwide also is limiting its options: a higher quality plastic may be available for a better price from larger, national firms.

NAVAL OPERATING BASE, ARKLADELPHIA

Purpose

The purpose of this case is to permit a discussion of the difficulties faced by a negotiator in a "sole source" situation.

Discussion

Sole source purchases can be most difficult. Because competition does not exist, the buyer is denied his or her most powerful weapon. Hence, such negotiation should be conducted by the firm's or the government's most capable negotiators. Threats can be a powerful negotiating technique; however, they normally should not be made unless the buyer has both the will and capacity to carry them out if necessary. Even then, they should be made calmly, gently, and directly.

Question 1:

Should Lt. Early question costs that appear to be caused by "inefficient management"?

Comment:

The negotiator should question costs that appear to be caused by "inefficient management," but from the attitude taken by Trustworthy Company's representative it is not likely to do any good. In anything but a cost-type contract, the buyer or contracting officer is in no position to be able to unilaterally disallow cost elements. If the buyer were able to get Trustworthy to accept a cost-type contract, the reported inefficiencies could even make the ultimate price higher than the fixed price quoted.

Question 2:

What action should Lt. Early take with respect to the contingency allowance of 3.3 percent?

Comment:

The basis for the contingency allowance of 3.3 percent, while insignificant in relation to the selling price, should also be attacked by the negotiator. It is possible that this item could be replaced by a provision for escalation in labor or material, or both, as appropriate. This may at least reduce the initial price, and a price increase would take place only if the elements to which the contingency was to apply actually were encountered during the production period.

Question 3:

What can Lt. Early do if the Trustworthy representative is unwilling to eliminate some of the unusual cost items?

Comment:

If the facts as to excessive costs are correct, it implies that the company is still able to sell this product because of one of two factors:

a. They have a limited life monopoly because of patents.
b. The product they sell does not have a market large enough to encourage other firms to market a comparable product to compete with this product.

If (b) is the case, and the Navy's requirement is continuing and substantial, the contracting officer can consider inviting other firms to copy the Trustworthy Company product. The government might then indemnify such firms from any damages resulting from patent infringement. This is drastic action, but it has been done on a few occasions. More importantly, the threat of this action could make the Trustworthy Company more willing to negotiate. If, on the other hand, it is determined that the Trustworthy Company has no patent rights, the Navy could develop specifications around the Trustworthy design and invite open competition on such specifications. In such cases the successful supplier could be required to produce a prototype for test and evaluation prior to entering into actual production.

NEW VALLEY POWER CORPORATION

Purpose

1. To review the role and operation of an integrated materials management system.
2. To study basic inventory and stores management practices.
3. to explore and resolve the human problems associated with changing to a new computerized MMIS.
4. To develop a plan to implement a new computerized MMIS in an organization.

Immediate Issue

- To determine the needs and concerns of using departments about the MMIS and recommend a plan of action to implement it.

Basic Issue

- To obtain cooperation and support from using departments in reducing inventory investment and developing a more effective company-wide computer-based materials management system.

Suggested Student Assignments

1. Design the basic elements of an inventory control and a stores system for this firm.
2. Why is the change to the new MMIS being resisted by using departments?
3. How should Joan Davis proceed? Develop a plan of action.

Possible Discussion Questions

1. What are the strategic implications of this situation for the Materials Group?
2. Analyze and discuss the highlights of David Chance's study.
3. Why do you think the Electric Systems and Generating Groups resisted using MMIS?
4. How should the MMIS be implemented?

Analysis

1. Strategic Implications

   a. Inventory Investment Cost
      - Inventory investment at an estimated average of $70 million.
      - Borrowing rate at an estimated average of 14 percent per year.
      - Thus, $70 million × 14 percent = approximately $10 million per year in interest expense, if we assume inventory was purchased with borrowed capital.
      - Conceptually, even minor reductions in inventory investment would produce major savings that would fall almost totally into company profit.

   b. Materials Group
      - The MMIS is a sophisticated system designed to serve integrated *Corporate* needs in five activities

- Accounts Payable and Cash Management are not normal purchasing responsibilities.
- The Materials Group is responsible for purchasing, storing, and disbursing for the entire corporation, which implies that NVPC is using the materials management concept.

2. Highlights of The Study

   a. One-week-old Information
- In fact, the *average age* was approximately three-months
- On the whole, inventory information is much too old to be of value to the operating departments.
- Could hardly expect using departments to place their ability to perform effectively in such a system.

   b. Physical Inventory
- Every 24 months is totally inadequate.
- Wonder why inventory is taken at all.

   c. Inventory Error
- Current accuracy rate is only slightly better than a coin toss.
- Excess inventory carried to avoid stock-outs, and to protect position on long lead-time items.

   d. Growing Inventory Investment
- It is possible that price increases account for much of the 14 percent increase.
- However, one would suspect that additional quantities are being held for protection against uncertain business conditions.

   e. Size and Make Up of the Inventory
- Normally, holding MRO items that represent approximately one-third of the total inventory investment is much too high. Proactive purchasing should improve this situation greatly.
- Study suggests that millions per year could be saved by reducing inventory investment.

3. Resistance To Using The MMIS

- Did not want to change the way things were done.
- Threat to cut inventory levels was perceived as a possible obstacle to performance.
- Electric and Generating Groups wanted inventory "JUST IN CASE" anything happened; they were accustomed to plenty of back-up stock.
- Inventory items actually were carried under three different systems; Electric and Generating Groups used a "Job Category" number system, Purchasing and Stores used manufacturers' "Part Numbers," and Accounting used a "Commodity Code" classification which was recorded only in dollars.
- Users wanted an "electronic catalog" which would permit them to sit at a computer terminal and get instant feedback on inventory. The new system should provide this capability.

4. Implementing The MMIS

- Put the user in charge of description (e.g., everything required to do a manhole repair).

      – Develop a purchasing description and then a storage description (where to store, how to store, shelf-life, etc.)

      – Coordinate the three descriptions—user, purchasing, and storage—into the computer system of MMIS.

      – Create the electronic catalog so that all users can get instant information.

What Did NVPC Do?

1. A modified, and highly effective, system was developed and implemented at a cost of nearly $4 million.

2. Most inventories were consolidated centrally.

3. An accurate electronic inventory catalog was an important part of the system.

4. Storage information and order-picking routines were included.

5. Complete document-matching capability for receiving and accounts payable purposes was included.

6. Initial inventory reduction of 40–50 percent was achieved, along with corresponding carrying cost savings.

NORTHEASTERN EQUIPMENT COMPANY

Purpose

The purpose of this case is: (1) to examine some of the management weaknesses and lost profits which occur when materials management functions are not coordinated and controlled, and (2) to explore methods of improving a poor materials management situation.

Discussion

The objective of all centralized materials activities, whether titled purchasing, procurement, materials management, supply management, or logistics management, is to reduce the *total cost* of materials and thus increase profits. Because of low profits, slow inventory turnover, higher than average selling prices, and slow deliveries, it is patently clear that material costs at the Test Equipment Division need to be reduced. All of the above named "profit leaks" have their genesis in higher material costs; hence, increased centralization and better control of materials activities are needed to improve this situation. The critical question facing the new division manager is: What materials activities should be centralized and more efficiently controlled to best reduce Northeastern's high material costs?

Question 1:

What would you recommend the new division manager do to make the materials management operation more effective?

Comment:

The case does not say whether the other three divisions of Northeastern are experiencing materials problems similar to those of the test equipment division. However, from a reading of the text, a perceptive student will deduce that they are. Material costs cannot be optimized when related materials organizational units are not integrated, clear channels of communication do not exist among coordinate materials units, and the corporate organizational plan itself creates innate conflicts of interest.

No information concerning the other three divisions and the corporate headquarters is given in the case except that all four are within 15 miles of each other. However, this is enough information to assure the reader that some form of centralized materials management organization at headquarters could reduce materials cost. The only question is how much and what form of centralization is needed. The appropriate degree of centralization in situations of this kind depends on the extent of the similarity of the commodities which are used throughout the four divisions. If the high usage commodities are similar, a high degree of centralization would be indicated and vice versa.

This does not mean that the individual items within a commodity group must be identical. Rather, it means that the commodity groups themselves which are used at the various divisions must be similar. For example, if two or more of Northeastern's four divisions used large quantities of two or more different kinds of basic chemicals, centralizing the purchase and control of these chemicals would result in both economic and manufacturing benefits. Similarly, benefits would accrue to Northeastern from centralizing the purchase and control of the many commodities which two or more of the four divisions jointly use in large quantities. These would undoubtedly include commodities of the following types: mill supplies, hand and machine tools, electrical supplies, automotive supplies, etc.

The degree of commodity similarity, therefore, is the first problem area the new division manager should study. From this study, he or she can recommend to the corporate executive vice president the degree of corporate centralization he or she considers appropriate.

Next, the division manager can proceed to combine all possible materials functions in the test equipment division. The combined functions should be placed under a materials manager who reports directly to the division manager. The case tells us that division material costs exceed 50 percent of total cost, and that the Division's profit performance is below average. The division manager, therefore, should realize that a materials manager is needed to gain control over the division's largest single element of cost and to reduce the present profit drains.

As the division is presently organized, a number of basic management concepts are being violated. Consider four: (1) Three departments, i.e., marketing, production, and purchasing, all have divided materials management responsibilities. (2) Only when a single department within a firm is authorized to negotiate prices and delivery schedules, can purchasing costs be optimized. This is not the case at the test equipment division. Both marketing and purchasing are buying. (3) Although production has only a small, divided interest in receiving, this materials management function is assigned to production. Were it assigned to a materials manager who has a major interest in the efficient performance of all materials functions, it would be better managed and better controlled. (4) Purchasing and stores are under production; this assignment creates an innate conflict-of-interest situation which makes efficient management and realistic control of materials difficult, if not impossible. When a production manager determines a purchasing manager's salary, tenure, etc., control of inventories is traditionally poor. Under such conditions, the purchasing manager nearly always agrees to higher levels of inventories than would be agreed to by a materials manager. Emergency purchases are traditionally greater in number when purchasing departments are under production than when they are not.

How can a subordinate tell his boss that his planning is unsatisfactory or that he should plan far enough in advance to allow for minimum purchasing and administrative lead times?

There is no traffic department; hence, it must be assumed that this important materials management function is completely decentralized and uncontrolled. The same situation exists in regard to value analysis and surplus disposal operations, i.e., either these functions are not being performed or they are decentralized and uncontrolled.

Appointment of a materials manager to be placed on the same organizational level as the marketing, production, and engineering managers appears to be the change most likely to remedy the entire array of the test equipment division's profit failures, all of which have their genesis in materials problems.

Question 2:

What could be done to make the purchasing operation more efficient?

Comment:

Establishment of a materials management department would concurrently correct many of the division's present purchasing inefficiencies, such as divided authority, overlapping responsibilities, and lack of centralization, coordination, and control as discussed under Question 1.

Better purchasing would result from specializing the two component parts buyers. To the extent possible, buyers should always become commodity specialists. If the two component parts buyers in this case were to specialize in specific groups of parts, rather than each buyer continuing to purchase similar parts for two different manufacturing operations from the same suppliers, many benefits would accrue. As a result of such specialization, each buyer would become more skilled in purchasing in his specialized field, duplications of purchases would be eliminated, and lower prices, lower administrative costs, and better service would result.

Both the government buyer and the assistant purchasing manager are now specializing in government regulations and contracts. This entails a loss of time and a duplication of effort. Additionally, an efficiency and communications problem exists between the government buyer and the other buyers who purchase materials used on government contracts. The government buyer must advise these other buyers what government clauses must be included in their contracts for materials to be used on government contracts. Because 40 percent of the division's business is government business, efficiency, accuracy, and avoidance of duplications is required in this complex government buying assignment to preclude a serious profit drain. A specialist is definitely needed. However, two specialists are not needed, and unnecessary purchases of similar materials by two buying groups is not needed. The case tells us that the government buyer is competent and is doing an efficient job. Therefore, purchasing operations would be improved and costs reduced if he alone were given the responsibility for making or coordinating purchases of government contract materials. This should be done.

Accordingly, the assistant purchasing manager should be relieved of all responsibility for government buying. His removal from these duties will preclude buyers receiving orders from two bosses under exceedingly poor conditions of communications and control. The assistant purchasing manager could be reassigned to purchasing staff studies, or/and troubleshooter duties, or whatever other duties the purchasing manager believes will best serve the department. If the assistant purchasing manager is given a line position, one logical assignment would be management of traffic, value analysis, stores, surplus disposal, and receiving activities.

Although the expediters are satisfactorily organized now, improvement would result if each individual were to concentrate on specific types of items, thus gaining the advantage of specialization. This change could be effected while relinquishing very little of the present flexibility of the expediting group.

THE OAKLAND SCHOOL DISTRICT

Purpose

The purpose of this case is twofold: (1) The primary objective is to discuss how the purchasing manager in a relatively small rapidly growing organization can improve the effectiveness and the efficiency of a paperbound, reactive purchasing operation. The focus is on the techniques to use in analyzing the operation, followed by the development of procedures and systems that can improve operating effectiveness. (2) A secondary objective is to expose the student to this type of operation in an institutional setting—specifically, a municipal school district.

Discussion

This case illustrates how the purchasing personnel in a rapidly growing organization can literally be worked to death by a horrendous, yet needless, flow of paperwork. As so often is the case in practice, the two culprits causing the difficulties are (1) excessively stringent financial procedures and controls, without recognition of the practical aspects of a professional purchasing operation, and (2) the utilization of purchasing policies and techniques which worked adequately when the organization was small, but which are totally unsatisfactory in a growing organization that expends a significant percentage of its operating budget for materials, supplies, and services. The key to an improved operating situation lies in the use of a proactive approach to purchasing management—and the recognition of the value of this approach to the school district by the district superintendent.

Question 1:

Identify the basic issues and management problems that Smith should consider in trying to improve the situation.

Comment:

The six basic issues Smith should consider are discussed briefly below.

1. *Excessively stringent internal financial policies.* Purchasing presently is being hamstrung by a series of counterproductive district financial policies that are stringent beyond the requirements of effective management and control.

    At the present time, no invoices are processed by accounts payable personnel until all details on the invoice match precisely the details on the purchase order or the change order. For items of major consequence, this is a good policy. For items of an inconsequential nature, it is a ludicrous policy that simply generates needless paperwork that serves no useful control purpose. Smith must somehow get this policy changed so that it distinguishes between major and minor matters from a control point of view.

    The stringent inventory policy should be loosened so that selected slower-moving C items can be carried in inventory, to preclude the issuance of an excessively large number of low-value purchase orders. Some type of max-min inventory control system can be coupled with use of the EOQ concept to keep the additional inventory carrying costs at a reasonably low level.

Present policy requires that each operating unit in the school district maintain excessively detailed records (purchase requisition, purchase order, and related supporting documents) for each expenditure of district funds. The degree of detail required prohibits the use of a petty cash purchasing arrangement for low-value items, as well as any kind of a user pick-up plan that is not fully documented with a purchase requisition and a purchase order. This policy also constrains significantly the use of blanket orders or systems contracting agreements.

The net result of these stringent financial policies is the deliberate creation of a small-order problem for the district purchasing department. All of the problems and disadvantages associated with the small-order problem are discussed in detail in Chapter 4 in the text. One of Smith's challenges at the present time is to attempt to reduce these constraints to a reasonable level.

2. *The need for additional analytical work.* The purchasing manager apparently has not conducted several important analyses of the purchasing operation, the results of which would help him develop a more effective overall purchasing strategy.

The first thing a purchasing manager must know with reasonable precision is the expenditure volume and pattern for major categories of materials. To do this, he should conduct an ABC analysis of the annual expenditures for the past several years. This will enable him to classify materials on the basis of their usage characteristics and value, a requirement for the subsequent development of purchasing strategy for each major family of materials. In conjunction with the ABC analysis, Smith should also make a frequency count of purchase order size. In the aggregate, he has determined that 35 percent of the orders placed last year were between $30 and $100 in size, and that 23 percent of the orders placed were for a purchase of less than $30 (accounting for approximately .35 percent of the dollars expended last year). The same analysis now must be extended and be done by specific material, by individual supplier, and by each individual buyer. This type of analysis brings into sharp focus the details of the organization's small-order problem. Very likely some consolidation of items is possible, and some consolidation of buys with certain suppliers is probably possible.

3. *Blanket orders and supplier relationships.* The purchasing manager apparently has not worked closely with key suppliers to develop cooperative, ongoing relationships. One of the things that he could have worked out with a number of suppliers would have been the use of blanket orders (and perhaps systems contract agreements) or other types of simplified ordering and invoicing operations. With the information from the two studies discussed in item number 2, if financial policies permit, Smith should attempt to handle many of the lower-value purchases for B and C items in this manner.

4. *Supplier base reduction.* Smith apparently has not attempted to reduce the number of suppliers with which the district deals. Although public entities that spend taxpayers' money are frequently forced to utilize a completely open competitive bidding process, it is often possible over a period of several years to modify this approach by developing an ongoing listing of a smaller number of qualified suppliers for each of the key types of materials purchased. In any case, it is unreasonable for an operation this size to deal with nearly 1300 suppliers. Since the department is in fact awarding over 80 percent of its dollar purchases to only about 15 percent of these suppliers, it is important that Smith's buyers attempt to cultivate this small group of suppliers and develop a more cooperative relationship with them. In other words, buyers should manage these selected supplier relationships more effectively, to the benefit of the school district.

5. *The need for increased use of annual contracts.* Related to the two preceding items, Smith's department apparently has not utilized annual purchase contracts to any great extent for high-value A items. Additionally, there is no evidence to indicate that any of Smith's buyers have developed an annual buying plan for each major material for which they are responsible. Both of these activities should become an integral part of the department's movement toward the utilization of a more proactive approach in the development of its procurement strategies.

6. *The need to develop cooperative programs to facilitate items 4 and 5.* Smith apparently has not been able to develop the following internal ongoing projects.

   a. Purchasing should take the lead in working with users throughout the district to develop a standardization program that standardizes needs and reduces the number of individual materials that have to be purchased.

   b. It is essential that Smith work with users of major materials to develop an annual forecast of material needs. While this is difficult to do with precision in a school district operation, for a majority of the key materials purchased, it is possible usually to develop approximate forecasts that purchasing can use to do its job more effectively in developing contracts and working with its key group of suppliers.

   c. If the purchasing department can get some support from the operations manager, it should take the lead in attempting to develop with key users a cost reduction program for the major materials the district uses. This can be accomplished through a number of the topics previously discussed, along with broadly based value analysis activities for selected high-potential items.

   In this connection, Smith probably can involve suppliers in such an effort in a number of cases. It frequently is possible in these kinds of cooperative endeavors to dovetail the needs of users and the purchasing practices of buyers more effectively with a supplier's operation and distribution activities. When looked at as a total buyer-supplier system, material requirements and operating systems frequently can be modified to the benefit of both the buyer and the supplier.

   It is incumbent upon the purchasing manager to attempt to develop these types of cooperative efforts that, given time and genuine commitment, usually lead to improved operations and increased cost effectiveness.

Question 2:

What additional information should Smith attempt to obtain?

Comment:

Question 1 discussed a number of analyses and activities that Gene Smith should undertake. In the course of doing these things, much useful information will be generated. In addition to this information, however, the following data will be useful in further refining the various courses of action that Smith may take.

   a. Additional breakdowns of orders placed in terms of dollars and number of suppliers, by general product classification, is needed to develop an analysis of which firms actually get the district's purchasing dollar for key materials.

b. Estimates of the work loads of individual purchasing personnel by time, distributed according to order size and material classification, will be useful in developing procurement strategy and in structuring individual buying and staff assignments.

c. Cost figures for operation of the purchasing department should be analyzed, and then projected for several years into the future, considering anticipated growth of the district.

d. At the appropriate time, Smith should obtain proposals from selected suppliers that are designed to reduce internal paperwork by means of simplified ordering and billing techniques, blanket orders, small-order pick-up plans, stock consignment operations, etc.

e. An analysis of characteristics of items presently carried in inventory, including an ABC classification and EOQ analysis, can be utilized in revising the procurement plan for inventory items as well as potential involvement of suppliers.

f. Smith also needs to calculate the incremental cost of generating a purchase order—and quantify the associated opportunity costs. The question to be answered is, How could buyers perform more effectively for the district if they had the time to devote to procurement activities other than processing a new purchase requisition every fifteen minutes?

Question 3:

How would you suggest Smith solve these problems?

Comment:

Gene must work through his boss, the district director for operations. He should not approach him until most of the analyses just discussed are completed, the data are in hand, and he has developed a concrete plan to modify purchasing operations and improve the department's cost effectiveness. This plan should be able to be presented effectively in a "before and after" type presentation. Such a presentation should show just how simplified ordering and billing term contracts, blanket orders, modified inventory operations, etc., can update the present outmoded system the district now uses. The director of operations is the logical individual to push such a program with the district superintendent. Gene must join him in this team effort, providing all of the information necessary to justify the policy changes necessary to implement the plan. In summary, Gene Smith must analyze existing operations carefully, identify the specific problems, develop a realistic plan for resolving most of them to the extent possible—then sell the plan to his boss—and, finally, assist his boss in selling the plan to the district superintendent.

OCR, INC.

Purpose

The purpose of this case is to discuss the quality problems of subcontracting with buyer-supplied tooling and subcontractor-diverted sources. The case also discusses the legal implications associated with these issues. Specifically, the case considers the extent of risk incurred by buyer and seller when responsibility is shared for parts produced.

Discussion

Firms make decisions to subcontract for reasons of economy, delivery, or merely to relieve an overload condition in the shop. In any event, they require the same quality standards that prevail internally. As a result, specific controls are established concerning how work will be subcontracted; these controls reflect engineering or quality control objectives along with other objectives of good purchasing.

Question 1:

Comment on the manner in which the purchase was made. Could the problems have been minimized—or eliminated—by some different approach?

Comment:

Answers to this question, of necessity, must be conjectural. No one can say with certainty whether some different buying approach would have worked better. However, the instructor should encourage broad discussion of possible approaches. For example, some may criticize the practice of splitting responsibility for the overall assembly by designating component suppliers and supplying fixtures. The assembly could have been bought according to a drawing and to specification, and the suppliers could have been held completely accountable. Others may claim that this invites a quality problem and that OCR must maintain full control over assembly, components, gauges, and fixtures. Still others may agree with this approach but point out that little coordination of assembly and component supplier was done by the buyer, and that this was the real cause of the problem.

Question 2:

What was the extent of Jones's liability? Of Brown's liability?

Comment:

It is clear that neither Jones nor Brown can be held fully liable for the failure of assembly and base-component to meet specifications. OCR has specified Brown to Jones, and precluded its going elsewhere. OCR has provided gauges and fixtures to both sources against which parts were to be inspected. Of course, both Jones and Brown agreed to meet print requirements, and this is a firm obligation under the purchase order. If it happened that parts produced from OCR tooling and inspecting to OCR fixtures did not meet drawing dimensions, both suppliers had an obligation to bring the matter to OCR's attention. Not having done so, they cannot disclaim all responsibility for rejection.

However, supplying gauges and fixtures (or any tooling for that matter) is always a risky business. For example, fixtures may wear because of high usage for the molder and assembler, who inspect parts on a 100-percent basis. Since OCR inspects less frequently—perhaps on a sampling basis—inevitably there develop variations in inspection criteria.

Addendum

Some instructors may be interested in the legal implications present in this case. The following analysis was prepared by Professor Betty Arnold of the University of San Diego.

Situation 1: Inspection Devices Not Supplied by OCR

Jones vs. Brown

The Uniform Commercial Code controls because the transaction involves the sale of goods, i.e., plastic bases, by Brown to Jones. 2–102.

Jones, as buyer, had the right to inspect the bases delivered by Brown before accepting them. 2–513. Since Jones never notified Brown the bases did not conform to specification, one of several events could have occurred. Jones could have omitted inspection or inadequately inspected. Also, the inspection devices could have been defective either originally or after some use.

If Jones failed to inspect or inadequately inspected, it is liable to Brown for the contract price. This is so because Jones has done nothing to reject the bases and because Jones's act of incorporating the bases in the total assembly is an act inconsistent with Brown's ownership of the bases—both of which constitute acceptance. 2–606(b) and (c). The effect of acceptance is to obligate Jones for the contract price. 2–607.

Additionally, since Jones has completed assembly and delivered the units to OCR, more than a reasonable time has passed for discovery by Jones of the nonconformity. Thus, since time for discovery has passed and Jones has given Brown no notice of any breach, Jones is barred from any remedy from Brown. 2–607(3)(a).

On the other hand, if the inspection devices, the fixtures and gauges, were initially defective or became defective upon use, then the outcome differs. The facts do not say who supplied the inspection devices. The assumption here is that OCR supplied them. It is further assumed Jones was entitled to rely on the accuracy of the devices. In such case, Jones could not have discovered the nonconformity before accepting the bases. Jones can, then, revoke its acceptance since the nonconformity substantially impairs the value of the bases to Jones—i.e., Jones cannot include nonconforming bases in the assembly. 2–608(1).

Jones must now promptly revoke acceptance and can only do so if assembly has not caused any substantial change in the condition of the bases. 2–608(2). Assuming Jones can and does rightfully revoke acceptance, it can either cover and have as damages from Brown the difference between the cost of cover and the contract price or have as damages for nondelivery the difference between the market price for the bases at the time Jones learned of the breach and the contract price plus any consequential and incidental damages less any expense saved. 2–711, 2–712, 2–713.

OCR vs. Jones

OCR has, after inspection, rightfully rejected the nonconforming assembly since OCR has promptly notified Jones of the specific defect and not signified to Jones OCR would accept despite the nonconformity. 2–601(a), 2–602, 2–606(a).

Since the parties have not excluded it, there runs from Jones to OCR an implied warranty of merchantability in the assemblies, i.e., a "guarantee" that the assemblies are fit for the purpose for which they were intended. 2-314. With the existence of this warranty the time for Jones's performance probably has not expired. Thus, Jones has a right to cure the defect. 2–508. Before OCR can proceed to sue for damages, it must permit Jones to attempt to cure.

If Jones does not promptly notify OCR it will cure, then OCR has the same damage options as those described for Jones.

Situation 2: Inspection Devices Furnished by OCR

If OCR supplied the inspection devices assuming both Brown and Jones were entitled to rely on their accuracy and assuming both Jones and Brown properly used the devices, then neither of them could have discovered the nonconformity. Neither of them would have any liability for the nonconformity.

THE OFFICE SUPPLIES HASSLE

Purpose

1. To explore the small order problem in the context of an office supplies purchasing operation in an institutional setting.
2. To identify and resolve purchasing problems associated with:
   a. Purchasing for a major institution in a small city.
   b. Providing optimal service for professional employees in a university setting.

Key Issues

1. The identification of the inefficiencies currently existing in the procurement of office supplies.
2. The development of one or more systems to improve the acquisition and supply of these items for university use.
3. Who should be responsible for the purchasing of office supplies? What type of controls should be used?
4. How can the inventory investment in office supplies be reduced?
5. How should Mr. Harrison address the issue of varying discounts for similar items from different suppliers?
6. The staffing and workload of the purchasing department.

Possible Student Assignments

1. Identify the major problems Mr. Harrison faces as the new purchasing director.
2. List and discuss the alternative solutions to these problems.

Possible Discussion Questions:

1. How will the use of the various alternatives increase the effectiveness of this part of the university's purchasing operation?
2. What can be done to reduce the amount of paperwork currently being done by the mail room, the accounting department, and Mr. Harrison?
3. What can be done to reduce the number of repetitive tasks performed by all involved departments?
4. How can Mr. Harrison involve his major university customers in the decision making process?

THE OLD OAK FURNITURE COMPANY

Purpose

The purpose of this case is twofold. First, it discusses the subject of retaining the goodwill of suppliers when they lose an order. Second, it forces the student to consider a number of fundamental purchasing principles during source selection.

Discussion

The case is interesting because it discusses a subject that is real to all buyers of material or services. When there are many suppliers competing in a marketplace, it is inevitable that some will get business and some will lose business. Those who lose business could easily become enemies of the buying company. Some will even be moved to write uncomplimentary letters to the buyer's boss or to the president of the firm.

It is important that buyers understand that the only contact many people have with a company is through its purchasing department. Good relations with all suppliers are essential. Good relations can be achieved by assuring all suppliers that they will be evaluated fairly. Salespeople are realistic; they do expect to be treated fairly. If they understand the basis for their evaluation, they can more readily adjust to the times when they will be unsuccessful in obtaining business. For example, suppliers can be told that the criteria for evaluation will be price, quality, and service with varying emphasis on each of these, depending on the material being purchased.

Some students will be "led down the garden path" by the supplier's letter. These students will accept at face value everything the complaining supplier has said and will immediately begin to condemn the purchasing department. When this happens, the instructor should ask such questions as, "Do you believe this is the only letter of this kind the president has received about his purchasing department?" Or, "Is there any evidence in the case that he has received other letters like this one?" (There is no such evidence.)

Question 1:

What should Petula's memorandum to the president contain?

Comment:

If this case is used as a written case, many students will actually write the memorandum they would send to the president. Therefore, this case can also be used to point out to the class the things they will need to learn about writing memoranda to their bosses before they enter the business world. Past experience has shown that many students will write a memorandum that is much too long and perhaps unclear. The instructor may wish to correct the memorandum for the student from the standpoint of good purchasing policy.

Before writing her memorandum, Petula must find out everything about the specific procurement involved, including all correspondence to and from the upset supplier. If the supplier lost the bid, as he stated, because he was "$75 high," Petula must emphasize in her memorandum the criteria her department uses for the evaluation of suppliers. The president should receive a comparison of the quality, capabilities, and experience of the firm awarded the contract with those of the complaining supplier.

Petula should point out that while past supplier friendship has value, it should not be the overriding consideration for making an award to a higher-priced supplier. If both suppliers are capable of providing the product involved and if the quality and service are identical, the low bidder should be chosen. It would be difficult to rationalize to a losing low bidder that he or she lost the bid for not being an old friend. This type of action would certainly ruin the purchasing department's reputation with its suppliers.

In strictly competitive bidding, quality and service of all competing suppliers have been prejudged as satisfactory. It should be known by all suppliers that price will be the determinant. It should also be known that there will be no "second looks" for $75, or any other sum.

Question 2:

Who should answer the supplier's letter and what should the answer say?

Comment:

A strong case can be made either for Petula answering the letter or for the president answering the letter. If the case is used in class, a vote can be taken on who should answer. The students on each side of the question can then be asked to defend their positions. Many companies would have Petula answer the letter as a display of confidence in the purchasing department. A blind copy of the letter to the supplier, in this case, would be sent to the president by Petula. This solution also would give Petula an opportunity to improve her relationship with the unhappy supplier.

Others would have the president answer the letter. They would reason that the president was the addressee, and therefore courtesy demands that he answer the letter. The students who take this position should be asked if they believe that Petula should send the president a draft of a suggested letter to the supplier in response to the president's memorandum. In companies where the top executive who received the complaining letter does reply himself, this is the usual policy. However, there are companies that pride themselves in having the president take as active a part in replies of this kind as possible. For example, Mack Truck and American Motors have followed this policy in the past.

Regardless of who answers the letter, it should be answered in a direct, straightforward manner. The letter should support the present purchasing department and contain a short explanation of how the unhappy supplier (and all other suppliers) were evaluated. The unhappy supplier should not be given information it can dispute. The supplier should be thanked for its past help and invited to compete for future business, and the reply should be friendly.

Unquestionably, the principle that most needs explaining is that the new purchasing department uses many purchasing practices in its overall program. When competitive bidding is used routinely, the successful bidder will be the lowest bidder. In this type of purchasing, there normally is nothing a supplier can recommend in terms of service, quantity, quality, and so forth. If the old purchasing group did routinely take such recommendations and use them as an excuse to permit a "second look," it simply was violating a sound purchasing principle and operating poorly. At any rate, the new group should be very careful to explain all changes in procedures to the company's suppliers. As discussed earlier, this action should preclude many complaints. Suppliers do not expect to "be given" orders; they expect to win them competitively. However, they do expect to be treated fairly and impartially. There is no reason for any progressive purchasing department not to discuss its policies with any supplier. In fact, all suppliers should be given copies of such policies as a technique for building company friendships and avoiding misunderstandings and disputes.

PACIFIC HEALTHCARE

Purpose

The purpose of this case is to discuss:

1. The policy issue of purchasing authority.
2. Considerations in dealing with internal customers.
3. The advantages and disadvantages of using different approaches to making the sourcing decision (e.g., competitive bidding, negotiation, long-term alliances, etc.).

This case can be used to look at many facets of purchasing. It illustrates the importance of having specific people delegated the authority to control the purchasing activities in an organization. Additionally, it addresses the issue of customer initiated purchasing activities, specifically single sourcing decisions. It also involves considerations relating to negotiation and competitive bidding, two major sourcing techniques that can be used to achieve an optimal purchase decision.

Analysis

Question 1:

What alternatives should Barney Rubble consider when solving the problem?

Comment:

There are many alternatives Mr. Rubble could consider. He could stay with Kodak and pay the original price. On the other hand, he could attempt to negotiate with Kodak to obtain a lower total cost and a more attractive procurement situation. He could also inform the Kodak sales manager that Pacific Healthcare is planning to open the procurement to competitive bids—and then take such action.

Question 2:

Should Pacific's purchasing policy allow for medical staff personnel to control purchasing decisions?

Comment:

As a general rule, it should not. However, in a few specialized cases where selected operating personnel have extensive technical product expertise, it may be in the best interest of the organization to delegate the final decision to such an individual or group.

In this case, however, Barney Rubble should change the purchasing policy (or perhaps its implementation) so that only purchasing staff members make the final decisions on purchasing activities. It is always good practice, though, to work jointly with the medical staff, encouraging them to submit ideas and input for analysis and consideration.

Question 3:

What are the advantages and disadvantages of staying with Kodak—or changing suppliers?

Comment:

By staying with Kodak, Pacific Healthcare is insured the usual product quality, reliability, and service. The two firms have worked together for a number of years and know what to expect from each other. Additionally, they can save the time and money that otherwise would be spent in searching for a new supplier. In addition, a major advantage to Pacific healthcare is the discount on equipment, maintenance, and service that Kodak currently provides, as a single supplier.

However, Pacific Healthcare is faced with paying a significantly higher price for the film if Kodak refuses to negotiate—a premium of approximately $120,000 to $246,000 per year. In exploring different alternatives, students should quantify and analyze the various alternatives, making some required assumptions in the process. In the final analysis *total* cost is the major concern, given acceptable product quality and service. Clearly, Pacific Healthcare is not practicing proactive procurement simply by staying with Kodak on Kodak's terms.

Question 4:

What actions could Mr. Rubble have taken prior to Mr. Howell's death to obtain reduced film prices?

Comment:

Top management should have established a policy dealing with authority in purchasing activities. Mr. Rubble should have solicited Mr. Howell's input, but Howell should not be permitted to assume full responsibility for the decision. For example, Mr. Rubble could have worked cooperatively with Mr. Howell in conducting carefully controlled tests on the five types of film for various elements of quality. If Howell played a key role in the testing process, it might have been possible to select the top two performers for Pacific Healthcare's use. This is just one of several approaches that might have been taken to genuinely involve Mr. Howell in the selection process.

Mr. Rubble also could have discussed the pricing situation with Kodak in an attempt to achieve a better overall deal for Pacific Healthcare. If this approach did not work, Mr. Rubble could then have informed Kodak of his intention to use the competitive bidding process as a sourcing mechanism for the next contract.

A PARTNERING AGREEMENT AT I.M.C.

Purpose

This case, while short and direct, can be used to discuss the marketing strategies of suppliers, the concerns of a manufacturing firm's purchasing office in their source selection, the ethics of dealing with unsolicited offers as they affect the firm's other suppliers and any subcontractors, and the legal issues of entering into such an agreement. The case requires no mathematical analysis or computations. It can be discussed with minimum outside research required by the student. The basic recommended outside research would involve discussions with various purchasing managers and lawyers and the investigation of what constitutes a partnering agreement. It is an excellent tool for introducing the student to case studies in general.

Basic Issues

1. What general factors and considerations should be addressed when determining whether or not to enter into partnering agreements?
2. What specifically should be considered by the purchasing manager to determine whether or not to recommend that I.M.C. should enter into this partnering agreement?

Suggested Student Assignments

-   If you were the purchasing manager, how would you address I.A.C.'s insistence that the sub-contractors not be allowed to share in the rebate program and that, in fact, they are not even to be told about its existence?

-   Would you, as the purchasing manager, consider this idea I.A.C.'s alone, or would you approach other suppliers about it? If so, what would be your approach?

Possible Discussion Questions

-   What factors should be considered by the purchasing manager before he makes his recommendation? From what other disciplines should he seek advice?

-   In this idea the exclusive property of I.A.C. since they approached I.M.C. with it? Can other suppliers be approached with this idea without harming your relationship with I.A.C.?

-   Is it ethical to keep this rebate program a secret from your sub-contractors?

-   Would you sell this program to the sub-contractors? If so, how? What would you tell them their benefits were? Would you tell them of any downside to the agreement? If so, what would you tell them the downside was?

-   If a current supplier finds your firm has started purchasing all of its aluminum from a single source, what will be their marketing attitude toward your firm in twelve months when this agreement ends without being renewed?

Analysis

The purchasing manager should be able to recommend a course of action as to the acceptance or rejection of any proposed partnering agreement. He should be able to reject I.A.C.'s offer without affecting its current or future relationship regarding price, delivery or quality. He should be able to accept I.A.C.'s offer without eliminating or reducing future service by the other available suppliers. He should be able to make either decision without compromising the ethical standards inherent and necessary in any purchasing office.

Key Points

1. Partnering agreements are not unusual; they are a standard marketing tool. Additionally, they are a standard tool of purchasing offices who want to lock in a firm price, one that is traditionally lower due to the supplier being assured that it does not have to compete for that firm's business for a set period of time. In the case of a volatile product like aluminum this is still a viable tool since 'escalation clauses', tied to the Producers' Price Index (PPI) or similar standards, can assure both buyer and seller fair pricing over a period of time. No partnering agreement should be considered the exclusive property of any supplier.

2. Partnering agreements must be entered into carefully to insure that other suppliers in the marketplace do not refuse to supply their goods upon termination of this single-source agreement. In a highly volatile, highly competitive marketplace there is less danger of this happening because each supplier is striving to increase its market share. The aluminum market falls into this category. There is still, however, a danger in harming a business relationship that has endured for over seventeen years. Suppliers who work well with a firm in the good times may be willing to work only with their best customers in the bad times.

3. The best of both of these worlds might be to give all suppliers an equal opportunity to be the 'partner'. This philosophy is no different than calling for prices on a daily basis on the spot market, as long as all firms understand the rules of competition and each has an equal opportunity to obtain the business, none will have a basis to hold a partnering agreement with their competitor against the purchasing firm.

4. As to the ethics of accepting a rebate based on the I.A.C.'s offer, there is, again, nothing wrong with accepting rebates as long as all sub-contractors know about the rebate. The rebate can be explained as a bonus to the partnering buying firm for allowing the sub-contractor to receive the other benefits of the partnering agreement, and it can be passed on in the form of bonuses to the sub-contractor for quality, timely work, etc. It is not realistic, however, to believe that such a rebate program could exist without the subcontractor hearing about it. This issue should be handled from strictly a business sense. By doing so, it will eliminate the ethics issue.

Teaching Strategies

1. Ask the students to identify the various issues within this case.
2. Assign individual groups to dissect the various individual issues and to report to the class on their analysis of those issues.
3. Have the students present the case to individual purchasing managers in the community to find out how those managers would have handled the situations.

4. Have the students take I.A.C.'s proposed agreement to various lawyers in the community and have them address the legal considerations of entering into such an agreement. Have those lawyers address the issues within the proposed agreement that they would advise their client firms to modify before signing the agreement.

5. Have students reach consensus on the proper business, ethical, and legal recommendation that the purchasing manager should make to the president of I.M.C.

THE PEACH COMPUTER COMPANY

Purpose

The primary purpose of this case is to examine the advantages and the disadvantages of two approaches to describing construction quality. A secondary purpose is to emphasize by discussion the essential prerequisite for using performance specifications, i.e., purchasing must unconditionally be able to preselect capable, honest contractors.[1] The case also serves to illustrate the applicability of industrial purchasing principles to the procurement of construction.

Discussion

This case vividly points out the savings in time and dollars which may be enjoyed when the proper type of specifications is selected. It also causes the student to focus on the advantages and disadvantages of two approaches to describing quality.

Question 1:

Should Don get any additional information? Explain.

Comment:

The ability to select capable and honest suppliers is prerequisite to the proper use of performance specifications. Donal Bright, the purchasing manager, must, therefore, ensure beyond doubt (1) that two, and preferably three or more, honest and capable suppliers (builders) in the area are available, (2) that they have open capacity, and (3) that they are willing to compete for this project. Discussions with purchasing managers in the area, the Associated General Contractors local office, the county building department, and satisfied customers are all sources of information.

In addition, it is absolutely essential that Peach Computer be able to develop an explicit description of the function(s) the new building is to serve.

Without precise knowledge of the availability of capable, honest contractors, and the ability to write explicit functional specifications, performance specs cannot be used effectively. Therefore, it is mandatory that Don get this information.

Should performance specifications ultimately be accepted by Peach as the preferred method of purchasing to be used, undoubtedly an outside firm or consultant would be needed to guide the preparation of the performance specs. It would be highly unlikely that Peach would have on its staff someone with the required knowledge of building contracts, contractors, and experience preparing performance specs in the building industry to do this.

Question 2:

Discuss the inherent advantages and disadvantages of the performance specifications method of describing quality.

---

[1] In construction purchasing, vendors and sellers are referred to as contractors.

Comment:

The four primary advantages of describing quality by performance specifications are (1) ease of preparation, (2) assurance of obtaining the precise performance desired, (3) lower prices, and (4) reduced time of delivery. The use of performance specifications encourages a depth of competition which can result in great savings. With performance specs builders are free to develop many alternative solutions to the purchasing company's requirements. It is this encouraged "competition of concepts" that permits savings over the competition resulting from inflexible materials and method-of-manufacture specs. Under this approach, the purchasing firm assumes the responsibility of selecting the "one best approach" and then obtaining price competition on just this one approach.

The disadvantages of performance specs result primarily from their being inappropriately used and from faulty selection of competing contractors. If considerable expense is required of competing contractors regarding research and development, or if a great deal of uncertainty exists concerning exactly what the buyer wants, then the use of performance specs would be inappropriate and needlessly expensive.

Question 3:

Discuss the inherent advantages and disadvantages of the plans and specs method of describing quality.

Comment:

The plans-and-specifications method is the most common approach to purchasing building construction. Its industrial counterpart, the materials and method-of-manufacture specification, is widely used to purchase defense hardware for the Department of Defense and nonstandard items for industry. The plans-and-specifications approach has two advantages. First, wide competition (on the "one best way") should result in attractive prices. Second, when purchasing manufactured goods, since the item is nonstandard, discriminatory provisions of the Robinson-Patman Act do not apply. Accordingly, lower prices may be obtained than through the use of commercial standards.

The plans and specs (materials and method-of-manufacture) approach to describing quality has several disadvantages. Of greatest importance, the full responsibility for the item's performance is assumed by the purchasing company. Use of this approach may also deny the purchasing company the latest advances in both technical development and manufacturing processes. Further, such specifications are relatively expensive to prepare and require more inspection to ensure compliance with the specifications than do performance specs.

Question 4:

Assuming that Don's investigation and analysis indicates that both methods are practical for use by Peach, discuss which approach Don should recommend.

Comment:

Assume that Don determines that (1) an adequate performance specification can be developed and (2) two or more capable and honest contractors who have experience with the performance-specification method of describing quality are available and are interested in competing for the work. The time and cost savings potential of the performance-specification method greatly favors its use over the use of plans and specifications to describe quality.

Question 5:

Explain why one method will require more active involvement on Don's part than the other.

Comment:

This question generally evokes considerable discussion. The plans-and-specifications (material and method-of-manufacture) method of describing quality requires very close monitoring of the contractor's performance. Most importantly, because buildings are constructed by a sequence of different trades (masons, plumbers, electricians, carpenters, etc.), deviation from the plans or specs must be noted, and/or corrected when they occur. Otherwise, they can become hidden by subsequent work, and they may not show up for years.

If a building purchased by using performance specs fails to function as planned, the responsibility is totally the buyer's. Therefore, great care must be exercised on Peach's part to be certain such specs include all essential features. To develop such specs takes considerable time and usually the help of an outside firm or consultant.

If an honest and capable contractor is selected to carry out the work under a performance specification, a somewhat more casual monitoring of his performance is possible. Inspection is relatively straightforward. Only one question must be answered: Does the building perform as specified in the performance specifications? If so, it is accepted; if not, it is rejected.

PEGASUS TECHNOLOGIES

Purpose

This case demonstrates the use of financial data and other information obtained from the income statement and balance sheets of potential suppliers in the sourcing decision. Students should be aware of the importance of financial data and the ability to "read" a company's strengths and weaknesses through its financial statements.

Discussion

In this case, Linda and her team members have prepared a comparative statement of the various ratios of each of the four suppliers. Further, industry averages show the strengths and weaknesses of the respective companies compared with the rest of the industry. Students tend to use industry averages as the most important measure of comparison. A word of caution is necessary at this stage. An industry average is just that: "an average." In most cases, one expects a desirable potential supplier to be *above average*. The average should be used as *one* of the tools of decision making, not the sole criterion. The case requires the student to analyze financial ratios and make his or her own judgement of a firm's capacity or ability to service the contract in an efficient manner. Once again, a note of caution: comparative ratio analysis is useful, but it is customary to analyze the ratios of each firm over a period of time, and not just one year as in this case. No mention has been made of delivery schedules or other terms of the potential contract. The intention is to restrict the analysis to "reading" of financial statements and arriving at a suitable conclusion based on a financial analysis of potential suppliers.

Question 1:

Briefly analyze the data provided in Exhibit 1 for each of the four potential suppliers.

Comment:

1. REESE CORPORATION

Reese is the largest corporation, but may not be very interested in a contract which would be less than 5 percent of its annual turnover. From a financial standpoint, the firm appears to be very sound. The liquidity ratios are satisfactory, even though the current ratio appears to be below the 2.19 industry average. Large companies do not need to hold as much in current assets as do smaller firms. All the profitability ratios are above the industry average, the price-earnings ratio is a strong 18.5, indicating that the market views Reese as a sound investment. The debt ratio of .14 indicates that the firm has a low degree of financial leverage and can raise additional funds in the debt market if needed. But this is not important to Linda's decision. The price quoted is $245, which is the second lowest. Expenditure on R & D is the lowest as a percentage of sales (2.3). However, students should consider that the $150 million spent by the company on R & D is more than the combined amount spent by the three other companies.

2. CAPOZZI

The price is competitive with Reese and Kruger, but a few points to consider are:

a. The low-price earnings ratio of 6.45 versus an industry average of 12.0. For some reason, the market does not view Capozzi very optimistically.

b. The production efficiency (utilization) is 91 percent. This is the ratio of actual output to existing manufacturing capacity. While this is fairly high, it is still the lowest of the four. The engineers on the team would probably be suspicious about this figure and may conduct further analysis.

c. The order would be 15 percent of the firm's present sales. Whether Capozzi views this as signifying a major customer is an important issue.

3. KRUGER

This is one of the smaller companies. If the order is placed with this firm, it would be about 46 percent of Kruger's total business. While the business would be extremely important to Kruger, there is also a certain element of risk involved. Financially, the firm appears to be stable, although it does have a high liquidity position. Emphasis is on technology which is evidenced by the allocation of R & D expenditure (8.3 percent of sales). The high price of $275 is perhaps the result of superior quality. Sales have been growing by 18.82 percent over the past three years, and the company has the capacity to expand production (installed capacity is 88 percent). However, the debt ratio of .45 may come in the way of borrowing additional funds at a reasonable rate of interest. The return on investment of 8.7 percent is the lowest of the four candidates and also well below the industry average of 14.2 percent. This is further reflected in the comparatively low price-earnings ratio of 7.15.

4. PAYNE

The most attractive feature for Payne is its low price. But Linda and her team are not likely to be swayed by this. After all, with two engineers on the team, and emphasis on quality, price will not dominate the decision-making process. At the present level of sales, almost all of Payne's capacity would be devoted to this contract. Unless Payne adds to its existing capacity, it may not be able to meet future demand without subcontracting part of its work. The installed capacity of 85 percent indicates that the company can absorb additional work without investing in new plant and equipment. The high debt ratio of .65 indicates the firm is very highly leveraged. Also, the times interest earned is a mere 2.6 versus an industry average of 6.0. This information will not be looked upon favorably by lenders. Thus, even if Payne is able to raise funds, it would find it expensive to service additional debt. Whether the company will be able to maintain its low price in spite of higher borrowing costs is a point worth considering. A look at some of the other ratios confirms the belief that Payne is an aggressive company. The liquidity ratios are lower than the others and that of the industry, credit is more relaxed (37 days versus an average of 30 days), inventory and fixed asset turnover are well above the industry averages. In spite of these risky strategies, sales have been growing at a phenomenal 32.1 percent per annum and investors have paid 34.5 times current earnings for shares of Payne.

Question 2:

Based on the information contained in Exhibit 1, which potential supplier looks most attractive? Why?

Comment:

On the facts presented, all four appear to be capable of servicing the contract. However, the company policy and the composition of Linda's team should provide a clue to the student. As mentioned in the case, Pegasus has always maintained a reputation for high quality and purchase prices have never been compromised on this issue. Hence, the difference in price would not be likely to sway the judgment of the individuals in the group. Further, two of the four members of the group are engineers. Engineers in general appear to view technology and quality as top priorities. Price is rarely considered that important by engineers. It is reasonable to assume that Arno Berg and John Harper would like to go with Kruger, where quality has been emphasized. Linda should like this too, since the contact would be 46 percent of Kruger's business. A shrewd negotiator would be able to use this fact as a weapon in negotiating a lower price. The financial analyst, Kevin Rice, is likely to view the low ROI and P/E ratios as signs of weakness at Kruger. However, the company is just four years old. High investment in R & D is bound to reduce earnings in the short run. The R & D investments would detract from ROI, in the short run. Since Pegasus is not looking at Kruger as an investment opportunity, there is no reason to be unduly worried by these lower than average ratios.

Reese also is a strong contender. However, being a large corporation, this is not an important contract to Reese. It has already stated that it would not be interested in any order of less than $500 million per annum. Even if Reese accepts the Pegasus contract, it would do so reluctantly. Pegasus would have little clout with Reese.

Capozzi's main drawback is the poor production efficiency. Engineers may view this as a major concern. However, another visit to the plant may set at rest any doubts about the ability of that firm to service the contract in an efficient manner. Otherwise, Capozzi seems to be a good choice. It is a large corporation and the order would be about 15 percent of total capacity.

Finally, the team should take a closer look at the Payne bid. No mention has been made in the case about the attitude toward risk of each of the team members. Payne is a risky venture, but with some encouragement from Pegasus, a strong bond and collaborative long-term relations could be created between the two companies. The industry recognizes the potential of Payne. If Pegasus is willing to fund Payne's growth, it could develop into a single source of supply of color monitors. Perhaps Kevin Rice will recommend that the company make a takeover offer for Payne so that in the future, all the components of the personal computer "package" would be manufactured in house. But such action is beyond the scope of the case.

In conclusion, therefore, Kruger Corporation seems to be the likely choice and Linda should recommend it. Students should mention the importance of conducting a preaward survey of all four potential suppliers before the final decision is made.

THE PERILS OF PRESUMPTION

Purpose

The purpose of this case is to discuss the basis for a sound value analysis program and how helpful suppliers should be rewarded under such a program.

Discussion

Tom went off half-cocked in his value analysis program by failing to realize that value analaysis involves many other departments in the company, particularly engineering. The program will not succeed unless it includes their ideas under policies and procedures set up with top management backing. Suppliers, too, should be made to understand the policy and realize that value analysis contributions will be considered along with other factors in the award of future Buzzy orders.

Question 1:

How can Tom start a sound value analysis program?

Comment:

Here is what Tom should do:

a. Enlist the active assistance of the chief design engineer in a joint value analysis program to meet the common 5 percent cost reduction goal. This will involve some "crow-eating" by purchasing, but Tom should explain to the engineer that he was mistaken in trying to do it alone. He should point out that he understands that final responsibility for design approval under value analysis rests in engineering.

b. Present the value analysis technique to the president together with engineering and ask top-level approval for the program. Value analysis may bring in ideas resulting in savings of 25 percent or more, and the president must assure the technical staff that these innovations will not be considered criticism of previous work. Rather, they are known to be the result of changes in technology, competitive situations, and more time to analyze, experiment, test, and so on.

c. Develop policy and procedures for handling value analysis and explain them to other department heads through meetings and written manuals. Describe purchasing's part in stimulating supplier suggestions, and offer purchasing's services as the agency to seek supplier help. Set up a value analysis evaluation committee for regular appraisal of value analysis projects and follow-up.

Question 2:

How should he inform the suppliers who can be genuinely helpful in this program?

Comment:

The policy should be presented to Buzzy's suppliers, including present suppliers, through a letter and a value analysis meeting should be scheduled within 30–60 days. Selected suppliers should be invited to meetings where items will be displayed tagged with annual purchase quantities. Teams of Buzzy buyers, engineers, plus manufacturing and cost personnel should be on hand to discuss items with suppliers interested in later quotations.

Buzzy must make sure that suppliers understand that value analysis efforts are to be competitive, too. Regular sources will be notified when it appears that the next purchase will depend on the best value analysis contribution. But suppliers' ideas will be protected, just as price is protected in routine bidding. However, purchases stemming from value analysis suggestions normally will be negotiated. Whenever possible, negotiations should include promise of a contract for one year's requirements. This kind of reward stimulates great interest and effort in the program.

Question 3:

What should Tom tell Dandy Products?

Comment:

Tom must explain to Dandy Products (the protesting suppler) that the company will have an opportunity to quote on any Buzzy redesign of the product in question—but not on the ideas of other firms on this contract. Also, Tom should point out that Dandy's position as a current supplier will be given consideration, and that the firm's experience with the product should give them a competitive advantage over other firms for making value-analysis suggestions.

PLACIDO ENGINE COMPANY

Purpose

This case addresses two key issues: (1) the use of "off spec" material, and (2) postaward activities required to receive the required quality of purchased materials.

Discussion

Much of the discussion which follows is based on the statement in the case: ". . . the purchasing department was further instructed to notify its casting suppliers that strict adherence to the *previously issued* Mil Spec M–3171 and the cleaning and corrosion prevention procedure prescribed by Placido *would NOW be required*" (emphasis added). It appears that Placido had issued definitive cleaning and corrosion prevention procedures but *had failed to enforce* them. In effect, incoming materials which deviated from the specification were being accepted. This practice commonly is known as "off specs." While the intentions of those involved (quality assurance) mandated adherence to specs, the result was a complete breakdown in supplier discipline and a waiving of Placido's legal rights.

Enforcing compliance with all specifications and other terms of contracts required diligence on the part of all who are involved: purchasing, inspection, Q.A., design engineering, and manufacturing engineering. The net result of enforcing such compliance is a disciplined supplier base that ships only materials which conform. This, in turn, allows the purchasing firm to reduce or eliminate inventories of purchased materials (cushions against possible defective incoming materials) and the need to rework or scrap materials during production.

Question 1:

Define and discuss the basic issues in the case.

Comment:

Placido is receiving numerous complaints from dissatisfied customers concerning corroded gearboxes on purchased engines. Investigation reveals that the corrosion situation is centered in the Turbo 110 engine and its magnesium castings.

Placido is accepting corroded magnesium castings from Placido's suppliers, and entering them into inventory for use in future production of engines. Quality assurance is processing defective castings for rework so that manufacturing can meet production schedules.

Ronald Penson, the senior buyer of castings in the purchasing division, has sent a stern letter to Placido's magnesium castings suppliers requiring strict adherence to the cleaning and corrosion prevention procedures.

Placido's suppliers quickly responded to the letter, stating that they could not adhere to the request, unless they substantially increased their costs and expended the time to retool and acquire new production equipment.

As noted in the "discussion," the continued acceptance of nonconforming materials has destroyed supplier discipline and resulted in the waiving of Placido's legal rights. Placido and Ron Penson have their work cut out!

Question 2:

What should Ronald Penson do?

Comment:

Ron (and Placido) have at least three viable alternatives:

a. Placido can redesign or reengineer the corroded gearbox castings.

+ An analysis of the current gearbox may reveal that the corrosion problem is engineered into the design. An example of this would be two dissimilar metals used in the design which compound the corrosion effect through electrolysis.

+ Engineering must work with materials and purchasing to determine if performance and reliability specifications can be met with materials other than magnesium. New technologies in manufacturing since the design of the old gearbox may allow this. Materials such as aluminum and titanium can be such substitutes. Although titanium is considerably more expensive to purchase, significant cost savings may occur due to less stringent storage and shipping procedures and machining practices.

− Redesign or reengineering of the current gearboxes can take a considerable amount of time before the new and improved gearboxes reach Placido's production line. This, in combination with significant redesign costs, makes this an unlikely alternative for a quick fix as required by the Executive Corrosion Task Force.

b. Penson and a team from engineering, quality, and finance can evaluate other sources of supply that have the capacity to comply with the cleaning and corrosion prevention procedures and negotiate contracts with the most desirable one(s).

+ Placido may want to change suppliers because it will take too long for the present ones to conform to the required corrosion procedures, or the cost of materials to Placido may be too high, even if present suppliers can conform. Placido will have to go through a supplier evaluation process that will take into account numerous factors of desirability for selection criteria. Criteria such as performance, capacity, reliability, costs, and cooperation must be analyzed. The most desirable suppliers will then be contracted with to deliver the required castings.

− The supplier evaluation process and the steps required to set up production by the new suppliers may be extremely time-consuming. Also, the current contracts that Placido has with its suppliers may preclude it from entering into new contracts at this time. A phase in period will be required as old contracts expire; this is the only way that this alternative can be feasibly undertaken.

c. The Executive Corrosion Task Force (ECTF), in cooperation with suppliers, can identify the factors causing the corrosion of the magnesium castings and make the necessary internal and external modifications to prevent the need for rework prior to production.

+ The ECTF, with the technical expertise of cooperative suppliers, will have to analyze the corrosion situation to determine the factors causing it. All divisions of Placido and affected suppliers will have to take an active role, so that an effective strategy is developed and implemented in fighting the corrosion problem. Areas of concern that may be contributing to the corrosive environment are material inspection, shipping procedures, manufacturing processes, inventory storage, and handling procedures. An effective inspection program can identify corrosion early, before it has a chance to spread and destroy material. The manufacturing process itself may use corrosive chemicals.

Shipping may use the wrong material container or method. Finally, improper inventory and storage procedures can also affect the corrosive environment.

Obtaining supplier cooperation may be difficult because the factors causing the corrosion probably are not under the suppliers' control. With cooperation, however, comes an invaluable source of technical knowledge and assistance to solve the problem. This would appear to contribute to a quick and timely approach, because all aspects (suppliers, materials, and processes) of the business and manufacturing environment essentially remain in place without drastic change.

Recommended Solution

The third alternative is the method that should be used to correct the problem! It identifies and attacks the elements of the magnesium corrosion situation.

- Placido (Q.A.) needs to develop a comprehensive inspection program or enforce the present one to identify defective materials upon receipt from the supplier before they enter production.
- Placido (purchasing) must developing long-term supplier-buyer relationships, through an early supplier involvement program, so it can nurture a cooperative and team spirit environment with suppliers.
- In this specific problem, Placido needs to contact the affected suppliers and discuss with them its corrosion problem. All possible factors that could cause the corrosion in the supplier's environment must be analyzed. The stern letter that Mr. Penson sent to Placido suppliers should be retracted until the exact cause of the corrosion is determined. If, in fact, corrosion cleaning and prevention procedures need to be performed, a mutually acceptable economic agreement should be negotiated if supplier costs increase. Placido should provide assistance to its suppliers in efficient manufacturing, financial, and management techniques so that they can control quality costs.

PRICE PRINTING SERVICE

Purpose

The purpose of this case is to show the importance of anticipating emergency situations by having a service contract established which would meet the firm's needs.

Discussion

This case addresses several important issues that are involved when developing a service contract: quality, responsiveness, overall costs, and purchasing's role in the contract. This is also an excellent case for discussing both a long-term solution as well as a short-term one.

Question 1:

What is Gregg's first objective in this situation?

Comment:

The buyer's first objective is to provide the services required to minimize the firm's all-in-cost (not necessarily the lowest purchase price).

Question 2:

What action should Gregg take to meet his immediate objectives?

Comment:

The issues presented in this question allow the student to estimate the all-in-cost associated with each source. The estimated costs are shown in the following table:

Source	Labor	Materials	Production overtime cost (5 men, $10/hr)	Opportunity cost (paper late $398/hour)	Total all-in-cost
Print Fixers	$900 × 2.5 = $2250	incl. 0	3 hrs at $50 = $150	0	$2400
Print Special.	$345 × 2 = $690	est. $750	5 hrs at $50 = $250	0	$1690
Maintenance Plus	$750 × 2 = $1500	0	8 hrs at $50 = $400	est. 3 hrs = $1194	$3094

In Addition:

- Advertiser's response/lost sales: Print Fixers will have no effect. Alternatives 2 and 3, however, may cause PP's advertising customers to be skeptical about future delays. PP also loses an additional $398/hour in advertising revenues for late delivery.
- Cost in customer loyalty: PP's customer loyalty could decrease as a result of late delivery of *FOR SALE* magazine. Customer loyalty is a nonqualtitative measure; however, it is very important in the company's overall success.
- Company's personnel response/impact on Gregg's reputation: Since Gregg is a new employee, he will have to be aware of senior employees' response to the decision. Gregg

must also take into consideration that PP has never been late for a production run. Any problem that arises will be Gregg's responsibility.

Question 3:

What long-term action should be taken on the procurement of emergency services?

Comment:

This question addresses the company's long-term solution. Price Printing should develop a statement of work for repair services. The creation of a SOW will get qualified purchasing personnel involved early so that both the customer and purchasing will know the organization's needs. The SOW serves as the basis of an agreement with a supplier for specific work to be performed. PP should contact each of the three repair companies. Gregg should try to negotiate a variety of key issues that are important in the development of the service contract, including:

- a not-to-exceed time and materials contract, including an hourly rate.
- markup on parts. (Such action will avoid contingency pricing in an hourly price which includes labor and parts.)
- an average time to complete repairs by taking total time of all repairs divided by total number of repairs.
- a priority clause guaranteeing that PP will be served first in case of an emergency.
- an evaluation of each visit to determine how the repair company is performing. The evaluation will be reviewed every four months with feedback to the supplier.

PRINTED CIRCUITS COMPONENTS
FOR A JIT FACTORY

Purpose

The purpose of this case is to familiarize the student with the conflicts between price, service, time, and quality that occur when selecting a source. Selecting satisfactory suppliers is one of procurement's major responsibilities, and when done correctly, can lead to optimal trade-offs between the four conflicting factors in a purchase decision.

Some important aspects of supplier selection include:

- Supplier goodwill
- Assurance of supply
- Supplier's size
- Supplier's financial condition
- Local, national, or international suppliers
- Management orientation
- Supplier's record of performance

When there is a good match between the characteristics of the supplier and the needs of the buyer, it is more likely that acceptable cost will result, delivery schedules will be met, quality will be sufficient, and good technical service will be available to the degree necessary. This case is an example of a good match between buyer and seller for most of the parts supplied, and for a very poor match for a few parts.

Question 1:

Compare the advantages and disadvantages of staying with Monitor versus switching to the new suppliers.

Comment:

One way for the student to begin this analysis is to itemize the strengths and weaknesses of each supplier. For instance, Monitor's strengths include being an industry leader, offering quality parts at lower costs, having a reputation at Acacia for being a competent supplier in general, and being the only supplier for five of the diodes. Monitor's weaknesses include being so big that his new business was not critical to it, having a bureaucratic, inflexible management, and demonstrating an unacceptably slow response time to change requests.

United's strengths include a real interest in supplying parts to Acacia, a willingness to conform to JIT specifications, being eager enough for the new business that Acacia would be a preferred customer, and being a U.S.-based firm (no currency or communication problems). United's weaknesses include having no history as a JIT supplier with Acacia, having no experience with JIT requirements, and charging a price 10 percent higher than Monitor's.

Taguchi's strengths are a familiarity with JIT and the automatic equipment used at Acacia. Its weaknesses include being an international supplier (potential currency or communication problems), having no history as a JIT supplier with Acacia, and charging a price 10 percent higher than Monitor's.

Other considerations the students should explore include how quickly the new suppliers would come up to speed, whether it would be useful to continue with Monitor in the short-run

while additional qualified suppliers are located, and how seriously supplier goodwill would be jeopardized by pulling the JIT parts away from Monitor.

Question 2:

What should Carl do now?

Comment:

There is, of course, no single correct answer to this question. In the class discussion there should be mention of how critical quality, service, timeliness, and cost are for the parts. The quality of Monitor's parts was so poor that production was repeatedly halted as a result. This is an extremely important factor for a high-volume, mostly automatic process. The service provided by the supplier is also of key importance in this case because of unusual specifications arising from the JIT environment, and probable engineering changes due to lack of experience Acacia has with the product and production process. The timeliness of delivery is also an issue, since JIT hinges on virtually no inventories and assumes weekly or more frequent deliveries. The higher cost of the new supplier's parts is probably not a critical issue; although 10 percent is a relatively big percentage increase, it is not very significant since the parts being re-sourced are relatively inexpensive.

The actual way Carl settled the issue was to transfer all but the five monitor-unique parts to United and Taguchi over a period of a few weeks. This has not resulted in any known damage to supplier relations, since the 440A parts were a tiny fraction of Monitor's total production. Both new suppliers have been able to meet the JIT packaging and delivery requirements without incident.

Question 3:

How could Carl have avoided the problems he experienced with Monitor?

Comment:

The most serious error Carl made in choosing Monitor as the initial supplier was the assumption that since Monitor was a competent supplier for ordinary parts, it would be competent for special-order parts as well. Carl should have considered Monitor's management orientation toward high volumes, and the size of the supplier relative to the size of the order he was placing. Finally, he should have balanced the slight cost premium for better parts against the notional costs of repeated line shut-downs and inventory stocking problems. By choosing the correct suppliers initially, additional costs associated with researching the parts could have been avoided.

THE PRIVILEGED FLY

Purpose

The purpose of this case is to discuss the interrelationships which exist among production, marketing, finance, purchasing, and traffic, while focusing on inventory and transportation problems.

Discussion

Used in conjunction with Chapter 2, this case provides an excellent "icebreaker." Also, the case can be used in the role-playing mode. When using the case this way, select six members of the class to play the various roles. Some instructors may desire to reserve the role of Joe Gish (the successful president) for themselves.

Question 1:

Discuss the basic inventory problem confronting this firm.

Comment:

Unless top management designates the specific size an inventory should be in percentage of stock-outs, which can be translated to approximate dollars, the manager of inventory is doomed to conflicts with finance, marketing, and production. Marketing and production usu-ally want the same kind of inventories—large. In this situation production will never be stopped for lack of materials, and marketing will not lose any order because of not being able to give immediate delivery. This desire for a large inventory creates direct conflict with finance and the practical problem of having a large number of dollars tied up unnecessarily.

As the level of zero stock-outs is approached, inventory carrying costs become increasingly difficult to bear. These costs increase at a geometric rate rather than at an arithmetic rate. Therefore, as a practical matter, most company managements establish an inventory carrying policy on a level of stock-outs they can afford. The manager of the inventory is then judged on how well he or she handles the inventory within these guidelines. Thus, management may believe that 2 percent stock-outs (this means that in an inventory of say 5,000 items no more than 100 should be out of stock at any one time) is acceptable because of the uneconomic cost of reducing this to 1 percent stock-outs. Therefore, the production manager's complaint of a single stock-out could be held to be without merit if the inventory manager is within the 2-percent figure established by management.

Many departments in companies not having inventory policies frequently blame the others for inventory difficulties. After a reasonable stock-outs policy is reached, based on probabilities of stock-outs, shutdowns, and costs, such interdepartmental fights stop. Inventory failures are now blamed correctly on faulty policies.

Question 2:

Air freight bills keep growing both in numbers and in total dollar value of freight transported. What are the factors that have contributed to the development of this situation? Do

they reflect efficient or inefficient management of purchasing, inventories, and production in firms such as this one? Discuss.

Comment:

The air freight part of this case involves the interesting question of the economics of using premium transportation as a means for reducing the size of inventories. Some national companies have eliminated regional warehouses and use air freight to provide as timely delivery as regional warehouses would have provided. It is the belief of these companies that the higher costs of air transportation are more than offset by the savings from not managing and carrying inventories in various parts of the country. Additionally, as the traffic chapter in the text points out, the price alone of air freight is becoming increasingly competitive with other forms of transportation. Because the air freight industry is in a state of rapid change, the instructor may want to obtain the latest information available on this subject before discussion of the case from such air freight lines as Emery Air Freight, Federal Express, or International Tiger. Most of the major passenger airlines (such as American Airlines and United Airlines) have also developed descriptive information that may be helpful in teaching of this case.

Question 3:

What should Joan Glass do?

Comment:

First, Glass must market to the president the need for a definition of policy on who should make the basic decisions on inventory and scheduling, since these are the key to freight charges, carrying costs, and customer order completions. The president's interest in teamwork should provide a logical starting point for this move. Glass much convince the president to establish a company policy on the number of stock-outs allowable and the size of the inventory.

Glass should avoid attacks on her fellow managers' positions, because this will do nothing but aggravate the situation. Rather, in her report for the president, she should concentrate on the fact that inventory appears to be the problem and that these kinds of problems would exist in any company where inventory policies are vague or lacking. Glass could also point out that she feels it would be appropriate to assign purchasing the responsibility for inventories. All departments concerned, however, must work together on the inventory problem. Better information in the form of sales forecasts, production schedules, materials requisitions, and alternate traffic costs are needed for better decision making on inventory. This will give Glass the tools needed to balance inventory carrying costs, freight charges, delivery schedules, order quantities, and customer requirements.

There are several ways that Glass can get this cooperation within the existing corporate structure. These ways include joint consultations with marketing, production, and traffic to develop a master schedule; round-robin reporting system; or a special liaison in purchasing to act as order coordinator. Other possible solutions to the problem include various forms of materials management with the new position reporting to the president and not production.

Question 4:

Should Glass suggest a materials manager?

Comment:

Glass must realize that the traffic cost crisis is only symptomatic of a more basic company problem: lack of policy and coordination in the materials area. The best solution to this basic problem probably is the establishment of a materials manager's job.

The $140 million sales volume would give solid support to an argument for creating a materials manager. If this company is average, over $70 million is being purchased annually. Usually this is more than a large enough volume to justify having a materials manager. If the materials manager concept is adopted, the traffic manager should report to the materials manager. Under the present organization he appears to be on the same level as the present top official in the materials area, the purchasing manager. However, in proposing the materials manager concept, the present purchasing manager should be aware of the fact that the present traffic manager as well as a person from production control could also logically be considered for the materials manager job. Although the production manager probably would attempt to have the materials manager report to him, rather than to the president, this attempt should fail. On the other hand, the attempt to get purchasing under him might not fail considering the president's personality and the marketing-production clique. The materials management attempt should not fail because it is widely accepted in management circles (including AMA and NICB courses, which the president attends) that materials management and production managers belong on the same organizational level.

Question 5:

Should Glass build up her inventories?

Comment:

Glass can only answer the question of inventory building *after* she has a statement of management's policies on size of the inventory. Rather than a larger inventory, she may need better *inventory management.*

As pointed out in the discussion section, rather than a larger inventory, extensive use of air freight may be the best decision. At first blush, transportation costs equal to the cost of a $955 part may seem excessive. However, this repair part might be needed only once every five years. If this company is average (average inventory carrying costs for metalworking industries are above 30 percent per year), it can be seen that it would be less expensive to pay a $955 air freight bill once every five years for such a part than spend $1425 keeping it in inventory. Unfortunately, far too many companies will keep a seldom-needed part on the shelf (with the danger of obsolescence and the probability of it not being needed for many years) rather than cheerfully pay for premium transportation at the time the part is actually needed.

A PROBLEM OF PRICE

Purpose

This case is designed to emphasize that even when the five prerequisites for using competitive bidding appear to be satisfied, more sophisticated management action may be required. Also, the case illustrates that negotiation is mandatory in some specific situations. This is one of those situations—as discussed in the text. Additionally, the case provides an opportunity to examine the adage that it may be less expensive in the long run to pay a premium today.

Question 1:

Under what conditions does competitive bidding normally assure the buyer of obtaining the lower possible price?

Comment:

When the following five criteria prevail, competitive bidding normally assures the buyer of obtaining the lower possible prices:

1. The dollar value of the purchase is large enough to justify the expense that accompanies this method of pricing.
2. The specifications of the item or service to be purchased are explicitly clear to both buyer and seller. In addition, the seller knows from actual previous experience, or can estimate accurately, from similar past experience, the cost of producing the item or rendering the service.
3. The market consists of an adequate number of sellers.
4. The sellers comprising the market are technically qualified to produce the required item and actively want the contract and are willing to price competitively to get it.
5. The time available is sufficient for using this method of pricing.

Question 2:

Under what conditions may a buyer fall into the "competitive bidding trap"?

Comment:

Buyers fall into this trap when they are purchasing highly technical items that:

1. are made to the buyer's own specification.
2. require special design engineering, tooling, and testing.
3. entail additional orders that are not initially expected, i.e., the total number to be produced is not known.

Question 3:

Which situation existed at Prestige Plastics for the *first* contract? Why?

Comment:

Prestige Plastics fell into the "competitive bidding trap" on the first contract since the requirement entailed additional orders that were not initially expected. Thus, the total number to be produced was not known and the cost of producing the total number, therefore, could not be either accurately calculated or estimated.

Question 4:

Which situation existed at Prestige Plastics for the current buy? Why?

Comment:

Once Prestige Plastics has fallen in the "competitive bidding trap," it will remain in the trap until it takes some positive action to remove itself.

Question 5:

Describe three approaches to overcoming Sue's pricing problem.

Comment:

1. While maintaining the integrity of competitive bidding is extremely important, it's also important to realize that there are some situations that superficially appear to dictate using the competitive bidding method of purchasing, but which really dictate using negotiation. In this case, large set-up costs are involved, and it appears that the low bidder, Chicago Chemical, amortized these costs on the initial Prestige Plastics contract for X-pane. (Even if all of the set-up costs were not amortized the first year, whatever percentage of them were gives Chicago this advantage.) Since then, Chicago Chemical has enjoyed a windfall profit by bidding a few dollars less per barrel than its competitors. (Remember, the competitors must recover their set-up costs.) Let us examine two aspects of these costs for Chicago's nearest competitors. Costs at Greater Sandusky Chemical (the second low bidder) are approximately as follows:

Set-up costs	$ 750,000
All other costs	2,085,000
Profits (10%)	285,000
Total	$3,120,000

Assuming, as appears to be reasonable, that Chicago (the low bidder) has already amortized its set-up costs, then its cost to produce the 10,000 barrels would be approximately $2,085,000. Allowing a generous profit of 10 percent (generous in that there is little risk and uncertainty), a price of $2,293,000 ($2,085,000 plus a 10 percent profit) for the 10,000 barrels seems to be extremely generous. It is likely that Chicago should have experienced learning both in the purchase of its raw materials and in its production operations. Accordingly, a price of $2,000,000 seems fair and reasonable for Chicago.

Sue should invite Chicago's marketing manager to her office to discuss the situation. (These discussions are really negotiations.) Sue's negotiating objective should be a price of $2,000,000. In this negotiation, Sue probably will need to explain her reasoning in order to get Chicago to budge from its current bid. While Sue does not have the best of negotiating positions, she does have a trump to play, assuming a continuing requirement for X-pane: if Chicago is unreasonable, she can award an order to the second low bidder at an estimated total annual cost of $3,120,000. The logic of such action is presented in the next section.

2. Assuming that Prestige Plastics anticipates a large requirement for X-pane for a number of years, it may be in the firm's best interest to break Chicago Chemical's virtually monopolistic position resulting from its cost advantage.

   Assume the following:

   a. Chicago chooses not to lower its price.
   b. Prestige anticipates purchasing a minimum of 10,000 barrels of X-pane for each of the next five years.
   c. Chicago will retain its willingness and ability to produce X-pane for one to two years, even if it does not receive award of the Prestige order this year.
   d. Chicago and the recipient of this year's order would not enter into a formal or informal conspiracy to keep the price of X-pane artificially high. (That is, Chicago and this year's supplier would bid competitively for future Prestige's business.)

   Now, observe the likely costs to Prestige (ignoring the effect of inflation or deflation) under two conditions:

   a. Award to low bidder (Chicago):

Year	
1	$ 2,970,000
2	2,970,000
3	2,970,000
4	2,970,000
5	2,970,000
	$14,850,000

   b. Award to Great Sandusky this year with active competition in the succeeding four years (with the assumption of reduced costs through learning):

Year	Supplier	Annual cost to Prestige
1	Greater Sandusky	$ 3,120,000
2	Chicago Chemical	2,000,000
3	Greater Sandusky	2,000,000
4	Chicago Chemical	2,000,000
5	Greater Sandusky	2,000,000
		$11,120,000

   Thus, under these assumptions, it is clear that it is less expensive in the long run to pay a premium today.

3. The third alternative open to Sue would be to extend the Chicago contract for a month (remember the first concern of purchasing is to keep the production line operating!). Then, assuming that Prestige anticipates a continuing requirement, prices may be solicited for a three-, four- or five-year period. This will allow Chicago's competitors to amortize their set-up costs over that same extended period and to reduce their average annual production costs (as a result of learning) to $1,820,000. Likely *annual* costs for the new producer over a five-year period would be as follows:

	New producer's cost
Set-up costs (1/5 x $750,000)	$ 150,000
All other costs	1,820,000
	$1,970,000

The annual cost to Prestige, including allowance for a 10 percent profit, would be $2,167,000, or $10,835,000 for five years. This is some $4 million less than if Prestige were to continue its present competitive bidding approach on an annual basis. Prestige would, however, assume a contractual obligation to either purchase at an average rate of 10,000 drums for each of the five years or to reimburse the new supplier for any unamortized set-up costs.

If this case is assigned after the chapter of negotiations has been assigned to the student, the instructor may want to ask the following question:

"Under what circumstances is it necessary to use negotiation to obtain a fair and reasonable price?"

The answer to this question is found in Chapter 15, Negotiation, under the heading "When to Negotiate."

Q 4: THE OUTSOURCING OF INFORMATION TECHNOLOGIES

More and more procurement personnel are becoming involved in the procurement of nontraditional services. Information technology represents one of the most crucial services to be addressed, partially because of the strategic implications and partly because of the cost and financial implications. (NOTE: This case can be adapted to any nontraditional purchasing requirement.)

1. What issues favor outsourcing?
    a. Cost
        (1) Inefficiencies may have entered in in-house IT process.
        (2) Outsources may take advantage of lower cost labor in India, the Philippines, Russis, Ireland, etc.
        (3) The outsource may be able to negotiate more attractive terms for both hardware and software.
    b. Excess hardware capability can be utilized by the outside supplier.
    c. The supplier usually will negotiate better licensing terms.
    d. A carefully structured contract may result in more responsive service.
    e. Specialization of effort should result. Outside suppliers are professionals—this is their only business.
    f. Suppliers frequently can negotiate more creative and realistic hardware leases.
    ·g. The outsourcing firm's management can focus its attention on more crucial issues.
    h. Outsourcing can improve the firm's balance sheet. The hardware/software assets can be converted to cash. A stream of probable future investments can be converted to variable expenses.
    i. Existing and potential new services will be more critically reviewed since IT will no longer be a free good (hidden in overhead).
    j. Companies with a low tech culture may have difficulty recruiting and retaining high "techos."

2. When would outsourcing not be appropriate?
    Large low-structured projects—ones where the IT systems are susceptible to significant evolution—are not attractive candidates. Responsiveness and trial by error approaches argue toward performing the IT in house.

3. What would be Mr. Rathswold's role if IT were outsourced?
    a. Establish the parameters of the outsourcing arrangement.
    b. Actively involved in sourcing, negotiations, and technical relations with supplier.
    c. Key player in determination of quarterly award fee (if any).
    d. Visualize and coordinate the long-term approach to interconnectivity. Plan networks, hardware/software conversion, and database accessibility.
    e. Assess the hardware/software alternatives and their capabilities, both present and future.

4. What fairly unique procurement issues must be addressed if Q4 were to proceed with outsourcing?

In addition to the traditional procurement issues, purchasing and IT must address the following:

- performance standards for systems response time, availability of service, and responsiveness to systems requests.
- flexibility.
- consider (and structure) an award fee provision to develop a carrot—not a whip—to optimize performance.
- investigate the cultural compatibility of the two firms.
- monitor/measure performance.
- build trust between the two organizations.

RANDALL CORPORATION

Purpose

Suppliers can get into difficulty on several fronts: manufacturing, quality, personnel, and management problems; labor relations difficulties; incoming materials; and financial problems. This case focuses on the issue of financial problems with a presently satisfactory supplier.

Discussion

A supplier's financial condition *should be* of particular interest during the preaward survey *and* during performance of the contract.

Question 1:

What is the relationship between financial soundness and supplier performance?

Comment:

When a supplier begins experiencing financial problems during contract performance, it is sorely tempted to (and frequently does) reduce the attention it pays to quality. Defective material is shipped in order to meet current cash needs (suppliers and employees). Further, since management's attention is focused on cash flow, late deliveries frequently result. Neither of these are tolerable! Thus, the professional buyer monitors his or her supplier's financial ratios.

Question 2:

What action should Bill take?

Comment:

Bill (and Randall) have at least three viable alternatives:

1. Work with Qualco's management to resolve the financial problems and possibly renegotiate Qualco's current contract, provided such action is determined to be in the best interests of both parties.
   + This would allow Randall to retain one of its most valued suppliers.
   + A partnership effort that includes problem solving would promote goodwill and strengthen working relations between buyer and seller. Such action could result in even better technical performance on the part of Qualco as well as improved financial performance.
   + Such action would give Bill Huff the opportunity to award all, or part of, the upcoming contract to his preferred supplier, Qualco.
   + By assisting Qualco to solve its financial problems, Randall could "protect" its substantial stake in mechanical subassemblies—for which Qualco is responsible for 40 percent.
   − Qualco's financial problems may be too far gone and be serious to remedy.

– Qualco's management may resent (and ultimately reject) Randall's efforts to assist Qualco in problem solving.

– Other suppliers may learn of Randall's willingness to assist Qualco, and they may demand equal or similar treatment (especially if special financial allowances are provided to Qualco).

2. Eliminate Qualco from list of qualified suppliers, transfer Qualco's subassembly share to other suppliers, and find another supplier as a replacement to Qualco.

+ This alternative would alleviate Randall's concerns that Qualco's financial problems might deteriorate to the point of bankruptcy, leaving Randall in a precarious position.

+ According to Bill Huff, there are many suppliers around the country who are capable of producing mechanical subassemblies of good quality. Therefore, Bill should not experience too much difficulty in eventually finding a replacement to Qualco.

– A major portion of the mechanical subassembly work (40 percent of the current total volume) would have to be offloaded to other suppliers.

– Randall would stand to lose a valued supplier whose superior performance (from a quality and delivery standpoint) might be difficult to replace in a short period of time.

– It would take additional time and effort to evaluate and select a qualified supplier to replace Qualco.

3. Randall Corporation could examine the feasibility of purchasing (Qualco (either a majority share, or full ownership).

+ Randall would control and maintain a steady supply of high-quality and on-schedule mechanical subassemblies.

+ This would provide a necessary infusion of cash to help Qualco overcome its financial problems.

+ Randall could offload more business (including the upcoming contract award) to its newly acquired (or majority-owned) firm, ensuring the company's success while perhaps strengthening Randall's position in obtaining additional contracts.

– This approach could prove to be more costly than using subcontractors.

– While attempting to resolve Qualco's financial problems through a partial or full purchase of Qualco, Randall may jeopardize its own financial position and resources.

Recommendation

Alternative 1 is recommended for several reasons. First, Randall and Qualco are substantially dependent on each other. Randall has a large stake (40 percent of its total subassembly volume) vested in Qualco. Conversely, Qualco's revenue has grown considerably since it became a supplier to Randall. Secondly, Qualco's performance is not marginal; on the contrary, the company has established a reputation of being a high-quality supplier with exceptional delivery performance. Randall Corporation would benefit by assisting Qualco in problem solving because, in doing so, Randall could better understand why Qualco is suddenly experiencing financial ills. At least this approach would place Randall in a more knowledgeable position to assess Qualco's situation, and make a more responsible determination on how to proceed rather than relying on hearsay and impressions.

RIO VALLEY STATE UNIVERSITY

Purpose

This case addresses some of the short-term and long-term aspects of services procurement.

Discussion

The procurement of services has increased in importance over recent years. The satisfactory purchase of cafeteria, janitorial, installation, and other services have an immediate impact on the morale of those benefiting from the services. Further, since contracted services frequently are very visible, their successful accomplishment can have an impact on the responsible buyer's image and future!

Question 1:

What should Eileen do to overcome the immediate problem?

Comment:

She could insist that Prestige fulfill the contract by complying with the one-year guarantee and repairing the carpet. The company was hired to perform a service and its performance was unsatisfactory. Not only could Prestige be held legally liable, its reputation could be on the line. Eileen should emphasize the long working relationship the two businesses have had in the past, and the positive one it would like to have continue into the future. This alternative is preferable and reasonable.

Should Prestige refuse, Eileen has two options: either to correct the problem in house or to select another carpet installer. Both options are time-consuming and costly. RVSU may not have the operating resources to repair the carpet in house, or the financial resources to hire a carpet layer. RVSU may have to resort to one of these options because it is necessary that the carpet properly adhere to the auditorium floor.

Question 2:

What should be done to ensure that such problems do not recur?

Comment:

In the future, a sound Statement of Work must be developed. The SOW must ensure that the contractor instructions are complete, accurate, and clear. It appears that RVSU did not go into satisfactory detail concerning subordinate objectives, after-installation service, and liability for noncompliance of the contract. RVSU should have ensured that the resulting contract motivated the supplier to meet these objectives. Compensation schemes in future contracts should reward contractors for good service and penalize them for poor service. Additionally, RVSU purchasing should monitor and have control over the progress of its suppliers. Eileen Boyd has been withholding five percent of payment until installers performed repairs during the installation; once the installation was complete, her management of the contract ceased. She was not even aware of the recurrent bubbling in the carpet for some time.

RVSU must realize that satisfactory performance is not only a function of the optimal source and price, but also the quality of the Statement of Work and aggressive management of the contract.

RIPLEY ENGINE COMPANY

Purpose

This case addresses several interesting aspects of developing a base of potential suppliers to receive a request for proposal (RFP).

Discussion

Lay people frequently assume that potential suppliers are beating at purchasing's door in an effort to be considered as sources of supply. All too frequently, such is not the case. Professional buyers who have not developed preferred supplier relations with a limited but viable supply base often attempt to enlarge their base. What should they do when a previously unsatisfactory supplier now appears to be very well qualified?

Question 1:

What are the arguments favoring Aerolog's inclusion on the list?

Comment:

Aerolog is rated as superior to its competitors in the following areas: financial status and, for the last two years, quality reputation. It is a close second on the rating of its managerial team and rate of growth. It has the most unutilized capacity (in absolute terms, considering utilization rate and sales volume). Were it not for the recent negative experience, Aerolog appears to be the best of the lot.

Question 2:

What are the arguments against Aerolog's inclusion?

Comment:

Aerolog was disqualified three years earlier. The political normative override makes inclusion of Aerolog on the RFP list a most sensitive issue. If Aerolog receives the award and fails *for any reason* both it and those selecting it will have been badly damaged.

Question 3:

What would you recommend?

Comment:

Several issues deserve attention prior to making a decision to include Aerolog:

- Are there only four domestic sources?
- Can foreign sources be utilized?
- Are there potential offset benefits from global sourcing?
- Has there been a change in management at Aerolog during the last three years?

- What was the basis of Aerolog's disqualification?
- Does Ripley have a policy for requalifying a disqualified supplier?
- What impact will Ripley's work have on each supplier's capacity utilization?

Based on the available information, it is recommended that Aerolog receive the RFP with the understanding by both Ripley and Aerolog management that Aerolog will receive the award *only* if Aerolog is clearly—and by a significant margin—the most attractive bidder (price and all other conditions considered).

In an industry with an apparent small base of potential suppliers, it is in Ripley's best interest to travel a path of reconciliation with a potentially attractive supplier.

ROBOTICS, INC.

Purpose

The purpose of this case is to consider the meaning of F.O.B. points, and to consider their significance when losses result en route.

Discussion

The instructor should develop discussions concerning the meaning of F.O.B. points and their varying advantages and disadvantages. Specifically, he should bring out the fact that F.O.B. points merely determine the point of transfer of title, but do not affect the basic terms and conditions agreed to in the contract.

Question 1:

What is the significance of F.O.B. points? What are the advantages and disadvantages of F.O.B. delivery point and F.O.B. shipping point?

Comment:

The selection of F.O.B. shipping points permits the buyer to exercise traffic management over the selection of carrier and the selection of routes. This can be an important benefit from the standpoint of reducing transportation costs to the minimum. However, because the buyer selects the carrier and route, he also bears the burden of filing claims in the event of damage to his purchase in transit.

When the buyer selects an F.O.B. destination, the selection of the carrier and route is the seller's and claims for damage must be made by him. However, the buyer is now precluded— unless the seller allows—from achieving cost reduction through his own traffic management. Even stating on the order "Ship cheapest way" will not necessarily give him the desired cost advantages.

Regrettably, particularly in smaller firms, many buyers, without having first determined the economies involved, select the F.O.B. delivery point simply to be relieved of two responsibilities: (1) determining the routing of the purchase, and (2) having to file applicable claims.

The buyer must determine and evaluate the risks inherent in not using the proper F.O.B. point, and then act accordingly. He must always remember that regardless of whether the F.O.B. shipping or destination point is used, all remaining contractual commitments are still binding.

Question 2:

Whose responsibility is it to file a claim with the carrier?

Comment:

F.O.B. shipping point means that title passes from seller to buyer at transfer to a common carrier. The carrier is then an agent of the buyer, and claims for damages en route must be made by the buyer. F.O.B. receiving point means just the opposite. However, F.O.B. points do

not cover basic purchase order requirements. In this case, the right of selection of carrier was agreed to by the seller, but later ignored by the seller. Payment of invoice in no way dilutes that right. Therefore, it would seem that Michigan Manufacturing Company is responsible for the loss, and the buyer should insist that Michigan Manufacturing Company press a claim.

To provoke discussion, the instructor should emphasize the fact that payment had been made, and that a cheaper mode of transportation was selected. This he should imply was for Robotics's benefit, and Robotics took advantage of it. Consequently, should not Robotics be responsible for the loss?

ROMMY PICKS A CAREER

This case is designed to assist a student who is about halfway through his or her graduate or undergraduate program, either at a 4-year college or junior college, address a problem common to many of our students: What will I do after I graduate?

While a purchasing and supply management career may not be the appropriate choice for all students, it will be for many. The arguments in favor of such a career selection are in two areas: financial and personal satisfaction.

In 1995, several of the University of San Diego's procurement majors started working in industry for base salaries of $35,000 to $40,000.

Of equal importance to people entering the procurement profession is the opportunity for challenge and personal satisfaction. Graduates in their early twenties work as equals alongside design engineers, product managers, and suppliers, who are 10, 20, and even 30 years their senior. One recent USD graduate represents his employer (a Fortune 500 firm with its principal Japanese supplier in Japan on a monthly basis. Other graduates have less glamorous jobs, but the nonroutine nature of their work and the opportunity to make a contribution allow them to know that "they make a difference."

Several purchasing majors wind up in industrial marketing. Feedback from several USD graduates who have gone this route is that the insight gained from the procurement program has been the key to their success. (Most such graduates become sales leaders at their companies in a very short time.)

We recommend that students who take this introductory course in Purchasing and Supply Management be required to go through the process of developing a written answer to the "Rommy Picks a Career" case to get them thinking about their career options and to attract the people who are going to become the leaders of this exciting profession in the 2000s.

RUHLING MANUFACTURING COMPANY

Purpose

The purpose of this case is to consider the nature and application of a requirements contract.

Question 1:

Should Epsilon's alternative proposl be considered?

Comment:

Epsilon has in fact proposed a requirements contract whereby Ruhling would be committed to purchase 100 percent of its motors from Epsilon if, as, and when they materialize. The additional benefits of carrying a 3-months' inventory and adjusting capacity to meet increased demand are common to this type of contract.

In directing this question, the instructor may find little willingness from the students to accept Epsilon's proposal. For example, some students may feel that Epsilon does not understand all of the costs involved. Therefore, the instructor should follow up on this point, asking about the economies of long runs and learning curves. After all, there is a saving to Ruhling of $4.25 a unit (using the $28.00 quote of Beta as a "low bid"), and projected over a yearly demand on 96,000 units during the first year, the savings would be over $400,000. Some students may oppose the proposal because it was not solicited by the buyer and because it was submitted after all the bids were in. At this point, the instructor might ask whether other bidders should be given the same opportunity to quote on a requirements contract.

Some students may oppose the proposal in principle, claiming that it is not suitable to the nature of the item or the purpose of its purchase. The instructor should look for specific justifications of this last approach to the case, as well as of all other approaches. The students may tend to "fence-sit," rather than take a firm position on the problem and defend it. By asking the class for a show of hands of those favoring the proposal and those opposing the proposal, the instructor usually can get undecided students to commit themselves on a course of action.

Question 2:

Comment on the practice of dual sourcing when part of the requirement is produced internally. Relate this to the advantages and disadvantages of a 100 percent requirements contract.

Comment:

The question of dual sourcing depends completely on the quantity and rate of demand and on the ability of one or more suppliers to satisfy it. Certainly where a minimum requirement is already being produced in-house, this is the paramount consideration. Of course, dual sources provide competition and a basis for comparing prices.

However, because the amounts to be purchased are divided, dual sources deny the buyer the maximum advantage of high quality/low price. Further, on the basis of internal estimate, Ruhling has a good idea of prices, and this is borne out by the close bids quoted.

Although the case refers to a 100 percent requirement contract, such contracts can be established on some other percentage distribution (such as 70 percent). The advantages of requirements contracts are that they consolidate periodic releases, or usage estimates, into an aggregate target figure, thereby permitting the supplier to price accordingly. Additionally, they entail minimum contractual risk (such as cancellation or obsolescence) with maximum inventory protection.

However, not all items lend themselves to requirements contracts, and it is entirely possible that the motors cited in the case do not. To begin with, they are of high unit value and entail large dollar commitments. They may entail frequent engineering changes and hence be exposed to risk of obsolescence. Their total requirements cannot be estimated precisely, so that sizable increases or decreases in demand could damage buyer and seller alike. Perhaps the more desirable method of buying would be by competitive bids for each new 6-month requirement.

In developing this question, the instructor should encourage both points of view: the pros and cons of dual sources and the pros and cons of requirements contracts.

SAMPSON PRODUCTS

Purpose

The purpose of this case is to expose the student to an operating situation that brings to light several very basic policy issues—in the areas of reciprocity, supplier relations, and purchasing strategy and procedure.

Question 1:

What are the basic policy issues in this situation? Analyze and discuss each of them.

Comment:

This case brings to light three major policy issues dealing with the topics of (1) reciprocity, (2) supplier relations, and (3) purchasing strategy and procedures. Each of these issues is discussed briefly below.

1. *Reciprocity.* From both an operations and a legal point of view, the matter of reciprocity is a delicate issue for which every firm should have a clear-cut policy statement. The policy should be applied rigorously and consistently.

    The pros and cons of engaging in reciprocity are discussed in the text, pages 233 through 236. Generally speaking, most buyers disapprove of the practice of reciprocity, even when legal, because it restricts their ability to achieve competition among potential suppliers. Thus it often constrains purchasing's opportunity to increase a firm's profit by reducing material costs. Sales personnel, on the other hand, often favor the use of informal reciprocal practices simply because they permit the expansion of a company's markets. Hence, despite the Sampson president's observation, reciprocity is neither a purchasing nor a marketing problem—rather *it is a top management problem.* The concerns of both purchasing and marketing must be considered and weighed appropriately in making the final decision. If management believes that it can expand sales permanently and add to the firm's profit legally by practicing reciprocity, then this is the decision management should make. Conversely, if management believes that profit will be increased by buying without the constraints of reciprocity, then that is the policy management should adopt.

    Undergirding the entire issue should be a thorough discussion of the legal aspects of the practice of reciprocity. The Justice Department views reciprocity as a commercial vehicle that potentially can restrict competition and trade in the marketplace. For firms that engage in reciprocity, the burden of proof rests on them to show that their actions involve no economic threats and that there is no intent to restrict competition. Consequently, many U.S. firms adopt a reciprocity policy that says in essence, "When important factors such as quality, service, and price are equal, we prefer to buy from our customers."

2. *Supplier Relations.* George Smithe has unwittingly created a potentially serious supplier relations problem. Sampson has been doing business with General for a number of years, and has recently consummated a five-year contract with General to purchase approximately one million dollars' worth of special alloy motor shafts. Hence, General has every right to assume that its shafts fulfill Sampson's needs well—and

that a positive and mutually profitable buyer-supplier relationship exists. For Smithe to deliberately request competitive bids for a large order of similar shafts without even discussing the issue with General, its ongoing supplier, lacks the elements of both common courtesy and professionalism in maintaining a positive buyer-supplier relationship.

Subsequently, in his two meetings with Mr. Jones and General's machine shop division president, Smithe's defensive actions contributed further to the deterioration of a good buyer-supplier relationship. Smithe should have anticipated General's aggressive actions, and he should have developed his own "game plan" for dealing with the situation in a mutually constructive, unabrasive manner. His decision to "fight fire with fire" could do nothing but lead to antagonism and jeopardize both the existing purchasing and the sales relationships Sampson had with General.

At the same time, Smithe has created a potential relationships problem with the other three firms he has asked to bid on the new job. He has invited General to rebid on this job and has not extended this invitation to any of the other bidders. Should General now revise its bid and be awarded the job, Smithe would be involved in a very unethical situation in which he has given information and favored treatment to one bidder, to the extreme detriment of all other bidders. If such actions occurred, Sampson's credibility with the other potential shaft suppliers would be completely destroyed—and the firm would likely end up with a reputation for being an unethical "price buyer."

3. *Purchasing Strategy and Procedure.* The obvious question is, Why did Smithe request competitive bids for the new shaft job in the first place? If he did his price analysis or cost analysis work effectively at the time he concluded the existing five-year shaft contract with General, he should have been certain that price and all other elements of the contract with General were completely justified and satisfactory. Unless his plan is to multiple source Sampson's shaft business (in which case he should not have asked General to bid), competitive bidding at this point in time should produce no new information that would be helpful in this sourcing decision. So, in analyzing this case, one is forced to conclude that perhaps Sampson's contract renewal/sourcing analytical procedures may not be as thorough and as stringent as they should be.

In view of the size and duration of the existing shaft contract, it appears that Smithe's most effective purchasing strategy would have been to negotiate directly with General to add the new job onto the old contract. General obviously should be interested in doubling the size of the contract. Because of the additional volume, General's cost should decline (perhaps the learning curve would also reduce production costs somewhat), permitting the negotiation of a new price significantly below the current $3.10. This approach, if handled properly during the negotiation, should produce a mutually beneficial win-win situation for both firms.

Question 2:

What actions should Smithe take? Why?

Comment:

Creative students will identify various courses of action that might be taken. At this point in time, however, it is difficult to predict what the success of any of them might be. Nevertheless, the steps involved in one logical approach are described below.

1. Smithe should first talk with Sampson's sales personnel responsible for motor sales to General. He should apprise these individuals of the recent scenario, so they can plan their approach to insure retention of the motor business with General.

2. Based on his previous actions, Smithe really has no viable alternative other than awarding the new shaft contract to the lowest qualified bidder. In all likelihood, this will increase Sampson's shaft costs, compared with the possibility of negotiating the new contract with General originally. However, the multiple sourcing arrangement will provide the advantages and additional source reliability that accompany the multiple sourcing approach.

   It is unlikely that General will cancel the existing contract, simply because it represents an attractive piece of business for five years and the machine shop division currently needs the business. Even if the contract were canceled, Smithe easily could resource with his new supplier or with one of the other bidders.

   It is also unlikely that General will discontinue its motor purchases from Sampson. In all likelihood, the motors are not being purchased by the machine shop division, and the purchasing division appears to be completely satisfied with Sampson's product quality and price.

3. It may be difficult to accomplish, but Smithe is obligated to attempt to improve his relationship with the General organization. The approach he takes will depend significantly on the personality of the individual he chooses to deal with, and also on General's attitude toward the entire situation after the dust has settled. One of the things that must be accomplished in these discussions, however, is an objective and friendly presentation of Sampson's policy on reciprocity. Since the existing contract still has approximately five years to run, it is imperative that Smithe try to mend his broken fences to the extent possible and attempt to reaffirm and continue the positive relationship that Sampson has enjoyed with General in the past.

4. It is clear that Sampson's procedures to be used in supplier selection and contract renewal (including the use of price analysis and cost analysis) must be reviewed carefully and firmed up. A good set of procedures in this regard, properly utilized, should ensure that this type of blundering, poorly conceived sourcing practice does not happen again. Whether Smithe will recognize the need for this type of procedural improvement is problematic. If he does not, perhaps his president will generate enough heat as a result of this embarrassing situation to make Smithe aware of this important need.

SDC CORPORATION

Purpose

The purpose of this case is twofold: (1) to help the student visualize the difficulties encountered in negotiating with and managing a foreign subcontractor, and (2) to address the basic issues involved in managing supplier quality.

Discussion

Negotiation as part of the procurement process encompasses preparation and implementation of a strategy to ensure that performance objectives are achieved. The essential objectives of negotiation include:

- Obtaining a fair and reasonable price for the quality specified.
- Ensuring that the supplier performs the contract on time.
- Exerting some control over the manner in which the contract is performed.
- Persuading the supplier to give maximum cooperation to the buyer's company.
- Developing a sound and continuing relationship with competent suppliers.

It is essential that the negotiation process be conducted in a cooperative manner to achieve mutually advantageous results. This case illustrates how negotiating in the international arena introduces additional constraints in obtaining a desirable distribution of benefits.

Question 1:

How could Tom Decker have avoided the problems with Hangsu?

Comment:

There are several things that Tom Decker needed to do before SDC signed the contract with Hangsu.

- SDC needed to develop a better method to communicate the performance requirements to Hangsu. Hangsu had a good tract record of producing similar components for the Japanese market; however, the component that SDC was procuring required new engineering. SDC gave performance specifications to Hangsu to complete the task. In this case, SDC should have been talking to the Hangsu engineers during the development process to ensure that the product would perform as required.
- SDC should have established a stringent performance test for both the Hangsu components and the final product. The Hangsu components should have been subjected to thorough testing upon receipt. This may have resulted in detection of the problem before the tracking units were assembled and before the product failed in the field.
- SDC should have considered the effect of currency fluctuations on the contract with Hangsu. The decline of the U.S. dollar has made the cost of the Hangsu components increase and subsequently has limited the value of using Hangsu as a supplier. SDC should have established upper and lower limits on the two currencies and set contingencies that would have protected both companies.

Question 2:

What negotiation skills should Decker rely on to achieve SDC's objectives?

Comment:

The student should begin by reviewing the many possible considerations involved in negotiating with foreign firms. The list below has been constructed to help Tom Decker achieve his objectives. It can also be used as a general outline for a negotiator to review before entering any type of negotiation

- It is important for Tom Decker to realize that negotiations with Japanese firms proceed very slowly. He must be patient. On the positive side, any delays will allow Tom the opportunity to refine and revise his negotiating strategy, objectives, and tactics.
- A thorough understanding of Japanese exchange rates (spot and future rates) will allow Tom Decker to determine the monetary impact of any agreements reached with Hangsu-MTC.
- Tom Decker should realize that when dealing with a Japanese supplier, he will never be communicating with a single individual having absolute authority to make a final decision.
- Tom Decker should realize that the Japanese take pride in their workmanship. Hangsu is a small family business, and the loss of customers due to a failure to meet the listed performance specifications could mean a "loss of face." Tom should exhibit confidence, power, and respect while indicating the potential loss of present and future business in the ETD market.

Question 3:

How can Tom Decker get the 3,700 units reworked to meet specifications?

Comment:

The discussion should focus on SDC's immediate difficulty getting the rework done quickly on enough units to satisfy the needs of the present client. The main problem resides in the location of the Hangsu components, which are currently in SDC's plant.

The following are viable solutions to this question:

- SDC could rework the components internally, which would leave the financial resolution of the contract with Hangsu in dispute and could precipitate a lengthy and expensive legal battle.
- SDC could find a local shop to perform the rework at less expense than using internal resources. This approach still leaves the Hangsu contract unresolved.
- Hangsu could send technicians to contract or oversee the rework.
- The units could be sent to Japan for rework.

Actual Outcome:

Tom resolved the problem by coming to an agreement with Hangsu wherein the rework costs were split on a negotiated basis. Hangsu sent its workmen to the SDC plant to rework enough units to solve the short-term crisis. The remaining units were sent back to Japan for rework. Tom used the Japanese sense of pride in their workmanship to motivate them to settle this issue to the long-term benefit of both corporations.

SELECTION OF A PRESSURE VESSEL MANUFACTURER

Purpose

This case has four objectives: (1) to discuss plant visits as a part of the source selection process; (2) to discuss the interrelated factors of price, technical capability, managerial capability and motivation, previous experience, etc.; (3) to discuss the implications of different types of contracts; and (4) to reach a decision concerning a choice between two capable potential suppliers.

Discussion

This case includes material from chapters 9, 10, and 12–15. Hence it can be used as a comprehensive written case, an examination case, or a class discussion case. The authors have found it to be excellent in all of the above applications.

Question 1:

What specific areas should the Oceanics group have investigated on its two visits?

Comment:

The major areas to be investigated during plant visits are:

Area	Atomic	Nuclear
Capability of management, including: planning, organization, coordination, and control	–*	+
Age and adequacy of facility and equipment	–1	*2
Stability of labor force	–	+
Appearance of plant	+	–
Laboratory and test facilities	+	i3
Production (in process and backlog)	i	i
Production scheduling and control	–	+
Materials segregation	i4	+
Purchasing efficiency including availability of critical materials	i	i
Financial stability	i	i
Adequacy of quality-control equipment, procedures, and personnel	i	i
Adequacy of design engineering: Are engineers customer oriented? Is the R & D budget adequate? (Are sufficient, adequatelytrained and experienced engineers available to be assigned to the current project?	i	i
Since both suppliers propose a cost type of contract, documentation on the efficiency of each supplier should be reviewed	i	i
Adequacy of cost accounting system	i	i
Subcontractors and/or divisions to be involved	n/a	–
Experience	–5	+
Management attitude	–	+

---

* Key: "+" = favorable findings; "-" = negative findings; "i" = ignored.

1Problems anticipated with clean room.

2Experienced workforce may offset age of equipment.

3The fact that the equipment was old does not indicate if it was adequate or inadequate.

4Asked question—no information adequate to reach conclusion.

5Experience with smaller units is helpful, but *no* substitute for experience with the same or larger-size vessel. (Ask the builder of the C-5A!)

Question 2:

Rate each supplier on each of the above items using information obtained on the field visits.

Comment:

Each of the areas which *should* have been investigated are rated in the list which follows the comment to question 1. It should be apparent that the Oceanics team was not well prepared for nor very thorough in its field visits. Many of the findings are more the result of feelings and impressions than specific facts. Yet, when this case has been used with experienced purchasing managers and buyers, the same findings and conclusions tend to result.

Question 3:

Based on the face value of the written proposals, which company appeared to submit the better proposal?

Comment:

The major differences in the written proposals are:

a. The estimated total cost is $1,232,000 vs. $1,560,000, with Atomic's estimated cost only 80 percent that of Nuclear Vessels.
b. Atomic is asking for a 10 percent fixed fee, while Nuclear is asking for only a token fee of $1.
c. While the overhead rate for Atomic is only 20 percent higher than that for Nuclear, the total cost per hour is 60 percent higher for Atomic.

	Nuclear	Atomic
Estimated shop rate	$16.00	$24.00
Overhead	$25.60 (160%)	$43.20 (180%)
Total cost per hour	$41.60	$67.20

These figures clearly show the problem when overhead is taken as a percentage of labor costs. When an almost identical percentage overhead rate is applied to substantially greater shop costs, the result can only be magnified total costs. In this case, the total hourly costs of Atomic are about 60 percent greater than those of Nuclear, once the overhead rate is applied to the direct labor costs. Thus, using the total cost figures for both companies, it is possible to see even more clearly the vastly fewer numbers of hours of work Atomic anticipates for this project than Nuclear anticipates.

Since Atomic is charging a 10 percent handling cost for materials, this actually can be viewed as an increase in the overhead rate.

Question 4:

Based on the proposal plus information obtained from the case history, which company is likely to be the better supplier?

Comment:

In spite of some detractions, Nuclear appears to be the more attractive potential supplier for the following reasons:

1. Experience with a larger pressure vessel. This experience is crucial in the minds of most of the experienced professional purchasers who have used the case.
2. Atomic's labor relations are of major concern.
3. Nuclear's apparently higher cost may be an illusion.

They have relevant experience on which to base their cost. As will be discussed in question 5, neither proposal guarantees the cost to Oceanic. Thus, the Atomic proposal may represent a buy-in.

Question 5:

What do you recommend?

Comment:

The awarding of a cost plus contract to either supplier is not recommended. Nuclear's agreement to accept the job for only a $1 fee is not what it seems. What Oceanic will be doing if it accepts either proposal is giving the supplier a blank check.

An interesting example of the ramifications of a cost plus contract is the purchase of steel plates by the supplier. If Atomic Products should have to purchase additional plating because of hidden flaws in earlier purchases, they would actually be paid a 10 percent premium, plus the cost of the additional plate. In short, they risk nothing while being assured a "fair profit."

It is difficult to choose between these suppliers. Nuclear's enthusiasm and experience weigh heavily in this decision. While Atomic's cost per hour worked is considerably higher, it may be a very efficient producer. An estimate of the total hours necessary to complete the project from each company would be a very useful piece of information.

A counterproposal by Oceanic is necessary. An incentive type contract offering a bonus for efficient performance could be useful in this case. If Atomic is as efficient as it boasts, its higher overhead rate and per-hour rates will not make it less competitive. A target figure of $1,396,000 could be set (a point halfway between Atomic's and Nuclear's estimates), with an upper ceiling of $1,600,000. Either supplier would be allowed 50 percent of any savings made under the target price and would, conversely, be allowed only direct costs, plus burden for any amount exceeding the target price. The $1,600,000 represents the upper contract limit and puts a ceiling on Oceanic's total contract liability. The "risk takers" should, in fact, be made to take risks.

SENATOR FOGHORN

Purpose

The purpose of this case is to explore two subjects: reciprocity and the use of retired political figures to help with marketing. The case also provides a platform for discussing idealism and the realities of the real world.

Discussion

Usually this is a popular case with students. It can be an effective examination case as well as a good case for class discussion. However, the interest (and humor) of Senator Foghorn sometimes obscures the important reciprocity considerations in the case.

In using this case, the instructor must keep in mind the differences (which are not always readily detectable) between: (1) reciprocity that tends to restrict competition and trade (which is illegal), and (2) reciprocity resulting from nonpressured purchases among firms that are friends that do not restrict trade or competition (which is legal).

There are two ways of viewing Senator Foghorn's proposal. Either the retired senator has honestly become an industrialist looking for business, or he is seeking financial gain based on his political connections. Either conclusion is supportable. Because some political figures have become wealthy in office or shortly thereafter, many students will find Foghorn's action suspicious. The instructor, therefore, may have to encourage the view that the former senator is offering something legitimate to Maryland.

In the electrical equipment industry, reciprocity is a basic fact of life, because major electrical manufacturers make equipment that has wide industrial and consumer applications. For example, Maryland's small horsepower motors could be used in a host of products such as vacuum cleaners or evaporative air coolers which almost anyone might buy. Another example might be light bulbs. In the electrical industry, the trucking company favored by an electrical manufacturer probably would be expected to be a buyer of its light bulbs. Thus, it is possible to defend the position that the former senator is only trying to do business in a manner common among companies in this industry; that is, swap a sale on a favorable value basis.

If it is true that Foghorn is offering something completely aboveboard, the reciprocity point should be discussed on the same basis as any other reciprocal decision. It would not be significant in this event that a powerful political figure is involved. The reason why the Maryland's plating facility is operating currently at only 60 percent of capacity while business is being given to outside suppliers should be explored. The question can be asked, "Is there a difference between taking business from another supplier to buy from a customer and taking business away from your own plant?" Many business executives feel quite differently (and keenly) about taking business from their own plant as compared to taking business from a supplier. If businessmen felt as strongly about taking business from a supplier, undoubtedly there would be much less reciprocity in industry.

Question 1:

Should Maryland become involved with Senator Foghorn? If so, to what degree?

Comment:

The answer to this question involves a consideration and reconciliation of three factors:

1. What does Senator Foghorn have to offer?
2. What will it cost Maryland to buy what Senator Foghorn is offering?
3. Are there any other considerations in becoming involved with the former senator?

A careful analysis of the facts will show what the former senator has to offer. It is known that he produced a plastics contract for Maryland. It is also known that the head of a large mail order house is now working with him. Thus, what he is offering on the housing contract can be calculated by computing the gross profit Maryland will make if it receives the order.

The cost to Maryland can be computed by an analysis of the price, quality, and service Foghorn's plating company will produce. It may be that Foghorn is offering competitive prices with good delivery dates on high-quality plating. Thus the direct cost in dollars to Maryland could be little or nothing. The indirect costs connected with the other suppliers and the company's own plating plant are another problem (to be discussed in question 2). A thorough analysis of the plating plant should be made, including a plant inspection and a review of the company's financial strength. The plant's major customers should be interviewed to gain an accurate picture of their experience with Foghorn's company.

At this point, it is logical to propose the question, "Assuming that there is nothing illegal involved, what if $100,000 of profit will be made by Maryland on the housing project and Maryland has to buy $50,000 of plated items which are worthless and must be junked?" It is entirely possible not to disturb either the present supplier arrangements or the Maryland plating plant to make a profitable deal with Foghorn on this kind of exchange.

There is the possibility that the former senator is utilizing his past public position for his own private financial gain. In this case, Maryland could be open to criticism, if not legal liability. This possibility should be checked with Maryland's legal department. Although Foghorn says that he prefers to work "behind the scenes" and be paid in the form of reciprocal purchasing, it might be possible to pay Foghorn directly for his services. Foghorn might be very valuable to Maryland as a high-level marketing figure if he would accept a permanent operating or consulting position on the Maryland staff.

Question 2:

Should business be taken from Maryland's own plating plant or regularly good sources of supply to satisfy Senator Foghorn?

Comment:

A decision to take business from the company's own facilities must result from a study of the capacity of the plating plant, its percentage of use, how far normal operations are above or below the break-even point, and so on. The same thorough analysis for make-buy decisions as discussed in the text should be made for this plant. If the Maryland plating facilities are operating at less than estimated capacity, the fixed costs must be amortized over a smaller volume than anticipated when the facilities were constructed. This raises unit costs. Any further reduction in work for the Maryland plating plant would further raise unit costs because fixed costs would be spread over a still smaller volume. Therefore, any reciprocal decision must accurately predict the economic impact on Maryland's own plating facilities.

Since Maryland is currently using only 60 percent of its plating plant, the potential use of Foghorn's company could be a blessing. It could force a make-buy analysis that otherwise might not be made. Thus, even paying Foghorn a premium price for his plating could result in a net saving to Maryland because of the closing of its own, inefficient plating facilities.

A decision to take business from present suppliers forces placing a value on the cost of risking the loss of sources of supply who have performed well in the past. Unfortunately, most businessmen do not weigh this consideration as carefully as taking work from their own plant. Logically, the same kind of analysis should be given to this possibility. Undoubtedly, present suppliers would be unhappy with the loss of Maryland business, and as a result of this loss they probably would retaliate by placing their electrical business elsewhere (but this is not certain). Maryland can compute the costs it would incur if this should happen and those suppliers should start buying their electrical supplies elsewhere.

There normally is a surplus of good, reliable plating firms available in all industrial areas. Therefore, Maryland should have no production worries in connection with finding good sources of supply if the reciprocal arrangement with Foghorn were to be stopped sometime in the future.

SHEER ELEGANCE

This case allows the instructor to delve into the issue of pollution avoidance in a far deeper manner than does the text. It is our observation that pollution avoidance is largely in a compliance mode, but soon will transition into a proactive mode. The most powerful driver will be economics, with regulation playing a key, but secondary role.

When an automobile assembler can save $500,000 through the use of reusable shipping boxes, both the ecology and the profitability of the assembler benefit. When a fast food chain switches from styrofoam to biodegradable paper, it improves its image as a responsible corporate citizen and—probably—its market share and profitability.

1. Develop a value chain from Mother Earth through Sheer Elegance to Mother Earth.

Figure 1: The Value-Chain Concept

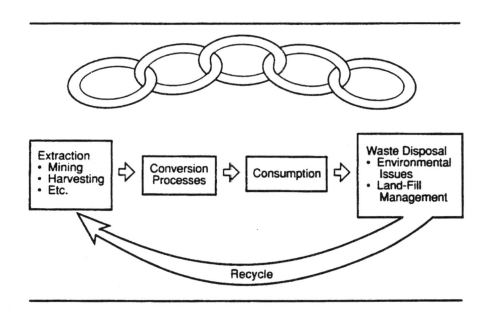

From *The American Keiretsu*, p. 9. © Copyrighted by David N. Burt and Michael F. Doyle; used with permission.

2. Identify points at which pollution may enter the value chain which, to some extent, are under the control of Sheer Elegance.

In order to develop ideas of how to minimize waste throughout the value chain, one has to know where waste or pollution is generated in the first place. If we look at the overall value chain (supplier-company-customer), we can find five main locations of pollution which may be totally or partially under the control of the manufacturing or processing company:

a. The first source of polluting waste is the specification imposed by a customer firm as we move down the value chain from Mother Earth to the next processing/manufacturing firm on to the final consumer.

b. The second potential source of pollution or waste is quality requirements which may force the supplier to produce the material in a nonstandard way. This nonstandard specification may make it impossible for the supplier to manufacture with its highest degree of efficiency, thereby generating waste. For example, Sheer Elegance orders

one type of product labels on a nonstandard specific type of paper. Since this type of paper generally is not requested by any other firm, the label manufacturer cannot optimize its material usage by combining different sizes of labels (even for different customers) in the same production run. The result is an above-average scrap rate of unusable material (salvageable material or waste).

c. The third type of pollution or waste generation is the interface waste that results from the geographic distance and the different process or quality requirements between supplier and customer. Geographic distance forces the supplier to transport the material while preserving the integrity of the product. This means the supplier has to use some form of packaging material which generally ends up in the waste stream, because it is not requested and therefore not needed by its customer, nor considered salvageable by the customer.

d. The fourth main location of pollution or waste generation is the company's internal processing of purchased materials. Internal waste typically originates from three main sources:

   (1) First, surpluses from production processes are inevitable. Not all production materials are wholly consumed in most manufacturing processes. Frequently, a residue is left. This excess is called scrap, and must be disposed of as surplus or waste. Surplus also results from wasteful production processes, or inefficiencies in general. This type of surplus can be either salvageable or waste. Either way, it remains unusable material for the original application.

   (2) The second source of internal waste that often ends up in the external waste stream is from obsolete or damaged stocks. Any warehouse operation, regardless of how efficiently it is controlled, also accumulates some salvageable or waste material from breakage, deterioration, and errors in record keeping. And finally, changes occur constantly in the designs and specifications of fast-moving technological products. As a consequence, obsolete labels, packaging materials, and the products and parts themselves constitute a continuing source of surplus (salvageable or waste) materials. A just-in-time approach to distribution greatly reduces such waste.

   (3) The third main internal source of waste is the interface between the company and its customer. This waste is largely composed of packaging materials. Today, packaging materials have evolved into a highly sophisticated medium which allows manufacturers to deliver their products to consumers, many times over great distances, with a minimum of damage, spoilage, or deterioration. In order to meet this goal, packaging performs a number of important functions during transportation, storage, and use. Included in these functions are:

   • Containment of the product to ensure its integrity and safety,
   • Protection of the product from physical damage, spoilage, etc.,
   • Convenience of use and consumer acceptance,
   • Compliance with legal and regulatory requirements,
   • Conveyance of information/data.

   Packaging is the largest, fastest growing, and most complex component of municipal solid waste (that is, municipal waste generated by homes and businesses, as opposed to industrial and agriculture waste.)

   (4) The final source (the fifth) is post-consumption waste, basically the portion of the product itself (including packaging) which is not consumed by the end

customer. Once the company specific locations are identified, the next step is to determine the waste composition of the combined sources.

These five sources of waste within the value chain are shown in Figure 2.

Figure 2: The Pollution Value Chain

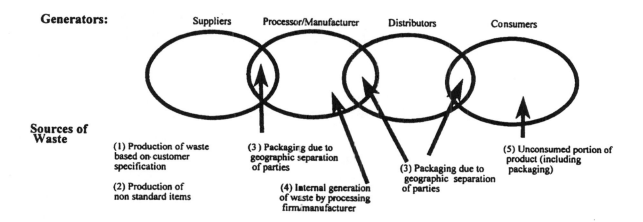

3.   How can pollution be avoided throughout Sheer Elegance's value chain?

Value Chain Pollution Avoidance (VCPA) goes back to the beginning of the value chain and tries to reduce the initial generation of waste throughout the complete chain. VCPA focuses on processes that prevent or minimize pollution from being created throughout the value chain. While traditional end-of-the-line approaches represent an add-on expense (collection, separation, transportation, etc.), the avoidance option is based on increased process efficiency. Companies committed to waste prevention will, similar to quality assurance, often apply statistical procedures to collect data to monitor the process along the value chain, with the focus of minimizing the impact of the different process variables. Waste avoidance, like quality assurance, is a systematic approach to optimize the efficiency of a *given process*.

To understand the importance of actual waste composition, it is necessary to analyze the different cost elements of waste handling. Waste is expensive. Each company pays for its waste in a variety of ways. The production of waste in the manufacturing process forces the company to use more material per unit. Generated waste has to be collected, sorted, stored, labeled, transported, and finally disposed. In each step the company "wastes" time and money resources on its waste. In order to effectively collect the different waste materials, the organization has to build an internal collection system. The different materials have to be sorted to ensure the safety of the environment and its employees (i.e., combination of different flammable chemicals). Storage space has to be provided to bridge the time gap between initial generation and final disposal. Depending on the type of waste (hazardous waste), special labels have to be applied to identify the materials and inform the environment about its specific handling. And finally, the company has to pay the waste transportation and the tipping or disposal fee for the different materials. Managing waste is expensive—and becoming even more so, as restrictions on environmental releases tighten and cleanup costs skyrocket. Disposal fees for hazardous wastes have risen as much as 300 percent over the past decade alone, approaching $2,000 per ton for some wastes. The EPA estimates that each year the nation's industries and municipalities spend $120 billion to treat or contain wastes.

However, it would be a costly misperception to believe that the company pays only for its own waste. The company also pays for its suppliers' waste by purchasing their outputs at higher prices, prices that include the costs of each supplier plus its suppliers' waste. Indirectly, the company even pays for the generation of post-consumer waste.

Today's customers are environmentally conscious to an extent that they will choose a product or even change to a brand that safeguards the ecological environment provided that cost is not excessive. However, it is not enough for the company to just know which of its product materials will end up in the post-consumer waste stream. Because of public confusion about the environmental impact of the different materials, from a marketing standpoint it is even more important to know which of the product materials are *perceived* to be environmentally friendly. For example, paper bags are *perceived* to be environmentally friendlier than plastic bags. In fact, plastic may be the better environmental choice, but it is not the better economic choice since its use can hurt sales. And as mentioned earlier, continuous pollution prevention will not survive in our business world, unless it makes economic sense. It is therefore, important to understand that companies lose customers *based on perception* and not necessarily on hard facts. One way the company pays for post-consumer waste is by losing its customers to more environmentally sensitive competitors who make consumers aware of this sensitivity.

The cost of waste is positively correlated to the type of material entering the waste stream. For example, if the waste is hazardous, the company has to provide a higher level of safety with the collection, sorting, storing, labeling, and transportation of the material. In addition, the company pays a substantially higher amount of money for the final disposal of more hazardous materials. Therefore, to determine the total costs of waste, management has to have the composition of the firm's waste analyzed. The organization has to identify the different types of waste, the quantity of each type and the amount of money (for collecting, sorting, etc.) that is spent on each type. This systematic approach enables the company to allocate individual cost elements to a single waste material or waste material group. The establishment of an effective waste control monitoring and documentation system is crucial for the efficiency of continuous pollution prevention.

However, because of the importance of both supplier- and consumer-generated waste, the company also has to integrate these sides of the value chain into the analysis of the total waste stream composition. Surveys can and should be used to collect supplier and customer data regarding the different types and quantities of waste the party generates. Both sides are elements of the value chain and both sides have, therefore, the potential to reduce total waste generation. Customers as well as suppliers are important information sources which cannot be ignored by any company concerned with pollution avoidance. A company that does not integrate both parties in the development of any kind of total value-chain concept will never reach its total potential of protecting the environment. One of the greatest challenges is to maximize value and minimize costs (including environmental costs) throughout the value chain. This challenge requires that manufacturers and firms in process and service industries, their suppliers, their distributors, and their customers must focus their collective efforts on reducing the total cost of pollution within their value chain.

The composition of the total waste throughout the value chain is a combination of many different materials. Waste documentation allows the value-chain leader (normally, the key processor or manufacturer) to identify the most costly and environmentally destructive waste materials throughout the value chain. Such cost is based on the quantity, the degree of hazardousness, or the customer perception of the waste. In order to establish a list with the most important (and first to address) materials, management should have the different materials ranked based on the Pareto concept. Normally, a Pareto list will reveal that approximately 20

percent of the waste materials cause approximately 80 percent of the total waste cost. This analysis helps the company get an overview over the actual cost impact of the individual waste materials. The final Pareto listing will also identify those materials which must be addressed first.

Value Chain Pollution Avoidance (VCPA) requires the application of statistical process control (SPC), monitoring procedures, and the involvement of the employees at firms along the value chain and the customer. VCPA includes all aspects of a company's business, from marketing (representing the customer's voice) to purchasing/supply management (representing the supplier's voice). The system requires the analysis of the entire value chain from Mother Earth, through suppliers, through the company itself, to the ultimate customer and, possibly, to Mother Earth.

4. If you were Mr. Scherer, what action would you recommend?

Like every other strategy in a business, the implementation of VCPA requires a detailed plan of action that delineates the different steps to be followed, as well as a basic time frame for implementation. The plan must be complete, so that everyone in every member of the value chain understands what is expected and when it must be done. The implementation plan detailed below describes the common activities a company is likely to encounter.

Each organization in the value chain should include in its mission statement a long-run vision and direction of what the organization is trying to become: the unique goal that differentiates the organization from competitors. It is important to realize that the need for a mission statement is not the stated purpose itself. The mission statement provides direction and significance to all members of the organization. A mission statement of a VCPA firm could include the following:

> Our company wants to protect the environment and natural resources related to all our operations worldwide through responsible management exercising excellence in environmental control.

Sheer Elegance will benefit from a wide variety of ideas and suggestions from its employees, with the empowerment of its employees and the establishment of challenging incentive programs. However, this alone will not be enough to integrate an effective waste prevention strategy. The company needs a systematic approach to evaluate the impact of its different operations on the environment. Many functions within the firm must be involved in pollution avoidance. Senior management should develop cross-functional pollution avoidance teams consisting of design, purchasing, supply, process and quality engineering, distribution, marketing, and finance, as well as customers and suppliers. Subteams from each member of the value chain actually carry out the step-by-step approach and report back to the top management of their company and the superordinate team consisting of representatives of all members of the value chain.

No waste management or pollution avoidance system will work unless it makes economic sense to do so. Doing what should be done, rather than what has to be done, means that economic objectives should be broadened to include intangible benefits like corporate reputation and employee morale—a "VCPA" goal should encourage technical innovations to prevent pollution at the source, through the methods of product reformulation, process modification, equipment redesign, and source recovery, while simultaneously ensuring the consideration of the environmental factors for the entire life cycle of the product.

VCPA is not a mechanical system that, once implemented, runs automatically. VCPA is like Continuous Quality Improvement (CQI), a philosophy that lives with and within the

members of the organization. A successful pollution avoidance program requires the involvement and visible commitment of top management to the waste-prevention philosophy by all members of the value chain. VCPA needs executive sponsorship to reinforce the importance of the policy to employees at all levels. Positive environmental awareness can be created through internal management speeches and publications, employee briefings, company slogans, publicly proclaimed emission-reduction goals, and incentive programs that reward initiative and innovation in meeting or exceeding environmental objectives. Top management has to prepare the organization for a new way.

One very effective and low-cost way of promoting the implementation of a sound environmental agenda within an organization is to incorporate environmental thinking into current programs, rather than creating new programs from scratch. The TQM concept is emerging in several organizations as an ideal vehicle for environmentally based quality programs. TQM encourages the emergence of ideas in the organization from the bottom up (empowerment of the individual employee), and it also provides a logical framework for environmental objectives.

Once the decision is made and management has agreed on those materials that are the first to be addressed, the cross-functional pollution avoidance team has to answer the following three questions:

1. Where is the waste material generated?
2. At what stage was it planned into the value chain?
3. Why was it built into the value chain?

Each waste material accumulates at some point in the value chain. The team has to follow the physical waste stream from the customer, over the internal value-chain links of the company, through the supplier to Mother Earth. End-of-the-pipe solutions are not the goals of VCPA. The team has to determine the location where the waste material is produced in the first place. Focusing on the internal process, this could be in the internal warehouse and logistic arrangements, the production process, or purchasing requirements. Once the physical location of generation is identified, the team has to go one step further. It has to analyze the remaining portions of the value chain, in order to find the link that caused this material to end up in the waste stream. At which level was this material initially integrated into the value chain? During the investigation phase of the new product, the development phase, the procurement plans, the production process, the warehouse stage, or the logistic phase? Once this second question is answered, the team can move along to address the third question: Why was it built into the value chain?

To meet the challenge of sustainable development, production must become more resource-efficient—adding more value while using less energy and raw materials and generating less pollution. This will require the redesign of both products and production processes, and it will require manufacturers to consider the entire life cycles of their products. To realize this goal, justification for the existence of each waste material has to be questioned. In Value Chain Pollution Avoidance (VCPA), the cross-functional pollution avoidance team must question the reason each material was initially built into the value chain. Such analysis could lead to redesigning processes, upgrading cleaning practices and material handling, reevaluating product design and choice of raw materials and solvents, or modifying product packaging, loading, and transportation.

For example, when 3M cut round respirator masks from fabric sheets at its Aberdeen, South Dakota plant, fully one-third of the fabric was wasted. Resin sprayed on the fabric to allow the mask to keep its shape prevented the scraps from being recycled back into the process. Engineers came up with a fiber blend that holds its form without resin. This change has allowed full recycling of 300 tons of fabric scraps per cutting and eliminated nearly 400,000 gallons of dilute resin wastes.[1]

This specific manner in which an environment and cost-based value analysis is performed cannot be standardized. The different members of a team possess unique analytical abilities and employ unique patterns of thought. However, management should require analysts to follow several general steps which are designed to stimulate and organize their efforts. Those commonly used are (1) the value analysis checklist, (2) the functional environment and cost approach, (3) the use of brainstorming, and (4) the use of suppliers and customers. The checklist consists of a number of general questions followed by several highly specialized questions for particular company characteristics. During the functional environment and cost approach, the question would be: Do particular functions performed by a single part justify its environmental impact and costs? The use of brainstorming stimulates creative problem solutions. Depending on personal preference, step number (4) can either be an isolated step by itself or, as we recommend, should be integrated into the first three steps. Value analysis possesses a tremendous potential. However, if its potential is to be realized, those responsible for administration for the value analysis program must adopt a broadly based management point of view. This is important, because the purpose of value analysis should be to optimize the *total* value-chain efficiency.

After evaluating the current system, the team members must reach a consensus on the parts of the system (including other members of the value chain) that must be changed and exactly how and when they should be changed. Once a general course of action has been agreed upon, a detailed plan can be developed. This plan will define all the process improvements the company and the members of its value chain must make in order to achieve an efficient VCPA system. In addition, the plan must also establish a realistic time frame for implementation and delineate the person or persons responsible for overseeing each improvement. As is true with TQM, complete and accurate documentation is the key to achieving the full potential of VCPA. All the elements, requirements, and provisions adopted by the company for its VCPA system must be documented in a systematic and orderly manner in the form of written policies and procedures.

5.   What role does supply management play?

Companies that adopt VCPA as the guideline for their environmental commitment put purchasing right in the middle of corporate environmental management: value for money and environmental issues. Environmental impact is a threshold issue in purchasing. Where appropriate, relevant environmental criteria are to be included in specifications, requests for offers, and evaluations of potential suppliers.

For example, it may be appropriate to specify recycled products or to require energy-efficient office accommodation. Potential suppliers should be required to provide information relating to the nominated environmental criteria just as they provide information on their financial situation, project management skills, and quality processes. Compliance with these criteria

---

[1] "Profits One," *Business Week* (January 3, 1992), p. 91.

could be determined during evaluation and offers not meeting them *may* be rejected, just as noncompliance with other aspects of the specification or request for offers may lead to rejection.

Selecting strategic suppliers is based on the development of specific measurement criteria for the sourcing of critical components. Supply management and, hopefully, other members of the sourcing team should carefully review the potential supplier's pollution avoidance capabilities against the established criteria. With the implementation of VCPA, having an environmentally sound management strategy should be the next criteria to be added to the list. The purchasing department is also the closest link to the supplier. When integrating particular suppliers into the processor/manufacturer's cross-functional pollution avoidance team, the purchasing department should be the one introducing individual suppliers. Supply management plays an important role within VCPA, but it does not have to play the leading role.

SIGNAL-TEK CORPORATION

Purpose

The purpose of this case is to discuss purchasing's role and responsibilities in new product development.

Discussion

Signal-Tek faces several issues which must be addressed in new product development: purchasing's role, engineering's role, supplier involvement, standardization, and management's commitment to these issues.

Question 1:

How can early purchasing involvement assist in low-cost and timely new product development?

Comment:

Purchasing personnel should be able to pass on information regarding new technologies and products that are available to the product design group. Purchasing can aid in source selection by discussing potential suppliers' quality programs, production capacity, lead times, delivery reliability, financial capability, and management stability and strength. During the design meetings, the purchasing department can stress the availability and economy of standardized components.

Question 2:

How does purchasing's involvement enhance an early supplier involvement program? What are the potential benefits?

Comment:

Suppliers can provide technical support in the early stages of design that can decrease material costs and improve product quality. Furthermore, early purchasing and supplier involvement can reduce start-up problems and delays.

When purchasing joins engineering in meetings with potential suppliers, it can address price and discount issues, quantity and quality requirements, lead time and delivery schedules, and financial capabilities. The supplier's responses to these issues will allow purchasing to further qualify the supplier.

Purchasing also will be privy to discussions between the engineer and supplier regarding possible design and component changes. These meetings will allow purchasing to gain some knowledge of component requirements and availability (especially in regards to unique components); however, purchasing needs to learn much more in order to be effective in new product development. Early purchasing involvement will allow purchasing personnel to realize their lack of knowledge and motivate them to upgrade themselves.

Question 3:

How can the division increase cooperation/communication between the engineering and purchasing departments?

Comment:

In the existing procurement environment, purchasing personnel lack the technical skills necessary to effectively assist the product design group. To address this issue, the division should hire a component engineer to serve as a mediator between engineering and purchasing. Although the component engineer will not be inexpensive, the investment should be recovered several times over just on this contract alone.

Question 4:

How will standardization improve the new product development process?

Comment:

The component engineer's expertise, together with purchasing's awareness of all material requirements, will be used to develop a standardization program, as well as a qualified supplier list.

By introducing a standardization program and materials catalogue, the number of parts can be reduced and catalogued for easy reference by the engineers. The design engineer's use of nonstandard or unqualified suppliers will cause delays, whereas the use of catalogue items will result in a shorter development time.

Question 5:

How does more effective purchasing involvement change engineering's role?

Comment:

The engineering department currently has too much latitude in dealing with potential suppliers. The engineers should concentrate on designing a reliable and timely product; they must work with purchasing to meet that end.

The engineers will be motivated to spend more time designing and evaluating new parts. Design engineering should move from its present assumed responsibility of selecting sources to a partnership responsibility as a member of the source selection team.

Question 6:

What can the division do to help expand purchasing's contribution?

Comment:

The division must recognize that it needs to invest in a training program for its purchasing manager and buyers in order to receive the full benefits from its procurement system. This training can take many different forms, including individual training at seminars,

trade shows, or classes conducted by engineers on how to read blueprints and specification sheets.

Signal-Tek Denver also should seriously consider hiring a technical/professional buyer. This professional buyer will assist in upgrading the purchasing department.

Final Comments

Management must be strongly committed to early purchasing involvement in all aspects of new product development including early supplier involvement. Management must stress standardization and limit engineering's role in procurement issues. Training purchasing personnel is a key to further success. The division's management must emphasize the importance of these issues to the entire organization. With such commitment, the division will be able to develop new products in the shortest amount of time for the lowest cost and still maintain the quality and reliability that gave the company the leadership position that it once enjoyed.

SMC TURBINES

Purpose

This case addresses some of the problems (opportunities) of supplier management. Specifically, the case focuses on the quality problem SMC is facing in the quality of sand castings purchased from outside sources.

Discussion

Supplier management is a very important part of procurement. It can lead to higher quality materials, more timely deliveries, and lower costs, thus better *value*. Purchased materials need to be addressed all through the procurement process in order to achieve the highest quality possible.

Question

What options are available to Greg through basic supplier management? What actions do you recommend?

1. Greg could suggest using the higher grade material so that 10 percent of the castings will be acceptable.

Comment:

The higher grade of materials could cost up to $25,000, over twice the cost of the present sand castings. Moving to a higher grade would require pre-qualifying all suppliers, costing both time and money. Although SMC would receive higher quality materials, the costs for purchased materials would more than double.

2. SMC could use a new design to alleviate the problems of the current sand castings.

Comment:

Due to the complexity of the situation, a new design might be in order. Some of the current designs may not be feasible with today's technology. However, sand castings cover a large variety of components that would require a lot of redesigning. It does not seem reasonable to assume that all of the problems can be removed through redesign.

3. Should SMC monitor the production process of each of its suppliers to see exactly where the problems lie?

Comment:

This kind of action would be very costly to SMC in the short run. However, once SMC can effectively determine the source(s) of the problems, it can provide knowledge and experience to ensure higher quality. Each of SMC's suppliers can work to come up with plans as a part of the monitoring process. Gantt charts could easily be implemented to chart techniques for planning and controlling. Weekly progress reports could be required from all suppliers.

Outcome:

SMC *is* currently monitoring every single step in the production process of its suppliers. Each individual problem is being addressed and being given an action plan to find solutions and ways of improving quality. SMC plans to reduce its supply base and concentrate on its best two suppliers in a further effort to improve quality.

SMITH-JONES ELECTRONICS CORPORATION

Purpose

This is a good review case that summarizes a number of key points with respect to three areas of activity: (1) proactive buying practices, (2) supplier selection and management, and (3) centralized/decentralized organizational considerations. The case highlights the interaction among these three areas of activity and points up the need for their coordination and integration if the purchasing function is to be managed well.

Discussion

At most of Smith-Jones's plants, purchasing is perceived as a group of subprofessional people who conduct "price auctions" to obtain the materials needed in the manufacturing operation. Ironically, analysis reveals that in many cases Smith-Jones is paying more for its materials than market prices, on the average, justify. Additionally, as might be expected, an excessive number of material deliveries are chronically late.

This situation is sometimes typical of that found in large organizations that largely decentralize the purchasing function, providing only minimal guidance and staff support at the central level. In organizations that tend to be engineering or production oriented, the potential value and productivity of a professionally organized purchasing function is often overlooked in plant management's zeal to excel technically. In such cases, it is imperative to have a strong central purchasing group at the corporate level to provide staff assistance to the plant operations to ensure that purchasing is a profit contributor to each plant's bottom line.

Question 1:

Identify and discuss the basic issues in this case.

Comment:

As noted above, the three basic issues in the case are (1) inadequate proactive buying practices, (2) inadequate supplier selection and management, and (3) centralized/decentralized organizational considerations. Each of these issues is discussed in the following paragraphs.

1. *The need for developing and managing a buying plan.* At the present time, most purchasing personnel tend to behave as order placers rather than as professional buyers. In many cases, buyers apparently do not know enough about the expected annual demand for materials, enough about the material specifications themselves, or enough about potential suppliers to do an intelligent job of planning for most material acquisitions and selecting qualified suppliers. It is imperative that buyers become more knowledgeable about all three issues.

   In the absence of assistance from the centralized corporate procurement staff, individual plant purchasing personnel must work more closely with design engineers in developing specifications that match supplier capabilities in the marketplace; they must also work more closely with master scheduling and production scheduling personnel to obtain the best information they can get about expected material demand for the ensuing 6 to 12 months. With more complete information of this type, individual buyers are then in a position to do a better job of assessing potential suppliers in the

marketplace—visiting a selected number of these firms—and in developing a much more thorough understanding of the operating, technical, and financial strengths and weaknesses of the key potential suppliers.

Following the course of action just suggested, each buyer is then in a position with respect to his or her own plant responsibilities to develop a 6- to 12-month proactive buying plan for the major materials handled.

2. *Inadequate supplier selection and management.* Armed with a more thorough understanding of the information just described—unique aspects of material specifications and operating requirements—for the more important materials, buyers can undertake a systematic supplier investigation effort. Based on the results of these investigations, a buyer can determine whether it will likely be most advantageous to the firm to utilize a negotiation or a competitive bidding approach in the supplier selection and pricing process.

The attitudes of buyers and other plant personnel at Smith-Jones toward suppliers and the role that they can play in Smith-Jones's success in its own marketplace appears to be a decade or so out of date. There is virtually no attempt by the buyers to "manage" their suppliers. Buyers apparently make no effort to develop ongoing relationships with their suppliers, and they make no effort to evaluate supplier performance, even in the most rudimentary form. Hence, the notion of collaborative purchasing or partnering plays no role in the Smith-Jones purchasing process.

As discussed throughout Parts III, V, and VII of the text, it is essential that for major materials Smith-Jones's buyers attempt to develop an ongoing cooperative relationship with key suppliers. The two groups must work together to ensure optimal effectiveness, cost reduction, and profitability for both firms.

3. *Inadequate development of the central corporate purchasing function.* Perhaps the greatest weakness in the Smith-Jones purchasing operation is its failure to utilize the central corporate purchasing group effectively. The three functions now being performed by the central group—large contract procurement, purchasing training, and policy and procedure administration—are good, but insufficiently done.

The actions recommended for individual plant buyers in discussing the preceding two issues are all worthwhile, but none can be completely effective without the assistance of the central purchasing group. This group should promote and develop professionalism at the plant level. It should also coordinate the needs of all plants for specific materials, policies, and operating and control procedures. It is top management's responsibility to attempt to achieve the major advantages offered by both centralization and decentralization by carefully blending the purchasing functional responsibilities and authority of the central group with the line operating responsibilities of individual plant purchasing departments.

To date, too much authority has been vested with individual plant managers to the detriment of their own purchasing operations. It is vital that the central purchasing group work with each plant manager and purchasing manager to develop a viable aggregate demand forecasting system for all major materials. When such a system is developed, it can be used in all plants and the aggregate corporate demand for given materials can be estimated with at least reasonable accuracy. In the case of materials that are used fairly heavily by several or more plants, it makes good sense to negotiate a one- or two-year corporate contract against which all plant users issue releases. Depending on the details of the situation, such a contract could be negotiated by the central group or it might be negotiated by the purchasing manager from one of the

leading plant users. In any case, it is essential that a corporate buying plan for each of these materials be developed and the benefit of the corporation's buying power be made available to all plants.

At the present time, no substantive market research is being done. This work should be done for all plants by a small group of skilled market researchers and forecasters at the central level. Two types of research should be conducted: (1) that dealing with fluctuating market conditions that are important in making buying plans for individual materials, and (2) research that is useful in developing information for price and cost analyses that can be used in evaluating the purchasing department performance at each individual plant, as well as at the corporate level.

Further development of more sophisticated operating policies and procedures should be undertaken by the central purchasing staff. These policies and procedures should focus on all aspects of the purchasing function necessary to ensure effective professional practice at the individual plant level. In connection with this effort, the central group should be responsible for the development of more rigorous and more effective training experiences for all purchasing personnel throughout the corporation.

Concluding Comment:

No discussion of this case is complete without addressing, at least briefly, the matter of implementation. How can George Brown effect constructive change in the Smith-Jones organization?

Brown has a tough job ahead of him, to say the least. Top management obviously does not recognize the significance of the problems resulting from its inaction in the purchasing area. George's chances for success are probably the greatest if he is able to define clearly and quantitatively the financial and operating impact of some of the problems resulting from the present mode of operation. If he can build a strong enough case for improved productivity and profitability, he should be able to get the attention of the corporate vice president responsible for the various operating divisions. An alternative approach might involve his working with several plant managers (and respective purchasing managers) to create an awareness and sensitivity to the magnitude of the potential operating improvements and cost savings they are foregoing. These plant managers, if sufficiently sensitized, could then take the problem to top management. In any case, George's mission is to concretely identify the more important problems, quantify the losses or potential benefits, and then sensitize the appropriate managers to the need for some changes in the present system.

SPRINGER-BRIGHTON ELECTRONICS

Purpose

The purpose of this case is twofold: (1) To expose the student to the logic and the mechanics of preparing a simple MRP Operations Plan and its accompanying Order Point Table; and (2) To require the student to identify and discuss the common types of operating problems associated with purchasing operations for an MRP driven system; of particular importance are the implications of these problems for a buyer in conducting source selection activities and developing ongoing supplier relationships.

Question 1:

Complete the ordering/operations plan for the Model 48A housing, and construct a table showing when you would expect order points to be reached during the first eight weeks.

Operations Plan For Model 48A Housings

Order Quantity = 140 Lead Time = 4 weeks Safety Stock = 80		Weeks → Firm Reqts.										Tentative	
		1	2	3	4	5	6	7	8	9	10	11	12
Requirements		40	40	50	40	40	50	40	40	60	50	50	50
Planned receipts			140	-	-	140	-	-	140	-	-	140	-
On hand, end of week	130	90	190	140	100	200	150	110	210	150	100	190	140
Planned order release		140			140			140					

Order Point Table For Model 48A Housings

Order Point = Lead time demand quantity + Safety stock quantity

Total Available Housings = Quantity on hand, EOW + Quantity on order

Week	Lead time Demand (4 wk.)	Safety Stock	Order Point	On Hand On Order	Total Available	Order Point Reached
1	40 + 50 + 40 + 40	80	250	90 + 140	230	Yes
2	50 + 40 + 40 + 50	80	260	190 + 140	330	
3	40 + 40 + 50 + 40	80	250	140 + 140	280	
4	40 + 50 + 40 + 40	80	250	100 + 140	240	Yes
5	50 + 40 + 40 + 60	80	270	200 + 140	340	
6	40 + 40 + 60 + 50	80	270	150 + 140	290	
7	40 + 60 + 50 + 50?	80	280	110 + 140	250	Yes
8	60 + 50 + 50? + 50?	80	290	210 + 140	350	
9	50 + 50? + 50? + ?	80	?	150 + 140	290	?
10	50? + 50? + ? ?	80	?	100 + 140	240	?

Comment:

The week during which an order for housings must be released can be determined in two ways:

1. The operations plan can be worked week by week on a trial-and-error basis. The quantity now on hand + planned receipts for next week – requirements for next week = the quantity on hand at the end of next week. This figure is then compared with the quantity required for the following week + safety stock. If the latter figure exceeds the former, an order must be placed to arrive during that week. Since the lead-time requirement is 4 weeks, the order must be released 4 weeks earlier. Using this procedure, week by week, the operations plan can be completed.

2. A more direct approach involves the construction of an order point table, as shown. In determining the lead-time demand, the analyst must always work one week ahead (e.g., during the first week, the lead-time demand is the quantity required for weeks 2, 3, 4, and 5). When the total quantity available for a given week is less than the order point, an order must be released during that week for receipt 4 weeks hence.

Question 2:

List and discuss briefly the types of operating problems you might encounter that could require replanning and rescheduling work. What are the implications for supplier relations?

Many unexpected circumstances can arise that may require replanning and rescheduling work by the buyer. Some of the more common ones are noted below:

1. The buying firm may experience a customer/production change in product demand. In most firms, sales forecasts need to be adjusted from time to time with changing market conditions.

2. Transportation problems may arise. Various carrier problems may result in delayed deliveries.

3. Lead-time requirements may change simply because of unexpected problems or modifications in the supplier's operation. Thus the buyer's order quantities and schedules may require revision.

4. Material quality problems may require additional time for rework, for return and replacement, etc. Hence the order schedule may require a significant adjustment from time to time.

5. Operating and capacity problems in the buyer's own shop may delay material requirements or may modify the requirements schedule because the job must be done on other equipment with different operating speeds and capacities. These variables obviously impact the MRP schedule.

Comment:

In most cases, these situations require the supplier to change its operating plans on short notice. Not all suppliers can or will do this willingly. Hence the buyer's initial sourcing job for MRP suppliers is more complicated and more difficult. He or she must locate flexible suppliers and provide sufficient incentives for them to function effectively in this mode of operation. As a firm moves toward JIT operation, this factor becomes increasingly important.

In the initial discussions and negotiations, these requirements for flexibility must be discussed in detail so the supplier is fully cognizant of the potential for such short-fused operating changes. The supplier should be able to demonstrate how it can provide the necessary flexibility in its shops—and realistic minimum time requirements (advance notice) for various types of operating changes should be determined. The point is that, to the extent possible, the major potential scheduling difficulties should be identified and discussed in advance. And they should be referenced and detailed as specifically as possible in the purchase contract.

SPRINGFIELD PURCHASES A GARBAGE TRUCK

Purpose

The purpose of this case is to discuss the basic problems involved in choosing between a local supplier and an out-of-town or out-of-state company, and the political implications of these problems in a city or state government purchasing department.

Discussion

The buy-at-home problem is common to all types of city and state purchasing. If a city or state buys at home, it does keep its tax dollars home. However, if a premium is paid to home industry, tax dollars can be wasted. Inefficiency and high costs can be encouraged in both producers and distributors. Cities and states which engage in such practices say, in effect, "Yes, I believe in the free enterprise system, but I want to modify it just a bit to protect local businesses."

If this modification to free enterprise is to be done equitably, as far as suppliers are concerned, the city or state must explicitly determine its policy, announce it publicly, and administer it fairly. The policy, for example, might be to give a 5 percent differential to city or state taxpayers. "Outside" suppliers, naturally, will not like such a policy, but if it is administered fairly, it becomes just another factor in supplier selection.

City and state purchasing departments are just as dependent on good supplier relations as industrial purchasing departments if they are to operate effectively. Cities and states have emergencies, need help with value analysis programs, standardization, service, preparation of optimum specifications, and so on, the same as other purchasing departments. To achieve these benefits which come from supplier help and cooperation, any purchasing department must, in the eyes of the suppliers, deal fairly and impartially. For these reasons, giving preference to any group of suppliers can be dangerous to any purchasing department. In large cities and heavily populated states where competition is intense and suppliers are plentiful and "hungry" for business, a preferential policy for local suppliers has an entirely different result from that in small cities or sparsely populated states having few suppliers and minimum competition. In the former case, the policy has little effect on pricing. In the latter case, the premium offered will actually be paid in high prices.

Question 1:

What factors should Sam consider in making a final decision?

Comment:

Mangler is the apparent lowest bidder. However, the award should be made on the basis of the lowest owning, operating, and service cost, not solely on initial purchase price (price is only one element of cost). Sam must assess total cost. He must evaluate pertinent factors such as differentials for fuel, lubrication, repair, and service costs. He must also estimate salvage value at the end of the useful life of the equipment and calculate a yearly depreciation rate. Parts and service on Mangler's compressors must come from a city 300 miles away, whereas SST has local mechanics and a stock of parts. This may mean additional expense in freight, service-call transportation, and an investment in Mangler parts stocked at the city warehouse. There is the

possibility that delays to compressor repairs in an emergency, such as a water-main break, might actually cause public suffering and complaints. Sam must put a realistic price tag on these factors.

Sam should get full information on all pertinent non-cost factors including such intangibles as the firm's attitude toward service before and after the warranty has expired. He should consult with the street department, other city officials such as the controller, local and state purchasing managers, and engineers who have had previous experience with these equipments. He should also check into both suppliers' financial reliability. Financially weak firms are notorious for their poor service and failure to meet warranties.

Sam cannot ignore the political aspects of the solution. He must investigate thoroughly SST's claim of layoffs and Mangler's claim it is a major customer of other Springfield firms. He also should get an honest appraisal of public opinion as viewed by the city council, the major newspapers, tax groups, and so on. His purpose in getting this information would not be to influence this particular bid, but rather to make recommendations for any changes in policy that might appear necessary—also, so that he can give facts to his boss, the mayor, to answer questions from any source.

Question 2:

What should that decision be?

Comment:

Suppliers submitted bids on good faith that Springfield will go through with the award of a contract, and the purchasing manager should honor this faith and choose between Mangler or SST. Sam should avoid possible charges of favoritism and bid-rigging. The kind of reputation resulting from such charges is certain to hurt the city in the long run. Sam's reasons for awarding the contract, therefore, should be based on concrete evidences of costs, soundly documented to withstand any probing questions from any source.

Springfield has had a long history of sound purchasing policy, good supplier relations, and square dealing. If Sam's evidence shows that Mangler's truck offers net savings over possible additional operating costs compared to the SST truck (spread over the life of the equipment), then he should buy from Mangler. If the evidence shows other savings on SST equipment that will more than offset the $4,240 cost differential over Mangler, then the order should go to SST.

Question 3:

What should have been done to avoid some of the problems Sam faced?

Comment:

The city might choose to have a stated policy favoring local suppliers by giving a stated percent differential to city taxpayers. The advantages and disadvantages of this approach are contained in the discussion portion of the case analysis. Since operating costs and service considerations will play such an important role in the selection of capital equipment, the Request for Quotation or Invitation for Bids should state that award will be made to the bidder whose equipment will be least expensive to the city, including considerations of initial acquisition cost; operating, maintenance, training costs, and likely salvage value.

STANDARD TELE-LINK CORPORATION

Purpose

This case can be used effectively to:
1. Explore the purchase of capital equipment in a high tech industry.
2. Discuss the various factors involved in making a lease or buy analysis.

Present Situation

Standard Tele-Link Corporation (STC) is responsible for operating a large international telecommunication network, as a common carrier. In this particular industry, firms are using cutting-edge technology, while technological requirements of the network environment currently exceed what the market has to offer. At the moment, STC is considering the acquisition of some advanced equipment to use in its telecommunication network operations. The basic decisions to be made are (1) should the equipment be acquired at this point in time, and, if so, which supplier should be used? (2) should the equipment be purchased or leased?

Analysis

Issues:

The major issues that must be investigated and assessed are:

1. What are the pros and cons of Channel-Net Products Company?
2. What is the capacity of the Channel-Net production facilities?
3. What is the technical significance of Channel-Net's new product?
4. How long will it be until a similar product is introduced by a competing firm?
5. What is the expected life of this technology—replaced by a more advanced technology?
6. Can STC develop this product itself?
7. Is Channel-Net Products a company STC might want to buy?
8. Why is Channel-Net's price so much higher than that of its competitors? Is Channel-Net a high cost operation?
9. Can STC justify paying Channel-Net the price differential?
10. Should STC buy or lease this particular equipment?

Positive Factors for Channel-Net:

1. Channel Net's product is the only one currently on the market that handles satellite links.
2. Channel-Net has a board of directors and a key group of investors who are major figures in the industry.
3. Channel-Net's current facility is only 20 percent occupied, leaving considerable room for growth.

Negative Factors for Channel-Net:

1. Its product price is three times the price of other suppliers, and all suppliers' products meet STC's spec requirements.
2. The new Channel-Net product has not yet been proven in a live environment.

3. Channel-Net is a small organization that has not yet developed a large sales volume; STC business would be approximately 80 percent of Channel-Net's sales.
4. Channel-Net does not do its own assembly operations; this contracted portion of the business could produce quality and delivery problems.
5. The competitive future for Channel-Net Products is uncertain.

Comment:

One of the reasons Channel-Net looks so attractive as a potential supplier is the fact that its product has a capability that no other competitor's product has at the present time. STC needs to assess how this particular product feature will affect its business from the standpoints of quality, competitiveness, and cost.

If this unique capability would give STC a significant competitive advantage, it certainly may want to utilize it. Since Universal Semi-Conductors is expected to have a similar product on the market within four months, it is probably reasonable to anticipate that the market will develop in this direction.

An important issue is the length of time this technology will survive before being replaced by a more advanced technology. If the time frame is short, STC will probably want to adjust quickly to get into the market during the early stages. The most important element in a market characterized by rapidly changing technology is to enter the market as quickly as possible.

The Lease–Buy Issue:

Channel-Net's purchase and annual lease costs are shown below, along with corresponding estimated costs for one of its competitors. A cursory review of the data indicates that if STC leases the product for approximately two and one-quarter years, the outlay will approximate the cash purchase cost. To make a more precise analysis of this data, however, students should conduct a discounted cash flow analysis, comparing the cost of leasing with the cost of buying.

	Channel Net		Competing Supplier	
	Purchase	Yr. Lease	Purchase	Yr. Lease
Processor	$56,000	$22,572	$18,667	$7,524
Channel Adapter	$25,740	$12,360	$8,580	$4,120
Line Adapter	$57,000	$27,936	$19,000	$9,312
Total (each)	$138,740	$62,868	$46,247	$20,956

A qualitative analysis of the situation produces the following factors that favor a leasing decision:

1. In all likelihood, the life of the unique technology will be relatively short before being replaced with the next generation of technology.
2. At the moment, the potential product quality and price of the new Universal Semi-Conductor product is unknown.
3. The uncertainty associated with the financial strength and stability of the Channel-Net organization appears to be significant.

SUNSPOT, INC.

The instructor should emphasize that a buying firm may have one, two, or three "partners" for the same item. The late Lamar Lee, Jr. advocated a dual sourcing approach to the procurement of many materials. Professor Lee recommended a 70/30 allocation of business. The supplier with 70 percent of the business would enjoy economies of scale and should be able to offer a low price. The 30 percent supplier would provide competition—he or she would yap at the heels of the big supplier to keep this supplier "honest" and efficient.

One of the recent drivers toward partnering is found in the Japanese approach to business. Frequently, the Japanese divide the requirement, whether 70/30, 80/20, or 60/40 among two partners. The Japanese frequently use the smaller supplier to discipline the "lead" supplier. If the lead supplier violates cost, quality, or delivery objectives, its volume of business is reduced for the next ordering period.

1. What are the most likely benefits of forming strategic supply alliances or "partnerships" with Sunspot's key suppliers?

    *   The technology of the two firms will complement one another.
    *   This encourages suppliers to invest in R&D, resulting in new, cost effective, and high-quality solutions to the buying firm's needs.
    *   Suppliers are encouraged to invest in equipment training and the appropriate management systems required to be an efficient, low-cost procedure.
    *   All-in-costs tend to be lower.
    *   Suppliers tend to be far more dependable than when receiving business on a sporadic basis.

2. What are the disadvantages or risks of such partnerships?

3. How can these disadvantages be offset?

    a. (2) Since there are fewer transactions, there will be pressure to reduce purchasing's head count.

        (3) Partnerships require more skill and more energy to initiate and manage than do traditional purchase orders. Personnel need to be reallocated—not downsized.

    b. (2) Supply "partners" can become complacent.

        (3) This happened to one of the authors many years ago! In order to avoid complacency, the buyer must actively manage the relationship.

    c. (2) Partnering can weaken leverage (clout).

        (3) The buyer must substitute good management technologies for the beneficial effects of competition.

    d. (2) Purchasing and audit control can be lost.

        (3) Such lost control occurs only in poorly structured and managed partnerships.

    e. (2) Early success can lead to overuse of the concept.

        (3) Not every product or commodity class lends itself to partnerships. Purchasing must exercise judgment on a case-by-case basis.

    f. (2) Every supplier wants to be your partner.

        (3) This sometimes appears to be the case, but many suppliers do not possess the capabilities or the willingness to become partners. Further, many requirements may not lend themselves to partnerships.

TEMPLETON ENGINE COMPANY

Purpose

This case introduces some of the complexities involved in dealing with a single-source supplier and some proven techniques for handling such situations.

Discussion

A single- or sole-source negotiation is a very challenging one, especially when the supplier is aware of its position. Under such conditions, the buyer's bargaining power is minimal. But the professional buyer does have several techniques at his or her disposal which will aid in obtaining a satisfactory price.

Questions 1 and 2:

What alternatives does Neil have? What are the advantages and disadvantages of each?

Comments:

1. Neil could accept the 6 percent increase.
   + He can go about business as usual and concentrate on maintaining the quality of cutting tools. The supplier will not have to take time away from daily operations to conduct potentially time-consuming cost analysis.
   − Precision Cutting Tools may feel that it has carte blanche to raise prices on any pretext. Mr. Carlson will have to explain to his boss why he chose not to investigate Precision Cutting Tool's request for a price increase. Templeton may eventually become less competitive with other jet engine manufacturers as a result of its inability to hold costs down. This loss of competitive edge may result in a loss of market share.

2. Neil can request that Precision provide a cost analysis supporting each element of cost that makes up its price. A cost justification review is mandated by government requirements placed on Templeton.
   + Such an analysis will ensure that Precision is charging only direct and indirect costs necessary for performance of Templeton's work and that the costs and rates are reasonable and are supported by fact. The analysis also will indicate the magnitude of Precision's profit rate.
   − The analysis may show that the *costs* and *profit* are fair and reasonable. But the analysis will not indicate if the *prices* are reasonable and competitive. Price analysis will be required to do this.

3. Purchasing research should be conducted to identify past and projected changes in the tooling industry. Items to be analyzed include prices, costs of inputs, capacity utilization, new suppliers, likely future demand, and so on.
   + This analysis will aid Mr. Carlson both in determining his course of action and in preparing for likely negotiations with Precision.
   − Cost of the research. Hopefully, Templeton has a dedicated purchasing research staff which will relieve Mr. Carlson of this task.

4. Conduct an internal value management review. A team representing purchasing, manufacturing, and design engineering should conduct a value analysis of the tooling. For example, are specified materials, processes, and tolerances realistic? If present relations or when future relations warrant, Precision should have representation on the V.A. team.

    + It is entirely possible that this V.A. study will identify areas of significant savings.

    − The study requires the assignment of already overworked professionals. In the long term, it may be appropriate to hire a dedicated value engineer.

5. Conduct a make-or-buy analysis.

    + It may be less expensive to make the tooling than to buy it from Precision at the new prices. Further, the study will help convince Precision that Templeton is determined to hold costs down.

    − The manufacture of tooling is a highly specialized business. In all probability it would not be practical for Templeton to enter this vastly different type of manufacturing operation for the volume of tooling it uses.

6. Conduct a search for acceptable competitors.

    + Precision will learn of this activity and may change its plans for the price increase.

    + New attractive sources may be identified.

    − Significant time and administrative costs will be incurred if Templeton decides to change sources.

7. Have Templeton's president or other senior manager call on Precision's president, discuss the desirability of a long-term collaborative relationship and multiyear contract which includes a mechanism for dealing with changes in Precision's costs.

    + The offer of a multiyear contract is a proven means of becoming a preferred customer.

    − This approach negates the possibility of identifying new sources which may have better technology, quality, and/or prices.

Question 3:

What should Neil do?

Comment:

Neil has only 60 days to take action. He should develop an integrated solution consisting of alternatives 2 through 6, as time permits. If he becomes satisfied that Precision's price increase is reasonably well justified, he should pursue alternative 7, preferably within 30 days. (To wait much longer would further weaken his president's position at the proposed meeting of presidents.)

THREE VENDORS AND A TUB

Purpose

The purpose of this case is to discuss the relationship among sales forecasts, engineering cost estimates, value analysis, and effective negotiation.

Question 1:

What factors must Charlie consider now?

Comment:

Because Charlie initially failed to prepare adequately for negotiations, a thorough review of the tub requirement is necessary before he can go back back to the suppliers for negotiation. Here are some of the factors Charlie must consider and how he should prepare for and conduct negotiations:

a. Determine from management how large a quantity commitment Rub-A-Dub is prepared to make on the basis of the marketing department forecasts. The quantity is extremely important in persuading suppliers that they must assume, along with Rub-A-Dub, some of the risks of the new washer. There is $8 million in sales for the supplier on just the first year's production of 50,000 washers alone, and a potential of $112 million over four years. Purchasing must have commitment authorization based on the best available sales estimates in order to use the negotiating leverage that this large purchase gives it.

b. Review all pertinent issues and data with the three suppliers and Rub-A-Dub's sales and engineering people. It is important to be certain everyone understands the quotation and specifications.

c. Reject all bids. This move is necessary to allow redesign and to open future bidding to other suppliers who may be likely prime or secondary sources.

d. Value analysis. Through value analysis, consider possible tub redesign into a more economical unit by changing materials, using existing tooling, more liberal tolerances, and so on. At this point, ask suppliers for cost reduction suggestions and invite them to participate in tub value analysis activities.

e. Cost analysis. Analyze the cost of the tub into the various cost elements of materials, labor, tooling, set-up and other preproduction costs, factory and administrative overhead, and freight and packing costs.

f. Make or buy. Since certain changes may have been made through value analysis, a make-or-buy analysis is in order. Bring in production and engineering people and anyone else whose knowledge would add to the decision. Consideration should be given to manufacturing some parts of the tub and purchasing the balance, with assembly to take place wherever it would be most economical.

g. New quotes. On the basis of changes made during value analysis and with the assistance of cost analysis, new quotes are needed on quantities such as 50,000, 150,000, 300,000 and up, in the authorized commitment range. Invite at least two other suppliers, plus the "old-line suppliers," to submit formal quotations.

Question 2:

How should Charlie prepare for and conduct new negotiations?

Comment:

Armed with the cost analysis and other information gathered, negotiate directly with the two or three suppliers whose quotes look most promising. They key to making this negotiation period most profitable is to plan carefully and:

a. Set definite goals or objectives for each negotiation period.
b. Select those people for your negotiating team that you need to make the plan work.
c. Follow a prepared agenda.
d. Set an advantageous time and place for each meeting.
e. Determine extent of authority of supplier's representative.
f. Use the technique of negotiation presented in Chapter 11 of the text.
g. If the cost goal of $160 cannot be reached, seek a management review to see if the figure which can be reached is acceptable.

THE TIDEWATER GAS AND ELECTRIC COMPANY

Purpose

The purpose of this case is to discuss an habitually weak area of modern purchasing: contract administration expediting.

Discussion

Modern-day purchasing entails three primary responsibilities: (1) participating in the determination of what to purchase, (2) the act of purchasing it and (3) the management of the resulting purchase order or subcontract. In most organizations, the third responsibility receives the least attention. Expediting and contract administration are necessary prerequisites to successful and professional purchasing. Determination of the "right" material to purchase, in the "right" quantity, at the "right" time, from the "right" source, at the "right" price can all go for naught if the resulting purchase order and/or subcontract is not properly managed, i.e., if the material is not available where and when it is needed. Late deliveries, quality problems, and indirect cost increases are the order of the day when expediting and contract administration are ignored or given inadequate attention.

Almost every purchase order or contract requires some degree of management. Each time a purchase order or contract is placed, the buyer should ask himself or herself how critical the purchased material or service is. The degree of criticality should determine the required level of management attention needed. On a simple, noncritical item or service, checking with receiving on the day the item or service is due may be sufficient. On more critical items or services (critical being a function of dollar magnitude or importance to the well-being of the organization), more aggressive management action is necessary. Calls to the supplier, plant visits, and even the placement of an inspector at the supplier's plant may be appropriate.

The situation at TG&E calls for the most intensive level of contract administration. By analyzing and discussing this recommendation, students will gain insight into the complexities of expediting and contract administration.

Question 1:

Explain your understanding concerning the importance of contract administration or contract management. Have you noticed, in the help wanted ads of big city newspapers, that there are always many ads for contract administrators?

Comment:

The terms "contract administration" and "contract management" are used in two significantly different ways. In some firms, the terms refer to individuals who manage or administer contracts under which the firm is doing work for its customer. In other firms, the terms "contract administration" or "contract management" refer to the administration of the firm's contracts with its suppliers. In this text, we use the latter meaning.

Contract administration frequently is as critical a function as is sourcing or pricing. (A major construction firm nearly always pays its expeditors more than it pays its buyers!) Contract administration has the responsibility of ensuring that what is ordered is received on

time, and in the quality specified. The purchasing function is not complete until the goods or services under contract are received.

Virtually all large city newspapers contain want ads for contract administrators. This is a critical function and good contract administrators are always in demand. In many companies, the path to appointment as a buyer and then as purchasing manger begins with a job as an expeditor (generally the lowest level of contract administration).

Question 2:

When does the purchasing department prepare for its expediting responsibilities?

Comment:

Planning and preparing for good expediting and subcontract management begins with the preparation of the Request for Bids. The buyer *must* decide the optimum degree of surveillance and management that is necessary to insure compliance with the terms and conditions of the purchase order or contract. These requirements must be contained in the Request for Bids and in the resulting purchase order or subcontract.

Question 3:

Assume that you are a management consultant. Develop a list of recommendations for TG&E's purchasing management.

Comment:

The consultant's most important recommendation is that the following three provisions regarding contract administration be included in all appropriate bids, purchase orders, and subcontracts:

1. Program plan including:
   a. Program organization chart—This chart shall designate the program manager by name and shall show the key members of his organization by name and function. The program nanager's functional authority shall be clearly defined.
   b. Milestone plan—All major milestones, including those of the supplier and his principle subcontractors, shall be identified on a time-phased basis.
   c. Funds commitment plan—This plan shall show the estimated commitments on a dollar vs. month basis and on a cumulative dollar vs. month basis.
   d. Manpower commitment plan—This plan shall show the estimated manpower loading on a man-hour/month basis.

2. Monthly progress report to be furnished to TG&E 30 days or less after the close of each calendar month. This report shall include:
   a. A narrative summary of work accomplished during the reporting period, a summary of work planned for the next reporting period, problems encountered or anticipated, corrective action taken or to be taken, and a summary of purchaser/supplier telephone discussions and meetings.
   b. A list of all action items required of the purchaser.
   c. An update of the Milestone plan showing actual progress against planned progress.

    d. An update of the funds commitment plan showing actual funds committed against the planned funds by time.

    e. A report on any significant changes in the supplier's program personnel or in the financial or general management structure, or any other factors which affect or might affect the supplier's performance.

3. Missed-milestone notification and recovery plan

    a. Supplier shall notify purchaser by telephone within 48 hours after discovery of a missed major milestone or the discovery of an anticipated major milestone slip.

    b. Supplier shall provide purchaser with a missed-milestone recovery plan within seven working days after the above notification.

In addition to the above, the consultant should include in his list of recommendations some of the practical necessities of contract management. For example, it should be stressed that it is impossible to manage critical complex contracts without the contract administrator's getting out to the plant or job site. Even when inspectors are assigned to monitor the supplier's progress, it is essential that the buyer physically inspect progress once a month, or more frequently.

A TIGHT BUDGET SOLUTION

Purpose

This case provides an opportunity to discuss marketing techniques that border on the unethical approach to business and, at the same time, may have some redeeming features.

Analysis

A seasoned veteran who serves as procurement manager for a large research laboratory was asked to study the case. His analysis is summarized below.

A Blatant Violation

The situation is so blatantly a violation of good business practice as to bring into question why Midwest Tech should do any further business with Condor. This is clearly an offer of a gratuity—if not outright commercial bribery—and should be avoided. If the offer has been communicated to the faculty, a memo disavowing the notice must be sent by Purchasing. Otherwise, it will lead to a rash of sole source requests.

The appropriate institutional response should be a "cease and desist" letter, which says that Midwest expects the value of the frequent-buyer points to be reflected in future prices.

Finally, Joe might seek another field of work. He obviously does not recognize his obligations to the institution paying his salary. On the other hand, management should recognize Joe's concern for and interest in helping his internal customers achieve their mission and fulfill their responsibilities to the institution. This is a laudable attitude for the institution's "team members" to display. However, the poor judgment he used in attempting to achieve this goal should be pointed out and discussed thoroughly with him.

Procurement Manager
A Large Research Laboratory

TOKISAN CORPORATION

Purpose

The purpose of this case is to illustrate a poorly designed purchasing system that is out of control. Additionally, the case exposes problems that can exist when a foreign management style is used in an American environment.

Discussion:

Immediate Issues:

1. What should TAI do with the CFC 111, and what should Jack do to assist in the timely resolution of this problem?
2. How should TAI management assess Jack's performance in this situation?

Basic Issues:

1. What should TAI do to ensure that purchasing policy is applied uniformly in the company?
2. Should TAI continue the "ringi" process, or abandon it for something better? Why didn't it work well in this situation?
3. How can TAI minimize language and cultural differences that can lead to problems?

Key Items to be Considered

- This is a foreign-owned company with a very different corporate culture.
- The top management has traditionally come from Japan.
- Japanese is spoken in the plant.
- Existing communication problems are exaggerated by language and culture barriers.
- Communication difficulties are not only a problem, they are a symptom of a failed process.
- There are two purchasing departments, whose activities are not coordinated, and only one is required to clear with plant safety.
- The purchasing system failed to catch the problem, but then the entire company failed to catch the problem until too late. The "ringi" system is designed to stop faulty purchase requisitions.
- There is no central authority that bears overall responsibility for purchasing activities.
- Environmental regulations were not known or considered.
- The Business Systems group originally was responsible for sales; it is now entering a gray area in terms of its mission and its capabilities.

Possible Student Assignments

1. If you were Jack, how would you try to "fix" the problem?
2. How would you approach the Japanese management?
3. If you were Yoshio, what would you do?
4. If you were Cyrill, how would you address the problem, and what process changes would you suggest?

5. The case can be set up as a role-playing exercise with students playing the characters mentioned. A rubber stamp committee can review and pass the "ringi."

Possible Discussion Questions

1. Given the "ringi" system, who should review purchase proposals, and why?
2. Should one person be responsible, or are decisions made by consensus better? Discuss the benefits and problems with each approach.

How TAI Handled The Problem

TAI spent two years trying to get rid of the 100,000 cans of coolant. In the meantime, the cans collected dust in storage. Because they remained in inventory for two years, there were two years of inventory-handling and storage costs, not to mention the foregone warehouse space that could have been used for other purposes.

Eventually they found someone to collect and use the coolant, but it cost them an additional $4 per can. (They had to pay to get rid of it!) Total cost estimates for this mistake ranged from $700,000 to $800,000.

The purchasing system was modified so that there is now only one *consolidated* purchasing department. The "ringi" system is still used. Decisions are made on a consensus basis with management establishing a general direction and making decisions when long-range plans dictate action. All "ringis" are required to be cleared by plant safety.

TRANSPORTATION SERVICE

Purpose

The purpose of this case is to discuss the issues involved in the purchasing of transportation services.

Discussion

This case provides an opportunity to discuss the issues involved in purchasing transportation services: price, quality, reliability, flexibility, capacity, and Caterpillar's unique certification program.

Question 1:

Develop a checklist of items to be considered when choosing a carrier.

Comment:

Items to be included on the carrier checklist are: price, fleet size, claim rate, delivery time, quality program, safety record, and financial stability of the company. Other items to be taken into consideration are tracking capability, number of employees, and flexibility.

Question 2:

What are the advantages of certifying the carriers?

Comment:

The advantages of certified carriers are the known and consistent quality of carriers' service, the carrier's involvement in planning how to meet the transportation needs, open communication in solving problems, and the use of competitive bidding.

Question 3:

Is price the most important factor in evaluating the carriers? Explain.

Comment:

Price is not the most important factor. Carrier capability and quality of the service is more important. Measures of quality include consistent on-time pick-up/delivery, equipment availability, claim rate, and service to particular locations.

Question 4:

What are the key factors regarding Caterpillar's carrier needs?

Comment:

Caterpillar's carrier needs have stemmed from the problem of damaged equipment incurred during transportation. To solve this problem, Caterpillar established a carrier certification program. This program is imperative to provide reliable and flexible transportation for JIT inventory, as well as providing damage-free products to its customers.

Question 5:

If you were selecting the carrier, what are the alternatives? Which carrier would you choose? Why?

Comment:

Alternatives:

	Carrier X	Carrier Y	Carrier Z
Price	$1.05/ton mile	$1.15/ton mile	$.95/ton mile
Fleet Size	10,000	9,000	9,500
Claim Rate	1.5%	1.0%	1.0%
Quality Prog.	No	Yes	No
P-U/D Time	Avg.	Above Avg.	Below Avg.
Safety Record	–	–	Excellent

Carrier X has the largest fleet; this should provide flexibility. The price is reasonable, however the claim rate is high and it does not have a quality program. Although Carrier Y has a higher price and the smallest fleet, it does have a quality program and a low claim rate. Another strong point for Carrier Y is its above-average pick-up/delivery time, which is a result of its quality program. Carrier Z has an excellent safety record and a comparable claim rate to carrier Y. It also offers the lowest price but its below-average pick-up/delivery time is not acceptable for Caterpillar's JIT inventory program.

Based on the above information, the optimal carrier appears to be Carrier Y. Carrier Y meets Caterpillar's Certification Program Standards. Although Carrier Y's price is high, its quality program will ensure Caterpillar's standard of damage-free equipment and on-time delivery for its JIT program.

UNIVERSAL MOTOR COMPANY
ACQUIRES SEMICONDUCTORS

Question 1:

UMC Concerns*

Top management identified six areas of *Strategic* importance to the firm's survival and future profitability:

I.   Technology Access/Control

II. Quality

III. Supply

IV. Time To Market

V.   Reduced Production Cycle Time

VI. Total Cost Management

*These items of concern are the *"Goals"* of today's Strategic Supply Management initiative.

Question 2:

Problem Statement

How can Universal Motor Company gain continuing access to defect-free state-of-the-art semiconductors in a long-term and optimum way?

Questions 3 and 4:

*Alternative #1**

Look for Foreign Sources:

+ Quality
+ Timeliness
+ Cost savings
+ New technologies

– Impact on U.S. standard of living
– Cultural issues
– Political constraints

*Based on the assumption that UMC is currently working with domestic suppliers only.

Alternative #2

Partner with Another Auto Maker (Buy):

+   Increase purchasing power
+   Reduce redundant operations
+   No investment required
+   Combine professional resources

−   High risk alternative
−   Cultural differences
−   Continued supply problems
−   Loss of control
−   Lose potential competitive advantage based on differentiation in the marketplace

Alternative #3

Make Option:

+   Control over management's six areas of strategic importance
        (quality, testing of packaged devices, defect-free)
+   Specialization (can achieve special packaging)
+   Core technology secured
+   Potential market advantages
+   Technology leadership

−   High risk option
−   Obsolescence
−   High investment (expensive—$50 Mil. for plant alone)
−   Time to market unknown
−   Lack of expertise (design engineers in short supply)
−   Cultural problems
−   Increased organizational complexity
−   Unknown R&D costs
−   High cost strategy (cost: 2–4 times more to produce)

Alternative #4

Make Some, Buy Some (Make: design, test of wafers, test I.C.'s):

+   Technology
+   Time to market
+   Proprietary process
+   Flexibility

−   Cost (2 to 4 X)
−   Investment funds ($50 million)
−   Span of responsibility and control

Question 5:

Recommendation:

Step 1:

Form a separate procurement strategy team for the semiconductor market. Look at needs over the next year or so and forecast purchase requirements for semiconductors. Invest in inventory to avoid production disruptions. Be willing to pay a premium for quality components. Look to other auto manufacturers and/or other industries to fill short-term needs.

Step 2:

Make a long-term investment in one of your suppliers:

1. Form a *Mandate Team*
2. Have the mandate team develop a supply strategy:
    a. Set up *Objectives* before meeting with suppliers
    b. Develop a comprehensive *Business Plan* (including an incentive program)
    c. Develop measurement criteria to decide the potential relationship
3. Analyze the supplier base; current and future*
4. Target 4 – 6 potential suppliers who meet the *Objectives*
5. Establish dialogue and refine selection through measurement criteria (looking at issues like quality, cost management, technology access, etc.)
6. Finalize source selection on the basis of meeting the company's objectives

*The assumption is made that UMC is experiencing a unique situation and that supply for semiconductors is readily available.

Question 6:

- Technology and quality
- Time of design
- Speed to market
- Custom versus standard
- Ownership of technology versus reliance on a supplier for technology
- Fill in the matrix

ACTUAL EVENTS

Universal had many competitors around the world. The competitors took several different approaches to the same problem. One of the competitors decided to integrate (make) the entire process of design, manufacturing, packaging, and testing. This auto firm manufactured about half of its total semiconductor requirements. This was similar to the computer industry. At the time, IBM manufactured well over half of its semiconductor requirements. Apple Computer had decided not to manufacture semiconductors at all. At the other end of the spectrum within Universal's market is another competitor who has, like Apple Computer, decided not to manufacture or design semiconductors, but just to buy semiconductors from the merchant market, and indeed to only buy custom parts that are available to the general market. A third competitor did a bit of both: they both made and bought custom and standard I.C.'s.

Universal's foreign competitors all had different approaches to this problem. Different companies in different countries were doing different things and there did not seem to be a pattern. Interestingly enough, however, moving forward to 1988 or 1989, a pattern does seem to be emerging. Most of the Japanese firms are indeed developing an internal semiconductor design and manufacturing capability. This is strange, given the fact these Japanese manufacturers have such outstanding relationships with their semiconductor and electronic suppliers, whom in many cases they own, or in which they have a strong equity position. In Europe, many of the auto firms also have a very strong equity position in their semiconductor and high-tech suppliers and the actual movement towards owning these firms and integrating this technology has been increasing over the past few years. There obviously is some trend forming after, let's say, 1985, but this was unknown to the researchers back in 1982.

Universal long felt that it would be a better idea to use customer parts that were custom manufactured for its specific requirement for two reasons: (1) this was a more efficient way to implement Universal applications, (2) Universal engineers thought that by using custom integrated circuits they could hide what they were doing with the electronics of the vehicle from their competitors. Trying to reverse engineer what Universal would do with custom integrated circuits was extraordinarily difficult.

As noted in the case, the firm that decided to manufacture integrated circuits would be taking a very high cost strategy. It's very possible that these circuits would cost two to possibly three or four times as much as the automobile company that decided to buy standard circuits. Evidently Universal managers decided that this cost penalty was worthwhile. They felt that the quality they could guarantee themselves and the technology that they could apply to their vehicles was worth a price penalty.

After much study and after many months of research, the team started to develop final recommendations. These recommendations took some unanticipated twists and turns. They agreed with the observation that the entire process did not have to be integrated, that they should integrate (make) the design portion of the semiconductor process, and that they should integrate (make) part of the testing and all of the tests of integrated circuits. In order to implement this recommendation, they would buy, or build up from scratch, a wholly owned subsidiary that would hire design engineers from the semiconductor industry and begin the task of designing circuits for Universal Motors. They then would expand the operation to include the testing of critical circuits that Ajax Motors had decided would require this additional level of quality testing.

The second piece of this puzzle was a series of strategies that included the supply base for semiconductors. It became perfectly obvious, once the first phase of the strategy was thought through, that there was a very large hole in this strategy having to do with the semiconductor manufacturing process technology. Once a design is started or committed, the sourcing of that

design has been set, since the design must begin by using design rules that are aimed at a particular supplier's process. Throughout the design process, the sourcing is "fait accompli." Once the product is designed, there is probably only the one fabricator in the world that can manufacture it. Therefore, it is, for all practical purposes, sourced, regardless of whether purchasing wanted to source it somewhere else or not.

Additionally, the design engineers could not handle or comprehend all the various kinds of manufacturing process technologies that would be available. Therefore, they would have to select a certain subset of these manufacturing design technologies that they would use in the design of semiconductors. This realization drove the idea of reducing the supply base to only those suppliers that would be selected to have their design rules and process manufacturing technologies included in the design phase of Ajax Motors' future plans. This produced both good news and bad news.

The good news was that by reducing the supply base, the relative value of Universal's purchases to a smaller subset of suppliers would be much greater. This would improve Universal's clout. This financial incentive would reward and incentivize the suppliers selected to give license agreements and process manufacturing technology to Universal for it to use in its designs.

Who should be in and who should be out of the supply base? This decision now reads on economic and technology considerations, because once these decisions are made they're relatively long-term in duration.

The bad news of the decision to downsize the supply base concerned risk. If Supplier A was picked instead of Supplier B, Universal wanted to be sure that Supplier A would have the technology going forward that Universal Motors would require for its vehicles. It would be very bad news indeed to wake up two or three years later and find that Universal had to buy products from Supplier B because Supplier A's technology would not meet its needs. This forced another piece of the strategy to be developed, which had to do with the technology road map. Universal scientists and engineers were sent off to develop a complete understanding of the technology requirements, as specifically as possible. Forecasting technology into the future is a hazardous occupation, but it was going to be necessary because those thoughts and ideas had to be incorporated into the plan so that the proper supplier selection could take place.

Last but not least was the burdensome issue of actually negotiating the legal requirements of these contracts to protect both buyer and seller with regard to the technology transfers, patent indemnification, warranties, liabilities, consequential damages, and issues that would have to be resolved between the firms prior to starting work.

There is another issue that needs to be addressed: selection of the supplier base. The first thing, of course, that has to be done is that every supplier in the world that manufactures or has the capability of manufacturing the products that Universal is interested in has to be identified. Every single one of these firms must be identified, every single one of these firms must be researched. Professional supply managers must start from the beginning because if they're going to develop the strategic plan, they cannot make unnecessary assumptions. So, the Universal research team had to exert due diligence on every possible candidate in the world that might supply Universal's needs.

Interestingly enough, this is more complicated than it sounds. Many firms have capabilities, internal to themselves, which they do not offer for sale on the outside. But Universal had to find out who these firms were. Think about this for a second; the firms do not offer these services outside for sale, but they have the capability of doing the work. Universal must identify them as potential suppliers for the purpose of this investigation, because they could be approached and talked with regarding whether or not they might, in the future, like to sell

some of this capability. An example would be IBM, which manufactured semiconductors, but only for its own use. A researcher could possibly fail to put IBM on the list because it is not a merchant semiconductor manufacturer. But in Universal's view, at this time, that would have been a terrible oversight because IBM had the capability to be a supplier. Therefore, it had to be reviewed because Universal executives don't know that IBM would *not* supply their need. Making such a decision for IBM (or another potential supplier) is not fair to Universal or the potential supplier.

Therefore, worldwide identification of all firms possessing the capability was, in execution, an extremely difficult task. After each firm was identified, a series of analyses had to be conducted on it: some financial analysis, as well as scrutiny of trends over time, including a ratio analysis of the firm, measured by standards within its industry; data analysis of R&D spending; a review of the firm's current patent portfolio and its patent portfolio history—which patents it held or lacked, or what its patent position was in the industry; an assessment of technology trends, scientists who worked for the firm, any turnover problems—retention of top scientific people. All this detail work had to be done in an effort to compare one supplier to the next. In addition, and a very complicated piece of this puzzle, every single technology a company offers or has access to must be evaluated. Firm C may have outstanding technology of one type, but mediocre technology of a second type. If Universal *needs* both technologies, obviously Firm C would not be the choice. So even though it may be possible theoretically for Universal to conclude that it could source all of its requirements with one supplier, from a practical point of view, that may not be possible because no one supplier has all the technologies Universal might be interested in. Nor is each potential supplier world-class in every area in which it conducts business or pursues technology. So the technology element, the historical element, and a firm's strength within its industry, both financial and technological, must be reviewed. Another consideration is its corporate attitude toward the auto industry. Has the company established a commitment or an interest in long-term partnership-type relationships within that industry? It is quite possible that the "perfect" supplier for Universal would not welcome the opportunity to serve Universal in a major way. The potential supplier might feel threatened by having such a large portion of business in that particular industry.

VIGARD MANUFACTURING COMPANY

Purpose

The purpose of this case is to discuss the many problems involved in selecting a source of supply, especially when time is short.

Question 1:

If you were Mr. Krause, what action would you take and why?

Comment:

This is an interesting case presenting many issues that should provoke a spirited class discussion. Selection of each possible supplier can be justified with logic. Therefore, differences of opinion among the class as to the best supplier are almost a certainty.

Discussion of the question "What action would you take if you were Mr. Krause?" normally brings forth different viewpoints without any direction from the instructor. For example, if Mr. X, the first student, says he would take Webster, the instructor would ask, "Why, Mr. X, would you take Webster?" After Mr. X gives reasons, the instructor would ask, "Does everyone agree with Mr. X's choice?" Someone invariably has another choice. If not, the instructor could ask Mr. Z, "Why wouldn't you take Bullock?" and so on. This kind of questioning will bring out the considerations for each potential supplier.

The considerations brought out should include:

Webster

For: It is the largest concern. It has excellent facilities and it is well organized. It has plenty of capacity to do the job on time. Also, its hourly rate of $17.60 versus Bullock's $18.00 is the lowest, and its maximum is almost the lowest—$22,500 versus Bullock's $21,000. The company is hungry for business because of losing its big account.

Against: The significant changes in pricing offered are annoying and could cause one to question Webster's ethics. Losing 80 percent of business because a major customer is pulling out is dangerous. This large loss of business could result in bankruptcy for Webster.

Hershey

For: Management is proved. Hourly price is not too high. Has the capacity and facilities to do job. It is more important to get the manual out on time than to save $12,690. It is a smaller company, and therefore easier for a man inexperienced in technical manuals like Krause to deal with.

Against: Guaranteed price is on the high side: $33,750 versus Bullock's $21,000.

Bullock

For: Technically able to do a good job. Has great initiative, ambition, and vision. Lowest guaranteed price and second-lowest hourly price. Good at improving attractiveness of layout and simplifying production. Bullock is very strong in the area of technical display.

Against: No trained staff or going organization. No office space. Source of capital from brother-in-law and so on, could take longer than time available to start production in less than one week.

Other questions for discussion could include the following:

Could Bullock be used as a consultant, or engaged on a retainer basis, so as to take advantage of his capabilities while using a going organization actually to produce the manual? This is a possibility, but it poses problems and probably isn't necessary. The company given the production contract might object to Bullock's advice, contending that their pricing and timing was based on using their methods. On the other hand, consultants are used for many purposes, and when their duties are spelled out friction is minimized.

How important is the manual? It is a selling aid as well as an operating aid. Therefore, improvements in style, format, and so on, could be most helpful. Conversely, a poor display in the manual could kill future sales.

After discussion of the case is complete, ask the class, How many would go with Bullock? Webster? Hershey? Catalogue? Put results on the chalkboard and comment on the fact that we have a "hung jury."

Summarize the case. The summary could well take a form such as this:

"Well, ladies and gentlemen, while there is considerable difference of opinion on the best source, the differences seem to turn only on two main points. First, you are all looking for the source that will give you the best performance. Those of you who like Bullock tend to base your selection on the technical skill, initiative, and ingenuity of Mr. Bullock and reason that he would be able to pull an organization together and get the facilities needed for performance.

"Now, others of you don't want to rely on one man like Mr. Bullock, despite his personal brilliance. You believe that a good organization with experienced management is essential. Some of you choose Webster, because of the facilities, organization, and management knowhow in that company.

"The rest of you distrusted not only Bullock, but also Webster, partly because of the possibility that Webster might fail, and partly because Webster, in revising his bid, appeared to be grasping for straws, to have perhaps some questionable interest. You didn't want to risk inadequate performance and hence turned to Hershey, even though you might be required to pay a premium as high as $12,390.

"The second difference turns on this matter of price. Those of you who selected Bullock and Webster considered a $12,390 savings important, and, in some instances, sufficiently important to warrant the risk of delayed performance. While those of you who selected Hershey either considered the $12,390 savings as unimportant, or believed that the hourly rate was the more important figure, and that Hershey has as much chance as Webster and Bullock of turning out the manual for around $21,200."

WVC INDUSTRIAL CHEMICALS COMPANY

Purpose

This case explores in depth an important aspect of contract administration—the follow-up function and the expediting process. The case deals with the planning of major follow-up activities and also with the handling of a crisis situation after a supplier has failed to perform satisfactorily.

Discussion

Inexperienced buyers too often assume that suppliers automatically will fulfill the promises sales representatives make when a contract is consummated. Experienced buyers know that contract performance must be managed. On the surface, follow-up activities appear to be rather simple and innocuous in nature. In practice, resolution of the detailed problems that threaten satisfactory supplier performance frequently are anything but simple. Compounding this situation is the fact that buyers frequently create their own future expediting problems by failing to realize that their requirements are unrealistic for the supplier, and they frequently do not understand the supplier's operation in sufficient depth to recognize where the potential problems might lie. This case addresses these issues.

Question 1:

What should Jan do now?

Comment:

The following approach and related considerations represent one sensible course of action Jan might follow.

Approach

   a. The first thing Jan must do is to find out what the problem really is that has caused the scrapping of the casting. She needs to be sure that Western understands the cause of the problem and has the ability to bring it under control.
   b. The next step in the process is to discuss with the supplier possible solutions to the problem. Since Jan's objective is satisfactory completion of the contract on time, she should be willing to use WVC's technical talent and resources to help resolve the problem if that is necessary.
   c. If Jan is not already familiar with the production scheduling and operations activities at Western, she needs to find out in reasonable detail what elements of activity make up the twelve-week lead-time requirement that Western quoted. Her obvious concern at this point is how much these activities can be compressed at the present time to bring the two scrapped castings back on schedule. A very logical approach at this point simply is to ask the supplier for his proposed solution that will not result in breach of contract performance.

Considerations

a. The supplier still has four weeks to complete the work on the contract. In all probability, this should be adequate because the supplier already has the patterns made and has had recent experience in working with this particular casting.

b. Jan has a great deal of leverage in dealing with the supplier in this case because:

- When the contract was agreed upon, the supplier literally *guaranteed* that it would meet the twelve-week delivery requirement.

- Jan should be sure that Western is aware of the fact that she is paying a substantial price premium for two reasons: first, because Western agreed to meet her delivery requirements and, second, because Western has performed well for WVC in the past—the two firms have a good ongoing relationship.

c. Jan should work out an acceptable schedule for the work yet to be done on the two castings, and she should require detailed progress reports at least twice a week to ensure that the schedule is maintained. She may also want to call the schedule in between reports just to ensure that the schedule is not slipping. Clearly, the Western scheduler should be willing to rearrange his schedule, and perhaps even to work overtime, to resolve the problem that his organization has created for WVC.

d. Jan should make sure that she discusses with the appropriate sales people in the Western organization possible future business that WVC may want to commit to Western. It should be made clear that Western's performance on the current job will obviously have an impact on the placement of any future business with the firm.

e. These castings are going to be used by WVC to fulfill a preventive maintenance requirement. Consequently, the WVC maintenance superintendent may well be able to rearrange his schedule to give Jan a little more time if it is required. In all probability, the installation of these pump housings is not part of a crisis situation. So Jan may be able to buy some time, if it is absolutely necessary.

f. If the problem with Western appears to be extremely severe, Jan may wish to consider other possible sources. However, this should be a last-resort solution because it will be costly, time-consuming, and frustrating for everyone. The specific questions Jan needs to answer are: (1) Does WVC own the casting patterns? If it does, this obviously will simplify the problem. (2) Can Jan "pull" the patterns from Western without difficulty? How long will it take? (3) What would be the cost and time requirements for other suppliers to pick up the job at this point and complete it for Jan?

Question 2:

If you had been Jan, how would you have handled the follow-up function?

Comment:

The following points are critical in planning the follow-up function properly.

a. At the outset, Jan must be reasonably confident that her lead-time requirement is in fact realistic with respect to the supplier's capabilities. All requirements must be communicated clearly to the supplier, and a genuine meeting of the minds must be achieved at the outset. In some cases, a buyer may have to work with his or her users to modify their requirements schedule to coincide with a realistic lead-time requirement for the supplier.

b. The key to proper follow-up planning is to ask the supplier the right questions.

(1) How much of the supplier's lead time is consumed in the following activities:

- Fitting the new job into the production schedule (waiting your turn)?
- The internal scheduling process?
- Actual production operations—pattern making, casting, and machining?

(2) Questions about operating details of the production processes—casting operations and machining operations. The things a buyer must learn at this point in the process in a very realistic way are the potential problems that a supplier anticipates in the various steps of the manufacturing processes that may produce significant schedule slippages. It is critical that a buyer understand enough about these details to assure himself or herself that the supplier either has the situation under control, or can adequately handle the types of problems that may occur.

c. Finally, as the contract nears consummation, the buyer should effectively preplan appropriate follow-up dates. Periodic progress reports should be required—and details should be worked out ahead of time with the appropriate supplier personnel. If the job is costly or critical, the buyer or a buying organization team should make on-site visits to see firsthand how the job is progressing. The status of each part of the job should be reviewed carefully—e.g., design, material acquisition, casting, and machining.

Concluding Comment:

To perform the follow-up function effectively, the buyer, or expediter, clearly must know the product and the supplier's production operations well. There is no other way to determine with confidence the reliability that can be attributed to the information received from the supplier. In the final analysis, there must be a mutual understanding and trust between the two parties.

THE WIDE, WIDE WORLD OF PURCHASING

Purpose

This case discusses several key issues involved when considering foreign sources of supply.

Discussion

Well over one-half of buyers in America purchase materials of foreign origin. Quality, timely availability, and cost are factors in such decisions. But purchasing from foreign sources raises problems and issues not encountered when buying from domestic sources.

Question 1:

What key issues, figures, and information should Charlie obtain?

Comment:

1. Because Charlie has only two weeks to study the whole cost-reduction problem, of which foreign buying is only a part, he cannot use lengthy procedures such as a test order. He should at least take the following steps:
   a. Request top-level clarification of policy on buying from foreign sources. Issues to be considered would include possible local political and labor problems, additional investment in inventory to cover the longer supply pipelines, and possibly sales difficulties to government or other customers with limits or exclusions on foreign components.
   b. Point out alternatives to foreign sources that might bring equal or greater overall price savings. These could include adding additional U.S. sources to bring prices down through competition, redesign of component, and value analysis with current or potential future suppliers.
   c. Review commercial and transportation problems with a purchasing agent familiar with import procedures so that Ruggles can at least be prepared to give management an idea of the problems involved.
   d. Check out technical problems with the foreign company's representative on standards, tooling, inspection, and packaging. This might include a request for samples of similar products for inspection. Get estimates for a trial order sample.
   e. Begin to check possibilities of adding U.S. sources to inject competition into the purchase and bring down the price. The present sole-source position of Newton is poor purchasing policy, and other American sources may give a lower price without the risks and extra inventory investment that foreign buying would entail.
   f. Offer a thorough value analysis program, along with additional sources, as an alternative to foreign buying. This will require top-management approval and extensive cooperation between purchasing, engineering, other departments, and present and possible suppliers.
   g. After preliminary cost analysis and management approval, proceed with a trial order for the component. Work out cost, inventory investment, and savings figures based on awarding, say, 10 percent, 25 percent, and 50 percent of the component purchases to foreign suppliers. Do not figure on awarding all the business to any one supplier, foreign or domestic. Make any contract subject to full approval of a trial run of the component delivered in the U.S.

Question 2:

What sources should Charlie use for his information?

Comment:

Charlies should investigate the reliability of the foreign supplier by checking its U.S. customers for quality, pricing, and delivery information. Newton's bank and Dun & Bradstreet can give information on Eurofabrik's financial resources, and Department of Commerce reports and the country's commercial or trade mission can supply general capability information. Ruggles also might seek information and on-the-spot inspection through some of Newton's foreign sales representatives or import-export agents that provide this service.

Ruggles should request the names and addresses of other U.S. firms Eurofabrik does work for and contact the purchasing agents involved. This will probably give him the best information on the quality and reliability of this potential supplier.

Question 3:

What should Charlie recommend?

Comment:

If Charlie finds through his investigation that Eurofabrik is a quality producer and can be relied upon to meet delivery schedules, he should recommend a trial order. The possibility of a substantial cost reduction in the total product cost cannot be ignored.

WORLD-WIDE INDUSTRIES

Purpose

This case discusses three items: how to get good pricing while negotiating for a second source of supply, the disadvantages of the "second look" in competitive bidding, and development of a new buyer.

Discussion

The solution to this case hinges on the distinction between competitive bidding and negotiation as methods for determining the right price. If the five criteria (see Chapter 10) exist for using competitive bidding, then this method of pricing should be used. However, if the competitive bidding method of pricing were used, Miss Baxter's position would be correct. To allow a "second look" at prices arrived at by the competitive bidding method of pricing is unfair to competing suppliers. In the long run, such practice is certain to increase costs to the buyer.

Suppliers quickly learn when buyers resort to second looks. For these buyers, unreasonably high prices are bid initially because it is known that additional bids will be requested. Suppliers are ever hopeful the bidding will stop at some point before their lowest offers are made. On the other hand, when suppliers know that they will be given only one opportunity to bid, they have no alternative to offering their lowest possible price on the first bid.

If the five criteria for competitive bidding do not prevail, then the purchase is being conducted as a *negotiation* and Mr. Hackman's position is correct. Moreover, as indicated in the case, the housing being purchased is for a new item to be introduced into the power-mower line. In such a situation a sales forecast would normally be made which would be expected to vary within a wide range. Therefore, because of these uncertainties, negotiation seems to be the more appropriate method of pricing for this contract.

It should be noted that under the competitive bidding method of pricing, the bids are the final step in the purchase. Under negotiated pricing, bids (or quotations, as some call them) are only the *initial* step. Discussion, analyses, and further bidding take place after this first step. The case speaks of quotations, and much other information given in this case, such as the buyer-and-seller discussion of the drawings and specifications, indicates that the sellers were aware that this was a negotiated purchase, not a competitive bid purchase.

Question 1:

Why was Mr. Hackman able to reduce the price? How did he know it was realizable?

Comment:

Mr. Hackman obviously knew his suppliers well and was accustomed to doing business in the manner described. He also apparently was certain that discussion with both suppliers, after analysis of the first bids, would develop the Tipton Machine Company as an alternate source before he requested any of the companies to bid, and he allowed them a second opportunity to be the "low bidder." While the decision to develop an alternate source has merit, the method used could leave Mr. Hackman open to criticism. If he did not wish Troy to have the contract, he should not have allowed them to incur the time and expense of bidding. He should have

removed them from the bidder's list for this purchase. Any inquiry from the Troy Iron Works concerning the reasons for not being allowed to bid could have been answered directly and satisfactorily by saying the buyer desired, in accordance with good business practice, to develop an alternative source. The only internal justification Mr. Hackman could use for allowing Troy to bid is that historically they had always been low bidder and he wished to use them as a gauge for determining when the lowest possible price was reached. Because of the very large amount of business presently given to Troy, this normally unacceptable practice might have been considered acceptable to Mr. Hackman on a one-time basis.

Question 2:

Did Mr. Hackman treat Miss Baxter fairly?

Comment:

No, Mr. Hackman did not treat Miss Baxter fairly. She is new on the job and is an assistant to Mr. Hackman who needs his help. His actions undoubtedly will tend to antagonize Miss Baxter and prevent the warm, personal relationship that should exist between a buyer and his or her boss.

Mr. Hackman should have explained the entire problem to Miss Baxter, together with his strategy for solving the problem, in his initial discussion of this assignment. After explaining the problem, Mr. Hackman should have instructed and worked with Miss Baxter in each step of the negotiations. Miss Baxter especially needs instruction concerning the distinctions between competitive bidding and negotiation as methods of pricing.

Question 3:

Can this type of buying approach be broadly applied to all commodities and industries?

Comment:

The buying approach illustrated in this case cannot be broadly applied to all commodities in all industries. Different industries, companies, and buyers within the same company employ different negotiation techniques. In some instances, unhealthy practices such as giving a second look to favored suppliers is permitted on competitive bids.

Essentially, the case under discussion involves a nonstandard product for which a major investment in tooling must be made preliminary to production. Total volume of production needed could not be estimated accurately as no one could know with certainty how well the new power mower would sell after its introduction to the market. The company estimated there would be considerable volume over the next 12–18 months. Because of these facts (uncertainty of design and exact quantity needed), costs could only be estimated. Mr. Hackman apparently assumed rightly that the estimates of costs in the first bid would initially include some contingencies which could come out on a second round of bidding after suitable negotiation and discussion of all facts attending the purchase.

Question 4:

Do you believe that Mr. Hackman or Miss Baxter was right is disregarding the high initial bids submitted by the third and fourth companies?

Comment:

Generally speaking on competitive bid purchases, if any bidder is invited to submit a second bid, all bidders should be so invited. However, on clearly specified negotiated purchases, such is not the case. In these situations, the buyer generally negotiates only with the lowest bidders after analyzing the initial quotations. This kind of action is most common when there is a large price spread between the low and high bidders. In fact, to save negotiating time, effort, and cost, many buyers use the first quotations as the means for sorting the interested from the not-so-interested suppliers.

Examples of
Student-Developed Case Analyses

A STUDENT-DEVELOPED ANALYSIS FOR
THE MUENSTER PUMP COMPANY

I. Major Facts

1. *The Muenster Pump Company* has manufactured **high quality** agricultural pumps for over forty years.

2. The company's **only plant** is located in the **small midwestern city** of Muenster.

3. The company is Muenster's **largest employer**.

4. **Bob Dorf**, president of the firm, is the **grandson** of the **founder**, Emil Dorf.

5. **Bob** and his family, along with **key personnel**, live in or near the **city**.

6. **Cordial relations** exist between the firm and the **city fathers**.

7. Since its founding, the company has always been as **self-sufficient** as possible.

8. Shortly after setting up business, Emil Dorf had **established a foundry** to cast pump housings and related items.

9. The foundry provides virtually **all** of the required **pump housings**.

10. Bob Dorf's cousin, **Terry**, is the **purchasing manager** for Muenster Pump.

11. After graduating from State University, **Terry** had worked as a **buyer** at a **large appliance manufacturer** in the southwest corner of the state. After two years of this work, Terry had **returned to Muenster**.

12. **Bob** had been **delighted** to have her back and **established** the **position** of **purchasing manager** by **consolidating** the buying **functions previously** performed by **him** and **other members** of the firm.

13. The **internal organization** of The Muenster Pump Company is the following:

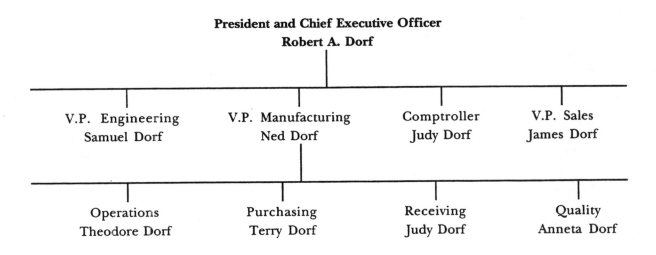

14. Terry *reports* to her Uncle Ned, who is the *vice president for manufacturing*.

15. Terry is an aggressive and conscientious buyer. She has *reduced material costs* from 60 percent of cost of sales to 50 percent in the two years since she assumed responsibility for purchasing.

16. Recently a *representative of Union Foundry*, a firm located in the southeast part of the state, called on Terry. The representative knew that Muenster Pump made its own cast pump housings. He claimed that *new developments in casting pouring* allowed his firm to offer extremely *attractive prices*.

17. Terry requested a *price* on the *L-1012 casting housing*, Muenster's popular size.

18. The L-1012 represents *60 percent* of Muenster's *demand* for casting housings.

19. The *pump* which incorporates the *L-1012* is sold to distributors for *$500*.

20. In a week a letter arrived from Union Foundry quoting a *price* of *$90 FOB Muenster*.

21. *Delivery* would be *120 days* after receipt of the *first order*, and *60 days* after receipt of all *additional orders. Minimum orders* were established as *100 units*.

22. Terry contacted *two* other *foundries* and obtained *quotations* for the L-1012 housing. The quotes were *$94* and *$98* FOB Muenster.

23. Terry met with her *Uncle Ned*, discussed her findings with him and asked how much it *cost Muenster to produce the casting housings in its own foundry*.

24. *Ned* was *not enthusiastic* about Terry's efforts in this area of the business.

25. Ned informs Terry that there is *more to this situation* than is apparent. The company produces a *quality housing* which is *not equaled in the industry*. He feels this is one of the primary *keys* to the firm's *success*! He also feels that the firm can *respond* to requirements *"much quicker than those city boys."*

26. Terry asks Ned if they assume *all his doubts could be overcome*, how much does it cost the firm to make the housing? Ned replies that there is *something else* involved. There are *16 men working* in their *foundry*, and if they stop making their own housings, they would have to *close down the foundry*. There is *no place*, he feels, in the company where these *men could work*.

27. At this point, Terry decides to *end the discussion* with her Uncle Ned and to return to her office.

28. Later that day *Bob Dorf* stopped by to see Terry. She *learned from him* that the *L-1012 housing cost* Muenster about *$180. Total overhead* was calculated to be approximately *200 percent*; therefore, *direct costs* for *materials and labor* for the housings would be about *$60*. Approximately *70 percent* of the *OH* is for *fixed costs* such as depreciation, taxes and executive salaries.

29. *Comparison of Relevant Costs:*

	Make	Buy
D.L & Materials	$60	
Variable OH	36	
Fixed OH that can be avoided by not making	0	
TOTAL RELEVANT COSTS	$96	$90

II. Major Problem

The Muenster Pump Company wants to maintain or increase profits by reducing production costs. One factor to consider is whether to continue making in-house or to buy outside the cast pump housings for the agricultural pumps.

III. Alternatives

1. The Muenster Pump Company can continue to operate exactly as in the past—maintain the status quo.

2. The Muenster Pump Company can buy the cast pump housings from Union Foundry and close its own foundry, laying off the foundry workers.

3. The Muenster Pump Company can buy the cast pump housings from Union Foundry and close its own foundry, but keep the foundry workers and retrain them.

4. The Muenster Pump Company can continue to make its own cast pump housings but with new equipment and technology.

5. The Muenster Pump Company can buy the L-1012 cast pump housings from Union Foundry, which is 60 percent of its housing requirements, and keep its foundry to make the other 40 percent. It can use the foundry's unused capacity to do subcontract work for other firms.

6. The Muenster Pump Company can buy the L-1012 cast pump housings from Union Foundry, which is 60 percent of its housing requirements. It can keep its foundry to make the other 40 percent with the idea that over a certain period of time it will lower the production of the foundry with the intention of eventually closing it.

7. Independent of the make-or-buy decision taken on the cast pump housings, the Muenster Pump Company should reorganize in order to create an integrated procurement system.

Assumptions

1. The decision to make or buy the cast pump housings will be a decision for *top management* with input from several departments such as production, purchasing, engineering, finance and marketing.

2. Terry, the purchasing manager, has performed an in-depth analysis or *preaward survey* of the prospective suppliers, including Union Foundry, and has found that these firms meet Muenster's standards.

3. The company is in a *strong financial position*. Sales are high and the company has little debt.

4. The *foundry equipment is old*. It has not been updated.

5. The company has *good labor relations*. There is *no union*.

6. Some of the *foundry workers* have been with the company a long time and are *near retirement*.

7. The $6 difference between the make and buy decisions represents *6.25 percent* ($6/$96) of the *cost of production*. This is a significant percent of costs.

8. *Ned Dorf*, vice president of manufacturing, *resents Terry Dorf*, the purchasing manager, because she was given some of his previous functions.

9. Muenster has not made a *quality analysis* to determine if its cast pump housings are "*over qualified*." Why is it that no other foundry supposedly produces housings of this quality? Is this level of quality really necessary?

Alternative 1

The Muenster Pump Company can continue to operate exactly as in the past—maintain the status quo.

Advantages

+ *Save jobs* in the short run
+ Not relying on *outside suppliers*
+ No *capital investment*
+ Maintain *cordial community relations*
+ Maintain pride in *self-sufficiency*
+ Assurance of *present quality*
+ No time and money spent on *contract expediting*
+ Maintain *good labor relations* with workers
+ No decision on what to do with *idle foundry*
+ Low position on *learning curve*

Disadvantages

- *More expensive*. It costs Muenster $6 more to make the cast housings than to buy them.
- *Loss of competitiveness*. Muenster is not taking advantage of latest technological advances; therefore, it will fall behind in technology and possibly not be able to lower production costs.

Alternative 2

The Muenster Pump Company can buy the cast pump housings from Union Foundry and close its own foundry, laying off the foundry workers.

Advantages

+ The *cost* of the pump housings will be $6 *less* than if it makes them.
+ *More competitive.* Muenster will be taking advantage of the latest technological advances.
+ *No capital investment*
+ *Save jobs* in the long run

Disadvantages

- *Bad labor relations*
- *Loss* of community *goodwill*
- *Expense* of *expediting* contract
- *Finding backup source* in order not to rely solely on Union Foundry
- *Loss* of pride in *self-sufficiency*
- *Lack of experience* in *negotiating* contracts
- *Internal staff problems*—family feud
- Decision on what to do with *idle foundry*
- *Expense* of *laying off* the foundry *workers*

Alternative 3

The Muenster Pump Company can buy the pump housings from Union Foundry and close its own foundry, but keep the foundry workers and retrain them.

Advantages

+ All the *same advantages* as with *Alternative 2*, plus
+ Maintain good *labor relations*
+ Maintain good *community relations*

Disadvantages

- Some *workers* might *not want to retrain,* and this would result in some bad labor relations and loss of community goodwill.
- *Expense of training workers*
- Problems due to *breaking up a group of employees* that have worked together a long time
- Lack of *facilities* to *absorb foundry workers*
- *Disadvantages mentioned in Alternative 2* related to dealing with *supplier*

Alternative 4

The Muenster Pump Company can continue to make its own cast pump housings but with new equipment and technology.

Advantages

+ *Remain competitive* in the long run
+ Maintain and possibly increase *quality*
+ *Decrease production costs* in the long run
+ *Less waste*
+ All of the *same advantages* as with *Alternative 1*, except that capital investment will have to be made and
+ *High position on learning curve overcome*

Disadvantages

- *Expense of acquiring capital equipment* and *new technology*
- *Expense of retraining workers*
- *High position* on *learning curve*
- *Risk* that *overhead* at Muenster is so much *higher than Union* that in spite of new equipment and technology, Muenster might not be able to make it cheaper
- *Worker resentment* of new technology

Alternative 5

The Muenster Pump Company can buy the L-1012 cast pump housings (60 percent of its housing requirements) from Union Foundry and keep its foundry to make the other 40 percent. It could then use the foundry's unused capacity to subcontract work for other firms.

Advantages

- + *Additional revenue* from foundry sales
- + *Increase expertise*
- + *Hire additional workers*
- + *No capital investment*
- + Maintain good *community relations*
- + Maintain good *labor relations*
- + All of the *same advantages as Alternatives 2 and 3* in relation to the L-1012 cast pump housing

Disadvantages

- *Workers* might still *resist changes.*
- *Expense* of changing over to *customer-oriented foundry*
- New image from lack of *self-sufficiency*
- *Deplete managerial* and **financial** resources
- *Disadvantages mentioned* in *Alternative 2* related to dealing with *supplier*

Alternative 6

The Muenster Pump Company can buy the L-1012 cast pump housings from Union Foundry, which is 60 percent of its housing requirements. It can keep its foundry to make the other 40 percent with the idea that over a certain period of time it will lower the production of the foundry with the intention of eventually closing it.

Advantages

- + All the *same advantages of Alternative 5* with the *exception* that there would not be any foundry revenue or increased expertise in foundry work or additional hiring of workers
- + *More competitive agricultural pumps*
- + Acquire *experience* in *negotiating* and *expediting* contracts
- + *Less workers*—some workers would be retired and jobs would be found for others

Disadvantages

- Some *workers* might still *resent change*
- *Community relations* might *suffer* in short run
- *Expense* of *retraining* some of the workers

 — *Expense* of *expediting* contract
 — *Lack of experience* in *negotiating* contracts
 — *Internal staff problems*—Uncle Ned
 — *Lack of experience* in dealing with *suppliers*
 — *Expense* in *retiring* some workers before time

Alternative 7

Independent of the make-or-buy decision taken on the cast pump housings, the Muenster Pump Company should reorganize its purchasing department in order to create an *Integrated Procurement System.*

To develop an Integrated Procurement System, Muenster should create a materials management department which would be on the same line level as engineering, manufacturing, comptroller and sales. Operations, purchasing and receiving would report to materials management. Quality would be a staff activity on a separate level, as shown in the following diagram.

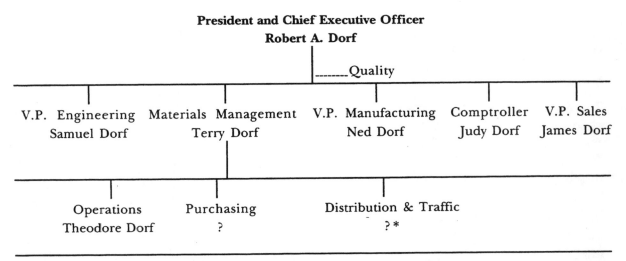

President and Chief Executive Officer
Robert A. Dorf

_____Quality

V.P. Engineering	Materials Management	V.P. Manufacturing	Comptroller	V.P. Sales
Samuel Dorf	Terry Dorf	Ned Dorf	Judy Dorf	James Dorf

Operations — Theodore Dorf   Purchasing — ?   Distribution & Traffic — ? *

*Muenster should consider having two different people as Comptroller and Distribution & Traffic. At present, Judy Dorf covers both positions.

An organization has the best degree of control over the cost of purchased goods and services when the various departments involved in the process operate as an *interdependent, integrated system.* The Integrated Procurement System begins in design engineering when concepts calling for alternative materials are being considered for the products. It continues as specifications are adopted. Before the first item is manufactured or purchased, the most critical make-or-buy analysis should take place. There should be further analysis of the make-or-buy decision during the manufacturing process or purchasing of an item. Make-or-buy decisions should be part of the *continuing strategic planning* process.

Value analysis techniques should be incorporated into the Integrated Procurement System since this allows the elimination or modification of anything that contributes to the cost of an item or task but is not necessary for required performance, quality maintainability, reliability or interchangeability. It is at this point that Muenster should make a decision on the quality of the cast pump housings to ensure that they are of required quality. Too low a quality will lose customers, and too much quality might increase costs unnecessarily.

The other departments will also feed their inputs to purchasing, and purchasing will return their ideas to these departments. It is an *interactive process*. It is a broad, pervasive, united effort which involves all the major departments of the firm.

There is usually some *resistance to change* in any organization, and in this case it is safe to assume that Ned Dorf will be one of the individuals who will offer resistance. He has assumed the position that the way the company is performing is the only way for it to perform successfully, and any changes he sees as threats to its success. Resistance from him and anyone else must be dealt with in the best manner possible. This is not an easy task.

It is of course necessary that the *president*, Bob Dorf, *support* the Integrated Procurement System. Without his support it would be very difficult to implement it. If he supports it, this will serve as an example to the other employees. The positive effects of the Integrated Procurement System could be shown with examples, such as the fact that a 10 percent decrease in material costs is one of the most feasible ways to double the profits of the firm.

The *implementation* of an *Integrated Procurement System* should be *handled* very *carefully*. Muenster is a successful company. Changes should be made in order to create a more successful company, not to adversely affect its performance.

IV. Choice and Rationale

Alternative 1

The Muenster Pump Company can continue to operate exactly as in the past—maintain the status quo.

For the Muenster Pump Company to continue to operate as it has in the past is a *potentially very dangerous situation*. In the first place, it seems to be more expensive for Muenster to make its own cast pump housings than to buy them from Union Foundry. The $6.00 difference in the make-or-buy alternatives would have to be weighed against the other expenses that would be incurred by no longer making them in the firm, such as laying off workers, retraining workers, expediting contracts, loss of community goodwill, etc. It is possible that these costs would lower the $6.00 difference significantly.

However, what seems to be the *deciding factor against* choosing this alternative is the fact that Muenster will become *less competitive* if it does not take advantage of the technological developments in its field. Some other company might do so and begin to produce a better quality pump at a lower price. This would affect Muenster's sales, market share and therefore profit. In the long run this could *threaten the survival* of the company. It is too great a risk for Muenster to take.

Alternative 2

The Muenster Pump Company can buy the cast pump housings from Union Foundry and close its own foundry, laying off the foundry workers.

This alternative has some *attractive points*. Muenster would be taking advantage of lower costs, and it would continue or increase its competitive base with the new technology. There would be some expense in negotiating and expediting the contract, which might reduce the $6.00 difference somewhat, but it would probably still be profitable.

The *negative factor* that must be considered in this alternative is the *effect* that this decision would have on the *workers, townspeople and family members*. To what extent would this decision

affect the relations between Muenster and its workers and neighbors? The reaction against Muenster might be very negative. It is possible that this negative reaction could be overcome or countered with the implementation of a worker incentive program, such as a profit-sharing plan, or some other similar idea.

This decision would create *problems* between the *Dorf family members* who run the company, and it very possibly could be a serious threat to the proper functioning of the company. For these reasons and the fact that the Dorf family has lived in this town for at least three generations, Muenster would probably not want to take this kind of action against the workers unless there were no other alternative, which there does seem to be.

Alternative 3

The Muenster Pump Company can buy the pump housings from Union Foundry and close its foundry, but keep the foundry workers and retrain them.

This alternative sounds like the *ideal alternative.* Muenster would get the best of both worlds: new technology, lower costs, the ability to maintain or increase competitiveness, avoidance of unpleasant labor and community relations. The only expenses would be that of retraining the workers and the expense of negotiating and expediting the contract.

However, this alternative is *dependent* on whether it is actually *possible* for Muenster to *retrain* and *keep* the displaced workers. Ned Dorf's statement as to the fact that there was no other place in the company to use these workers might possibly be true. Or it might be that the company can find a place for some of the workers but not all sixteen of them. Since *ideal situations do not usually occur in reality*, it is safe to assume that it would probably not be possible to retrain and keep all sixteen workers. Muenster would have to lay off most of them, and then the company would be back in the same situation as in Alternative 2.

Alternative 4

The Muenster Pump Company can continue to make its own cast pump housings but with new equipment and technology.

In choosing this alternative, Muenster would *remain competitive* in the long run. The workers would have to be retrained to use the new equipment and the new technology, but eventually they would maintain or better the quality of the housings and lower the cost of production. Muenster would avoid the problems associated with laying off the workers.

However, there are many problems that would develop in choosing this alternative. Muenster would have the expense of retraining the workers plus substantial capital and technological investments to make. The workers might resent the changes and put up barriers to the new technology. The company would have to start high on the learning curve and lose some of its competitive edge in the short run. Muenster's *overhead costs* are so much higher than that of a small foundry such as Union that in spite of the new equipment and technology, it might *not be able to make the housing cheaper*. There is also the *risk* that the *new equipment and the new technology* might again in a few years become *obsolete*, and then Muenster would be faced with this same situation again, except that now the company would be in *debt* for the capital expenditures it had made before.

Buying new foundry equipment and technology puts *heavy emphasis* on the *foundry*, and it is probably not in Muenster's best interest to spend so much in this area. Muenster should *concentrate its efforts and resources* in the area where it is most *successful*, and that is the production of *high-quality agricultural pumps*.

Alternative 5

The Muenster Pump Company can buy the L-1012 cast pump housings from Union Foundry, which is 60 percent of its housing requirements, and keep its foundry to make the other 40 percent. It could then use the foundry's unused capacity to do subcontract work for other firms.

This alternative *combines points from the make decision and the buy decision*. The make decision would keep the company from having to lay off its foundry workers and avoid all the problems related to this action as previously discussed. The buy decision would give the company the advantage of new technology and lower price in its most competitive product.

However, the decision to keep the foundry at capacity production, even though this would produce additional revenue, would place it in an area that is new to the company. This is the area of a *customer-oriented foundry*. The foundry would then have to be in *competition* with other foundries. Eventually the company might have to make *capital investments* to continue to be competitive. The expense involved in changing to this type of foundry business might *deplete* its *managerial and financial resources*. The company might find itself spreading its resources too thin. Thus Muenster might find itself facing the same decisions as in Alternative 4.

Alternative 6

The Muenster Pump Company can buy the L-1012 cast pump housings from Union Foundry, which is 60 percent of its housing requirements. It can keep its foundry to make the other 40 percent with the idea that over a certain period of time it will lower the production of the foundry with the intention of eventually closing it.

This alternative presents all the *advantages of Alternative 5,* and it does not have the disadvantage of Muenster's having to enter a new area of business unfamiliar to it. Also, since Muenster is going to become more competitive with its agricultural pumps due to their lower production costs, it is possible that the company could increase its sales. It might try developing foreign markets for its pumps. This increase in sales might create additional jobs in the company.

Muenster should review each of the *sixteen foundry workers' cases on an individual basis*. Some of the workers are probably at or near retirement age. Others, who are willing to move from Muenster, could be helped by finding other foundry jobs for them. Some could be retrained for other jobs with the company. The thing to remember, and what Muenster must emphasize, is that in order for there to be *jobs in the long run for all the workers, Muenster must remain competitive.* In order for Muenster to remain competitive, it must take advantage of new technologies. In an age of constantly changing technologies, it is better to be able to take advantage of these changes quickly by changing suppliers than to be tied down with large capital investments that may quickly become obsolete.

Muenster should have some kind of information dissemination system so that the workers and townspeople could be aware that Muenster is facing these problems. Muenster might still face a certain amount of worker discontentment and community resentment, but this is a *risk it must take in order to survive.* It is hoped that as time goes on, the workers and townspeople will see that this was the best possible solution under these difficult circumstances.

Aside from making this decision on the foundry, Muenster should *implement* the *Integrated Procurement System* that was previously discussed. The Integrated Procurement System will allow Muenster not only to make this kind of *decision as well as possible, but to consider its possibility even before it is actually faced with it.* The Integrated Procurement System will help make Muenster a better company than before by keeping it current on all levels.

A STUDENT-DEVELOPED ANALYSIS FOR
SELECTION OF A PRESSURE VESSEL MANUFACTURER

Facts Pertaining to the Case

In an attempt to select a supplier for a pressure vessel intended for use in its nuclear system, Oceanics, Inc. must determine which of two suppliers is best equipped to meet the product specifications in the most cost-effective manner.

A committee comprised of the buyer and a design and manufacturer engineer evaluate proposals submitted by Atomic Products Company and Nuclear Vessels, Inc. These are the final two of 18 companies that have submitted proposals for the vessel project.

In addition, as part of its preaward survey, this committee visited the production facilities of each company to review both facilities and meet those responsible for completing the job. It is, however, the buyer's responsibility to present a final recommendation to management.

The facts as they pertain to each of the formal proposals are as follows.

Atomic Products Company

Strengths

- Total price estimate $1,232,000 for labor
- Facilities located in N.Y., close to Pittsburgh locale
- Has equipment as know-how to perform task
- Requires no subcontracting
- Guarantees all workmanship and materials
- Committed to 6-month delivery date

Weaknesses

- Fixed portion of bid $112,000
- Hourly rate $24/hr + 180 percent overhead
- Added 10 percent handling charge to materials
- Has never made a vessel of this dimension
- Did not invite Oceanics to review facilities

Nuclear Vessels, Inc.

Strengths

- Fixed fee of bid $1.00
- Cost per man-hour $16.00 + 160 percent overhead
- Material surcharge avoided
- Extensive experience in this size vessel
- Has produced products for Oceanics before
- Willing to negotiate repair costs
- Invites inspection of facilities

Weaknesses

- Total price estimate $1,560,001
- Will subcontract forgings
- Will ship F.O.B. Houston in six months of *thereafter*
- Guarantees only workmanship. Oceanics will have to absorb plate rejection and repair costs.

After the committee had an opportunity to survey the facilities and meet the management, the facts as they pertain to the preaward survey are:

Atomic Products Company

Strengths

- Manager of production led Oceanics through tour
- Machines new and well maintained
- Felt productivity superior to competition
- Housekeeping excellent
- Laboratories excellent
- QC facilities and inspection state-of-the-art
- Adequate testing facilities
- Atomic is a potential customer as well as supplier

Weaknesses

- Sales representatives have been unable to reach procurement offices despite the fact Atomic is a potential customer.
- President did not appear enthusiastic, in fact, did not tour with the group or answer questions.
- Management seemed immune to the fact they were a top contender for this million-dollar project.
- Production manager expressed concern over the cleaning specifications and indicated a facility would have to be constructed outside the main area.
- Had never contracted for a vessel this size although capacity available.
- President did not meet until end of tour despite advance warning.
- Unwilling to explain end use of several projects in manufacturing.
- No manifest evidence of material control structure.
- President asked Oceanics to "let him know if you want us to do the job."
- Atomic is a union shop with a history of major job strikes.

Nuclear Vessels, Inc.

Strengths

- President offered to pick Oceanics group up from airport and make other travel arrangements
- Held business meeting on the night of group's arrival until 1:30 a.m. at a country club
- Chauffered Oceanics to facility the next morning

- Oceanics met with vice presidents of sales, manufacturing, and engineering, and other key people.
- Had no reservations about meeting any of the specifications
- Had extra equipment available in nearby El Paso plant.
- Never been unionized; employees had profit-sharing plan
- Used task-force approach to follow projects through completion
- Effective control between floor and management
- Experienced construction of larger vessel and adjusted organization according to that experience
- Demonstrated an effective material control organization

Weaknesses

- Machines were older and smaller than Atomic's
- Outside subcontractor or other facility would have to be used to meet tolerance levels required by Oceanics
- General working conditions not as adequate as Atomic's
- Higher estimated cost ($1.56), the result of less adequate equipment

Problem Statement

Failure to select the proper supplier will prevent Oceanics from meeting its implied profit objective for the nuclear system.

Assumptions

At the onset, some items relevant to analysis of this case must be assumed by the reader.

1. Evaluation of the previous 16 proposals was done effectively based on some predetermined criteria.
2. Of the 20 companies invited to submit proposals, some were foreign manufacturers. Those were dismissed on the basis of limited production runs and insufficient repeat business.
3. There can be no shared supplier contracts because of the nature of the item.
4. The limited source of suppliers (2) is insufficient but not within the scope of this analysis to address.

Identifying the Objective

To select the source, the buyer must decide which of the two firms can provide the right quality in the material at the most reasonable price and within the technical and service requirements mandated by Oceanics specifications.

The Options

There are only two options available for meeting the objective outlined. Each has distinct advantages and disadvantages which need exploration.

1. Award the contract to Atomic Products Company.
2. Award the contract to Nuclear Vessels, Inc.

Analyzing the Options

To evaluate the advantages and disadvantages of either option, a set of criteria must be established. Those criteria must address specific areas of concern as reviewed in the preaward tour.

Option 1—Award the contract to Atomic Products Company

A. Equipment and Facilities

Advantages

> + Atomic has the latest machinery for producing the vessel. In addition, it has the better productivity record according to the production management.
> + The facilities are well-organized and clean.
> + All of the machining will be done in the facility.

Disadvantages

> − There is no available space to construct a surgically clean work area to meet the cleanliness specifications required by Oceanics. A temporary facility will have to be built.

B. Production and Quality

Advantages

> + Atomic has satisfied the preaward committee that it's able to meet quality specifications and manpower requirements on smaller vessels.

Disadvantages

> − While the capability to produce larger vessels is in place, Atomic has never received a contract for such.
>
> − Further, in the plant tour, the production manager was unwilling or unable to identify an adequate material control program.

C. Purchasing/Financial Resources

Advantages

> + The Oceanics committee must investigate the financial stability of the Atomic Products Company if a contract is to be awarded. Should there be a problem in this area, raw materials may be unattainable which may be required to finance more than total costs estimated in the proposal.

Disadvantages

> − The Oceanics sales team had been unable to contact the procurement department despite the fact that Atomic was a potential customer.

D. Accounting System

The Oceanics committee did not review this system in its tour of the facility. In the interest of assessing appropriate costs to the vessel project and delineating those from other special jobs in process, however, further investigation is warranted.

E. Managerial

Advantages

+ The production manager conducted the facilities tour.
+ The president said that he would be pleased to meet with the group when they arrived.

Disadvantages

- Atomic's management did not take a marketing approach to this project.
- The president did not meet with the Oceanics committee, despite an appointment, until after the facilities tour.
- Further, the president did not offer to follow through on the proposal.
- Other than the production manager, no other responsible party was visible despite an express desire by Oceanics.

F. Industrial Relations

Advantages

+ Atomic has 2000 unionized employees working under one roof.

Disadvantages

- There have been several major strikes against Atomic in the past few years.
- The production manager implied an inability to "compel . . . workers to wear (garments) to adhere to surgical requirements" within the confines of the building.
- The fixed fee cost of $112,000 and the $24/hr + 180 percent overhead are the direct results of a union shop.

G. Past Performance

Advantages

+ Good with smaller vessels
+ Management boasts a good productivity record

Disadvantages

- There is not track record for projects of this size.

Option 2—Award the contract to Nuclear Vessels, Inc.

A. Equipment and Facilities

Advantages

+ There is adequate equipment for the job.
+ There is additional equipment in an El Paso plant.
+ Facilities clean.
+ There is adequate room for the cleaning facility.

Disadvantages

- Older facilities than Atomic's
- Older facilities mean higher cost per man–hour to complete the job.
- Overall facility not as good as Atomic's

B. Production and Quality

Advantages

+ Had supplied Oceanics with quality products in the past
+ Floor organized and all parts tagged by end use.
+ Production work load divided into task forces that include quality, scheduling, and expediting.
+ Experienced with large vessels which induced them into changing internal organization for closer follow-up.

Disadvantages

− Overall building not as clean as Atomic's

C. Purchasing and Financial Resources

Advantages

+ The concerns here are essentially the same as those outlined in the Atomic evaluation.

Disadvantages

− The cost estimate here is $328,000 higher than Atomic's. Oceanics should investigate this further.

D. Accounting System

Although Oceanics has had previous dealings with Nuclear, the effectiveness and adequacy of this system should be reviewed similarly to the manner outlined in the Atomic appraisal.

E. Managerial

Advantages

+ This appears to be a marketing-oriented organization.
+ Management takes a professional approach to presentation.
+ Vice presidents of 4 functions and key personnel met with Oceanics.
+ There appeared to be effective control over the shop floor.
+ A project engineer is given daily status reports of each project.
+ Management appears willing to revise its organization to meet demands of the product.
+ This is a congenial, professional group of people.

Disadvantages

− Nuclear may have been overly solicitous with Oceanics.
− The limousine, country club, and other perquisites only serve to drive up the direct costs.

F. Industrial Relations

Advantages

+ A union has never been formed here.
+ Employees are on a profit-sharing plan.
+ Good labor-management relations on the shop floor.
+ Fixed fee cost of $1.00 and the $16 per man-hour are indications of a stable work force and work flow.

Disadvantages

- None perceived

G. Past Performance

Advantages

+ This is an experienced supplier.
+ There is experience in supplying vessels of this size to the industry.
+ There is no perceivable problem with meeting the delivery date required.

Disadvantages

- Nuclear has run into problems with large vessels in the past on first-time production runs.

Evaluating the Options

The solution to this problem must address the following concerns, as implied by the Oceanics Management Committee:

1. The quality of the vessel is the biggest concern.
2. The delivery date is six months.
3. The rigid technical specifications must be met.
4. The price must be competitive.
5. The managerial, financial, and production organizations must be capable of handling the project.

To objectively evaluate these five areas of concern, a 100-point rating matrix will be used.

Factors	Maximum Points	Atomic	Nuclear
Technical competency	10	8	10
Production capabilities:			
• Facilities	10	8	7
• Equipment	10	9	7
• Material control	10	7	9
• Cleanliness	10	8	7
Ability to meet schedule	10	8	8
Price	10	10	8
Managerial, financial, & production organization	10	5	10
Quality-control staff	20	18	17
Total	100	81	83

Justifying the Outcome

Since Nuclear Vessels, Incorporated, scored 83 of 100 points and Atomic Products Company scored 81 of 100, the objective choice is Nuclear Vessels, Inc.

However, Oceanics should not accept the initial proposal of $1,560,001 without further negotiation. The bid may have been hastily prepared, and as Oceanics is a repeat customer, more adequate financial consideration is in order.

Finally, the issue of plate repairs and rejected materials needs clarification. Since Atomic offered to sustain the costs of all repairs in accordance with specifications, Oceanics's buyer has some basis for negotiating this item as well.

The language in the proposal in reference to delivery date is also unacceptable as stipulated. Since the Oceanics committee has determined six months as the date of delivery, then any slips in that time should be the responsibility of the supplier. The Oceanics buyer must negotiate those costs with the Nuclear management committee.

PART IV

Examination/Quiz
Questions and Answers

CHAPTER 1
PURCHASING: A PROFESSION IN TRANSITION

1. The term "supply management" describes both the purchasing function and the procurement processes.

   T F

2. The following elements: (1) determining the organization's requirements, (2) selecting the optimal source, (3) establishing a fair and reasonable price, and (4) maintaining mutually beneficial relationships with the most desirable suppliers, constitute which of the following:
   a. the supply strategy
   b. the backbone of the purchasing function
   c. the four stages of purchasing
   d. the strategic focus

   a b c d

3. Most organizations rate themselves very accurately with regard to their place on the continuum of purchasing and supply management stages.

   T F

4. In the past, typical *purchasing* duties involved:
   a. conscientiously controlling inventory
   b. preventing line shutdowns
   c. reducing cost
   d. managing supplier relationships

   a b c d

5. Materials coordinators manage the tactical activities while supply managers develop and implement supply policy.

   T F

6. The appropriate position for an organization's supply strategy is:
   a. in the center of the strategic business plan
   b. as a sub-strategy of the organization's conversion strategy
   c. fully integrated into the strategic business plan
   d. different for each organization

   a b c d

7. In making the transition from purchasing to supply management, shifting from internal processes to value-adding benefits can mean reducing the time to market by 20 percent to 40 percent.

   T F

8. Low value-adding supply activities are best handled in a centralized manner so fewer people spend their time on them.

   T F

9. The reason that there may be fewer people assigned to purchasing as a result of taking a strategic focus is:
   a. true supply management allows for more efficiency
   b. there will be fewer suppliers to manage
   c. more and better access to data will reduce the time required for decision making
   d. the caliber of purchasing professionals will be higher
   e. all of the above

                                                                                 a b c d e

10. Depending on the project at hand, cross-functional teams can either be on-going or ad hoc.

                                                                                 T F

11. A recent NAPM survey revealed that many of the traditional purchasing activities are actually better handled by a team. An exception to this would be
    a. supply market analysis
    b. quality requirements determination
    c. specifications development
    d. none of the above

                                                                                 a b c d

12. The value chain exists within an organization and is responsible for ensuring that all purchased materials and/or services are in the right quality and at the right price.

                                                                                 T F

13. The challenges involved in managing strategic alliances do not include:
    a. knowing when the relationship has reached the end of its useful life
    b. handling technology sharing in a sensitive yet open manner
    c. monitoring who is getting the most benefit out of each transaction
    d. making sure that communication is effective and timely

                                                                                 a b c d

14. It will be increasingly important for purchasing professionals to have technical degrees.

                                                                                 T F

CHAPTER 2
THE ROLE OF PURCHASING AND
SUPPLY MANAGEMENT IN BUSINESS

1. Over the past fifty years, in American manufacturing operations the reduction of unit labor costs has increased the relative magnitude and importance of material costs.

   T F

2. Since the early 1990s, the strategic emphasis on purchasing has been enhanced the most by purchasing participation in cross-functional teams for which three of the following activities?
   a. product design
   b. long-term MRO contracts
   c. supplier qualification and selection
   d. commodity management

   a b c d

3. Most companies generally use two sources of supply: *inside* manufacture and *outside* manufacture. The production department is responsible for inside manufacture, including production scheduling; the purchasing department is responsible for outside manufacture, including the scheduling of outside production.

   T F

4. Industrial buyers perform all the following functions, *except*:
   a. participate in determining what products a firm should manufacture.
   b. select suppliers.
   c. integrate purchases with sales forecasts and production schedules.
   d. procure needed capital for financing the production of the firm's product(s).

   a b c d

5. In most companies decisions about reciprocity dealings are usually made by the marketing department.

   T F

6. A firm can *always* generate additional profit by:
   a. increasing sales.
   b. decreasing unit production costs.
   c. increasing prices.
   d. all of the above.

   a b c d

7. The purchasing function is of equal importance in all cycles of a firm's life cycle.

   T F

8. The supply management concept typically encompasses a broader range of operating activities than does the materials management concept.

   T F

9. A firm's overall performance can be accurately measured by its profit on sales revenues.

   T F

10. Purchasing can contribute to top management's efforts to improve ROI by increasing the firm's profit margins and asset turnover rate.

                                                                                          T F

11. A production schedule that fails to provide sufficient lead time for a firm's purchasing department can result in:
    a. special production runs.
    b. increased transportation costs.
    c. increased production costs.
    d. production stoppages.
    e. all of the above.

                                                                                  a b c d e

12. In the majority of American industry, the proportion of material cost to total manufacturing cost exceeds 50 percent.

                                                                                          T F

13. The "purchasing function" is always managed by the "purchasing department."

                                                                                          T F

14. Management can improve performance in all of the following ways *except by*:
    a. increasing sales faster than investment.
    b. increasing sales faster than expenses.
    c. increasing expenses in response to a proportional increase in sales.
    d. reducing investment more than sales.

                                                                                     a b c d

15. As specialization in manufacturing developed, the cost and importance of materials in the manufacturing process increased as unit labor costs decreased.

                                                                                          T F

16. Optimum quality, safety, and performance of product design are the primary concerns of design engineering.

                                                                                          T F

17. The primary objective of a purchasing department is to acquire materials at the lowest possible unit cost.

                                                                                          T F

18. The procurement management concept encompasses a wider range of supply activities than does the purchasing management concept.

                                                                                          T F

19. Utilization of the materials management concept accelerated dramatically after the oil embargo and subsequent materials shortages during 1973 and 1974.

                                                                                          T F

20. On which of the following do sales forecasts have the greatest impact?
    a. customers
    b. production schedules, engineering, and manpower needs
    c. production schedules, purchasing schedules, capital budgeting, and marketing activities
    d. a firm's competitive position in the market

                                                                                    a b c d

21. There is a direct correlation among interest rates, material cost savings, and profits.

                                                                                    T F

22. In most industrial firms, purchasing has been recognized as a professional management-oriented function for only the past twenty to thirty years.

                                                                                    T F

23. Because of the nature of its responsibilities, purchasing has continuing relationships with most other departments in the firm. With which of the following departments does purchasing usually have the least direct relationship?
    a. design engineering
    b. operations/manufacturing
    c. material control
    d. marketing

                                                                                    a b c d

24. A firm's *overall* production costs nearly always can be reduced by purchasing larger quantities of the materials needed for production.

                                                                                    T F

25. The *major* advantage of a materials management department most commonly is:
    a. sales are increased.
    b. customer services functions more effectively.
    c. greatly improved coordination between purchasing and production control results.
    d. communication between production and inventory improves.

                                                                                    a b c d

26. Current business management theory recommends that materials management entail an integrated management approach to planning, acquisition, conversion, flow, and distribution of production materials from the raw materials to the finished product state.

                                                                                    T F

27. Physical distribution management, in the conventional view, includes all of the following activities *except*:
    a. inventory control.
    b. sales order processing.
    c. traffic and transportation.
    d. acquisition of production materials.

                                                                                    a b c d

28. Purchasing's relationship with the various production departments and design engineering departments is particularly important, because production and design engineering actions frequently impact significantly the cost and availability of the materials purchasing must acquire in the marketplace.

                                                                                    T F

29. Although similarities exist between the activities and functions of materials management and physical distribution management, the skills required to perform these are quite different.

T   F

30. When a firm implements a systems approach to coordinating and managing materials, this action principally results in:
    a. increased profits.
    b. increased conflicts among the various managers.
    c. a need for more employees.
    d. a reduction of the price of the materials acquired.

a b c d